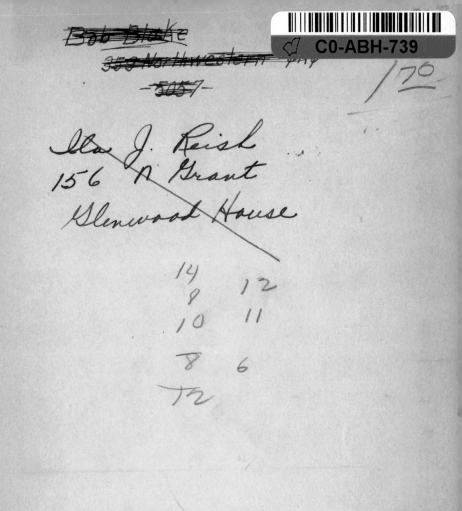

C0-ABH-739

~~Bob Blake~~
~~350 Northwestern~~ Hwy
~~5057~~

170

Ila J. Reish
156 A Grant
Glenwood House

14
8   12
10   11

8   6
12

Experimental Foundations of General Psychology

by

WILLARD L. VALENTINE

PROFESSOR OF PSYCHOLOGY, NORTHWESTERN UNIVERSITY

REVISED EDITION

NEW YORK

FARRAR & RINEHART, INCORPORATED

PUBLISHERS

REVISED EDITION
FIRST PRINTING, APRIL, 1941

COPYRIGHT, 1938 AND 1941, BY WILLARD L. VALENTINE
PRINTED IN THE UNITED STATES OF AMERICA
BY QUINN & BODEN COMPANY, INC., RAHWAY, N. J.
ALL RIGHTS RESERVED

PREFACE TO THE FIRST EDITION

THIS book was written to help supply the need in a first course in psychology for reviews of contemporary experimental work, presented in such a way that the beginner can understand them. This contribution is neither an exhaustive nor a critical review for professional psychologists; controversial issues have therefore been avoided. It is concerned mainly with the application of the scientific method to behavior problems, an area of major concern among the generally recognized objectives of the first course. The book reviews a sample of the literature in each of the subject-matter fields traditionally treated in the first course. It discusses details of experimental procedure in each area, and attempts to give some insight into the enormous amount of labor behind the formally written reports of experiments. Each chapter purposes to digest enough material to show why the generalizations that are made in the text appear reasonable in the light of our present knowledge.

I have had to select the material rigorously. There are innumerable excellent experiments that contribute to so small a part of the total picture that they could not be included. Many others were eliminated because they were too technical for beginners, or because they treat of phenomena so remote from everyday experience that they remain incomprehensible to the beginner even though the instructor may labor valiantly to point out their significance. On the other hand, some relatively trivial experiments were included because they have proved over a period of years to be of interest to beginners, however little they appeal to the professional psychologist. The present integration of materials appeared to me the best possible integration of the interests of both student and teacher.

The experience of a single person imposes a severe limitation on the accomplishment of such an integration, but in the case of this book this restriction has been relieved by counsel from many colleagues. Dr. Frank Stanton prepared the chapter on *Market Research,* and Dr. Donald B. Lindsley wrote the section on "Brain Waves." Dr. F. C. Dockeray selected some of the material and criticized some parts of the manuscript. Dr. Charles Bird, who read all the manuscript, made innumerable useful criticisms, as did Dr. Frank A. Pattie, Jr. Two of my students, Milton M. Parker and Robert Harper, read the rough draft from the student standpoint, and their aid helped to clarify many of the statements made here. Mr. Harper and Mrs. E. W. Senderling worked assiduously with the proof. To all of these colleagues and friends I owe a debt of gratitude.

It is a pleasure to acknowledge the co-operation of many authors, editors, and publishers in granting permission to use the longer quotations. In each instance appropriate credit is given in the text.

W. L. V.

Columbus, Ohio
May, 1938

PREFACE TO THE SECOND EDITION

THE plan of the first edition of this book has been somewhat modified in the present revision because of the numerous suggestions offered by various teachers who used it. My design, carried out in the first edition, was to write a series of detailed descriptions of important experiments, with the barest essentials of interpretation and systematization. This volume, as I planned it, served simply as a supplement to any one of the standard texts and left the problem of exposition to the text and to the instructor. However, users of the book in its first edition felt that more integration was needed in order to make even this supplementary function most effective. To this end the addition of interpretative comment has been a major part of the revision.

One of the major obstacles to the beginning student's understanding of psychological phenomena has always been the extensive technical vocabulary with which they are usually described. With this in mind I have carefully re-examined all the material, old and new, to eliminate as much of the technical vocabulary as possible.

New material has been added to most of the chapters, some of which have been rearranged internally as well as in the relation they bear to the book as a whole. There is an entirely new summary chapter.

The chapter on market research has been dropped, not because I have failed to recognize the existence of an important field of activity in which the work of Gallup, Roper, Stanton, and Starch is outstanding, but because this chapter could not be properly integrated with the rest of the book. It is unfortunate that this material must be omitted, because even a "Foundations of Experimental Psychology" must today be concerned with facts gathered under other than laboratory conditions.

The chapter on perception remains unchanged. Although more recent experiments have been made in this field, they are not of a type that lends itself to the treatment here accorded similar topics.

I have preserved the intent of the first edition in developing a series of broad generalizations which, for the benefit of the immature reader, are set in italics.

The suggestions of Professors Charles Bird, Ernest Hilgard, and John McGeoch have been immensely valuable to me in the work of revision. I am also indebted to Mrs. Marjorie Lisle who has helped me to simplify the presentation of technical matters.

W. L. V.

Evanston, Illinois
April, 1941

TO THE STUDENT

IN this book we shall be concerned principally with psychological facts and principles on which there is a majority, if not a universal, agreement. The experiments that are referred to by no means exhaust the list. If he had the patience to do it, one could rewrite this whole volume and arrive at exactly the same conclusions in each chapter, mentioning not a single specific item, with a few exceptions, that I have chosen. I have left out great sections of material that have traditionally appeared in psychology texts. In the selection of the material that appears here my criterion has been its utility to a young person who in all likelihood will have only one course in psychology. To that end there is frequent reference to the practical application of the principles developed.

This book is not designed to prepare a person for an advanced course in any special branch of psychology, nor is it planned to give him any rigorous system of psychology. Above all it is not a handbook for graduate students.

It will find its most useful purpose in providing some insight into how a psychologist goes about collecting the information he needs and what he does with it after he collects it. It also attempts to show why professional psychologists make some of the investigations that seem so important to them, but which to the outsider look like busy work without purpose.

This book will find its greatest value if it is used in conjunction with one of the standard texts, which will furnish the framework for understanding and for systematizing the items of information contained in this volume.

INTRODUCTION

WHEN a person learns a poem by heart, decides to take a blonde to dance rather than a brunette, expresses himself in favor of the New Deal, changes roommates because he can't get along with the one he is leaving, fails an examination or enters a law school, there is a reason for his action. These are only a few examples. Everything that he has ever done, is doing now, or ever will do is caused by something else. No action is ever spontaneous—uncaused. Even if a person honestly cannot give a reason for making a choice, there is no proof that it had no cause. Many forgotten conditions affect us: others that affect us now we cannot identify, however obvious they are to others. Some that are perfectly obvious to us cannot ever be detected by others however hard they may try to penetrate our privacy.

For a long, long time some people have believed that the relative position of the planets on the date of one's birth had a major effect in the determination of one's destiny. But to substantiate this view there has never been offered any evidence that would stand close examination.

The length of certain lines in one's palm has been credited with indicating how long he will live, whether he will marry and how many times, and with what success. But again the evidence offered is shaky and the reasoning processes used in arriving at the prognostication violate practically every known rule of ordinary logic.

The height of one's forehead, the length of his nose, the size of his mouth and the shape of his ears, the length of his fingers and the breadth of his hand, together with every other known item of physiognomy, have been shown time and time again to bear no relation to temperament, attainment, aptitude, vocation, or economic condition. But more about this in Chapter II.

These pseudo determiners of destiny are considered so silly by psychologists that most textbooks don't even mention them. What the positive factors are will depend for exact statement upon the particular author one is reading, but no one of them would quarrel with this: The factors which determine a person's behavior are (1) his heredity; (2) his biography—the things that have happened to him; (3) his surroundings and his internal condition at the moment under consideration. Nothing is said about stars, or luck, or charms, or curses, and there is no place to fit these things into the psychologist's blueprint. On the other hand, physique—length of fingers and so on—does pretty definitely belong in the hereditary category. And if, as we have already suggested, these factors are not pertinent ones, then they will have to be eliminated on an entirely different basis from the first-named group. There is not a single specific condition that can have an effect on behavior but that can be placed in one or more of the categories mentioned. *These categories are not intended to be mutually exclusive.* Suppose that we wanted to classify the effect that one grain of caffeine sulphate has on a person's behavior. There is no question (as has been proven experimentally) but that how much caffeine he was in the habit of taking in coffee, tea, and soda-fountain drinks would have its effect. This fact would come pretty definitely in the personal biography category. But his reaction would also be conditioned by various physiological factors which are both conditions of the moment and are also affected by a remote hereditary determiner.

Perhaps one reason why there is practically no disagreement on the threefold classification above is because it is too broad. Were we to become more specific, objections would be forthcoming. The elaboration of the specific elements of these topics is the burden of the remainder of this volume.

In Chapter I we digress from this main theme to see what it means to prove something by experiment. The experiment is a special method of observing which makes one more certain of one's results.

CONTENTS

LIST OF FIGURES

EXPERIMENTAL FOUNDATIONS
OF GENERAL PSYCHOLOGY

I

THE NATURE OF THE PSYCHOLOGICAL EXPERIMENT

OUR arithmetic teachers would have us believe that the study of arithmetic, or of mathematics generally, increases our power to reason. So wholeheartedly do they *hope* that this statement is true that they have convinced us, almost universally, that it *is* true. This kind of thinking—believing that a thing is true because we hope that it is true—is called "wishful thinking." It is indulged in by Latin teachers who say that the study of Latin increases our understanding of the English language, therefore everybody should take Latin. It is part and parcel of the thinking of people who believe that all kinds of unpleasant tasks, just because they are distasteful and hard, are good for our moral fiber.

Can we accept the statement of our Latin teachers and our arithmetic teachers or others who have led us to believe in the efficacy of what are called the disciplinary studies? What proof do they have for this belief? Can we believe a psychologist just because he asserts that these beliefs are in error? Whom can we believe? On the face of the matter the psychologist is just as likely to be wrong as his opponents. But if we press the point further we find a basis for the assertion of the psychologist that is totally lacking in the case of our Latin or mathematics teacher. What they hold to be self-evident the psychologist makes it his business to question.

1. LATIN

It is frequently observed, and correctly so, that students who take Latin in high school are abler students than those who don't. But to go a step further and say that they are abler *because* they take Latin is not justified. This inference was shown to be false by a study made about twenty years ago.[1] (This is not the only evidence available, but it is one of the simplest demonstrations.) The grades received in English by Iowa City High School students who were taking Latin or German, but not both, were compared.

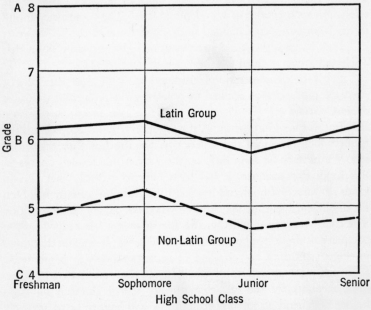

FIG. 1.—The difference between the median grades of high school students who are taking Latin and those who are not. Notice that the same difference that is present in the senior year is also obvious in the freshman year.

There were 184 in the Latin group and 120 in the German group. The grades were first converted into points and the median number of points in English for the 184 Latin students was computed for the first year's work. This turned out to be somewhat above a B, in the A B C D E system of marking. The same operation for the German group gave a number midway between a B and C. This result was for the first year's work. For the second and succeeding years

[1] J. M. Wilcox, "The Effect of Latin on High School Grades," *School and Society*, 1917, 6, 58-60.

the same condition obtained. These results can best be shown by a graph, from which it is clear that the Latin students as a group are superior in English marks to the German students, and that the superiority does not increase as the four years are completed. It is, we should agree, a reasonable expectation that if Latin is effective in making English grades better, then more of it should have more effect. No such condition was demonstrated. The superiority found in the freshman year extended unchanged through the senior year; it did not become greater as time went on. This can only mean that a selected group decided to take Latin in the first place.

This little demonstration illustrates one of the first principles of scientific procedure as applied to psychological problems: the most *obvious factors are not always the effective ones in producing a result.* In this case a hidden cause, the selection of abler people, was the factor which produced the superiority, not the Latin experience itself. We have to be constantly on the lookout for hidden factors of this kind. For instance, it has been asserted recently that certain kinds of nursery school and kindergarten training actually heighten the intelligence level of the children who take part in these activities. The controversy over whether this is true or not has hinged on the adequacy of the control over this selective factor. It may be that more intelligent children are enrolled in nursery schools to begin with. If anyone wants to determine which one of these alternative explanations accounts for the fact that nursery school children *do* score higher in general on intelligence tests, he will have to be particularly careful to obtain a comparable group of children who are not in nursery school but who are equal in ability to the nursery school group at the beginning of the experiment.

2. MATHEMATICS

A belief hard to kill is that which holds that arithmetic in grammar school, algebra and geometry in high school, and higher mathematics in college, as they are ordinarily taught, are the proving grounds for reasoning processes that will later be effective in dealing with problems not contained between the covers of a book. This

A Sample of the Reasoning Problems

Tommy said, "All the boys in our Sunday school except me have gone this morning for an excursion." Just after he said that another boy who went to the same Sunday school was seen playing in the street. Was Tommy right in what he said? You must give a reason for your answer.

A table is on the right-hand side of a chair, and a blackboard is on the right-hand side of the table. Is the blackboard on the right-hand side of the chair or on the left-hand side of the chair? You must say what makes you give the answer you do.

John and James both walked from a town called A to a town called B. John walked first to a town called C, and then, without stopping, he walked from C to B. But James walked on a road from A to B which did not go through C. Can you tell who went the shorter way? If you can tell, say what makes you think so. If you can't tell, say why you can't tell.

All butchers' shops in a long road were painted red. If you were in that road and you saw a shop painted red, would you be certain that it was a butcher's shop, or would you not? You must give a reason for your answer.

A gardener made three circular flower beds and planted flowers all around the edges. The first flower bed measured 80 feet round; the second and third measured 60 feet round. If he placed the flowers six inches apart, how many plants would he require?

Two men, Jones and Brown, set out together to walk to a town 160 miles away. Jones walked 10 miles a day, while Brown walked 8 miles a day. When Jones reached the town how many days' journey would Brown be behind him?

notion has been subjected to experimental test in a way which illustrates another method that psychologists frequently use to determine the truth of a belief uncritically held.

In order to make the case for arithmetic as strong as possible, a British investigator, W. H. Winch,[2] arranged to have very special instruction provided for a small group of girls whose average age was about twelve years. This instruction was designed to treat of general principles—to dig below the surface of problems; to get at the basic principles. The emphasis was such that the girls understood that it was more important to be able to give a correct reason for taking a step in the solution of a problem than it was to get all the computations correct. In planning his experiment to test how much improvement in reasoning would result from this extraordinarily complete arithmetic, Winch had developed a series of problems in reasoning, samples of which are shown on page 6. You will notice that although reasoning is necessary, no computation is required. The plan was to test reasoning by seeing how many of these problems could be solved before and after a ten-week period of this special training in arithmetic. The results follow:

LOGICAL REASONING TEST SCORES

Pretest	35 examples correct
End test	49.5 examples correct
Gain	14.5
Per cent gain	41.4

From this table what can we conclude? Can we say that the gain of 14.5 examples shows the result of the special instruction? Obviously not. Many other factors besides the special training may have had an effect on the scores. In the first place, the girls were ten weeks older when they took the second test. In tests of this kind for people of this age, ten weeks can make a considerable difference in the maturity of the subjects. Many things could have happened to them, both in and out of school, which would sharpen their perception of the relations demanded in problems of this kind. One factor which would certainly tend to raise the score is that the

[2] W. H. Winch, "The Transfer of Improvement in Reasoning," *British Journal of Psychology*, 1923, 13, 370-81.

end test was an exact repetition of the pretest. Even if they didn't know how they fared on the first test there would be a certain familiarity about the problems on meeting them again ten weeks later that certainly would not tend to lower the score. We can observe only that the increase in score is not great. The girls did not double or triple their pretest scores. The gain was considerably less than half the initial score, but this fact may be a function of the test itself and, on another one designed by someone else, the gain might be a great deal more.

Thus far Professor Winch may have seemed to be a most naïve experimenter, since *to make measurements is not enough*. Professor Winch knew this, of course, and in planning his experiment he gave the pretest to a relatively large group of girls. From these he selected two subgroups of approximately the same number, arranging them so that the average score on the reasoning test was, within a few tenths of an example, the same for both groups. One of these groups, the one that received the special arithmetic training, we shall call the "experimental group." The other was held in reserve; it did not get the special training—although in other respects it was as like the experimental group as it could be made. It is called the "control group." In this instance the control group could not be dismissed from arithmetic for a period of ten weeks; instead it was given ordinary grammar school arithmetic. The teacher provided was described as a "forceful" one and the usual emphasis on the mechanics of computation at the expense of the general principles filled the time. Here is what happened:

LOGICAL REASONING TEST SCORES

Pretest	34.8 examples correct
End test	38.8 examples correct
Gain	4.0
Per cent gain	11.5

We now have a basis for answering our question as to just how much influence we could expect ordinary experiences in and out of school to contribute to the total gain. The control group gained 11.5 per cent of the pretest score as compared with 41.4 per cent gain for the experimental group. Thus the special training accounts for a gain of approximately 30 per cent.

Notice, also, that the ordinary arithmetic in school, together with all the other factors—increased maturation, the identity of the end test with the pretest, and so on—produced a gain of only 11.5 per cent. In order to make a complete study, another group which made, on the average, identical scores with these two would also be useful. In the ten-week period we would excuse this third group from all arithmetic. At the end of that time they would presumably gain something—an amount somewhat less than 11.5 per cent. The contribution of ordinary grammar school arithmetic cannot be very great—the margin is not large enough to allow it to be much.

Summary of the two studies.—We have examined two examples of a supposed relationship between two things. The first was a simple study whose only claim to scientific value is that it involved an actual listing of students' grades in English, and a comparison between those who were and those who were not taking Latin. This is not, strictly speaking, an experiment. It is a study of collected records or data made with a definite plan in mind. That plan allowed for a comparison between two groups, one which had a certain property (having had Latin), and another which did not have this property. The comparison showed that there was just as much superiority in the freshman year of high school as in the the senior year. From this study we should infer, therefore, that *for some reason Latin classes are composed of the better students in the first place.*

The second instance showed that *ordinary grammar school arithmetic did not cause any considerable increase in reasoning ability,* although special methods and subject matter can produce comparatively higher gains.

Aside from the factual outcome of these two studies, we have also learned two fundamental methodological principles. First, *the most obvious factors in a situation are not, simply because they are obvious, the effective factors* in accounting for a result. As a matter of fact, it might be said that *all of science everywhere has been concerned principally with discovering the nonevident causes of natural phenomena.* To be scientifically sophisticated means, among other things, to be skeptical about any generally accepted cause which is supposed to be self-evident and therefore not to require rigorous proof. To elaborate on this point would take us too far afield, but as we proceed to present the many experiments that make up this book it would be well to consider each of them in the light of this generalization. The second principle we have learned can be called the Principle of Control. In planning an experiment we must have some basis of comparison—this usually, but not always, means that a control group has to be organized. *The control group has the same properties as the experimental group except one, that one being the factor under consideration.* These principles are easy to learn, but to apply them is a difficult accomplishment. The selection of a control group is not easy, a fact upon which we shall comment from time to time. The principal difficulty is that we never can be *absolutely certain* that the control is sufficiently similar to the experimental group so that they can be considered identical.

3. ROD DIVINING

Another simple experiment which illustrates a typical psychological experiment, and further elaborates the Principle of Control, is found in the method used by Foster [3] in examining the claims of a rod diviner. A rod diviner, or dowser, is one who claims to be able to locate water and minerals under the surface of the ground by the dipping of a branch held in his hands.[4] Generally, a **Y**-shaped branch of a willow tree is used. Held in the two hands by the two shorter parts, it is extended horizontally in front of the diviner. As he moves across the area where it is hoped water will be found, the rod suddenly dips at a fairly precise spot and the well diggers are

[3] W. S. Foster, "Experiments on Rod Divining," *Journal of Applied Psychology*, 1923, 7, 303-11.
[4] "The Divining Rod—A History of Water Witching," *U. S. Geological Survey Pamphlet*, p. 416, 1917.
   T. Besterman and W. F. Barrett, *The Divining-Rod an Experimental and Psychological Investigation*. London, 1926.

instructed to go ahead. The diviner claims that he has no part in the movements of the rod, but that, under the influence of sub-surface conditions, it bends sharply downward in ways that he cannot control.

A seventy-year-old diviner called at the Psychological Laboratory of the University of Minnesota and asked that his "powers" of divining be subjected to experimental test. He had documentary statements from engineers and others in Wisconsin, Minnesota, West Virginia, and Texas covering a period of forty-five years and attesting to the success of his method in locating not only water, but oil, natural gas, iron, gold, and silver. Here is an example of a phenomenon which a newspaper reporter, a novelist, or even a lawyer would accept as true, without further examination, based on the man's story supported by documents of a long career of successful divination. Documentary evidence of this kind, however, finds no ready acceptance in scientific circles. The explanation that will usually occur to a layman is that the man must have some special power that ordinary people do not have. Let us see how the psychologist proceeded in examining the claims and in explaining the phenomenon.

On March 26, 1923, in the presence of two other psychologists, R. M. Elliott and Donald Paterson, and with their co-operation, Foster made the following experiment. It was first determined that the rod would move downward for a cardboard box which contained a few coins. The diviner reported greater vigor in the movement when two gold watches and a silver watch were added. Of course, the diviner knew when the box was empty, and he knew what and how much was added at these preliminary preparations. This is an important point.

Accuracy of the positive judgments.—A large table was moved to the center of the laboratory and chalk marks were made on it in such a way as to provide fourteen squares, each twenty by twenty inches. Each square was numbered. The floor directly under the table was marked in squares corresponding exactly in number and design to those on the table top. The area under the table was shielded from sight on all four sides by a wall made of cardboard.

On the floor on one of the squares the experimenter placed the box containing the metal. He then left the room and another experimenter brought the diviner in. The diviner mounted the table and walked slowly over the squares until, by a system of checking in both directions, he finally indicated where he thought the box was located on the floor beneath. He was not told whether he was right or wrong. As a matter of fact, the experimenter who recorded the judgment did not know himself where his patrner had placed the box, so that he was unable to communicate, by his facial expression, by the sound of his voice, or by his manner, any pertinent information. These precautions are all a part of the observation of the Principle of Control. There were thirty-two trials made, two for each of the fourteen squares, *and four in which the box was not on the floor at all.* These four negative trials were made without the diviner's knowledge, of course, and his response on these trials was just as prompt, just as positive, as it was in the twenty-eight times the box was actually present. In these twenty-eight trials the correct square was indicated only once. By the laws of probability he should have gotten two of these twenty-eight right by mere guessing, so that his performance in this part of the experiment must be considered a flat failure. The Principle of Control is observed here by instituting the trials in which there was nothing on the floor. *There is no evidence at all that he could locate a box of metal under these conditions although he was positive of his success outside the laboratory in locating hidden and lost watches by his method.* And, it must be remembered, he had documents to support his claim.

A second test was begun at once. None of the three people concerned knew as yet how the first test had come out, because the two experimenters had not compared their independent records of placement and judgment.

In the second test, the diviner stood on top of the table and attempted to judge how much metal was in the box when it was placed out of sight under the table on which he was standing. The judgments were made in terms of "nothing, weak, fair, strong and very strong," depending on the vigor of the rod movement. He had in the preliminary preparation, when knowing what was going into the box, been able to judge with ease whether only coins, or coins plus one, two, or three watches were in the box. He said that the difference between these steps was pronounced. But under the test conditions, when the box contained nothing five times and each one of the four positive amounts five times (making twenty-five trials in all) he was successful only six times. If he had been guessing, we might expect that he would get five right, anyway, so that his success here, considering that there were only twenty-five trials, can be said to be no better than random guessing.

We might really expect that the diviner would have done much better in this test, because in order to conserve his energy (he was seventy, remember, and had already climbed upon the table thirty-two times in the previous experiment) he was not required to leave the room between trials this time. Although he could not see the experimenter, it is conceivable that small noises made in changing the amounts in the box, placing the box on the floor, or the tone of the experimenter's voice in calling "Ready," however careful the experimenter might have been, could have been a source of considerable information.

Tests made out-of-doors.—Another test was made out-of-doors and more closely resembled the conditions in which diviners usually work as they locate water and minerals. In this test he was required to identify the probable course of water mains leading to two campus buildings. An experimenter who knew the true locations accompanied him and recorded the observations on a rough map. Two probable courses were recorded. One missed an actual water main by 15 feet at one end and 50 feet at the other. The length of the course was about 250 feet and connected two buildings. The second course missed a sewer outlet by about the same amount. In the case of the second building a course of 80 feet was indicated correctly, but it ended in a visible hydrant. Any observant person could have done as well without a rod. A second water main leading into the building was passed over without any indication from the diviner. These results indicate that *where surface cues are available and where inadvertent signs from people who know the true locations*

are possible, diviners are more successful than they are under labora-
tory conditions.[5]

Although we shall not examine it now, there is evidence indicating that people can take advantage of barely perceptible signs or cues in directing the course of their behavior without being aware that they are using them. Not all diviners are charlatans.[6] Like this man, they are honestly convinced that they have some capacity that ordinary people do not possess. Like most of us, they don't count their failures and they attribute their successes to the wrong factors. What these factors are can never be found out by interviewing the people involved or by collecting documents, however wholeheartedly they may be attested. *To obtain evidence that will stand the test of mature reflection concerning psychological matters, trained investigators must control all possible factors by special tests.*

4. MIND READING

The tiny changes in facial expression or posture on the part of one person, which are used as signals for directing the behavior of another, were suggested as part of the effective factors which enabled the diviner to perform with more accuracy outside the laboratory than within. No actual demonstration of the efficacy of these factors was made. It remained for Stratton[7] to show, in another experiment, just how effective they can be.

A young Moravian known as Eugen de Rubini appeared in San Francisco in about 1920 and impressed a social gathering, at which Stratton was present, with his ability to find hidden objects. A common object was carefully hidden while de Rubini was out of

[5] F. A. Barrett, *Proceedings of the Society for Psychical Research,* 1897, 13, 2, 280; 1900, 15, 130-383.

E. R. Pease, *ibid.,* 1884, 2, 79-94.
[6] Charlatans resist a scientific examination of their claims. In this connection the student will find McComas's *Ghosts I Have Talked With,* Williams and Wilkins, Baltimore, an interesting account of investigations of spiritualistic mediums.
[7] G. M. Stratton, "The Control of Another Person by Obscure Signs," *Psychological Review,* 1921, 28, 301-14.

the room. Then a person who knew the location of the object held on to one end of a delicate watch chain while de Rubini held the other. The guide thus led him to the proper location of the object, although he disclaimed any direct knowledge of having done so. The guide could be selected from the members at random. There was no collusion between two partners as there frequently is in stunts of this kind. After a few warming-up trials, the watch chain could be successfully discarded. The most obvious cues, visual and auditory, were not necessary for de Rubini, who, in fact, told the guide on several occasions to stop giving him these perfectly obvious signs. He was also unusual as a public performer in that he made no claim of being able to read minds. He had to be assisted, he said, to the hidden object as a blind man would have to be. There must be, by the guide, continual mental correction of his false movements and a corresponding assent when his movements were right. His manner was wholly unfurtive; according to the descriptions of the psychologists who observed him, he was dreamy and receptive rather than aggressively on the lookout for cues. Since he was willing to serve as a subject in an experiment, an experiment was made in an effort to find out just what the cues were.

He was first asked to take a brass bowl from a table in front of him and place it on one of two chairs to the right and left of him as directed "mentally" by the guide. The results of the experiment, which was repeated ten times, are shown in the following table.

Number of trial	1	2	3	4	5	6	7	8	9	10
Direction intended	R	R	R	L	R	L	R	L	L	R
Direction taken by de Rubini	R	R	R	L	R	L	R	L	R	R

Except for the next to the last trial the directions were all as intended. Hence the subject was 90 per cent right. This is impressive, or rather would be impressive in a social gathering where more than ten trials, if that many, would seldom be required.

The next experiment, however, which was very similar to the first, gave somewhat different results. In it, de Rubini, as the subject, was required to place a small vase on either one of two small books about fifteen inches farther from him and to the right and left respectively. This time, without going into detail, suffice it to say that he got only three correct placements, an accuracy of only 30 per cent where 50 per cent might have been expected from a random placing.

In another experiment ten small volumes were placed flat, side by side so that they formed a row about six feet long. The subject was to designate which volume the guide was thinking of. The subject could pick up and handle any of the books in making a decision, but the one that was opened counted as his choice. Under these conditions chance success is very markedly reduced. When there are only two possible choices, random guessing should result in 50 per cent accuracy if enough guesses are allowed. But where any one of ten things can be right, we would expect the subject to get only one book right in ten trials if he were just guessing. Since he actually got thirteen right in twenty trials, he wasn't just guessing.

In order to find out just what he was doing, it was necessary to eliminate the possibility that he was receiving slight cues by any of the sense organs. He was reluctant to be blindfolded, but he had no objection to having his ears plugged. All of the auditory controls that were instituted seemed to have no effect on his accuracy. He was finally persuaded to wear blinders which eliminated his peripheral vision, not only on the sides but above and below as well, leaving only a restricted field in front of him. Under these conditions there was a marked reduction in his successes. In other experiments the guide was screened from the subject; in still others he stayed so close behind that the subject could not see him. In all of these experiments in which vision was interfered with, there was a marked reduction of the number of successes until in a total of sixty trials they did not exceed what might have been expected on the basis of chance alone. On the other hand, in all cases where no special precautions were taken to guard against visual cues, the successes ran definitely above chance expectation.

In one series in which the subject wore blinders and ear plugs and where the guide was completely screened, *there was not a single success in ten trials*.

Stratton concludes: "de Rubini received visual aid from signs unintentionally given him by each of the persons who acted as his guide—signs which indicated whether he was approaching or was going away from the right objects. These signs were exceedingly obscure, rarely evident to the experimenters watching the guide. . . . The hints seem to have come from fleeting glimpses of the guide's changes of place and posture caught in the very margin of vision and perhaps without any conscious intention of the subject to notice or use them. Upon these, when touch was excluded, his truly remarkable power seems to depend." [8]

These two experiments on divination and mind reading are further examples of the application of the Principle of Control. When the diviner reacted to the empty box he showed that the contents of the box had nothing to do with his response. *When de Rubini failed in his apparently remarkable achievements during the time he was temporarily deprived of his vision, he demonstrated that he was not reading minds but was reacting to visual cues.* That the auditory controls did not affect his results indicated that he was not influenced by what he heard.

5. EXTRA-SENSORY PERCEPTION

Recently the popular magazines and the radio have carried stories to the effect that psychologists at Duke University had *proved* that when no ordinary sense cues were used and when the subjects were allowed to examine only the plain backs of the cards, certain subjects could still tell with considerable accuracy which one of five cards was going to be turned up next in a pack of twenty-five (five each of five different forms). These experiments have thus served to reopen an area of controversy that traditional psychology had long regarded as permanently settled.

In the simplest experiments the subject tried to place the deck of twenty-five cards in five piles in front of him, separating them into suits by *looking at their backs.* Since a close examination of the cards disclosed no visible clues and since some subjects could

[8] *Op. cit.,* p. 314.

Part of Radio Script for One Program

NARRATOR:—Two of the characters on the Duke University ESP cards will be used in this experiment. So jot down on your paper. Cross and *Star*. [Italicized words were emphasized by announcer.] I'll repeat. A cross and a *star*.

ANNOUNCER:—*Alone* in a room *high above the streets of Chicago* are ten specially *selected* ["S" sound suggestive of STAR] telepathic *senders—five* men and *five* women. [Five—characteristic points of star not cross.] The *selecting* machine to be used has been prepared to *select* at random one of those two ESP *characters*—either a *star* or a cross. You will hear the machine operate—a bell will ring—and those ten *senders* will concentrate upon the *character selected* each time. The machine will operate *five* times. Each *selection* must be and will be either a cross or a *star*. There will be no blanks. During the *five second* intervals *see* if the *single* thought in the minds of those *senders* comes to you.

NARRATOR:—Write down your impressions in consecutive order. Do not hesitate or try to reason these out. Write them down as *soon* as you get them. The machine will *select* number one.

do better than they were expected to on the basis of chance alone, the experimenters jumped to the conclusion that no known sense department was used and that some hitherto unknown avenue of perception must be available; hence the term "extra-sensory perception," or, as it is frequently abbreviated, "ESP." Not only was such a conclusion premature (partly because previous work by other people had shown that very slight cues from the backs of cards of this kind can be used as sources of information about them) but the work soon became entangled with telepathy and even clairvoyance. In telepathy another person looking at the right side of the cards is instructed to concentrate on the symbol while the "receiver" attempts to catch what the "sender" is thinking about. In clairvoyance the subject tries to anticipate or to prophesy which card is going to be turned up. It is needless to say that experimental psychologists had for a long time regarded both telepathy and clairvoyance as distinctly pseudo phenomena unworthy of serious consideration.

The Zenith Radio Corporation did much to popularize the acceptance of the "proof" offered by Rhine and his associates by presuming the actuality of telepathy in a series of Sunday evening chain broadcasts lasting from September 26, 1937, to January 2, 1938. In the programs the Duke experiments were given considerable prominence, and people brought before the microphone related from personal experience dramatic examples of telepathy and clairvoyance. A few minutes of each period was devoted to what the Zenith Corporation called "telepathic experiments" which will be described in detail later in this section. A further evidence of this popularization of an unwarranted presumption of telepathic communication is found in at least one reference to the Duke experiments in the widely circulated picture magazine *Life*.[9]

Although the Duke experiments began ten years ago so that enough time has elapsed for these people to adopt controls that other psychologists think necessary, they have not taken advantage of the criticisms offered to them. These criticisms are much too

[9] Francis Sill Wickware, "Dr. Rhine and ESP," *Life Magazine,* 1940, Vol. 8, No. 16, pp. 86-95.

detailed to be related here.[10] Suffice it to say that in the early experiments the experimenters did not even deem it necessary to separate the two people involved in the so-called telepathic communication. The performance of de Rubini mentioned above shows that they should be apart. That the Duke experimenters continued to get positive results [11] when the subjects were separated can be explained in terms of the conditions surrounding the various experiments. In one instance where no cards were used, the "sender" merely thought of one of the five symbols while the receiver in another room called out the impression he had at the time. The sender wrote nothing until after the receiver made his choice. It is perfectly obvious that there is an opportunity that error may creep into this method of recording, particularly if the sender is convinced of the reality of telepathic communication. Moreover, he may be perfectly honest and simply misunderstand the receiver, who is in another room. In a long series of runs he may occasionally forget what symbol he has just "sent" and record a "hit" where there was none. Only a few errors of this kind are enough to push the number of recorded hits above chance expectancy.[12]

A control for this experiment would involve the use of a recorder for both the "sender" and the "receiver"; at the end of the experimental period the records of these two people could be compared and the matches added for the series. Specially prepared

[10] One hundred twenty-nine different articles, pro and con, have been reviewed by John L. Kennedy, "A Methodological Review of Extra-sensory Perception," *Psychological Bulletin,* 1939, 36, 59-103. Also see J. B. Rhine, *Extra-sensory Perception After Sixty Years,* Henry Holt and Company, New York, 1940.

[11] If there are five cards each of five symbols, then on the basis of chance alone we should expect that five would be right out of each twenty-five on the average. Some phenomenal runs of twenty-one out of twenty-five have been recorded under uncontrolled conditions. (See J. B. Rhine, *New Frontiers of the Mind,* Farrar & Rinehart, Inc., New York, 1936, pp. 77-79.) These runs are not consistently maintained. A consistent average of only six in each twenty-five would indicate that some factors other than random guessing were operating. One difficulty in these experiments has been that no limit to the number of runs has been set at the beginning of the experiment. As with poker, or any game, the stopping time may make a great difference in the final result.

[12] C. E. Kellogg, "New Evidence (?) for Extra-sensory Perception," *Scientific Monthly,* 1937, 45, 340.

blanks which would allow the two records to be placed side by side for comparison would materially reduce the errors.

As far as the Duke experiments are concerned, most psychologists believe that the results are due to uncontrolled factors in the experimental situation. They do not think that it is necessary to postulate a special source of perception over and above ordinary vision, audition, touch, and the like. But, even though these factors are ruled out as possibilities to be used in explanation, as they may be when the subjects are separated, there are still possibilities of error in recording, in selecting cases, and in certain attitudes that can best be illustrated by discussing the Zenith experiments in more detail.

The script of a part of the broadcasts is given on page 18. It shows the general outline of the procedure although its details were varied on different dates. It turned out that small differences in the script or in the program immediately preceding had an effect on the response of the audience. More than a million replies from the fifteen broadcasts were analyzed by Louis D. Goodfellow,[13] who listed the responses from the original data. That there were definitely preferred patterns in the responses was his most important finding. In the circle-square choice, for instance, almost no one guessed either five circles or five squares, while 16 per cent of all the audience guessed either CIRCLE, CIRCLE, SQUARE, CIRCLE, SQUARE or its reverse—SQUARE, SQUARE, CIRCLE, SQUARE, CIRCLE. It is evident that the *patterns* here are identical and can be represented by the symbols A, A, B, A, B. Whether one starts with a circle or with a square is determined by other factors that we will explain in a later paragraph. Another favorite pattern is A, B, B, A, B, which had a frequency of approximately 15 per cent. Still another is A, A, B, B, A, with a frequency of 12 per cent. It is obvious that if one of these preferred patterns *happens* to be selected by the spinning wheel, then an unusually large number of hits will be recorded; and *in the absence of these detailed data a careless person would jump to the conclusion that telepathy was the only explanation.*

[13] Louis D. Goodfellow, "A Psychological Interpretation of the Results of the Zenith Radio Experiments in Telepathy," *Journal of Experimental Psychology,* 1938, 23, 601-632.

These patterns of response could also result in an unusually large number (more than would be expected by chance) of zero scores, e.g., suppose that the machine chose A, A, B, A, B, where A is CIRCLE and B is SQUARE and for some reason an unexpectedly large number of people started out with SQUARE. Then in five responses not a single one would be right. Whether one starts with a CIRCLE or with a SQUARE is determined by a large number of personal factors and by the suggestions immediately preceding the attempted telepathic receiving. In the excerpt from the script given on page 18 the suggestions for starting with STAR are shown in italics when STAR and CROSS are the choices to be made.

Some of these suggestions may appear to be far fetched. There is no way to *prove* from these data that the repetition of the *s*-sounds, the mention of "five" and the phrase "high above the streets of Chicago," actually did cause a considerable number of people to start their five guesses with STAR. But it is a characteristic of suggestion to be subtle. If it is not, it would cease to be a suggestion and become a command, whereupon the audience might be expected to refuse to modify its choices in the intended direction.

There were several instances in which the tests were repeated, i.e., the same symbols were used although the machine in the studio chose a different pattern, of course. Now—had telepathy been a factor, *one would have expected a change in the audience response, but the fundamental pattern of response remained the same in most instances. When it did change, then the immediately preceding suggestions were a better explanation than telepathy* because these changes frequently made the audience wrong.

6. RED AND ANGER

"A lively little Jersey cow whom I had known all her six years of life chased me through a barbed wire fence when I was wearing a red dress and sweater, and never did so before or after. I changed to a dull gray, and re-entered the corral, and she paid no attention to me, and let me feed and water her as usual."

This is the statement of a California woman experienced in the care of cattle who was among those questioned by Stratton in an effort to find out how widespread among cattlemen is the widely accepted notion that red is particularly exciting to cattle. She was one of eleven who supported the belief; the other fifty-three questioned were against it. The majority held that in a complex natural situation there are many things besides the color that are effective in producing the excitement so often reported. In commenting on the old saying "like waving a red flag before a bull," one cattleman remarked, "I have found that to wave anything before a bull is dangerous business." The implied statement here is that the waving —the movement, not the color—is the signal for the bull's charging.

Stratton [14] tried to find out the truth of the matter by arranging an experiment in which the effectiveness of red compared with other colors could be determined by actually watching the cattle in an experimental situation in which the various factors could be controlled.

He made four banners, two by six feet each, of white, black, red, and green cloth. They were attached lengthwise to a line of such height that the cattle could easily move under them. Small herds of cattle were observed at one time. The description of a herd of twelve, two bulls and ten cows, is typical of all the cattle observed.

I urge the herd gently toward the colors. At a distance of forty or fifty feet, the nearest cows stand at attention, the bulls remain behind. One of the bulls then moves to the front, and there is a general slow movement forward with some gentle snorting. The other bull remains in the rear, feeding. Cautiously coming to the flags, there is much halting, with most attention to the *white*. Four cows sniff the white, and back slightly when it flutters towards them. Then one of the bulls smells of the *black* for a time; the other bull stands near the red, facing it, but with little or no sign of interest in it. One of them sniffs the *white,* glances at the *red,* and turns again to the *white*.

The five-year bull, when slowly driven along the line of colors now fastened along a high fence, showed perhaps a slight start at the *white;* and after passing this color he returned and sniffed it. Moving again

[14] G. M. Stratton, "The Color Red, and Anger of Cattle," *Psychological Review,* 1923, 30, 321-25.

past the colors, he gave at most a glance at the red, then stopped between the *green* and the white, and gazed up the hill. Again, he goes to
the *black* and stops with perhaps a sniff at it, then turns and passes close
to the *red* and stops with his rear to this color.[15]

As a result of more extended observations than are recorded
here Stratton concludes:

1. There was no strong excitement from the colors as a whole or
from any one of them. There was interest, hesitation, mild mistrust
toward all and any of the banners, as toward strange things.

2. None of the colors caused any reactions that could be recognized
as anger.

3. Brightness and movement, rather than hue, caused responses in
the cattle. A slightly greater interest and mistrust was shown toward
white than toward any other; toward a fluttering banner rather than
toward a still one.

4. There were no differences in the reactions of bulls, cows, steers,
or calves.

The California woman who was so certain that her red dress
and sweater caused the cow to charge her must certainly have been
wrong. What the cause was we are not able to say, but we may
infer that she left something very important out of her report.

7. BLOOD AND EXCITEMENT IN CATTLE

Failure to recognize a true cause and its confusion with the
mere accompanying circumstances are found in the almost universal
belief that the smell of blood is exciting to cattle. "The smell of
blood," writes one cattleman, "always excites cattle of either sex,
causing them to bawl, paw the ground." Another man writes: "A
freshly dehorned cow with bleeding horns seems to excite the other
cattle; they are apt to follow her and appear to be somewhat afraid
and suspicious, and yet show a tendency to fight her. I dehorned
a few cows near a pen containing a grown bull. He certainly be-

[15] *Ibid.*, p. 322.

came excited and acted as though he wanted to fight. It took a week or more to quiet him down."

Stratton [16] has also subjected these notions to test. He used both horse's blood and cow's blood and presented them generally on a white cloth which was soaked with the blood and then laid on a piece of burlap. The cloths were tested first without any blood on them at all to see if those without blood caused any excitement. The results of this control were negative: There was no excitement. But when the wet and crimson cloths saturated with freshly drawn blood were presented, the results were also negative—again there was no excitement. There was never any pawing of the ground or bawling. Usually the animals came singly to the blood, sniffed, or licked it and passed on. There was some avoidance, but it was mild. The results were identical for both the horse's and the cow's blood, a fact which shows that there is nothing peculiar about cow's blood itself as a producer of excitement.

Stratton surmises then that the excitement from blood universally reported by cattlemen is actually a reaction not to blood but to the noise and confusion which usually accompanies the letting of blood, as in dehorning. The cries of pain and alarm and the excitement of the people who are caring for the animals are among the factors which are not mentioned when all of the excitement is attributed to the sight or smell of blood although they are always inextricably combined in a stimulating situation. Stratton's experiments were reasonably free from all these complicating factors so that the effect of the sight and smell of blood alone might be examined. When these conditions were met there was no excitement on the part of the cattle.

Summary of the chapter.—The principal purpose of this chapter has been to show how impossible it is, without the use of an experiment, to know what really is causing the behavior we observe. An experiment is simply a controlled observation. By control we mean that we can hold factors constant or vary them in a prescribed manner and watch for a resultant change in behavior on the part

[16] G. M. Stratton, "Cattle, and Excitement from Blood," *Psychological Review,* 1923, 30, 380-87.

of our subjects, either human or animal. Six of the seven sections relate the outlines of extremely simple experiments. The first one makes use of simple counting [17] and record keeping—no more. The second involves a measurement before and after a group of children has had a certain experience. The third experiment showed how under one set of conditions a diviner failed to locate hidden objects and how he was more successful under other conditions. The fourth experiment makes the factors, hinted at in the third, themselves the principal objects of control in the successive elimination of opportunities to use the various senses in a mind-reading performance.

The fifth section concerns itself with a more complicated experiment. At least the people who have written about it make it appear to be complicated, but had the problem been clearly envisioned in the beginning and had the experiments been planned beforehand to fit the scientific formula, the details would have been easier to relate and the outcome more certain. The two last experiments show how, when all factors are kept constant but color, one color is not more effective than another in producing excitement in cattle, and that the same thing is true for the sight and smell of blood.

By selecting instances in which widespread misconception is prevalent I have chosen, in this first chapter, to illustrate the principles of the scientific method as they apply to understanding human

[17] Floyd Ruch, in his *Psychology and Life,* Scott, Foresman and Company, Chicago, 1937, relates how counting and record keeping are valuable in changing an opinion regarding the superiority of the various nationalities. He tells of a young chemist who had studied in Germany and who in a social gathering said that the Germans were clearly superior to other nationalities in their contribution to chemistry. The statement resulted in an argument during which neither party succeeded in convincing the other. Some months later Ruch asked the chemist to list ten major contributions to the science of chemistry. He said nothing about the argument. In the list the chemist made—and to the layman it looks like a good list—contributions made by both Englishmen and Frenchmen clearly outnumbered those made by Germans. The young chemist had probably been thinking about the contributions the Germans have made to a limited field in chemistry. In his thinking, when no count was made, this limited contribution colored the whole of chemistry and led him to make an unwarranted generalization.

and animal behavior. From studies I have made [18] I know that about 90 per cent of the people who register for psychology in a large state university believe that the study of Latin automatically will improve their understanding of English. Many people suppose—and without foundation—that mathematics will increase their ability to reason or that games like chess will develop their abilities to concentrate. Mind reading, divination, telepathy, clairvoyance, and the ability of cattle to recognize danger in the color red and in the sight and smell of blood—all are firmly believed by the typical undergraduate. Merely to say that these things are misconceptions is not enough. Reasons for disbelieving them are given in this chapter. The same principles of scientific methodology which are illustrated here could have been made explicit by a formal—but to most readers less interesting—discussion of the scientific method in the abstract and by an illustration with laboratory experiments on lifted weights. The remainder of this volume continues to develop the plan set forth here.

[18] W. L. Valentine, "Common Misconceptions of College Students," *Journal of Applied Psychology,* 1936, 20, 633-58.

II

PHRENOLOGY, PHYSIOGNOMY, GRAPHOLOGY, AND CHARACTER ANALYSIS[1]

HIDDEN behind the complicated names that serve as a title to this chapter is one of the most complicated stories of bad reasoning and faulty observation that we encounter any place in human history. Had we all grown beyond the childish beliefs encountered in this chapter, the situation would have academic interest only; but it is not all history. It is estimated that several hundred millions of dollars are spent each year on the various fraudulent schemes for analyzing character and personality based on the shape of hands and the type of profile a person has. Some of these schemes are described by Dorothy H. Yates in an aptly titled book, *Psychological Racketeers*. Every student will want to read this little volume which is a record of a teacher's visits, sometimes in the company of her students, to the various quacks that prey on the gullible. Most modern psychological rackets trace their ancestry to a very famous Viennese physician, one Franz Joseph Gall, a brilliant but rash gentleman of a century ago.

1. PHRENOLOGY

Dr. Gall's magnum opus was a contribution which in some editions ran to six volumes and contained one hundred plates. The title of this work was the *Anatomy and Physiology of the Nervous System, Together with Observations on the Possibility of Determin-*

[1] In connection with this chapter every student will enjoy reading Joseph Jastrow's delightfully written *Wish and Wisdom,* D. Appleton-Century Company, New York, 1935, especially pages 230-303.

28

ing Mental and Moral Qualities in Men and Animals by the Contours of Their Heads. It contained some sober anatomical in-

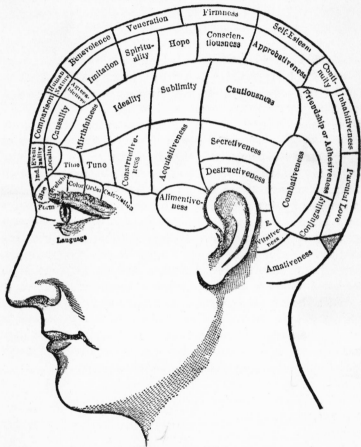

FIG. 2.—A phrenological chart. (After Spurzheim.)

vestigation, and at the time it was written it was not unreasonable to investigate the *possibility* that mental qualities could be determined by the contours of skulls. But Gall soon forgot the tentative nature of his hypothesis. He became a propagandist intent on proving his point.

It seems that his first observations of a phrenological kind were made when he was nine years old. He observed that boys in school who displayed elaborate retentive capacities also had bulging eyes. The brain responsible for the good memories back of the eyes was, he thought, pushing them forward.

Aside from his own uncritical observations at age nine, Gall was doubtless influenced by the teachings of the Swiss priest Lavater whose books on physiognomy[2] were widely read about 1800. Physiognomy differed from Gall's phrenology only in ascribing potency to the face rather than to the skull. But Lavater was responsible for a very clear statement of the position of the phrenologists when he wrote, "The cavity of the skull is visibly fitted to the mass of substances it contains, and follows their growth at every age of human life. Thus the exterior form of the brain, which imprints itself perfectly on the internal surface of the skull, is, at the same time, the model of the contours of the exterior surface." Regardless of Lavater's assertion to the contrary, one has to examine only a few skulls in any modern collection to see that there is little or no relation between the external surface contours and the formation of the brain within. Figure 3 shows how the thickness of the skull wall varies in two different specimens. Figure 3 is of particular importance because it is taken from a skeptic's book published in 1839. The only explanation for an assertion so contrary to fact is that some people see what they *hope* to see. They entertain only those facts that are congenial to their bias, fabricating where necessary, merely suppressing difficult items when invention is not demanded.

Some further insight into the logic of phrenologists is revealed in Gall's discovery of the seat of attachment or friendship (Fig. 2). He once knew a woman who was noted for the many friends she had. Since there was a bump at the back of the skull, the back of the skull must be the determiner of a person's "adhesiveness," as it came to be called. This kind of evidence could be continued for the twenty-odd "organs" that Gall thought he had discovered and the

[2] Physiognomy has a history extending back to Aristotle, who believed that the principal characteristics of animals were exhibited by human beings whose faces resembled the animal.

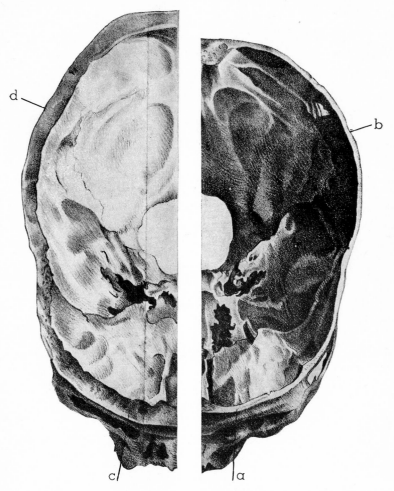

Fig. 3.—A section through a thick-walled skull on the left;
a thin-walled skull on the right.

score that were added by his followers. There is positively no relation between the *assumed* functions of various parts of the brain and the actual function as later determined by physiologists. A further discussion of this problem will have to be deferred until we reach Chapter XX.

Aside from their faulty notions of anatomy, phrenologists are also far from right in asserting that "friendship," or adhesiveness in their verbiage, is something that a person can have in so many cubic centimeters. Some people are more generally friendly than others, but a description of this friendly behavior reveals that "friendliness" is not the kind of thing that can be measured like the area of a table top or the volume of a pail.

Phrenologists stop at nothing. Advice today, as a hundred years ago, is offered without reservation. A phrenologist just can't be wrong. For example, physicians are said to require "large perceptive organs so that they may study and apply a knowledge of anatomy and physiology with skill and success; full destructiveness, lest they shrink from inflicting pain; large constructiveness to give them skill in surgery; large combativeness, to render them resolute and prompt." This is only part of the list, but it grows tiresome to read much of such drivel. *Not a single shred of evidence is offered to support any of these contentions.* You are expected to believe that the phrenologist, because of some studies that he is terribly vague about, is competent to advise you on what vocation you are best suited for. The procedure of the modern psychologist is quite different. It is described in detail in Chapter III. Suffice it to say here that any psychologist worth listening to is extremely humble in the searchlight of modern demands made on him. He feels uncertain and ignorant; he is not able to predict by *any* method, with certainty, how successful a person will be in any vocation.

2. PHYSIOGNOMY

After Gall's death early in the nineteenth century phrenology and physiognomy became more confused than they had been before. We read in a popular book written in 1859,

Now, since coarseness and fineness of texture indicate coarse and fine-grained feelings and characters, and since black signifies power, and red ardor, therefore coarse black hair and skin signify great power of character of some kind, along with considerable tendency to the sensual; yet fine black hair and skin indicate strength of character, along with purity and goodness. Dark-skinned nations are always behind the light-skinned in all the improvements of the age, as well as in the higher and finer manifestations of humanity. So, too, dark-haired persons, like Webster, sometimes called "Black Dan," possess great power of intellect and propensity, yet lack the finer and more delicate shadings of sensibility and purity. Coarse black hair and skin, and coarse red hair and whiskers, indicate powerful animal passions, together with corresponding strength of character; while fine or light, or auburn hair indicates quick susceptibilities, together with refinement and good taste. Fine dark or brown hair indicates the combination of exquisite susceptibilities with great strength of character, while auburn hair, with a florid countenance, indicates the highest order of sentiment and intensity of feeling, along with corresponding purity of character, combined with the highest capacities for enjoyment and suffering. And the intermediate colors and textures indicate intermediate mentalities. . . .

Straight, even, smooth, and glossy hair indicates strength, harmony, and evenness of character, and hearty, whole-souled affections, as well as a clear head and superior talents; while stiff, straight, black hair and beard indicate a coarse, strong, rigid, straightforward character. . . .

Coarse-haired persons should never turn dentists or clerks, but seek some out-door employment; and would be better contented with rough, hard work than a light or sedentary occupation, altho mental and sprightly occupations would serve to refine and improve them; while dark and fine-haired persons may choose purely intellectual occupations, and become lecturers or writers with fair prospects of success. Red-haired persons should seek outdoor employment, for they require a great amount of air and exercise; while those who have light, fine hair should choose occupations involving taste and mental acumen, yet take bodily exercise enough to tone up and invigorate their system.[3]

The quotation makes it clear that analogy is the favorite logical method of the phrenologist as it is for all lazy thinkers. Palmistry serves as a further example. A long line in the palm means a long

[3] O. S. Fowler and L. N. Fowler, *A New Illustrated Self-Instructor in Phrenology and Physiology*, Samuel Wells, New York, 1859.

life; a short line a short life; a squarish rugged palm means a firm rugged nature; a long finger here a deep seriousness; another long finger, no loss for words. Again there is no testing of hypothesis; the palmist must know enough about the person so that the judgments independent of the appearance of his palm have some verisimilitude, or else the information about his character is so vague and general that it could not help but be true for almost anybody.

As proof of this latter statement let anyone write a typical character analysis and hand it to a group of friends individually. Ask them how many of the statements are true of them. Be careful to make the statements either *boldly flattering or only mildly critical*. You will be surprised at the results. This test is frequently made in classrooms. After a few meetings of the class the instructor says, "Now, I have been studying you people for a few days and I want to try an experiment. I have written a short analysis of your character here and I want you to underline all of the things that I have said about you that are true." Papers conspicuously labeled with each person's name are distributed and the students set to work. The majority of the statements will be marked as true; their flattering nature has assured that they will be. Then it is revealed to everyone's discomfiture that every character analysis is identical with every other one.

3. BLOND AND BRUNET TRAITS

Paterson and Ludgate[4] found one physiognomist[5] who described traits supposed to be related to color of the skin and hair with sufficient detail so that the traits and alleged relation to complexion could be studied experimentally. Most physiognomists are not consistent. Their work will stand no careful comparison of what is said on one page with what is announced on another. Blackford

[4] Donald G. Paterson and Katherine E. Ludgate, "Blonde and Brunette Traits: A Quantitative Study," *Journal of Personnel Research*, 1922, 1, 122-27.
[5] Katherine M. H. Blackford and A. Newcomb, *The Job, the Man, the Boss*, 1919, p. 141.

held that blonds "always and everywhere" are positive, dynamic, driving, aggressive, domineering, impatient, active, quick, hopeful, speculative, changeable, and variety-loving. Brunets present just exactly the opposite of these traits: They are negative, static, conservative, imitative, submissive, cautious, painstaking, patient, ploddy, slow, deliberate, serious, thoughtful, and specializing. On the basis of these and other physiognomical relations, Blackford made sweeping generalizations relating to vocational guidance.

	Per Cent Required by the Hypothesis		Per Cent of 187 Actually Who Were Said to Be Described by the Adjective	
	Blond	*Brunet*	*Blond*	*Brunet*
Blond traits				
Positive...........	100	0	81	84
Dynamic..........	100	0	63	64
Aggressive.........	100	0	49	50
Domineering.......	100	0	36	36
Impatient..........	100	0	56	51
Brunet traits				
Negative..........	0	100	16	17
Static.............	0	100	28	31
Conservative.......	0	100	51	61
Imitative..........	0	100	39	40
Submissive.........	0	100	25	26

In order to subject these claims to experimental test, Paterson and Ludgate prepared a sheet of paper on which the 26 traits were listed in random order. These papers were given to a group of students who were asked to select from among their acquaintances 2 blonds and 2 brunets. In 4 separate columns, one for each person rated, they were to place check marks if it could be said that the person under consideration could be described by the adjective supplied. In this way judgments were made on 187 blonds and 187 brunets.

After these sheets were collected the results were tabulated and percentages computed as shown in the table.

We reproduce only part of the data. The remainder tells the same story. In order for the hypothesis to be substantiated in the positive and dogmatic way in which it is stated, it is necessary that we have numbers closely approximating 100 under the word "Blond" for the 5 blond traits. In this same column these numbers should drop to very close to zero with a corresponding rise in the brunet column and they should be very close to zero in the upper right-hand quarter of the table. None of these conditions obtains. *We must conclude that there is no relationship between the adjective that a group of judges will use to describe a person's behavior and the kind of complexion he has.*

For several years this little exercise has been required of beginning Ohio State University students and in no instance has a relationship between complexion and behavior been shown. Paterson and Ludgate's results are uniformly substantiated; Blackford's claims are uniformly negated.

In a more complicated study Cleeton and Knight[6] were able to examine intensively the relationship between the physical characteristics of face and hand, and the behavior that would be described as judgment, leadership, originality, or impulsiveness in thirty different subjects. These psychological investigators ran into the problem of measuring "psychological traits," like frankness, that the physiognomists so glibly talk about as though there were complete agreement on what these labels refer to. Just what is a "frank" person? What kinds of things do frank people say and do that establish their frankness? How completely do people agree in their judgments on abstract qualities of this kind? Cleeton and Knight solved their problem by allowing only intimate acquaintances to make the ratings. They then pooled the ratings of several different raters in such a way that they were fairly certain that another group of raters describing individual John Jones, one of their thirty subjects, would say the same things about him. *Technically this procedure is known as establishing the reliability of their ratings.*

[6] G. U. Cleeton and F. B. Knight, "Validity of Character Judgments Based on External Criteria," *Journal of Applied Psychology,* 1924, 8, 215-29.

They secured 122 physical measures on each of their 30 subjects and then made comparisons between the ratings and the 122 physiognomical signs. In all the 201 comparisons which they could make from their data not a single relationship could be found. In fact, their data were so monotonously regular in exhibiting no relationship that we will not reproduce them here.

4. GRAPHOLOGY

The same use of analogy that we have seen in phrenology, physiognomy, and palmistry is evident in the work of people who claim to be able to read a person's character by the kind of handwriting he exhibits.

There are at least three different kinds of graphology. First, there are those people who are interested in detecting forged documents and the like. That is a story entirely apart from psychology. Then there are those persons who consider handwriting a kind of expressive movement, like the gestures that a person uses. That story is the interest principally of social psychologists.[7] Although the experimental work from this angle is of the highest caliber, we cannot go into it here. The third kind of graphology asserts, without evidence, that character and handwriting are related: that ambition is related to lines that slope upward; pride is related to lines that slope downward; bashfulness to fine lines; force with heavy lines; perseverance with long bars on *t*'s and reserve with closed *a*'s and *o*'s. The use of the crudest kind of analogy here is self-evident.

Hull and Montgomery[8] have subjected these latter claims to experimental test, using as subjects seventeen members of a medical fraternity at the University of Wisconsin. Each man was asked to

[7] G. W. Allport and P. E. Vernon, *Studies in Expressive Movement*, The Macmillan Company, New York, 1933.
[8] Clark L. Hull and Robert Montgomery, "An Experimental Investigation of Certain Alleged Relations between Character and Handwriting," *Psychological Review*, 1919, 26, 63-74.

write in his own manner, in his own room, at his own desk, and with his own pen, a paragraph from a popular magazine.

When he had finished writing, each subject was supplied with a set of sixteen small cards, each containing the name of one of the other subjects. The subject was directed to arrange the cards in the order in which the sixteen subjects ranged according to ambition, putting the most "ambitious" person first and the least ambitious last. The rank thus accorded to each of the other subjects was recorded by the experimenter. Then the cards were carefully shuffled and given to the subject again. This time he ranked his fraternity brothers in "pride."

From the seventeen rankings obtained in this way, an average position for each subject on each of six traits was obtained. These measures constituted the best estimate that could be made of the graphologist's traits of ambition, pride, bashfulness, force, perseverance, and reserve. It remained to measure the slope of the line, the fineness of the lines, the length of the *t*'s, and the open or closed character of the *o*'s and *a*'s and to relate these measures to the character ratings.

When these comparisons were made *there was not a single item that showed any consistent relationship to the estimates of character by seventeen judges who were intimately acquainted with the people they were judging.*

The only conclusion possible is that the graphologists who assert a relationship between handwriting and character or behavior traits based on analogies of the one with the other are sadly in error. In order to protect one's self against the charlatans in this field it is only necessary to ask for an objective demonstration of the relation which the graphologist asserts. If the only evidence forthcoming is the authority of the graphologist, one may safely conclude that he doesn't know what he is talking about, however persuasive he may appear.

Summary of the chapter.—Efforts to understand human nature have not always been scientific. The systems of phrenology, physiognomy and graphology that we have examined in this chapter typify any pseudo-scientific system—under whatever name—advanced by whatever self-styled psychologist today. These systems are nonscientific because they make no use whatever of the scientific method. Their proponents do not develop hypotheses which can be tested for truth, nor do they make any effort to formulate the kinds of hypotheses that are susceptible to testing. They assume the truth of their hypotheses at the outset: their hypotheses become dicta backed only by the authority that the charlatans are able to muster.

To the uncritical and the untrained this authority always carries a good deal of weight because it is supported by what seems to be an exact accuracy of statement. But this accuracy turns out to be a pseudo accuracy accomplished in three ways: first, the generalizations are so broad that they have to be true to a degree; second, the generalizations are flattering, never critical; third, they are supported by selecting cases that demonstrate or illustrate the dictum—other specific cases that do not fit are glossed over or ignored. By the proper selection of instances one can prove anything at all true provided somebody doesn't ask: "And how about all these other instances?" The charlatan has to evade this question.

The charlatan employs principally the logical method of analogy. There is nothing wrong with the method, but the analogies are made on the basis of superficial resemblances between nonexistent psychological traits like "force" and immaterial properties like "breadth of stroke" in handwriting.

The modern psychologist with adequate training in the scientific method would urge, as a substitute for these engaging short cuts to understanding human nature, the long and rigorous road which scientific method and principles provide. Science is a hard taskmistress.

The outlook must seem rather hopeless to the student who has read with understanding the preceding pages, which have denied the validity of a fairly large sample of what he may have considered sound knowledge or self-evident truth. He may find himself convinced that the psychologist is an iconoclast, but whether he thinks of the psychologist as a knight on horseback jousting with Ignorance or as a bad boy letting the air out of automobile tires is probably a matter of personal preference; there are both kinds. But in the rather short history of scientific attempts at understanding human beings there has been built a definite body of constructive facts. The next chapter introduces some of these.

III

APTITUDES

Definition.—Whenever a person can learn a thing quickly and effectively, he is said to have an aptitude for it, or a special ability with respect to it. Whenever his learning is startlingly rapid, he is said to be talented in the particular field under consideration. Talents are most frequently thought of in connection with artistic, literary, or professional fields; but the term really only expresses the notion of extraordinary excellence and may be applied to the more mundane fields of mechanical art, athletic activity, or even clerical responsibility.

Heredity and aptitude.—In the prescientific era, which in this field extends well into the present, there was a good deal of nonsense written about aptitudes, special abilities, and talents. *Aptitudes were held wholly to be hereditary "gifts" of a special kind.* The phrase "gifted musician" or "gifted artist" meant that the person in question has been endowed by his heredity with special talents of an artistic kind. The expressions "he wasn't cut out to be a physician" or "teachers are born, not made" reflect the same notion of behavior causes—human nature is what it is because of special hereditary endowments or ineptitudes along specific lines.

Hypostatization.—It should be obvious that the error of nominalization (hypostasis) has crept again into our thinking about talents as it has in our thinking about all psychological factors.[1] When we say that a person has a special ability as a public speaker, or is particularly adept at mechanics, we are not explaining why he is facile in these fields. The name cannot be the cause; it is a short description of the condition.

[1] When we hypostasize we attempt to explain a phenomenon by giving it a name rather than by seeking out its cause.

40

If a boy wants to become a physician it is common to search through his ancestral tree to try to find the reason. Rather than fall back on a poorly understood inheritance of special ability as the *sole* cause, we should investigate alternative possibilities of explanation. A boy may *conceivably* become a physician because he is motivated to be like his family doctor. The occupation of a physician may have appealed to him because he soon observed that a doctor is a highly respected man in a community. An early interest in medical practice could conceivably be as important as hereditary background in determining his vocational choice. *We cannot state with any finality or even with any accuracy to what extent a successful career as a physician is dependent upon inherited structures as contrasted with acquired tastes, aptitudes, or skills.* But fortunately we do not have to face this problem in order to understand the nature of aptitude. *What a person has learned in the past and the degree to which he has learned it is indicative of what and how he will be able to learn about new things in the future.* For instance, an aptitude for medicine is a manifestation of a present condition of interests and attainment which indicates that the individual will learn quickly about medical things.

Before entering upon a discussion of the complicated professional fields and the special abilities which are usually accepted as being paramount in persons who succeed in them, let us see how one goes about determining the nature of talent in a simpler situation.

1. CLERICAL APTITUDE

Considerable success has recently been attained in separating clerical workers from nonclerical workers by the use of tests for what is called "clerical aptitude." [2] These tests are not concerned with whether an individual is a blond, whether his fingers are long, or how he dots his *i*'s and crosses his *t*'s. In the construction of a clerical aptitude test the first prerequisite is a careful description of

[2] Dorothy M. Andrew, "An Analysis of the Minnesota Vocational Test for Clerical Workers," *Journal of Applied Psychology*, 1937, 21, 18-47; 139-72.

Job Analysis of Clerical Occupation

Much of a clerk's work has to do with papers: memoranda, correspondence, and records. On the papers are words, symbols, numbers. These he reads, compares, classifies, transcribes, or passes judgment upon, and in the course of so doing makes decisions which, except in the more routine operations, may require a high order of technical knowledge and good sense. The tools of his trade include the pencil and the pen, and sometimes the slide rule, the typewriter, the duplicator, the bookkeeping or calculating machine, the filing cabinet, the card index, and similar aids in classifying, cataloguing, finding, rearranging, identifying, copying, computing, or otherwise manipulating for a purpose the papers and symbols used in recording and communication. It must be remembered, however, that a clerical worker's speed and accuracy in the mechanics of using these tools, essential though they are, rank lower in value than the correctness of his thinking about the problems which the papers present. A clerk may be called upon to do other kinds of work also, such as to use the telephone, receive visitors, make purchases, organize and supervise the work of others in the office. But as a clerical worker, the abilities indispensable to the effective performance of his duties are those which enable him to handle the problems arising in connection with his paper work judiciously as well as rapidly.[3]

[3] W. V. Bingham, *Aptitudes and Aptitude Testing,* Harper & Brothers, New York, 1937, p. 151.

the clerical occupation. This is called technically a "job analysis." Its purpose is to determine, if possible, the most important phases of clerical aptitude, and the essential abilities which they seem to require.

The job analysis shown on page 42 for the clerical occupations shows that they require at least four *different* kinds of abilities:

1. The ability to observe words and numbers and to perceive instantly what is on the paper.

2. The ability to make correct decisions regarding the questions these symbols raise.

3. The ability to handle the tools of the trade with facility.

4. An ability with elementary schoolroom skills of adding, multiplying, spelling, punctuating, capitalizing, and understanding the meaning of words and expressions.

Measuring clerical aptitude.—The most hopeful attempt to measure these abilities has been made within very recent years by the Minnesota Employment Stabilization Research Institute. The test constructors have rather closely followed the above outline of abilities in preparing a collection, or a battery, of tests designed to measure clerical ability. The first test of the battery, as dictated by the job analysis, is a test of number- and name-checking performance. The speed and accuracy with which a person can perceive similarities and differences between pairs of numbers and names is obtained. These are some sample items:

307—309

4605—4603

2063849102983—263349102983

Hulme Co.—Hulne Co.

L. T. Piver—L. T. Piser

Keely Institute—Kelly's Institute

The direct relation between these operations and the job requirements is perfectly obvious. The operations are identical. No vague "ability" is to be measured. If a person has learned to make promptly the discriminations required of him, he can make a good score on the test. This learning is presumably definitely limited by the physiological structures one possesses. But as we have pointed out, the problem of inheritance does not have to be faced in a practical problem like this. A clerk of considerable experience may not be superior to a person who has much less experience. But just which structures are involved and how much they are involved we do not know.

The second requirement—that of being able to understand relationships between symbols and to make decisions regarding them —is met by the use of one of the standard "intelligence" tests. These tests really measure how well one can understand the meaning of words and symbols as we shall see in a later chapter. The particular tests used at Minnesota as part of the clerical battery were the Pressey Senior Classification Test and Senior Verification Test. Both of these tests are heavily loaded with items that overlap with the fourth requirement, a mastery of simple schoolroom skills. They test how well the skills of spelling, punctuating, capitalizing, and so on, have been mastered as well as what is usually called "intelligence."

The third requirement is measured by the performance on three kinds of manipulation tests. The first is called the Minnesota Rate of Manipulation Test. Sixty wooden discs about $1\frac{1}{2}$ inches in diameter have to be placed in just slightly larger holes in a board. The placing has to be done in a specified way and the time required is a measure of hand and arm dexterity. Dexterity in handling the same objects with the fingers is measured when the subjects are required to pick the discs out of the holes with one hand, turn them over with a thumb and finger movement, transfer them to the other hand, and replace them in the same hole.

Finger dexterity is measured by the O'Connor Finger Dexterity Test. The time required to place small metal pegs, three at a time, in one hundred small holes, is the score. This is a task which is different from, though related to, what is demanded in the Rate of Manipulation Test. The small size of the objects demands a finer co-ordination of the small muscle groups of the fingers.

The ability to use a small instrument, a task requiring even finer discrimination and co-ordination, is tested by means of the O'Connor Tweezer Dexterity Test. The same pegs that are used in the Finger Dexterity Test must be inserted in somewhat smaller

The Minnesota Rate of Manipulation Test

The O'Connor Finger Dexterity Test

The O'Connor Tweezer Dexterity Test

Fig. 4

(Courtesy of the University of Minnesota Press. From Paterson and Darley, *Men, Women and Jobs*, facing p. 10.)

holes, one at a time instead of three at a time, and with a small pair of tweezers instead of with the unaided fingers.

Thus we see that there is nothing mysterious about a "test." In a testing situation the subject is merely active with respect to certain stimulating objects that are placed before him. He is constantly doing that anyway, whether or not he is being tested. It is true that the objects and symbols placed before him are of very highly selected kinds. The subject's reactions may be circumscribed or restricted in various ways, and there may be the pressure of finishing in a certain time limit. All this irritates some people and creates in them an unfavorable attitude towards tests and testing, but such an attitude should not keep us from learning the advantages of testing procedures. Of course, there are good tests and poor tests. *The ultimate standard by which tests should be judged is whether they prove to have high validity.*

The meaning of validity.—Briefly, *an indication of validity is an indication of how accurate the title or label at the head of a test really is.* If a test constructor asserts that a score a person makes on his test is indicative of some property or attainment or ability that a person has, he has to prove it. He proves it by determining the validity of the test.

Questions of validity do not generally arise in tests for simple schoolroom skills. A test of spelling involves the same activity that one is testing; one doesn't have to prove that it is a spelling test. Everybody would agree that a spelling test is a spelling test, or that an arithmetic test really tests what the label says it does.[4]

But if a psychologist asserts that he has an instrument which will select the people who will make the best salesman out of all the people who want to become salesmen, then he has to *prove* the assertion by showing that people who are already successful salesmen score high on his test and others who have been discharged or are about to be discharged or who have become discouraged and have quit because they were not successful in selling or did not like it, make low scores. The production in selling is called the *criterion,*

---

[4] This assumption is open to challenge, but we do not want to pursue the question any further here.

and if it is highly valid, the test must agree with the criterion all the way down the line and not just differentiate the extremes (cf. page 57). Parenthetically, no such test for salesmanship exists.

The validity of the clerical battery.—In keeping with these principles a person who designs a battery like these clerical tests *has to demonstrate that the battery does actually discriminate between persons who succeed in the clerical occupations and persons who are successful in other occupations that require different abilities.* This procedure is a marked contrast with that of the phrenologist or graphologist, to whom the necessity for this kind of proof would never occur. From our discussion of experimental and control groups in Chapter I, it is obvious that the individuals in the contrasting occupational groups should be the same age, same sex, of the same social level, and so forth, except for occupation. The profile shown in Figure 5 exhibits the average performance of two adult groups of workers—garage mechanics and men office clerks. The mechanics are only slightly above the mean of an unselected adult population in all of the tests that we have used for measuring clerical aptitude, while the clerks are distinctly above the mean in the same tests. For women a similar condition exists when retail saleswomen are compared with women office workers. Thus the validity of the battery is demonstrated. The nature of aptitude generally is further elucidated by the addition to the men's battery of a "mechanical assembly" test and a "spatial relations" test. These are tests of "mechanical ability" and, for our purpose, it is not necessary to describe them. They show that the garage mechanics are not just generally of lower attainment than men office workers. When tests are used that tap the abilities they exercise in their occupations then they become superior. For the women, although there is a clear-cut difference for the clerical battery, i.e., the first three tests, no tests were used which permitted the retail saleswomen to show in what respects they were superior to the women clerks.

2. INDIVIDUAL DIAGNOSIS

As a digression from our main theme at this point, let us consider Figure 6, which exhibits a profile of a single student.[5] He stands very near the bottom of the distribution in a college aptitude test, in the American Council Test, and in the Iowa English Examination. His high school scholarship record is also below average. If we had only these tests, we would be forced to conclude that his ability generally was very low, but the inclusion of a general science test and the dexterity and mechanical assembly tests shows that we have here a case in which there is a special ability in dexterity and mechanical assembly. In this case rank incompetence in the abilities required for scholastic success is associated with a manipulative ability that puts most college students in the class of "also rans." This case, however, is not typical.

Popular belief to the contrary, it is not true that low ability in the intellectual fields is invariably associated with high ability in the mechanical field. The patterns of aptitude and ineptitude must be determined for every individual. *There is no generalization that will permit us to predict what we will find in behavior segments which are as yet untested, from the results of tests in areas that are not closely allied with these.* This problem will be discussed at greater length in a later section of this chapter.

The meaning of the labels in Figures 5 and 6.—It is necessary at this point to make still another digression from our main theme in this chapter. The careful student has observed the labels "Sigma Units" and "Centile Rank" in Figures 5 and 6. Since both of these units are used extensively in psychological work, an understanding of them is essential. They are both units for comparing the performance of one person on several different tests or of many people on the same test in order to find the comparative standing of individuals or groups. Whenever we have the problem of making this

[5] Adapted from E. G. Williamson, *Students and Occupations*, Henry Holt and Company, New York, 1937. Every student should consult this helpful volume.

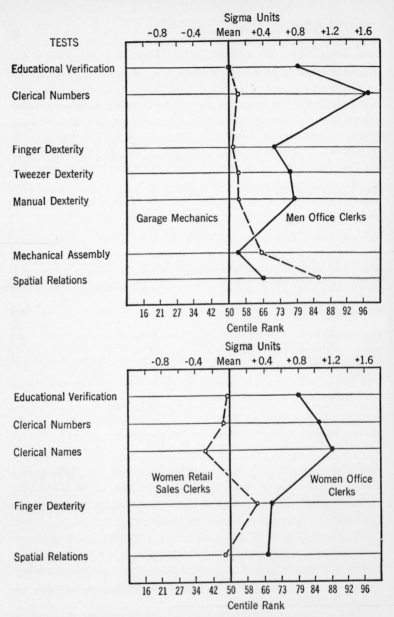

FIG. 5.—Profiles of different occupational groups. (After Paterson and Darley.) The central tendency of a group of subjects is shown by the heavy line in the center of the charts. The extent to which men office clerks exceed this mean is shown in the top chart by means of a series of solid lines. Garage mechanics do not stand as far above the average, except in two tests as shown by the broken line. The lower chart is to be read in the same way.

comparison, we need to state a given person's standing on a test with considerable precision. In comparing heights, for instance, we could say that a given man is 5 feet 10 inches, and that this is somewhat above the average. The use of centile ranks, however, would allow us to be more precise in our statements, because we can com-

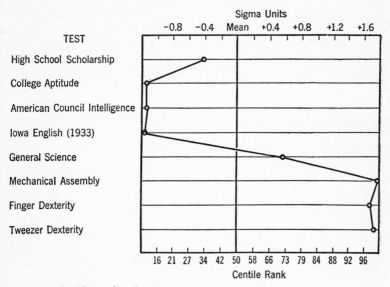

Fig. 6.—The profile of an individual student. This is an unusual case because this boy stands in the lowest 10 per cent in three of the tests and in the topmost 3 or 4 per cent in three others.

pute that a height of 5 feet 10 inches is in, say, the 75th centile. Interpreted, this means that 75 per cent of all men are of this height or below. Out of every 100 unselected men we should expect 25 to exceed the height of the man we are studying.

If we want to find this same person's standing in weight we may use the same process. Our man may weigh 190 pounds, which might turn out to be in the 90th centile. Therefore we could say that this man was further removed from the central tendency in weight than in height.

The real value of this technique is not apparent, however, until we are confronted with the necessity of comparing several different

measures on the same person or on groups of people. In comparing
the garage mechanics with the male office clerks we have seven
different measures on each group. In the first two tests the scores
are in terms of points—the number of correct items resulting from
the testing procedure. The finger, tweezer, and manual dexterity
tests, however, are scored in terms of the time required to perform
the various tasks. Now to try to compare the scores directly—points
with seconds—results in having to deal with incommensurables, an
error which any high school student should be able to recognize.
By transferring the raw scores into ranks, the ranks can be compared without consideration of the units which determined them.
Even when the units of measurement are the same—seconds, for
instance—to compare them directly leads to ridiculous conclusions.
A much longer time is required to complete the tweezer dexterity
test than the finger dexterity test, but since this is true for everyone the total time is not important. The relative standing, or rank,
however, is.

The same interpretation could be made from sigma units
although the procedure is less direct. Each system has some technical advantage that we will not discuss here. Notice, also, that
nothing has been said about the method of computing either derived unit. Our emphasis is on interpretation rather than on computation. For the latter the reader is referred to some standard text
in psychology or elementary statistics.[6]

What is an ability?—The results of a test of any kind are stated
in some units of performance. One cannot observe an aptitude directly: what one does observe are marks on paper symbolizing the
selection that was finally made out of a whole series of possible responses. In non-paper-pencil tests, movements of fingers and other
members are the processes under observation. These symbols (pencil
marks) and co-ordinated movements constitute performance. Per-

[6] There are many sources: Three recent ones are Henry E. Garrett, *Statistics
in Psychology and Education,* Longmans, Green and Co., New York, 1940;
E. F. Lindquist, *A First Course in Statistics,* Houghton Mifflin Company,
Boston, 1938; and G. Milton Smith, *A Simplified Guide to Statistics,* Farrar
& Rinehart, Inc., New York, 1938.

formance, however, needs to be explained. When there are observed relations between different performances, for example, it becomes useful scientifically to assume an underlying ability which is responsible for the fact that the relations obtain. This underlying ability is an abstraction. It cannot now be observed nor will it ever be observed in the future regardless of how sensitive our tests are made.

The difference between an aptitude and an accomplishment.— Some tests are labeled "aptitude tests" and some are labeled "achievement tests." The difference between them is not very clear cut in practice. In an aptitude test the items and the kinds of performance required are relatively uninfluenced, even by extended practice. An achievement test, on the other hand, requires the kind of performance that will exhibit the degree to which a given operation has been mastered. The usual classroom examinations in school subjects, if carefully prepared and well standardized, are typical achievement examinations. The fact that a good aptitude test presents a situation in which there is but little improvement with further practice does not necessarily mean that the responses were not learned in the first place. They are usually learned responses which have approached an ultimate physiological limit.

3. ACHIEVEMENT AND APTITUDE

The degree to which a person has achieved a mastery of certain school subjects can sometimes be taken as an index of his aptitude for them, and for similar subjects when other techniques for the measurement of the more fundamental components are not available.

This is the condition that exists in the selection of candidates for many of the professional fields today. One can take advantage of the similarity of the professional subject to the preprofessional requirements where the job requirements have not yet been analyzed sufficiently to make true aptitude testing possible. Consider medicine, for instance. We would like to know how to test the aptitudes required for success in medical school, but an adequate description of just what is demanded for this success has not yet been worked out with the same precision and detail that has produced such favorable results for clerical positions. Among the requirements that have been mentioned are a facility for learning the Latin and Greek polysyllables that make up so much of medical nomenclature, an aptitude for exacting detail, and a few other specifications which are so general that they cannot be measured. It has further been said that:

Surgeons and dentists are craftsmen in addition to being medically trained. Clearness of eye, delicacy of tactile discrimination, steadiness and strength of hand, dexterity of fingers, are obvious necessities. Quite as indispensable is aptitude for visualizing vividly in three dimensions; for it is necessary to see in their true positions and to manipulate the forms observed in a dentist's little mirror or in a laryngoscope; also to picture correctly the highly complicated unseen structures beneath the body surface—arteries, nerves, muscles, tendons, joints, glands, vital organs—perhaps at the end of a probe. Add to these abilities the grit and steadiness of nerve as well as of hand, without which surgeon, oculist, or dentist is prone to disastrous slips at critical junctures, and we have the aptitudes most commonly mentioned as more essential for surgery than for general medical practice. It is, however, hard to imagine how any practicing physician can do his work without frequent resort to the exercise of these same abilities in at least some degree, if he ever has to remove a child's adenoids, drain a suppurating fester, reset a dislocated shoulder joint, deliver a baby, or take a sliver from an eyelid.

So far as the professional schools are concerned, it is, to be sure, in the dental school rather than in the medical that a seriously large number of failures are directly traceable to lack of manual and mechanical aptitudes. Students who successfully pass the first two years of basic biological, physiological, and anatomical courses, not infrequently have to be dropped in the third year because they cannot master both the mechanical intricacies and the manual techniques of dental practice. . . .[7]

[7] W. V. Bingham, *Aptitudes and Aptitude Testing,* p. 184.

The charts in Figures 7 and 8 show how premedical grades are related to two criteria of success in medical school, whether or not the student was graduated and regardless of the average or grade he made if he was graduated. Notice that the general trend is in the upward direction, indicating that those who do best in premedical courses also do best in medical school. Slightly over 70 per cent of those in the lowest decile were graduated, while more than 95 per cent of those in the highest received a degree. Figure 7 shows the average grade for those in each decile. The interpretation of the term "decile" is exactly the same as "centile" except that the basis is tenths rather than hundredths. "The lowest 10 centiles" and "the lowest decile" are equivalent statements. (Cf. page 47.)

In a search for a better method of selection than is available in the premedical grades, the American Association of Medical Colleges has sponsored what has come to be known as a "Medical Aptitude Test." Changed every year, the test comprises generally about six parts which are designed to measure

1. Comprehension and retention
2. Visual memory
3. Memory for content
4. Logical reasoning
5. Scientific vocabulary
6. Understanding of printed material

There is much in common between this test and a general intelligence test, but a knowledge of the subject matter of premedical courses is required for any passable performance. As an "aptitude test," its approach is very indirect. Involving, as it does, so much highly specialized information, it would be more appropriate to call it an achievement test.

The results of its use have been surprisingly good, notwithstanding this criticism. Figures 7 and 8 show the relationship between graduation and "aptitude" decile. Only 40 per cent of the lowest decile were graduated, while 100 per cent of the top decile finished their four years in medical school. Figure 8 shows the relation between grades in medical school and "aptitude" decile. By comparing Figures 7 and 8 which are drawn to the same scale, it is evident that when it is a matter of predicting success in medical

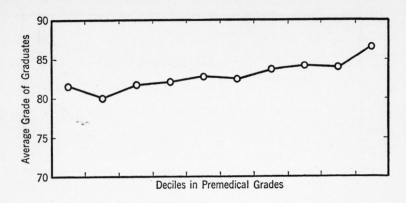

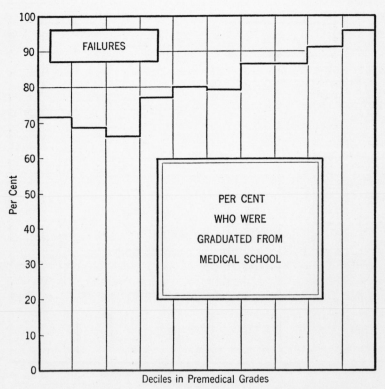

FIG. 7.—The relation between premedical grades and success in medical school. (After Moss.)

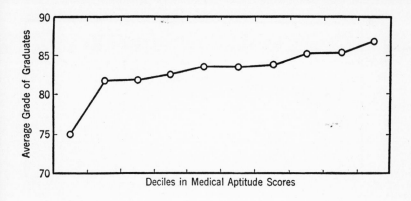

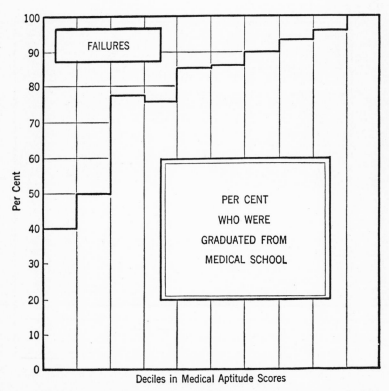

FIG. 8.—The relation between medical aptitude scores and success in medical school. (After Moss.)

school, the medical aptitude test score is of better prognostic value than the grades in premedical subjects. It is probably a better instrument for measuring the actual mastery of premedical subject matter than are the premedical grades themselves. Cramming or cheating might conceivably be more of a factor in determining grades than they are in determining test scores.

APTITUDE TEST SCORES

ABOVE 200: THE HIGHEST TENTH

Rated 2 or 3	Rated 1

Average Rating 1.8

APTITUDE TEST SCORES

BELOW 100: THE LOWEST TENTH

Rated 4 or 5	Rated 2 or 3	1

Average Rating 2.3

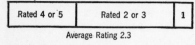

FIG. 9.—Medical aptitude and rating of success as an intern. (After Moss.)

Does the medical "aptitude test" predict success after graduation?—The superintendents of hospitals having three or more interns who had taken the test were sent rating scales to apply to the interns under their supervision. The ratings were to be made on a scale from 1 to 5; 1 was the highest and 5 the lowest rating. The definitions of these ratings given to the superintendents were:

(1) means "comes up to the best intern the hospital has had"
(2) means "is good, above average, but not equal to the best"
(3) means "is equal to the average intern the hospital has had"
(4) means "is below the average intern, but better than the poorest"
(5) means "is among the poorest interns the hospital has had." [8]

The chart shows the results of this survey. The average rating of those who were in the highest tenth of the Medical Test Performance was 1.8. As a group they were "above average." Forty-two per cent of them were rated "1." The others were rated either "2" or "3." None was rated either "4" or "5." Those in the lowest tenth present a contrasting picture. Barely 10 per cent were rated "1." Thirty-eight per cent were rated "4" or "5." This study shows

[8] F. A. Moss, "Medical Aptitude Tests," *Journal* of the American Association of Medical Colleges, 1936, 11, 275.

that as far as the extremes are concerned, the aptitude test can be used to predict how well *groups* of students will do as interns. The factors which are required for success as an intern still remain to be discovered. When they are, it is obvious that the prediction of success will be improved if they are taken into consideration.

The lack of a criterion.—We have been skirting a problem which is discussed in the technical literature under the topic "criterion." *A criterion is an objective measure of the mastery of one's job.* In some occupations, particularly those of a mechanical nature, the establishment of a criterion is relatively simple. The number of finished castings; the number of relays assembled; the number of soldered connections made—have all been used as criteria. In selling life insurance, the amount of insurance sold has long been a firmly fixed criterion of success in the occupation. In schoolwork grades have been used as the criterion, as in the top part of Figures 7 and 8; in other cases the attainment of some goal like graduation has been used, as in the lower parts of these same figures. But after entrance into the legal and the medical professions, as well as into other professions, standards of this kind do not exist, so that in order to establish a criterion the tester has to resort to the use of rating scales in an effort to get quantitative measures of the subjective estimates of supervisors and colleagues. Unsatisfactory as these scales always are and in spite of the fact that they may be a great deal less valid than the aptitude test score itself, there would never be any way of finding out whether these criticisms were true unless there were an objective criterion with which both the ratings and the aptitude scores could be compared. It is felt that in some fields the objective standards do not and cannot exist. Consider, for instance, the number of obscure painters, who even if they had been known well enough by their colleagues to be rated, would certainly have been placed at the lowermost category, and who at some later time have been recognized as masters of their craft. Numerous writers have been neglected or reviled by their colleagues, but later generations have turned the tables completely. Thus, by the very nature of artistic accomplishment, standards are constantly changing so that aptitudes can hardly be said to exist except with reference to a particular time in a particular culture.

4. ARTISTIC ABILITIES

Ability in music, painting, sketching, the plastic arts, dancing, decorating, architecture, and poetry has long been considered to be solely the product of hereditary endowment. Genetic charts have been made which purport to prove that since artistic talent runs in families, it must be inherited.[9] People who make assertions of this kind are a great deal more enthusiastic than the more level-headed geneticists, who generally hold that a talent in the artistic field is so complex that it defies genetic analysis. There is here, as in all other fields, a structural substratum which is necessary for the development of artistic talents. But the necessity for such a structural foundation has to be developed from theoretical considerations rather than from observable items of information. If there is any difference in the brain or the ears or the muscles of a competent musician which distinguishes him from people who are inept in music, we don't know now what that difference is. *To assert that the possession or the absence of these talents is wholly determined by structure is entirely without foundation.*

It also goes without saying that no attribute of physique, like long tapering fingers, holds any consistent relation to artistic skill. The oft-asserted relation between long fingers and artistic temperament is just so much nonsense because we have no notion of what artistic temperament is: we have no criterion for it.

Musical aptitude tests.—There are several tests available which purport to measure musical aptitude. Since the test items are auditory stimuli, instead of being printed on paper as most tests are, they are presented by means of a phonograph. One of the best

[9] H. M. Stanton, "The Inheritance of Specific Musical Capacities," *Psychological Monographs,* 1922, 31, 157-204.

known is the Seashore Test,[10] named after its originator, long Dean of the Graduate School at the University of Iowa. There are six double-faced records comprising the test. The first test presents one hundred pairs of tones alike except for a difference in pitch. Beginning with easily observable differences, they come closer and closer together and consequently become harder to discriminate as the test proceeds. The second test measures how well the subject can discriminate between tones of different loudness. He has to say, of each pair, whether the second is louder or softer than the first. As in the pitch test, there are one hundred such pairs to be discriminated. The remaining three tests are more difficult to describe and should be heard in a demonstration for a more complete understanding of the task required of the subject. Suffice it to say here that they are aimed at testing how well the subject can judge time, discriminate consonance, and discriminate rhythmic patterns and recall melodies. It is clear from the nature of these tests that Seashore considers the complex musical aptitude to be made up of simpler abilities which can be tested. His job analysis includes more factors than the five comprising the test, but tests for the others have not yet been developed.

These tests have been studied by several investigators, prominent among whom are Esther Allen Gaw, Hazel Stanton, L. H. Lanier, Joseph Peterson, and Paul Farnsworth. One of the problems which concerned these people is that of reliability.[11] Any test, whether for musical aptitude, clerical aptitude, general intelligence, or for some school subject, must be reliable. *High reliability means that people who take the test for the second time rank in approximately the same way that they did the first time they took it.* If there is little relationship in the relative standing of people between two administrations of the test, then the reliability is low, and, of course, the test is worthless. The data on the reliability of the Seashore Test is ambiguous. Some investigators have reported satis-

[10] C. E. Seashore, *The Psychology of Musical Talent,* Silver Burdett & Company, Newark, 1919.
[11] For a summary of all this literature see Paul Farnsworth, "An Historical, Critical, and Experimental Study of the Seashore-Kwalwasser Test Battery," *Genetic Psychology Monographs,* 1931, 9, 291-393.

factory indices of reliability; others, working with different groups of students of differing ages, have found low reliabilities. *One must conclude that these tests are still in an experimental stage.* If one withholds a musical education from a child who does not do well on these tests, there is the likelihood that a serious blunder is being made. On the other hand, a high score does not by any means ensure success in choosing music for a career or even for a satisfactory avocation. Notwithstanding, Hazel Stanton [12] has found that a combination of the Seashore score and a score from a standard intelligence test is useful in predicting the success of students in the Eastman School of Music; at the Ohio State University, however, they have not proved to be valuable.[13] When we have contradictory evidence like this it usually turns out that there is a difference somewhere in the two situations. It is possible that the objectives of the two schools of music are entirely unlike so that a test that satisfactorily predicts an outcome in one place will be useless in another. Since medical education is much more standardized than musical education, the outlook for developing even more adequate aptitude tests is much more favorable in the former field.

Students interested in the psychological studies relating to design, painting, sketching, and the development of artistic appreciation in adults and in children will want to read the contributions made from the Iowa Laboratory under the direction of Norman C. Meier.[14]

Summary.—Aptitudes are abstractions. They are inferential constructs, like "gravity" or "force" in physics, which are used to

[12] Hazel M. Stanton, "Prognosis of Musical Achievement," 1929, University of Rochester, Eastman School of Music.
Hazel M. Stanton, "Psychological Tests—a Factor in Admission to the Eastman School of Music," *School and Society,* 1929, 30, 783-891.
[13] M. E. Wilson, "The Prognostic Value for Music Success of Several Types of Tests," *Music Supervisors' Journal,* 1930, 16, 71-3.
[14] Norman C. Meier, "Diagnosis in Art," *Yearbook* of the National Society for the Study of Education, 1935, 34, 463-76.
     C. A. Ruckmick (Ed.), "Studies in the Psychology of Art, Directed by Norman C. Meier," *Psychological Monographs,* 1933, 45, 1-188.
     N. C. Meier (Ed.), "Studies in the Psychology of Art, Vol. II," *Psychological Monographs,* 1936, 47, 1-175.
     N. C. Meier (Ed.), "Studies in the Psychology of Art, Vol. III," *Psychological Monographs,* 1939, 51, 1-158.

explain behavior. Being abstractions, they never can be observed directly. Neither can they be inherited; one doesn't inherit an abstraction. Nor can they be learned, and for the same reason. The structural and maturational features of an organism, together with its past experiences, determine its behavior. The sum total of all these features determines whether one is to exhibit this or that kind of behavior. Theoretically, a deficiency in one of these aspects can be compensated for by a substitute function from some other area, at least within certain ill-defined limits. But the knowledge of the characteristics that a person has now can be used in predicting the kind of person he will be later after a certain course of study or a training period in the acquisition of certain skills and attitudes. Not all features of his present attainment are equally valuable in making a prediction. Which ones are significant can be determined only by testing the items that are thought to be important on a priori grounds. This testing involves the use of a criterion and a comparison between the criterion and test results. In the mechanical and clerical fields some progress has been made, but in the professional and artistic fields, progress is less satisfactory. This lack of progress is due to the fact that as yet no satisfactory criteria in the latter fields have been established.

IV

INHERITANCE

FEW problems are older than those pertaining to the relative importance of heredity and environment in determining human behavior. Few have more practical significance. If it is true, as some hold, that man's personality is wholly determined by heredity, then education in its broadest sense should merely allow growth to proceed with the least possible interference from people and circumstances. If it were possible to determine accurately what a person is innately best fitted for, his training should take place along these lines and no others. Since, according to this view, environment offers only an opportunity for inborn traits to develop, the only hope of racial improvement lies in allowing only those persons of unusually gifted hereditary backgrounds to have progeny. Some even argue that a gifted person will grow into superlative achievement in spite of environmental handicaps of the harshest sort, and contrariwise, opportunity is wasted on those who are innately incapable. This is an extreme hereditarian's viewpoint.

Another opposed view throws the burden of responsibility onto the environment. Opportunity, it is said, is the fundamental determinant of human behavior. People fail to achieve useful wholesome lives, not because their germ plasm is defective but because poverty and restriction have so limited their horizons. One should concentrate on eliminating poverty and on equalizing opportunity, rather than on mating selectively if he would improve national well-being. This is an extreme environmentalist position.

The tremendous social impact of these two opposed ideas is obvious. The first fits in with an aristocratic political philosophy, and people who think in aristocratic terms have done all that they can to foster it. The second view fits the democratic ideal of equal opportunity for all and the more recent extension of this notion to include abundance and wealth of opportunity rather than half-open doors. Slum elimination projects have their origin in social beliefs of this kind.

What is the answer? Which group is right? What compromise position can be worked out which is best in accord with the facts?

The scientific way to approach a problem of this kind is to marshal whatever facts we are reasonably certain of and to arrive at some sort of an hypothesis that can be tested by an experiment. It has been suggested that the relative merits of these opposing beliefs could be evaluated if we transferred a group of American boys to some remote primitive tribe and allowed them to grow up in a preliterate environment, and conversely with a group of primitives. Just to *suppose* what would happen if we transplanted a group of Hottentot boys to Central Illinois and took an equal number of Illinois boys to Central Africa is outlawed at the beginning because the rules of the scientific game demand that we actually try out our bright ideas, and not just talk about them. It isn't at all likely that we ever could actually make an experiment of this kind because public opinion would be opposed to it. But frequently what would be morally outrageous as a planned experiment actually does take place as a result of circumstances beyond the control of organized society. An example of this kind of occurrence will be described shortly when we relate the story of the Wild Boy of Aveyron, but let us examine first an experiment with animals as subjects which was designed to test the point of view of heredity.

1. ANIMAL EXPERIMENTS

The experiment was conducted by R. C. Tryon, a psychologist of the University of California.

One hundred forty-two rats chosen at random were required to traverse a long and complicated pathway nineteen times. At the end of the path the animals were rewarded by finding food. A system of pathways like this is known as a maze. It is an instrument of wide use in psychological investigations, because it presents a series of alternative paths to food. Some of these are more direct than others. Hungry clever animals soon learn to take the most direct route in the shortest possible time, but hungry, dull, and stupid animals take the wrong turns on many more occasions, and in doing so require a longer time to go from the starting point to the food. The number of blind alleys they enter in successive attempts to get from one end of the maze to the other is taken as an index of how quickly they are learning.

The total number of blind-alley entrances for each rat in its nineteen trials showed that the rats, like humans, differ in the quickness with which they learn a new task of this kind. Some rats entered as few as seven or eight blind alleys. Others, with equal opportunity to make errors, entered as many as 214 culs-de-sac. The remainder ranged between these two extremes.

When this part of the experiment had been completed, the bright rats were segregated and bred together as a group, and the dull and mediocre rats were bred together as another group. Their progeny were kept separately and required separately to run the same maze that had served to divide the preceding generation into bright and dull performers. Reference to the F_1 (first generation) progeny in Figure 10 shows the records made by these individuals when each had completed nineteen trials. The horizontal axis of the graph refers to the total number of blind alleys entered, a number which ranged from close to zero to approximately 214. The figures on the vertical axis refer to the percentages of bright and dull groups respectively, according to the total number of errors committed.

If we examine the series of graphs, one for each successive generation, we see that in the F_1 progeny there is little difference between the records made by the bright and dull groups. However, as the process of selective breeding is continued, and bright individuals are consistently mated with each other, while the dull individuals are also inbred, we observe that the curves for the respective groups become more and more distinct and separate from each other. Finally in the F_8 individuals (or eighth generation) there is practically no overlapping in ability between the two groups. In Figure 10 the intervening generations F_2, F_3, F_5, and F_7 are not shown.

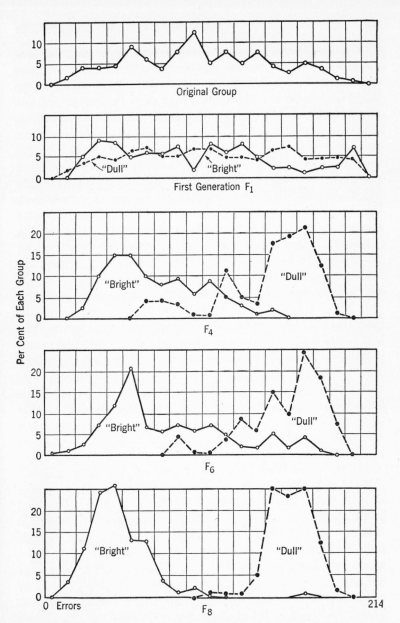

Fig. 10.—The errors that rats made on a standard maze through eight generations of selective breeding. The "brightest" and the "dullest" rats in each generation were inbred, a procedure which in eight generations produced two distinct "types" of "bright" and "dull" rats with little overlapping.

One can see how impossible it would be, from the standpoint of time alone, to make an experiment involving several human generations. To make such an experiment with human subjects would take something like two hundred years. But aside from the time required there are many other practical considerations which make this type of experimentation with human beings impossible. Although our principal interest is in people, not rats, we can only infer that something very much like this would happen if we were rigorous in our selection of human subjects over many generations.

In the absence of experiments with people, there have been attempts to gather information about old families whose social and political history is known. One of the most famous of these is an early study by Goddard called *The Kallikaks*. It recounts the known history of two lines of the descendants of Martin Kallikak, a revolutionary war soldier. One of these lines had its origin in the mating of Martin and a normal woman, the other through an illicit affair that Martin had with a feeble-minded girl. The genealogy shows clearly that there is more feeble-mindedness, poverty, and social viciousness in the illegitimate line than in the other. But how much of this asocial conduct and general worthlessness is due to the fact that the line started with a feeble-minded girl and how much is due to the social level and economic insecurity of this branch of the family cannot be determined. Observations on other families, like the Edwards family of New England, which show an unusually large number of successful people, are likewise ambiguous in this respect.

The only conclusion which we may draw from Tryon's experiment with the rats is that two so-called "pure lines" have been produced through selection. *Inbreeding among the bright individuals results in bright progeny, and inbreeding among the dull individuals results in dull progeny.* Experimental evidence of this kind serves to establish the fact that the ability of the rat to learn the maze has a biological basis and, further, that the differences in this ability are genetically determined. Differences in ability to learn a thing, among human beings as well as among rats, are probably determined by many hereditary factors. *But because Tryon's ani-*

mals learned promptly in this maze does not necessarily mean that they will learn all other things with as much facility as we find here. What the precise relations are between the abilities of the rats on other kinds of learning tasks is the problem on which Dr. Tryon is now working.

2. THE WILD BOY OF AVEYRON [1]

In the year 1799, a group of sportsmen found a lad roaming in a French forest who later came to be known as "the wild boy of Aveyron." [2] Presumably he had been living on roots, berries, and such other provender as might be found in the woods. When discovered he was naked, scarred, and unkempt, and sought to resist capture by hurriedly climbing into a tree. Although he appeared to be fully eleven or twelve years old, he was quite unable to talk and was without knowledge of the most rudimentary habits of personal cleanliness. He was taken to Paris and subjected to a long period of methodical and painstaking education by a young French physician, Itard. Despite the fact that considerable progress was made toward fitting him for the complexities of civilized life, the training on the whole was regarded as unsuccessful.

The hereditarian explanation of the boy's behavior.—The customary way of explaining the fact that a human being of this kind does not respond well to the efforts of those who would civilize and educate it is to say that he is feeble-minded. It is inferred that even if such children had lived under civilized conditions, they would still have failed to duplicate the accomplishments of normal individuals. This reasoning carries with it the assumption that because these children were not up to the average for their ages when their re-education was discontinued, there must have been something wrong with them in the first place. In fact, going one step further, it is often argued that the "wild" children were

[1] Adapted from W. N. Kellogg and L. A. Kellogg, *The Ape and the Child,* McGraw-Hill Book Company, Inc., New York, 1933. Used by permission.
[2] Jean-Marc-Gaspard Itard, *The Wild Boy of Aveyron.* Translated by George and Muriel Humphrey, D. Appleton-Century Company, New York, 1932.

probably abandoned *because* they displayed idiotic or imbecilic tendencies at a very early age.

The environmentalist explanation.—But there is a second way of accounting for the behavior of the wild boy. He may actually have learned, in a literal sense of the word, to be wild in the same way that a Caucasian child reared among Chinese grows into the Chinese customs and language, or a baby that has been kidnapped by gypsies knows in later years only the gypsy manner of living. He need not originally have been feeble-minded. He may have been so profoundly impressed with the experiences of his earlier years that the later efforts to teach him the reactions of the average educated child did not bear full fruit. *He had passed the age where the learning of civilized commonplaces was easy and natural, and had already consumed the most formative years in learning other things.* The wild animal cannot be thoroughly tamed unless its taming starts soon after it is born, which, paradoxically, is before it has actually become wild. Heredity, in this explanation, becomes of secondary importance; education and training are the powerful causal factors.

Here, then, are two complete but entirely distinct methods of accounting for the same phenomena.

Which view is correct?—We can never know for certain which of these views is the correct explanation of the behavior of abandoned children. We could get a clue as to which is more likely to be true if we knew something about the hereditary background of a new case, but we should have to place a normal human infant in uncivilized surroundings and observe and record its development *as it grew up in this environment*. Since an experiment of this kind can not be carried out with a child, we must fall back on animal subjects.

3. THE APE AND THE CHILD

It would be both possible and practical to reverse these conditions. Instead of placing a child in a typical animal environment, why not place an animal in a typical human environment? Why not give one of the higher primates exactly the environmental advantages which a young child enjoys and then study the development of the resulting organism? [3]

If such an experiment were to produce dependable results, it would admit of no halfway measures. To carry it out in any comprehensive manner one would have to obtain an infant anthropoid ape, as young as possible, and rear it in every respect as a child is reared—even to the most minute detail. The animal subject would have to be bottle-fed, clothed, bathed, fondled, and given careful human treatment in every phase of its daily existence. It would have to be placed in a perambulator and wheeled. It would have to eat with a spoon as soon as it was able to feed itself at all. Its mistakes would be gently and persistently corrected as are the mistakes of a child. It would have to be made a thoroughly humanized member of the family of the experimenters, who would serve respectively in the capacities of adopted "father" and "mother." Many of the highly developed customs of our society might thus become integral parts of its behavior equipment in much the same manner that they are built into the human baby. As far as its immediate surroundings are concerned, the animal must never be given the opportunity to learn any other ways of acting except the human ways. This means that the *psychological* as well as the *physical* features of the environment must be entirely of a human character. That is, the reactions of all those who come in contact with the subject, and the resulting stimulation which these reactions afford the subject, should be without exception just what a normal child might receive.

Things we must avoid.—Instances of anthropoid apes which have lived in human households are of course by no means unknown. But in all the cases of which we have any knowledge the "human" treatment accorded the animals was definitely limited by the attitude of the owner and by the degree of his willingness to be put to boundless labor. If an organism of this kind is kept in a cage

[3] W. N. Kellogg, "Humanizing the Ape," *Psychological Review,* 1931, 38, 160-70.

for a part of each day or night, if it is led about by means of a collar and a chain, or if it is fed from a plate upon the floor, it is not unreasonable to suppose that these things must surely develop responses which are different from those of a human being. A child itself, if similarly treated, would most certainly acquire some genuinely *unchildlike* reactions. Again, if an organism—animal or human—is talked to and called like a dog or a cat, if it is petted or scratched behind the ears as these animals are so often treated, or if in other ways it is given *pet stimuli* instead of *child stimuli,* the resulting behavior may be expected to show the effects of such stimulation.

The incidental nature of the proposed training.—The training of the ape must be what might be called *incidental* as opposed to *systematic* or controlled training. What it would get from its surroundings it would have to pick up by itself just as a growing child acquires new modes of behavior. It would be necessary to avoid deliberately teaching the animal, trial by trial, a series of tricks or stunts which it might go through upon signal or command. The things that it learned would have to be its own reactions to the human stimuli about it, not meaningless rituals elicited by a sign from a keeper. The spoon-eating training, to take a concrete example, according to the plan should be taken up only in a gradual and irregular manner at mealtime, as the subject's muscular coordination fitted it for this sort of manipulation. There could be no attempt to labor mechanically through a stated number of trials, rewarding or punishing the animal as it might succeed or fail. Such a proposed procedure, it will be readily seen, is loose and uncontrolled in that it precludes the opportunity to obtain quantitative data on the number of trials necessary to learn, the number of errors made, or the elapsed time per trial. It has the advantage, nevertheless, of being the same sort of training to which the human infant is customarily subjected in the normal course of its rearing.

Conclusions that could be drawn.—At the completion of our experiment we should be in a position to make definite inferences regarding the two organisms:

(1) If the chimpanzee had failed to develop as did the child but

remained instead on a subhuman level, then we could say that hereditary factors were dominant and that training did not seriously affect the resulting organism. Development along divergent lines within the same environment would show the importance of heredity. It could be maintained, should such results be secured, that the ape, given full opportunities to acquire a complete repertory of human reactions, had progressed only part of the way.

(2) If the chimpanzee in the human situation acquired many characteristically childlike responses, such results would show the importance of the human stimuli upon its growth. The extent to which the subjects learned to react in the same ways *despite their different heredities* would demonstrate the effect of the common cultural environment.

(3) In addition to showing environmental influence, the presence of identical responses in the ape and the child would also show that the heredities of the two, although different, were at the same time similar enough to permit like reactions to the same stimulation. Yet without the special influence of the civilized environment to serve as an activating cause in bringing out these likenesses, they would surely never come to light.

This plan was actually executed by Professor and Mrs. W. N. Kellogg of Indiana University. Now no one, we hope, will be foolish enough to suppose from reading a proposal of this sort that either of the Kelloggs had so far lost his senses as to presume that one could make a human being out of an animal. There are obviously many natural differences between man and the apes which no amount of environmental equalizing can overcome.

The accomplishment of the experiment.—No one can appreciate the detailed nature of the preparations required for the accomplishment of an experiment like this. The experimenter had to obtain a leave of absence from the University of Indiana, where he was teaching, and move his family to Florida for the duration of the experiment. This arrangement involved the co-operation of numerous colleagues and administrative officers. No college professor is wealthy enough to be able to take a year away from teaching without salary. As is true in most cases of this kind, an appeal was made to a foundation for the necessary money to furnish living expenses. The demands made on foundations are so numerous that each request must be carefully scrutinized. This involves convincing other people of the merits of the proposal. When all of the arrangements had been completed and the Social Science Research Council had agreed to grant Dr. Kellogg a fellowship there was already a history of several years' preparation that one never hears about in the formally written reports on experiments.

On June 26, 1931, a young female chimpanzee in the colony of the Anthropoid Experiment Station of Yale University at Orange Park, Florida, was separated from her mother, in whose cage she had previously been living. This little animal, named Gua, had been born in captivity in the Abreu Colony [4] in Cuba on November 15, 1930. She was turned over to the Kelloggs following the separation and was soon thereafter taken to their home, where her humanizing was begun. Her age at that time was 7½ months, or almost exactly 2½ months less than that of the Kelloggs' only child, Donald, who had been born August 31, 1930.

These two individuals lived together as companions, playmates, and members of the same household until March 28, 1932. Their surroundings and treatment were as nearly alike as it was possible to make them. At that time, 9 months after the initiation of the research, Gua had attained the age of 16½ months, while Donald was 19 months old. The experiment was then discontinued and the ape was returned by a gradual habituating process to the more restricted life of the Experiment Station. During the nine months a continuous series of tests, comparisons, observations, and experiments made upon the two subjects covered nearly every phase of their structure and behavior for which there were measuring facilities.

We select for digest here only a few of the observations made

[4] The story of a colony of great apes maintained by Mrs. Abreu, a wealthy resident of Havana, is found in R. M. Yerkes, *Almost Human* (1925). Mrs. Abreu's interest in apes was principally sentimental, but she did allow interested and qualified persons to make scientific studies of her animals. These studies by Yerkes and Bingham were responsible for the opening of the Orange Park Station of Yale University.

during the study; for the complete account the student is referred to *The Ape and the Child*.

By the end of the first week Gua was always dressed in diapers and shoes, and on one or two occasions she had been clothed in a romper suit as well. Within the same period she began to sleep in her crib (although at first without a full equipment of bedding), and she was regularly fed from a spoon and a cup in her high chair. By the end of the second week, she permitted the cutting of her finger nails and before the fourth was over she was daily submitting to the application of a toothbrush.

General description of play activities.—The human infant served as Gua's most intimate playmate for nearly nine months, and she in turn filled a similar role with regard to the child. It is safe to say that Gua was the first playmate Donald had ever had, aside from his parents. He correspondingly became the first playmate of the little animal, excepting only her mother, with whom she lived during her earlier cage existence. The initial reactions of the subjects toward each other should for this reason be of particular significance.

From the moment they first entered each other's presence there was evidence of curiosity and interest on the part of both. The interest seemed to be more marked in the case of Donald than of Gua. When they were seated side by side, the child reached for the ape and touched her, although at that early stage she would make no corresponding advances. They were not subsequently brought into close proximity for several days, but continued to eye each other from a distance. Donald, as before, seemed to persist in this behavior more than the chimpanzee. As soon as they had been moved together for the second time, she immediately *extended her lips in a series of exploratory kisses* which touched the child upon his face and lips. At first he seemed startled but made no avoiding reactions and subsequently cooed his pleasure.

Mutual attachment of the two infants.—As examples of the mutual attachment which grew up after their initial meetings, it may be pointed out that Gua almost always, if not prevented, would make her way in some manner to the child. She would go to him if he was in his walker, climb into his lap if he was seated in his high chair, and frequently sit upon his foot or his leg if he was on the floor. She would even follow him away from the protection of those who cared for her. If he had not yet awakened from his nap when she awoke from hers, she could hardly be kept from the door of his room, to which she would go, and, during the later months, which she would open.

Once, during an unavoidable absence on the part of the two observers, the subjects were left at home taking their noonday naps in charge of a maid who was new and somewhat strange to Gua. The ape, then 10½ months of age, awakened before either of the experimenters had returned. A report of her activities as obtained from the attendant is as follows: When Gua awakened and found herself alone with the strange person she began screaming and ran from one room to another as if in search of a familiar face. Her cries aroused Donald, to whose door she had not yet gone. Immediately upon hearing the noise he made, she rushed to the door of his room and hammered on it with both hands. When she was permitted to enter, she became quiet at once and remained in the presence of the child without further disturbance.

On another occasion, about two weeks after this incident, when the subjects were playing beside each other in the same room with both the adults, one of the observers without warning accidentally upset a chair. This made a sharp clatter near Gua as it struck the floor. Instead of running toward either of the grown-ups—a reaction to be expected under such circumstances—Gua rushed to Donald, threw both arms around him, and hugged him tightly, crying the while.

On his part, Donald began to toddle to Gua as soon as he was dressed and put down on the floor in the morning. His first act was then to greet her by stooping forward and hugging her. The same procedure would usually be repeated whenever she had been screaming or even if she had only been scolded. The little animal in her turn began about this time to take what appeared to be a protective attitude toward the child, particularly if the two were out of doors. When they held hands as they walked together, it was Gua at first who did the actual holding. If their grip broke for an instant, it was she again who stopped, waited for Donald, or went after him and seized his hand in hers, although the child became the aggressor in this act at a little later date. When Donald would cry, she would run to him, and if he was being carried by someone she would often slap the holder.

The kinds of things they learned.—At the age of 10 months the chimpanzee released a door latch by turning the door knob. Her first success in such a task was accidental, however, since she was hanging by one hand from the knob at the time so that the torque-like pull of her weight on one side of the handle caused it to turn. Just when accidental door opening, which thereafter became quite common because of her increasing tendency to hang upon door knobs, gave way to deliberate door opening, it would be difficult to say. For some months Gua was more likely to cry, or to lie down on the floor and look beneath a door, to put her fingers under it, or to slap it, than she was to manipulate the knob itself. The child never succeeded throughout the entire nine months in releasing a single door latch, possibly because of the shortness of his reach. He would, nevertheless, touch the knobs with his fingers and rattle them almost whenever he approached one.

By the time the ape had attained the age of 13½ months, she was observed to unlatch the front door of the house in a manner which appeared anything but accidental. This she accomplished by climbing upon a small piece of furniture beside it, reaching from the furniture to the knob with her right hand, and turning the knob successively to the right and to the left by extending and flexing her arm. As soon as the latch was released she pulled the door open at once.

Gua also formed a connection between electric light switches and the appearance of the light. The response, which she picked up without instruction or assistance, consisted in hooking the index finger over the movable part of the toggle switch and pulling it downward. Yet neither could extinguish the light by pushing the switch upward for more than a month, when Gua alone achieved this result. Donald tried frequently, but he was never successful, probably because his hands and fingers were not sufficiently sturdy.

The child proved, on the other hand, to be much superior to the

Excerpts from the Kelloggs' Protocols

July 5, 1931.

Donald placed in baby pen. Gua is on floor outside of pen. She goes towards him, reaching through the bars with her right hand. *They hold hands.* Donald seems delighted. She touches him gently on the abdomen with her closed fist. He gets hold of her hair and pulls it. She reaches through the bars with her right hand, and extending her index finger she touches his hand lightly. She loses her balance while sitting and falls back. . . . Donald soon afterwards falls likewise from a sitting position to his back, and cries.

July 10, 1931.

He stands in his play pen holding the rail. He is apparently so delighted when she approaches that he lets go with one hand as if to reach for her and nearly loses his balance. He laughs with almost every breath. . . . Gua goes to side of pen. Donald falls down, first to a sitting, then to a lying posture. He is picked up and placed again in a sitting position. He leans forward towards her so far that he then falls forward. Raises his head while lying prone and looks through the bars at her. She reaches in to him, pulls his head down and kisses it. She touches his face and hands. . . . Both seem to be very interested and strive to get nearer to each other.

July 11, 1931.

He is so excited he pants, vocalizing at each exhalation. He repeatedly stands up in his walker and then sits down again stamping his feet in this manner. He seems to like to see her fall down and invariably laughs aloud when she does. She is very active, moves rapidly and awkwardly, and probably falls oftener than usual. She moves towards him, bites at the counting balls on his walker, and pushes the walker with her hand. He reaches for her head and touches it. He evidently attempts to go after her in his walker as she moves away but jumps up and down in his excitement and pushes the walker backward instead. He cannot push it forward very well as yet.

July 13, 1931.

They are placed on a bed together. Donald reaches towards Gua. She "smiles." Seems very complacent and friendly. He puts his finger in her eye.

He then gets upon his stomach and while in this position he slides himself backward by pushing with his hands. He accidentally slips off the bed by this means before he can be caught. He is not hurt but cries loudly. Gua appears terrified at the noise and excitement and although she utters no sound, she rushes to me and buries her head in my lap.

She continues to kiss Donald frequently on approaching him. This is usually the case when she climbs up in his high chair, making contact with his bare foot which she kisses.

chimpanzee at the game of pat-a-cake, for Gua was here a hopeless failure. Toward the last she would slap the extended hands of one of the adults when told to pat-a-cake but she never learned to respond with typical handclapping. Her inability to acquire such a simple reaction is all the more surprising in view of the fact that she was given almost daily opportunity for such play for several months, while the human infant was not so persistently encouraged.

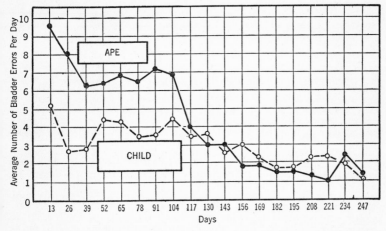

FIG. 11.—Average number of bladder errors per day for the ape and the child. The points plotted are the averages of 13-day periods. (After Kellogg.)

Miscellaneous observations of this sort are obviously conflicting with regard to the relative learning ability of the two subjects, so that we must turn to more precise experimental techniques in order to throw light on this important comparative problem. In this connection it is to be noted that probably the most exact and certainly the most persistent training through which the average human baby is conducted is in learning to control the bladder and bowels. Such training is begun usually at the age of less than a year and may continue as long as three or four years. If properly managed it is an invariable, methodical, day-and-night procedure which few subsequent endeavors in the lifetime of the individual can equal in either regularity or extensiveness. Here, then, should be an excellent field in which to compare the learning abilities of the two organisms, without modifying their ordinary childlike surroundings or conducting them through unusual or irregular processes of training.

Throughout the 9-month period of training in both bladder and bowel control, nearly 6,000 responses of the ape were tabulated, of which a little over 1,000 were errors. The child, in his turn, reacted more than 4,700 times, of which about 750 were errors.

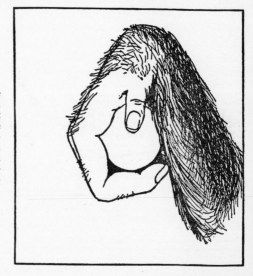

FIG. 12.—The chimpanzee grasps a bulky object like a ball, by pressing it against the volar surface of the forearm. The wrist will allow the palm of the hand to bend in this direction much further than it is possible for a human being to do. (After Kellogg.)

Manual dexterity.—In manual dexterity, particularly with regard to the grasping of small objects and the making of fine, coordinated finger movements, the ape, it is well known, is inferior to man. The finest prehensile movements of which Gua was originally capable were made with the lips. In getting a morsel of food from the tray of her high chair, or in picking up such a minute object as a pin, her reactions at the beginning were invariably to stoop forward and use the mouth. There are good reasons why this should be the case: (1) The lips of the chimpanzee form an important tactile organ with an apparent capacity to feel and manipulate small objects considerably surpassing that of the corresponding human parts. (2) The length and awkward shape of the hands and fingers preclude their being employed with as much efficiency as human hands and fingers, as, for example, in making the fine thumb-and-finger pincer movement. (3) In the beginning, when primates can walk only on all fours, it is much easier for them to carry objects in their mouths than in their hands. This in itself predisposes toward a greater use of the lips.

To encourage Gua in an increased use of her hands and fingers,

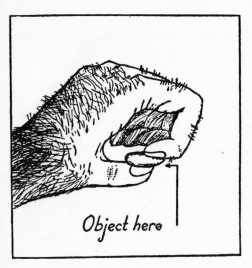

Object here

FIG. 13.—In a few instances Gua picked up small round objects like beans between the nails of the thumb and index finger. This movement was as near as she ever came to the more accurate thumb-forefinger opposition of the child. (After Kellogg.)

toys and tidbits which were held out to her were not released if she tried to take them with the lips. This method seemed to be generally effective, and its use was soon followed by a change in behavior in which the hands came to be employed with greater frequency and proficiency.

That Gua's *coarse* or *gross* hand movements were relatively clumsy may be accounted for in part by the backward limitations in the angles of movement of the wrist and finger joints. The gross grasping response for her involved not only the closing of the fingers but usually the movement of the wrist toward the arm as well. It consisted of a sort of rolling-up on the object in a manner which sometimes suggested the curling movement made by the end of an elephant's trunk (see Figure 12). The thumb was seldom used in such reactions. Her ability to bend the wrist and fingers backward, often in addition made it difficult for her to release objects from her grasp. Thus in her efforts at building with blocks she could put one block upon another readily enough, but she did not seem able to get her long curved fingers away from the second block without upsetting the whole tower, even though it might consist of no more than two blocks.

What shall be our criterion in the separation of those responses of the ape which show the particular effect of the human environment from those which seem not to do so? As a test upon each act we shall ask the following question: *Could the chimpanzee possibly have developed this behavior had she been reared without the pertinent stimuli of the civilized surroundings?* If the answer is "yes" or "doubtful," we shall classify the response as probably independent of the special influence of the human situation. If the answer is "no," then we shall feel justified in classifying the act as dependent upon the civilized environment.

Behavior that would have developed without human surroundings.—That Gua's mouth was more mobile as an organ of prehension is independent of the civilized environment. The same was true of her more consistent avoidance of bright lights, her (apparently) keener hearing, and her many distinctive emotional reactions. Similarly we should place her greater propensity to bite and chew, her inability to pick up small objects with the fingers, and her deficiency in articulation in this category. Her further deficiencies in exploration and manipulation, her attention to stimuli for only a relatively short time, and her inferiority in imitation seem also to us to belong under this heading. She was superior in muscular co-ordination and faster in her involuntary movements, stronger, and remembered better than the child.

These characteristics we think are independent of the specific humanizing features of the environment in which Gua lived. Certainly this need not mean that the influence of some sort of environment cannot be proven in every one of them. But it does mean that *they would probably have developed much as they did in almost any environment which permits healthy and regular growth.*

Since Donald's performance was about average for his age, the respects in which the ape surpassed him are the respects in which she was generally more advanced than the average child approximately as old as herself. They cast no necessary reflection upon the child, but are rather points of special credit for the ape. She may thus be said to have become "more humanized" than the human subject.

Behavior dependent on the human environment.—Here we would place her skipping, her greater co-operation and obedience, her tendency to kiss for forgiveness, her skillful opening of doors. Her more frequent sly behavior suggested the mischievousness of a lively boy, while her superior anticipation of bladder and bowel reactions were an obvious mark of progress. Her striking ability to eat with a spoon and to drink from a glass compare with corresponding abilities of children much older than she.

We conclude, therefore, that *it is possible to list a group of behavior items which depend principally on the bodily structure of the ape that would occur in any environment.* But at the same time, *Gua became surprisingly humanlike and, in the respects that we have mentioned, was actually superior to Donald.* These items we infer are dependent on the human environment in which she lived for nine months.

Summary of the chapter.—There are two opposing views relating to the efficacy of heredity as an explanation for differences in human ability and attainment. Which of these views, if either, is correct cannot be discovered by direct experimentation with people for various practical reasons. We have to depend on experiments with animals. One of these, Tryon's, shows that the biological basis or bases for maze learning can be manipulated genetically. "Bright" and "dull" rats can be developed by selective breeding. But "bright" and "dull" as they refer to a particular maze may not be significant designations for other learning situations.

The experiment with Donald and Gua is a record of observations on two animals entirely different from the genetic standpoint who were reared in like cultural environments. In those acts in which the structural anatomical features are extremely important, the ape remained an ape, but in many ways she became humanlike in her reactions and in some instances actually exceeded the performance of average human youngsters her own age. Cultural modification and molding ordinarily begin with birth and progress in an integrated way with the anatomical development of the organism. These anatomical structures are inherited. No amount of environmental similarity ever makes them more alike.

V

MATURATION AND GROWTH

ASIDE from the general questions of the relative influences of heredity and environment that we have considered in Chapter IV, there is another important determinant of behavior generally called *maturation,* or more simply, *growth.*[1] *The factor of growth itself without any co-operation from the environment except that involved in sustenance of the organism can account for some limited types of behavior.* This hypothesis has been subjected to experimental test in several different ways and with several different kinds of animals as subjects. We will take up the simpler cases first.

1. EXPERIMENTS WITH FROGS AND SALAMANDERS

The psychologist Carmichael selected frogs and salamanders as his experimental animals. In both of these species there is considerable development in the larval stages that in mammals is accomplished in the uterus of the mother, and is therefore hidden to the inquisitive eye of the scientific investigator. Another important reason why these species are used is that the behavior of these animals is relatively very simple. It is always best to try out an idea in the simplest possible manner. When explanations are possible in the simple organisms, then it is time to progress to those forms that are higher in the evolutionary scale and more complex.

[1] Although the terms *growth* and *maturation* are frequently used interchangeably, they are, strictly speaking, not synonymous. Growth implies chiefly an increase in body size. Maturation implies an increase in the complexity of the bodily tissue, or differentiation. Both usually occur together, although not necessarily. It should be clearly understood, therefore, that the development of behavior depends on the increased differentiation of the body tissues, or maturation, even though the word *growth* is occasionally substituted.

At the beginning of this century it was discovered that the drug chloretone could be used to anesthetize small animals like tadpoles so that they would continue to grow normally but would be entirely unresponsive to any kind of stimulus. Under the proper concentration of chloretone in water the larval growth is somewhat slowed down, but it continues in its essential respects while the animal remains absolutely inert. If the concentration is made too strong, the animal will be killed or will develop in abnormal ways. Therefore it is absolutely necessary to maintain the concentration at just that point where the skeletal muscles will not respond, but where the vital maturation processes will not be interfered with. This condition exists when a concentration of approximately 4 parts chloretone to every 10,000 parts water is used. For almost a quarter of a century this discovery was only an interesting scientific fact. No one had taken advantage of it until Carmichael set to work to make use of it in answering this riddle about the relative influence of growth and experience in animal development.

Method.—He collected frogs' eggs, and the eggs of a little salamander, not so well known but almost as numerous as the frog in certain parts of the country. At times these eggs can be found in ponds where frogs and salamanders live. They come in clusters known as clutches and are imbedded in a jellylike substance from which they have to be removed one at a time and transferred to small laboratory dishes, one to each dish and with the dish properly labeled with the specimen number.

After a few days, the embryro can be observed directly through the transparent egg. At this stage it does not move at all. It has no eyes, ears, or limbs—these are all supplied in the next few days. In the normal course of events the animal soon becomes free-swimming and at this point we come face to face with a very important question: Does the animal learn to swim, or does it simply grow up to a certain stage of adulthood at which it begins to swim regardless of the opportunity to learn? Do the stimuli that play on the maturing animal from the outside have anything at all to do with the swimming response, or would it occur irrespective of these outside influences?

This general question had been tried out experimentally before. In one widely quoted [2] experiment, birds had been confined in small cages where they could not have possibly flown and where the experimenter thought that exercise of the wing muscles was not possible. Confined birds, when released, flew as well as those that had not been confined. These results do not impress us today because it is easy to see that it would have to be a very close-fitting cage that would absolutely remove the possibility of wing exercise. The wings could be moved even if they could not be used in typical flying movements. There was not complete control over the effect of practice. *Even a little practice may be very effective.* In Carmichael's experiment, however, there is an opportunity to prevent all muscle movement by anesthetizing the animal. Indeed, the two experiments, even though they are aimed at answering the same question, are not at all comparable because the young bird, after hatching, is a much more mature animal than the Amblystoma larva.

Results.—At a stage well in advance of the normal appearance of the swimming response, Carmichael [3] removed half of his developing frogs and salamanders to the anesthetic solution. The other half were allowed to develop normally. The latter group constituted a normal series with which the responses of the experimentally anesthetized animals could be compared. When the unanesthetized controls had been swimming freely for some time, the experimental animals were placed in tap water, one at a time, and their responses to a slight touch on the side of the head with a slender glass rod were noted. On the average, for the first twelve minutes there was not any response at all. Then, in response to the touch, they bent, some toward and some away from the side upon which they were stimulated. The responses continued more promptly, more precisely, more vigorously, until by the end of thirty minutes, on the average, they were swimming freely—swimming so well, as a matter of fact, that it was very difficult to distinguish them from the normal ani-

[2] D. A. Spaulding, "Instinct, with Original Observations on Young Animals," *Macmillan's Magazine,* 1873, 27, 282-93.
[3] Leonard Carmichael, "The Development of Behavior in Vertebrates Experimentally Removed from the Influence of External Stimulation," *Psychological Review,* 1926, 33, 51-8.

mals that had not been anesthetized and by this time had been swimming for five days.

Interpretation of the results.—If it were possible to release the experimental animals from the anesthetic instantaneously, it would be possible to infer that the whole half hour was just a period of very rapid learning in which enough was learned to make up for the five days' practice on the part of the control animals. But no such inference is possible because we know that the usual effects of drugging dissipate slowly, not instantaneously. Or we could infer that the whole half hour was the period required for total recovery from the chloretone and that no learning at all took place. But this would not be a reasonable inference because it entirely neglects the possibility that learning may take place. We are left, then, with the only other reasonable interpretation, namely, the half hour is partly a period of recovery, partly a period of rapid learning.

If we are really scientifically inquisitive, a "maybe yes," "maybe no" conclusion of this kind will not satisfy us. Like Carmichael, we will seek a method of evaluating the period of recovery from the anesthetic. He reasoned this way: If it took animals who had already been swimming as much time to recover as it did those who had never swum before, then the whole half hour would be a recovery period, the learning time would be zero. If it took practiced animals only half as long to recover, then we could reasonably infer that fifteen minutes were required to eliminate the effects of the drug. The other fifteen minutes would be devoted to rapid learning.

Further experimentation to test this hypothesis.—In order to find out which condition was true, the whole experiment was repeated, this time with the salamanders alone.[4] The members of a group were kept anesthetized as before until their control mates had been swimming for some time. They were then released from the anesthetic and their recovery watched as before. But this time after being allowed to swim freely for thirty-six hours, they were re-anesthetized and for twenty-four hours they were held as inert as they had been before their thirty-six-hour period of free-swimming.

[4] Leonard Carmichael, "A Further Study on the Development of Behavior in Vertebrates Experimentally Removed from the Influence of External Stimulation," *Psychological Review*, 1927, 34, 34-47.

Results.—At the end of their twenty-four-hour period of inac-
tivity, Carmichael again transferred them to tap water. Carefully
he timed the interval of recovery and again, as it had been before, 12
minutes were required to obtain a first movement and a half hour
was required for complete recovery. Since there was no difference in
the recovery time, whether for the first or second experience, the
whole thirty-minute period must have been consumed in removing
the effects of the chloretone; consequently, the learning time was
zero, or in other words, learning did not take place.

Interpretation.—Growth processes in the animal determine
whether or not the swimming response occurs. When a certain maturational age is attained, regardless of whether or not the animal
has been anesthetized, the response occurs; therefore one may not
truly say that a larval frog or salamander learns to swim. Rather
than this, one should say that *when a given level in maturation has
been attained, swimming is the natural outcome of the relations
which exist between the organism and its environment.*

But where is this growth? Is it in the muscles themselves, in the
sense organs, or in the nervous system of the organism in question?
It took the anatomist Coghill just about a quarter of a century to
answer this question, but he did finally find an answer.[5]

Significance of Coghill's work.—Students, in general, are not
likely to appreciate the tremendous drive that would keep an investigator at a task for so long a period of time, particularly when
that task involves the inconsequential end that this one seems to
have. Who cares what element in a salamander's anatomy is responsible for his ability to swim? Most people would not spend a week
or a day or even an hour to find out. Of what value is it to know
this fact? It is not likely that Coghill himself had any final interest
in Amblystoma, but he did have a nagging curiosity about human
behavior. He got it in a first course in psychology when he was an
undergraduate. He saw clearly that there were numerous riddles
in human psychology that could not be solved until somebody had
adequate explanations for kinds of behavior that are much simpler

[5] C. E. Coghill, *Anatomy and the Problem of Behavior,* The Macmillan Company, New York, 1929.

than human nature. Sometimes this simple behavior appears to be so far removed from human nature that there does not seem to be the remotest connection between them. Coghill's discovery, taken by itself, is comparatively slight. Seen in its proper perspective, it is of the utmost significance. What this significance is we will try to make clear, but first let us see why the problem was so difficult of solution.

The proposed experiment.—In the first place, one has to know a great deal about the behavior of Amblystoma. The general plan of the experiment requires us to find some behavior items (swimming, simple as it seems, is much too complicated) that occur regularly in all Amblystoma and at approximately the same time in all specimens. In its early embryonic stages Amblystoma is inert. Then, as development proceeds, it will turn its head away from the side which is stimulated. Now there must be some difference between an inert animal and one that will turn its head. Taking several of each kind, we kill them, fix them, and make cross sections of them, slicing very thin sections from the tail to the head. Each section is only a few thousandths of a millimeter thick. As many as 2,000 sections, each one about $\frac{1}{100}$ of a millimeter thick, are mounted separately for a single animal and each is observed by means of a microscope in order to find some difference between those specimens that do and those that do not bend the head. (The specimen shown in Figure 14 is about $\frac{2}{3}$ of an inch long.) The skill required to make the sections alone is no mean accomplishment, as some students of biology can tell you. But aside from that, additional skill in being able to detect microscopic differences between the specimens is a further preparation that demands thorough training and endless patience. If you remember having looked through a microscope for the first time, you are aware of what has been called in another connection "a blooming, buzzing confusion."

By careful scrutiny of the behavior of the salamander, Coghill detected five stages in its development, all being accomplished normally before hatching:

1. The inert, or nonmotile stage. The embryo is perfectly impervious to stimulation of any kind.

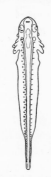

FIG. 14.—Nonmotile stage.

2. The early flexure stage. A light touch produces a movement away from the side stimulated. The movement is slow and is performed by the serial contraction of the muscle segments. As the embryo advances in age, the muscular action extends further down the side until the entire trunk is involved.

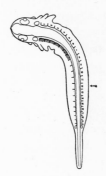

FIG. 15.—Early flexure.

3. The coil stage. The extension of the bending reaction promptly down the entire side of the embryo causes it to assume a tight coil form. Stage 3 grows directly out of Stage 2.

FIG. 16.—Coil.

4. The *S*-stage. A wave of contraction starts as if the animal were going to execute a coil, but before the wave has passed the entire length of the one side, a new contraction starts at the head on the opposite side. This causes the embryo to assume an *S*-shape. An instant later the reverse S (Ƨ) takes its place.

Fig. 17.—*S*-stage.

5. Swimming. When the *S*-reactions are sufficiently strong and fast enough, the embryo is propelled through the water. Stage 5 involves nothing new; it is merely an improvement in co-ordination over Stage 4.

Incorrect explanations.—So much for the behavior which is observed. Now to proceed to an *explanation* of this observed behavior. We could say that Amblystoma bends away from a slight touch near the head because it "does not like the stimulus" or because the "stimulus is painful." Such explanations, however, are not really explanations at all. They endow the animal with human characteristics. A man might *say* that he has bent his head away from an *unpleasant* stimulus, but we must remember that this embryo is not a tiny human being. It is a small bundle of developing tissues, principally muscles and nerves from the standpoint of our interest; therefore our descriptions must involve muscles and nerves and the relations between them and the external surroundings—and nothing else.

Scientific explanation.—*Stage 1:* A living embryo that will not respond to stimuli. What could the possible reasons be? There might be something wrong with the muscles, the sense organs, the sensory pathways, the motor pathways, or the central connecting fibers. Which is it? The muscles, even during the nonmotile state, are capable of contraction. This fact was shown by stimulating them directly by means of a sharp needle. When the needle was in-

serted through the skin directly into a muscle cell, that cell contracted. The effects were confined to the one cell, however: there
was no effect on the surrounding cells.
So the difficulty is not with the muscles.

Stage 2: There did not appear to be
any difference in the sensory or motor
pathways between those animals that did
and those that did not respond. But there
was a difference in the cells that connected
the sensory to the motor paths. In the
nonmotile stage these connecting cells
were undeveloped, but in the bending
stage they had extended themselves so that
they bridged the gap between the sensory
and the motor processes, a fact established
by direct observation under the microscope. When the final connecting link had
completed its growth, there was movement now where before there was none.
*There can be no doubt that the difference
between behavior and no behavior is entirely explained by the growth of a single
neuron in the central nervous system
through a distance of less than 1/100 of a
millimeter.*

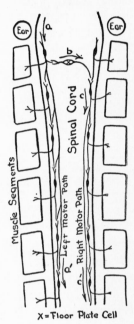

X = Floor Plate Cell

Fig. 18.—Figure to explain
bending.

Stage 3: But why the coil stage? Unlike the bending stage,
which is either present or not present, the coil stage is an outgrowth
of bending. The bending merely progresses farther and farther
down one side of the larva. This is explained by the fact that growth
starts at the head end of the larva and proceeds in the tailward
direction so that the same growth processes which explain the bending reaction occur successively at lower and lower levels and constitute an explanation of the coil stage.

Stage 4: In the S-stage there are two additional growth processes on the part of the nervous system. One of these processes involves the axons of the motor pathway and is simply an extension of Stage 3. But a curious new process is also under way: in each muscle cell there appears a sensory fiber. These fibers grow as collaterals of the sensory neurons which supply the skin. Therefore the contraction of a muscle cell has the same stimulational effect as contact in Stage 2. If the animal is then stimulated near the head on the outer skin, a contraction results on the opposite side, as we have seen. But instead of the process stopping here, as it has in previous stages, the contraction of the muscle produces a further stimulation which is transmitted to the muscles of the other side. These two wavelike contractions, progressing down each side of the animal, produce the S-shaped form that we have described.

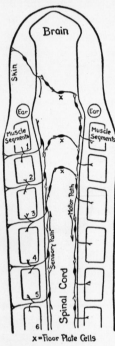

x = Floor Plate Cells

Fig. 19.—Showing the growth of proprioceptive collaterals in the motor pathway.

Stage 5: There is nothing new in the swimming stage. When the growth processes that we have described progress farther down the sides and when these S-stages become rapid enough, propulsion through the water results.

Entirely aside from the factual information regarding growth and maturation that they provide, these experiments of Coghill's and Carmichael's will give to the reflective student further insight into the scientific method as it applies to problems of behavior. You will observe that scientific explanation is really a series of descriptions. First we need accurate and detailed descriptions of the behavior under consideration. In obtaining these descriptions we almost always need to employ various instruments of precision such as microscopes and stop watches and measuring devices of other kinds. Explanation of this carefully described behavior is then made in terms of other descriptions, this time of the relationships that obtain between sense organs, nervous system, and muscles and glands. A curious person might still want to know how the sense organs, muscles and glands ever came into being. If he pursues his objective far enough he will find another series of descriptions in embryology relating to the origin of these structures. If he still asks "why?" the embryologist will refer him to the geneticist, who in turn will give him another set of descriptions. This process constitutes scientific explanation.

2. GRASPING AND CREEPING

Is growth as powerful in determining the behavior of children as it is for the laboratory animals that we have just seen? At least three lines of evidence indicate that before the school age, at least, it is. One of these lines stems from careful observations that have been made on the development of creeping [6] and of grasping.[7]

These studies involve only a description of the behavior, as we shall see, and are not explanations in neural and anatomical terms, but they reveal fairly definite patterns of response which follow on each other according to an invariable sequence, and consequently are strongly suggestive of explanation in the same terms as Coghill has used for Amblystoma. The other two lines derive from attempted modification of this sequence by allowing special opportunity or imposing special restriction on either (a) a group of children, or (b) a single child. In order to obtain controls for these experiments, in (a) another group of children has to be used; in (b) the most fruitful control has been the identical twin of the child whose environment has been experimentally modified.

[6] Louise B. Ames, "The Sequential Patterning of Prone Progression in the Human Infant," Genetic Psychology Monographs, 1937, 19, 409-460.

Arnold Gesell and Louise B. Ames, "Ontogenetic Organization of Prone Behavior in Human Infancy," Journal of Genetic Psychology, 1940, 56, 247-263.
[7] H. M. Halverson, "An Experimental Study of Prehension in Infants by Means of Systematic Cinema Records," Genetic Psychology Monographs, 1931, 10, 108-285.

Grasping.—In the development of both creeping and grasping the Clinic of Child Development at Yale University has made intensive studies over a period of years. The method used in these studies is strikingly like that we have seen in the previous section on Amblystoma. Of course, human infants are not sacrificed to find out just which neurons are responsible for a movement of the arms or legs, but the behavior descriptions are attempted in about the same terms that Coghill employed, and it turns out that the various stages of development in both creeping and grasping follow upon each other in a way that forces us to infer that maturational processes play a dominant role in this behavior development. Instead of attempting to make all of their observations directly, these experimenters have made extensive use of motion-picture sequences which are taken at specified intervals and provide a permanent record of the infant's behavior. These records can then be studied at leisure so that we are certain that nothing observable has been overlooked.

Newborn infants do not reach for and manipulate objects. When they do commence to make contact with objects it is found that larger objects are first reacted to by squirming and twisting the whole body and by random flailing of the arms. This reaction is definite enough so that it can be said to constitute a *stage* in development. A second stage involves raking and corralling movements with both hands. The hands themselves seem to be under the dominance of the arms, the wrists have very little independent action, and the elbows do not take part in adjusting the movements to the extent that they do in the adult. Most of the activity seems to be under the nervous and muscular control of the large muscles involved in making movements of the whole arm from the shoulder. Among the other stages are backhand approaches, where the back of the hand is directed toward the object; circuitous approaches, where the hand describes a wide arc in approaching the object; direct plane approaches, where the surface of the hand is parallel to the top of the table; palm grasps, in which the object is held against the palm by all five fingers; thumb-forefinger oppositions, where the object is grasped between those two digits alone. These responses follow one another in approximately the sequence enumerated here. They seem to be different from the development of the behavior of simpler organisms like the larval Amblystoma in that the stages are not quite so well defined. As a result one can find several of them present at one period of observation. Then, too, an infant frequently will have progressed to one of the more advanced stages and, for some reason, will then revert, for several days, to a more primitive way of behaving. Not all infants develop at the same rate, of course.

One principle is evident here which Coghill also demonstrated with Amblystoma (his experiments justifying this principle are not related here): *The direction of maturation is from the shoulder toward the finger tips,* or, more technically, in the proximo-distal direction.

Creeping.—The same kind of patterning has also been observed in creeping. To begin with, when an infant is placed prone at an early age the head is barely lifted from the supporting surface, if at all, but by sixteen weeks most infants will use their arms first and then the hands to raise the chest as well as the head from the surface. At about thirty-two weeks, on the average, they will thrust the knees forward so that the entire torso is off the floor. After that time some six or eight weeks longer are required before creeping develops as a well-executed response. One investigator has distinguished fourteen stages in this process. One frequently hears of children who suddenly one day walk unaided. In these cases it is extremely doubtful that they have been afforded the opportunity to exhibit the stages that normally would precede this relatively mature response. It is true that some infants seem to skip a given stage, but not many of them do. It is also true that certain infants develop highly individual ways of executing parts of the whole pattern, but here again, when we try to see the essential features of a long-time development, we are struck with the similarity in the way in which infant after infant develops. One reason why this pattern is not perfectly obvious is that the development extends over so long a time. Other animals develop so quickly that we can remember from the terminal stage what the first stages looked like; not so with the human infant. Without the use of motion pictures taken at weekly or biweekly intervals, it is likely that we would not even now be able to stage this behavior so precisely. These motion-picture views may be seen over and over again until the observer has exhausted all they have to offer.

As was the case with grasping, it is felt that the way one phase leads into another is better explained by some sort of fundamental growth process. The other alternative—that learning is principally responsible—throws too much weight on the uniformity of the environment. Environments are not usually uniform enough to account for the sameness with which specific kinds of behavior is exhibited. Moreover, when special attempts are made either to enrich or to restrict the environment, at least some behavior is practically unaffected by these changes. It seems more accurate to say that an infant *grows* to *grasp* or to *creep* than to say that he *learns* to do these things.

3. HOPI CHILDREN

Two investigators [8] observed that among the Hopi Indians of Arizona we have a social situation which is made to order for the student of maturation and its effect on behavior. The intrusion of the white influence upon the Hopi villages has caused, in some families, a decline in the ancient practice of binding infants to cradleboards. Formerly, all Hopi children were securely fastened to a board as soon as they were born and kept there during most of their infancy, being removed only for bathing or changing, operations that required only a few moments at the most. Hence we have two groups of Indians—the more progressive who do not restrict their infants, and the more conservative who maintain the practices of their ancestors, at least in this respect. These two groups had the same racial and social background until the impact of the white man's culture, so that without manipulation by an experimenter they naturally form a control and an experimental group. The average age of walking for sixty-three Indian children who

[8] Wayne Dennis and Marsena G. Dennis, "The Effect of Cradling Practices upon the Onset of Walking in Hopi Children," *Journal of Genetic Psychology,* 1940, 56, 77-86.

were kept on these boards was 14.95 months. Compared with white norms this is at least a retardation of a month or possibly more, but when compared with forty-two Indian children who were not cradled on the boards, we find no significant difference: the average age for unaided walking was 15.05 months. *Had the control group not been available we might have rashly assumed that hampering movements in early life produces a retardation in the onset of walking, whereas it really does not.*

4. NURSERY SCHOOL CHILDREN

In a study of the permanence of certain skills when an unusual opportunity to practice was afforded, Jersild used the entire enrollment of a New York City day nursery. There were twenty-three children between the ages of four and six who were tested for their strength of grip by an instrument called a *dynamometer,* which is simply a divided hand-piece that the children tried to pull together against the resistance of a spring. Connected to the hand-piece was a dial, calibrated in kilograms so that the strength of each child's righthand grasp could be measured directly.

Each subject was given practice on the instrument on each Monday, Wednesday, and Friday while school was in session for a three-month period, or a total of forty-three practice periods consisting of four separate trials for every child. One might think that during so long a period of time the interest of the children would definitely lag; that they might not work at a maximum level of performance; and that the results would then be inaccurate in expressing the child's full capacity. The experimenter himself was somewhat concerned about this factor before the experiment was under way. But let us see what really happened.

Immediately following the initial tests, there appeared to be a decline in the interest shown by some of the children, but this condition quickly gave way to what seemed to be whole-hearted enthusiasm for the project. The experimenters entered into the project with appropriate abandon; cheer-leader tactics while the child was squeezing the instrument, congratulations, handshakes, and applause when a past record was broken, a red-penciled entry of the score when a new high was attained, and other devices gave the project much of the flavor of an athletic event. Soon after the experiment was begun the experimenters were enthusiastically welcomed by a cluster of children whenever they were seen to enter the day nursery. The children asked to be given their turn, requests for additional trials were frequent. The subjects further expressed good will by means of Christmas cards, Valentines, etc., to the experimenters. If only one experimenter appeared, inquiries were made concerning the other, and if a new record was established by a given child requests were made that the tidings be brought to the absentee experimenter.[9]

Results on just twenty-three children would be useless unless we had something with which to compare them. Forty other children in different nursery schools in the city were examined in order to find twenty-three other children that were in age, height, weight, and strength of grip the equivalent of the experimental group. When these were selected, they were kept as controls and the practice which the experimental group had was denied them. After the three-month period, the control group was tested again, with the results shown in the following table.

AVERAGE DYNAMOMETER SCORES
(Kilograms)

	NUMBER	Av. AGE (Mos.)	WEIGHT (Lbs.)	INITIAL Nov. 1930	AFTER PRACTICE Feb. 1931	June 1931	Oct. 1931
Experimental Group........	13	63.9	43.2	9.9	15.1	17.0	17.2
Control Group...	13	63.3	43.3	9.5	12.3	13.6	16.0
Differences......	..	0.6	−0.1	0.4	2.8	3.4	1.2

The records of ten of the twenty-three subjects over this period of eleven months were incomplete in some respects, a troublesome factor in all extensive experiments. Children become ill at the critical time of testing. Some move to other localities and some cannot be

[9] Arthur T. Jersild, "Training and Growth in the Development of Children," *Child Development Monograph*, No. 10, 1932, p. 26.

reached for other reasons. The original groups must always contain about twice as many children as the number on which the experimenter hopes to have complete records.

These factors reduced the original twenty-three in each group to thirteen. There was a difference of only 0.6 of a month in the average age of the two groups and a difference of only 0.1 of a pound in their weights. There was on the average a difference of only 0.4 of a kilogram in their initial strength of grip. Three months later, after forty-three practice periods, the experimental group had gained on the average of 5.2 kilograms, *but not as a result of practice alone.* During these three months they were also growing. *What this group would have gained without practice in this period we can never know.* The closest we can come to knowing is to observe that thirteen other children just like them, at the end of the same three months, had made an average score of 12.3 kilograms. If we compare the 15.1 made by the experimental group to the 12.3 made by the control group, we see that only about one-half of the gain of the experimental group can be attributed to practice.

Permanence of practice effects.—Is this superiority of the practice group a permanent gain? If it is not permanent, then we need not be so concerned practically if a child fails to have an opportunity for early practice.

Five months after the end of the practice period, and with no further practice having been given to either group, we find a greater difference than that which existed immediately after the close of the practice session. Apparently the advantage is not only maintained but increased. However, at seven months after the end of the training, the advantage had almost disappeared. We would be forced to conclude, then, that *in this function training can produce a temporary advantage, but that shortly after the close of the practice period the comparative advantage is lost.* On the other hand, the trend of the data indicates that if practice were continued indefinitely, the practice group would widen its lead indefinitely.

Interpretation.—Of course it is obvious that the effect of practice is not completely eliminated from the control group. Everyday experiences in which the hands are used involve practice. It is only for the added formal practice which was afforded the experimental group that the conclusions hold. It might very well be that the formal practice in this instance constitutes only a very small increment to the incidental practice involved in the performance of daily tasks and that the impermanence of the advantage is due to the fact that "practice effect" in this experiment is really very small. If a function that is not so commonplace as strength of grip were subjected to the same experimental procedure, more permanent effects might be observed.

Production of tones and intervals.—A function of this kind can be found in the production of tones and intervals not included in the vocal range of the child. Eighteen three-year-old children were given tests on their ability to reproduce the eleven pitches, middle C, D, E, F, G, A, B, C, D′, E′, F′, and twelve intervals within the octave. The experimenter judged whether or not the child was singing the note sounded. Some of the children were soon making a perfect score by reproducing each of the eleven pitches each time so that the series had to be extended by adding G, A, B below middle C, and G′, A′, B′, C″ above the previous range, or a total of eighteen notes. The intervals were increased to twenty-two. There were fourteen pairs of children in the pitch series and thirteen pairs upon whom there were complete data in the interval series. The results are shown best in a table.

	No.	Age in Mos.	Initial Test 11 Notes Jan. 1931	After 40 10-Min. Practice Periods May 1931 Initial	Extended Test 18	After No Training Oct. 1931	
						Initial 11	*Extended*
Experimental....	14	39.1	4.7	10.8	16.0	10.9	16.8
Control.........	14	40.1	4.5	6.2	7.9	7.0	10.2
		12 Intervals			22 Intervals		
Experimental....	13	39.5	4.4	11.8	19.0	11.3	18.7
Control.........	13	42.0	4.5	7.6	9.0	7.4	9.8

Comparison between the groups.—Here the two groups started with about the same initial accuracy of 4.7 and 4.5 on the average out of eleven notes. After forty ten-minute practice periods, the experimental group averaged 10.8 with the eleven-note series while the control group, which had had no practice, managed to average only 6.2. Four months later, without any additional practice for either group, the practice group was still ahead and the gain in the reproduction of intervals was maintained. This can only mean that *as far as vocal ability is concerned, early practice gives a permanent advantage.*

Interpretation of the two experiments.—Taking these two experiments together, it would seem at first that we have two distinctly divergent sets of results. The strength-of-grip experiment demonstrates that practice is ineffective in increasing performance except for the duration of the formal exercise. On the other hand, the vocal experiment indicates a positive permanent value of practice. In the first function, improvement comes through an increase in strength, which has a pretty definite physiological basis. In vocal training the physiological basis is present, but the experiment is set up in such a way that an increase in score is made by adding new items to the repertoire. Training which prompts the child to make full use of his entire repertory of achievements may produce substantial results. In the latter function, therefore, *a child who receives training may achieve a range of skill that, if left to develop at his own pace, he would not normally acquire, if at all, until a later time.*

5. IDENTICAL TWINS

This last principle is illustrated in an experiment in delayed vocabulary training conducted by Strayer on one of a pair of identical twins.[10] The method is similar to the control-group technique in that one of the twins is given special training while the other is

[10] L. C. Strayer, "Language and Growth, the Relative and Deferred Language Training, Studied by the Method of Co-twin Control," *Genetic Psychology Monographs*, 1930, 8.

given none. This experimental device is called "the method of co-twin control." *Since identical twins have identical genetic back-grounds, differences that appear cannot be attributed to differences in innate capacity: they must be due wholly to the opportunities provided.*

Method.—The general plan of the experiment was to train formally Twin T and to keep Twin C as a control in a nonverbal environment during the training of T. Twin T was given an hour and a quarter of formal training each morning. This training consisted in presenting some object to the subject, naming it, and attempting to secure some repetition from the child. There was an attempt to keep the training in the nature of a game. The objects used—a ball, wooden duck, shoe, red paper cap, stuffed cat on wheels, and so on—were selected with the play requirement in view. After some progress had been made, instead of saying "What is it?" the experimenter commissioned the child to carry out simple commands, such as "Bring the *duck* to me," "Put the *ball* on the chair." At the end of a week, a picture book was brought to the child and she was asked to "Put your finger on the *baby*," "Show me the *doll*," "Where is the *wheel?*"

Daily records were kept of the number of times a given word was repeated by the experimenter, the number of responses by the child, her errors and her successes. A dictaphone record was also made.

While Twin T was being trained, C was by no means neglected. The experimenter spent about half as much time with her as with T. Many of the same games were played, but they were silent. Expressive gestures—nodding, smiling, pointing, beckoning, and head shaking—were not accompanied by words as they ordinarily would have been. Music was not eliminated and in many situations where the nurse or experimenter would ordinarily have talked with the child they now hummed.

Results of delayed training.—The principal results of the experiment are shown in two figures. Figure 20 shows the number of words that each child could say, plotted against age. Twin T's curve shows the kind of a growth curve that we have come to expect in

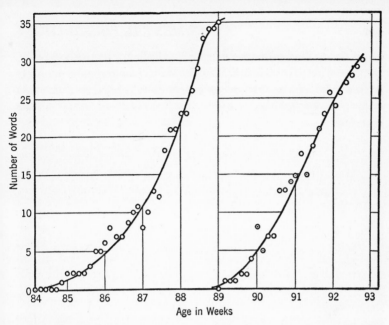

FIG. 20.—Results in delayed vocabulary experiment. Twin T was trained from the 84th week; Twin C's training did not begin until the 89th week.

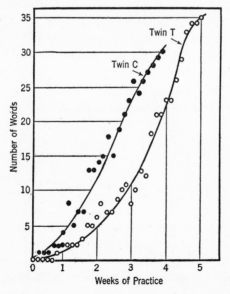

FIG. 21.—The same results, but the beginning of the training for each child is taken at the origin. This procedure shows more clearly how C learned faster than T.

experiments of this kind. The characteristics are a slow beginning followed by a more and more rapid rise. The flattening of the curve on the thirty-second, thirty-third, and thirty-fourth days does not mean that the word-acquisition process was slowing up. The inference would be that this relatively flat place showing little improvement on these days would be followed by a sharp rise as it was on the twenty-ninth day. Twin C's word-curve starts at zero words as did T's. There is no question but that after thirty-five days of practice, there is a marked difference between the two twins, who had been almost identical in language development up to the time that they were separated. When the same practice is instituted with Twin C that had previously been used with T, C improved markedly.

The learning curve is steeper from the beginning. A given amount of practice, when it was delayed five weeks, resulted in greater accomplishment for the more mature child. This is shown more adequately in Figure 21, which is simply Figure 20 replotted to show the effect of practice. Weeks of practice rather than age are plotted horizontally. It becomes immediately evident from these curves that when the training is delayed, improvement is more prompt. In four weeks Twin C accomplished almost as much as Twin T did in five. It would have been instructive to continue the experiment so that both twins would have had the same amount of practice, but unfortunately Twin C developed a kidney infection which made the precise completion of the experiment impossible. The beginning of the infection *may* have accounted for the slowing up of the learning rate in the few days before the end of the experiment.

Summary.—In summary, these data show two things: First, when one of a pair of twins is kept in a nonlanguage environment while the other is instructed in vocabulary, the differences between the respective vocabularies of the two twins become increasingly apparent. *Training is effective in producing an apparent psychological difference between two organisms of identical genetic background.* Second, *when training is instituted later in the life of the control twin,* the progress made is more pronounced since *a smaller number of practice periods produces the same result in terms of ac-*

FIG. 22.—The child rolls the steel ball through a pathway between posts by tilting the platform towards herself, away from herself, to her right, or to her left. There is only one way for the ball to go. The child has to discover which way this is. She cannot tell by looking at the apparatus because the difference between the true pathway and all the blind alleys is not visually discernible. (Courtesy of the Institute of Child Welfare, University of Minnesota, John Anderson, Director.)

complishment. Presumably maturational factors are responsible for the progressively greater value of succeeding practice acts.[11]

6. PERMANENCE OF ADVANTAGE

We still have to settle the question of just what kinds of responses are permanently susceptible to the influence of practice and what kinds exhibit only a temporary advantage which may not be

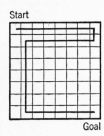 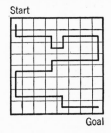 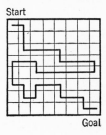

FIG. 23.—The three pathways.

even very appreciable. Jersild's experiments on strength of grip and on vocal ability indicated that these two functions were different in this respect. Strayer's experiment shows that training has a marked effect on vocabulary. But from these data we can certainly deduce no general principle.

In an experiment conducted at the Institute of Child Welfare at the University of Minnesota we have a distinguished contribution to this problem.

The effect of difficulty.—A task was set for preschool children which involved the same *kind* of manipulation but of three different degrees of difficulty. The child holds a square boxlike affair in his hands. There is a glass top to the box and a steel ball can be seen inside. By tilting the box, the ball can be caused to roll. But it will roll only in predetermined directions. A series of carefully

[11] This conclusion is of extreme importance to the elementary school where present practices require that children learn skills, that undoubtedly in the light of their maturational level, had better be delayed.

adjusted machine-screw heads will allow only one pathway to be followed. The child cannot tell by looking at the apparatus which way the ball will go. It is also clear that the pathways can be as simple or as complex as desired. The three used are shown here. Again, it should be understood that the child could not see these patterns. They had to be discovered by tilting the platform. The time required and the number of tilts made was a measure of the success of the learner in mastering this problem.

Figure 24 shows the time required for the children to master the hardest and the easiest tasks. The intermediately difficult task is omitted from the figure because it merely complicates the picture. The curves showing the number of errors made are also eliminated for the same reason.

Equating the groups.—One group of children, who worked on the easy problem, was divided into two subgroups shown at the bottom of the graph as dotted and solid lines. These two subgroups were not selected until after four practice periods so that the experimenter would have some actual basis for asserting that the groups were equivalent. That they are *not* identical is shown by the fact that the dotted and solid lines are not *exactly* superimposed, but they are close enough together in performance so that one could say they were, for all practical purposes, groups of equal performance. The same is true in all these respects for the two subgroups, control and experimental, that worked on the hardest task.

Training the experimental group.—After the fourth day, the control groups in each case rested. For the experimental groups the day of practice marked "1" is really the fifth day. For twenty-six days the experimental groups continued to work, those on the hardest maze reducing their average time from about seventy to thirty seconds. Those on the easiest problem reduced their time only about four seconds in the same interval.

Test after practice.—In the period marked "Test" the control groups again go to work on their respective problems. For the experimental groups there is no distinction between the test period and the previous practice periods.

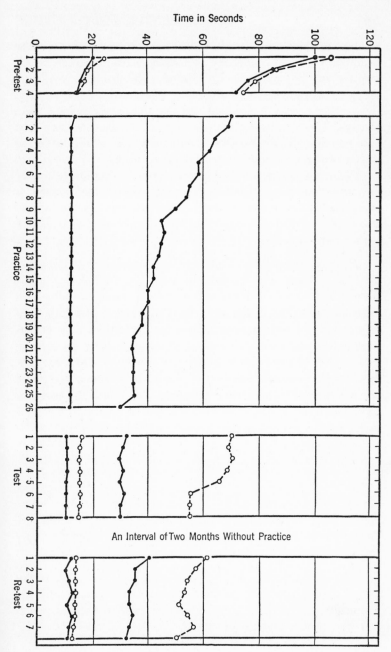

FIG. 24.—The results for the easiest and the hardest problem.

Results.—The appearance of the curves in the "Test" period shows that the difference between the control and the experimental groups is much greater for the hardest problem. For the easiest problem, although there is a difference, it is not marked. A further retest conducted two months later shows that the difference between the practice and the nonpractice groups on the easiest problem has practically disappeared, while for the more difficult task there is still a pronounced difference in favor of the trained group.

This result enables us to conclude that the difficulty of the task is an important factor in determining whether or not a relatively permanent advantage is gained by formal training. The complexity of the vocal responses which showed a superiority even after a period of no training is probably accounted for on this basis. Those experiments which show that the effects of training are ephemeral and confined to the period of practice and shortly thereafter have been made with simple tasks.

Summary.—The ramifications of this chapter are somewhat extended in that instances involving frogs and salamanders, Indian children, nursery school groups, and identical twins have been cited. The specific reactions studied in this variety of forms involved swimming, grasping, creeping, walking, language, and simple motor skills. All of this detail should not be allowed to obscure the fact that all these instances are directed at understanding how the behavior that we observe in adult organisms ever comes to be in the first place. In all these instances it is clear that structure is important, but at the same time it should be obvious that structure (inheritance) alone cannot account for behavior and that the really important determinant is the interaction between structure and environment.

VI

INTELLIGENCE

AT the beginning of this century, the Paris school directors were faced with the problem of the continuing increase in the enrollment in the elementary schools. A large part of the crowding was due to the fact that there was a large number of failing students. The directors appointed a special committee to find out which ones of these retarded students were capable and which ones were incapable of learning the ordinary classroom skills. The notion that some pupils were innately incapable and that others just weren't interested was then relatively new. The educational philosophy which charged school authorities with the responsibility of providing special facilities for the misfits in a system designed for the capable was just beginning to develop.

1. BINET'S CONTRIBUTION

The problem of finding a method for predicting the school achievement of children before their routine schooling had progressed very far was an intensely practical as well as a puzzling one. There was little to start with. One of the members of the commission, Alfred Binet, had for some twenty years been interested in the problem of reasoning and, as a matter of fact, it was the publication of his book, *L'étude expérimentale de l'intelligence* (1903), that had been instrumental in his appointment to the commission on special classes.

L'intelligence was a study of Binet's two little girls, who had told him what they were thinking about while they solved various problems which he had proposed. He learned from this experience that there was nothing in problem-solving that corresponded to the kinds of things that in the decade preceding 1903 had been assumed to be related to it.

In America, Cattell had examined and recorded the breadth of skulls, the hair and eye color, and the strength of grip and speed of movement of Columbia University students, but the newly developed correlation methods had shown as early as 1901 that there was no relation between any of these things and the marks that Columbia University students were receiving in their courses.[1]

Method of demonstrating the validity of the tests.—In a previous study[2] that he had made himself, Binet had developed a method of testing out some of the things that were held by other psychologists at the time to differentiate between the dull and the clever students. Briefly the method consisted of this: Out of a class of thirty-two students, he selected two groups. One group consisted of the five best students in the class, and the other was made up of the six poorest. Binet reasoned that if the good students excelled the poor ones in his tests, the tests could then be made to serve the purpose of separating new students of unknown ability into two groups. One group would include those who, in the course of the educational process, would eventually prove to be good students. The other group would be found to contain the duller members of the class. In his preliminary tests, Binet measured the ability of these two contrasting groups of students to make tactual discriminations, to count small points placed close together, to count the beats of a metronome, to copy printed material, to reproduce a design which they had seen for a brief period of time, and to make

---

[1] Clark Wissler's *The Correlation of Mental and Physical Tests* (1901) which examined the Columbia University data can be held responsible for retarding for almost ten years any further work in this country on the problem of intelligence. He showed that class standing correlated with reaction time to the extent of —.02; with association time +.08; with logical memory +.19; and with auditory memory +.16. He demonstrated that the correlation technique, itself, was adequate to find a relationship where one did exist. The correlation between the marks in the various subject matter fields was uniformly high. The study demonstrated that with the tools when available, psychologists could not detect beforehand which people would be successful in college.

[2] Alfred Binet, "Attention et adaptation," *L'Année Psychologique,* 1899, 6, 248-405.

reactions quickly. When the tests had been given and the results recorded, it turned out that some of the tests did not differentiate between the two groups at all. In some cases, the duller group actually exceeded the superior. In other cases, there was no difference at all between the groups, but in some tests, particularly the copy test, the metronome test, and the design test, the bright children were clearly superior to the dull. We see, therefore, that Binet had succeeded in isolating, by means of a scientifically controlled experimental procedure, tests of certain factors which were obviously involved in the process which differentiated good students from poor ones. Some of these tests, in improved form, are still in use today. Today we would be dissatisfied with Binet's procedure. For instance, we would not be content to take just one class of students as a fair sample of all pupils; we would demand larger groups for the two extremes. Nevertheless this technique was a beginning in the right direction and is followed in principle today.

The age scale.—Binet's major contribution to the field of testing, aside from demonstrating the kinds of items that would have to be included in an intelligence test, consisted of his development of an age scale. This notion was not completely developed until 1908, and in that year he published, with his co-worker Simon, the first instrument that could really be called an "intelligence test." The new notion that was elaborated in this test was that of scaling the items in difficulty and classifying them according to the average age of the pupils who could pass the respective test items. The scale started at the age of three years and, at this level, enumerated five things that a normal three-year-old child could be expected to do. They were the ability

1. To show his nose, eyes, and mouth when asked by the examiner.
2. To enumerate certain objects in a picture.
3. To repeat two figures.
4. To repeat after the examiner a sentence of six syllables.
5. To be able to give his surname.

These items were not the product of Binet's imagining of what youngsters ought to be able to accomplish. They were based on actual observation of three-year-olds. Items placed at other age levels in the scale were selected on a similar basis.

At four the child was expected

1. To name a key, a penny, and a knife.
2. To repeat three figures.
3. To differentiate between the length of two lines.

The scale continued through five, six, seven, eight, and nine years, with the items becoming increasingly difficult. At nine years, for example, the child was expected to be able

1. To give the date completely—that is, the day of the week, the month and the year.
2. To give the names of the days of the week.
3. To give definitions of common objects that involved more understanding of definition than simply to say a chair "is to sit on."
4. To be able to retain six different ideas that he could get from a passage which he read.
5. To arrange five blocks in order of their weight when the difference between them was rather small.
6. To be able to make change in certain denominations.

The scale continued with more difficult items on to the ages of ten, eleven, twelve, and thirteen.

A comparison of Binet's early scale with a modern intelligence test would show this scale to be rather crude. He expected the children to be able to pass all of the items for a given year in order to be given credit for that year. Thus a three-year-old child would have to be able to do all five things enumerated in the three-year level to be considered normal. If the child was not able to do all of them, he would be said to be subnormal. If this same three-year-old could do all of the things that the normal four-year-old could do (that is, pass all of the tests at the four-year level) when the child himself was only three, then Binet considered him to be definitely superior. These descriptions were all qualitative. He did not say how much the child was advanced or retarded in any precise quantitative manner. His method for measuring subnormality consisted of subtracting the highest year-level in which the child succeeded on all of the test items from the chronological age of the child.

A revised scale, published in 1911, involved (1) a rearrangement of some of the items that had been found upon further use of the scale to be either too difficult or too easy for the ages at which they were originally placed, and (2) a part method of scoring; that is, the child was given credit for as many test items in a given year which he passed correctly. Now, in the new scale each year was divided into five parts corresponding to the difficulty of the five expected things for each age group; therefore each item which was passed contributed .2 of a year to the child's score. If he passed all of the three-year-old items and three of the four-year-old items, his score was 3.6 years. This was a definite improvement in that it was a more accurate and a finer method of describing the child's accomplishment.

The content of these Binet scales and the method of scoring them are the basis for most of the work that was done later in Europe and in America on measuring intelligence. With very little change this 1911 scale could be used today to pick out the definitely retarded in any school system.

2. THE I.Q.

It is only since 1916 that we have started to arrange the tests more precisely in the order of difficulty and have been able to specify with considerable accuracy how much a child is either accelerated or retarded in his development. As we have seen, Binet spoke of acceleration in qualitative terms, merely saying that the child was either superior or inferior to others of his same chronological age. Now, thanks to the American psychologist Terman, we see that a developmental age can be related to a chronological age by means of a ratio between them. Thus, if a three-year-old child accomplishes what average four-year-old children accomplish, his development with reference to other children of his same age can be expressed by the ratio 4/3, or 1.33. If he is four and accomplishes only as much as three-year-olds are expected to do on the basis of three-year-old tests, then his ratio is 3/4 or .75. In his revision of the Binet scale in 1916, Terman employed the term "intelligence quotient" [3] for the ratio and multiplied this quotient by 100 in order to get rid of the decimals. Thus the intelligence quotients, or I.Q.'s, in the above examples would be 133 and 75. It is obvious that in such a scheme normality is expressed conveniently by an I.Q. of 100. Terman also named what we have called the development age the "mental age" of the child, in contrast to the "chronological age." Terman revised the 1911 Binet scale [4] on the basis of new measurements on item difficulty made in this country principally with California children. This test has come to be known as the Stanford Revision of the Binet-Simon Test from Terman's position as professor of psychology at Leland Stanford University.

A word of warning.—The concept of intelligence quotient is frequently misapplied. Thus students ask for their "I.Q.'s" when they have in mind some test of college aptitude which was given to them as freshmen. It should be perfectly clear that the notion of I.Q. applies directly to the rate of development in childhood and can be applied to adults only by extrapolation beyond the ages at which year-to-year increases in accomplishment (mental age) are evident. *One can truly speak of the I.Q. of an adult only by estimating what his I.Q. would have been had it been determined when he was in the elementary grades,* for even after he is twelve years old it becomes more and more difficult to separate one age group from another.

It turned out as a result of wholesale testing of conscripted men during World War I that the average mental age of this tremendous sample of nearly two million men was in the neighborhood of twelve years. In the succeeding twenty years we had newspaper editorials deploring the "intelligence" of the "average American adult." There was no point to all this wasted pessimism because the editorials could, on the basis of the findings, have just

---

[3] William Stern had suggested the use of "mental quotient" to express this notion as early as 1904.
[4] L. M. Terman, *The Measurement of Intelligence,* Houghton Mifflin Company, Boston, 1916.

as well been pointed toward an appreciation of the accomplishments of children. There are obvious differences between mature men and callow youths, but they are not to be found in the stuff from which intelligence tests are constructed.

3. TERMAN'S CONTRIBUTION

Terman's revision of the Binet test, in addition to introducing the concept of the I.Q. in a practical form, was superior in many other respects to the original Binet scales. In the first place, Binet was forced to work with relatively small numbers of mostly stupid children. Terman attempted to get a large number of children here who were more representative of the total population. On the other hand, Binet and some of the other workers who had used the Binet scale, notably Goddard, were principally interested in separating the subnormal from the remainder of the population, Terman succeeded in detecting brilliance among children as well as stupidity. The title of the Ph.D. thesis, "Genius and Stupidity: A Study of Some of the Intellectual Processes of Seven 'Bright' and Seven 'Stupid' Boys," which was published in the *Pedagogical Seminary* ten years before the Stanford Revision, is indicative of his early interest in the higher end of the intelligence scale. His *Genetic Studies in Genius,* published in 1925, is an account of studies of a thousand gifted children.[5]

Terman used better criteria than his predecessors for the inclusion of the items at the various age levels. The whole scale contained ninety items. Fifty-four of these were from the original Binet scales and the remaining thirty-six were entirely new. The tests were completely rearranged as determined by the results of their application to the nine hundred California children whom we have mentioned before. There were minute directions on how to administer the tests as well as complete and detailed directions on

[5] The concept of the I.Q. permitted him to define precisely what he meant by genius, viz., any child who could score 130 I.Q. points or above. Similarly, anyone who scores below 70 is considered feeble-minded; normality, by definition, ranges from 95 to 105.

how to score them, so that a considerable amount of close study and fairly intensive practice were required of anyone making these intelligence measurements.

Standardization.—The amount of labor involved in adequately standardizing a test of this kind can be appreciated only by reviewing some of the things which it is necessary to do. If we want to determine that a given item is a satisfactory test of the six-year development, that item must be passed by a majority of children who are exactly six years old. Furthermore, it must be failed by a majority of children who are less than six years old and it must be passed by all of the children who are more than six years old. Of course, it is impossible to obtain enough children who are *exactly* six years old out of an available population; hence Terman allowed a variation of one month on either side of six years. *Majority* was defined as 75 per cent of all those of a certain age. *All* of the children means 100 per cent of them. This means that the responses of large groups of children to each one of the ninety items have to be studied in this painstaking way. The mere labor of administering the tests in the first place is also no small item in the total picture. Since this test is given to each child individually rather than to groups of children, it is often called an individual test. This does not mean that there is no group comparison, however. The standardization group determined where a given test item would fall on the final scale so that every time a child is given a test, he is being compared in effect with a group of children, even if they are not in the room with him at the time the test is given to him.

Practical results of a testing program.—The results of instituting a program of mental testing in a school system are set forth in one of Terman's early studies in which he says:

> The so-called "retarded" children are in reality usually from one to three grades above where they belong by mental development; the real retardates are the underaged children who are generally found from one to three grades below the location which their mental development would warrant. In other words, the problem of retardation is exactly the reverse of what it is popularly supposed to be.

The first grade is the most critical. It is there that retardation scores its worst record, for usually about one-third of the pupils fail of promotion by the end of the first year. Accordingly, it is especially important that in the first grade the raw material with which the school is to work should be correctly evaluated.

In one study by Dickson the mental ages found in a first-grade group ranged from three years to almost eleven years. One-third of the pupils were below a mental age of six years; 90 per cent of this group failed to win promotion. On the other hand, 15 per cent of the group were above the mental age of seven and one-half years. Doubtlessly, many of these could readily enter the second or third year.

The success of a teacher is judged largely by the absolute standard of work she is able to secure from her pupils. How unfair this may be in individual cases is illustrated by the following facts for five first-grade classes tested by Dickson. The median I.Q.'s of five first-grade classes were 87, 76, 85, 108, and 112. There was thus a difference of 36 points in the median I.Q.'s of the higher and lowest classes. The best class was fully two years above the lowest in terms of average mental age; the lack of progress in the latter room was so evident that the teacher was in despair and the superintendent doubted her efficiency. One might suppose that the teachers of these classes would have been keenly aware of the difference in the intellectual make-up of their groups. They were not, however, except in the vaguest sort of way.

It appears that the standards of work which are maintained in the first year of the average California high school cannot be satisfactorily met by pupils with a Stanford-Binet mental age below thirteen years, and that below the mental age of fourteen the chances of success are not good. It also appears that children with an I.Q. below 80 rarely succeed in entering a California high school, and that those with an I.Q. below 90 rarely graduate. A large majority of those who drop out have an I.Q. considerably below 100. The typical high school offers little work which can be mastered by pupils of much less than average intelligence. A nation falls short of the true ideals of democracy which refuses to furnish suitable training for a third of its children merely because their endowment does not enable them to complete a course of study which will satisfy the requirements for college entrance. High schools at present are in a sense "class" schools.[6]

[6] L. M. Terman, "The Use of Intelligence Tests in the Grading of School Children," *Journal of Educational Research*, 1920, 1, 20-32.

The following table indicates the grade location of 263 eleven-year-olds and their mental ages. Four of the 263 eleven-year-olds were in the first grade. Their mental ages ranged from five to

GRADE LOCATION OF 263 ELEVEN-YEAR-OLDS BY
STANFORD-BINET MENTAL AGE*

(Correlation is 0.81)

MENTAL AGE	GRADE								TOTAL
	I	II	III	IV	V	VI	VII	VIII	
18							1		1
17							3	1	4
16						1	2		3
15					2	5	6	1	14
14				1	6	13	2		22
13				3	12	18	1		34
12			1	2	22	12			37
11			2	10	42	6			60
10			6	15	20	1			42
9		2	3	14	6				25
8	1	5	6	2					14
7	1		1	3					5
6	1								1
5	1								1
Total	4	8	21	47	110	56	15	2	263

* From L. M. Terman, *The Intelligence of School Children,* Houghton Mifflin Company, Boston, 1919.

eight years. Two of the eleven-year-olds were in the eighth grade. Their mental ages were fifteen and seventeen.

This table warrants special study because there are numerous other comparisons that will occur to the wide-awake student.

4. THE 1937 REVISION

Before progressing to a further study of the results of a testing movement, let us examine in some detail a more recent revision of the Binet scale. This revision was published in 1937, but preparations for it had been underway for several years preceding that date. The number of tests was increased from 90 to 129 and two equivalent forms of the test are provided. This made 258 items in all. More than 3,000 subjects were examined in order to standardize the various items, and the full time of seven people, working as examiners in different parts of the country, was required for two years.

THE DISTRIBUTION OF EMPLOYED MALES IN THE UNITED STATES AND THE LIVING FATHERS OF THE CHILDREN IN THE SAMPLE*

OCCUPATIONAL GROUP	PERCENTAGE OF EMPLOYED MALES	PERCENTAGE OF LIVING FATHERS
I. Professional	3.1	4.5
II. Semiprofessional and managerial	5.2	7.8
III. Clerical, skilled trades, and retail business	15.0	25.5
IV. Farmers	15.3	14.9
V. Semiskilled occupations, minor clerical positions and minor businesses	30.6	31.4
VI. Slightly skilled trades and other occupations requiring little training or ability	11.3	9.4
VII. Day laborers (urban and rural)	19.5	6.6
Total number ·	38,077,804	2,757

* From L. M. Terman and M. Merrill, *Measuring Intelligence,* Houghton Mifflin Company, Boston, 1937.

The Stanford-Binet test had been criticized because the nine hundred California children were not representative of all of the children in the United States. For some states, particularly, the tests were too difficult. It is also known now, but not so well recognized in 1916, that there is a definite relation between the socio-economic level of a child and his intelligence. It was not clear in the earlier standardization whether this factor had had an influence in making the tests too difficult for the majority of the population. In the new standardization procedure, therefore, in order to take care of the first objection, seventeen different communities in eleven different states were sampled. A special effort was made to obtain an adequate sample of the rural population. This had not been done previously and we now know that, in general, urban children do test higher than rural children. The occupational groups according to the 1930 census figures were used as a reference in selecting the standardization sample. The table shows the occupational group and the percentage of employed males in the United States in 1930 in these different occupations and the percentage of the standardization group where the occupations of the living fathers could be ascertained.

The authors note that the rural sample is still inadequate despite the fact that special precautions were taken against this very fault. This is very largely due to the extreme difficulty in moving from locality to locality in the country as compared with the ease with which large numbers of children can be obtained in the cities. The discrepancies between the lower occupational groupings and the inability to obtain children in the testing is explained by the fact that a large number of these people in the census were young men who were unskilled by reason of lack of experience and training and who had as yet not established families; Negroes included in the census were not included in the standardization groups.

5. THE EFFECTS OF PRACTICE ON TEST SCORES

Many people who use intelligence tests in practical situations are not acquainted with all of the factors which affect a person's score on a test. Many of them believe that practice, for instance, can make little difference in a test score, because in an intelligence test one is supposed to be measuring something that a person inherits: *Heritable features of human make-up are not subject to practice, of course.* Some tests have only one form and the directions generally state that practice effects are insignificant particularly if as much time as a year elapses between successive testings. Test manuals that make statements like this are very misleading. Thorndike found as early as 1919 that when trials were given in immediate succession, a

repetition of a test raised the scores 10 per cent on the average, and
if a second repetition (a third test) followed an additional 4 per
cent increment was imposed. The psychological knowledge of too
many testers is entirely derived from overly optimistic test manuals.

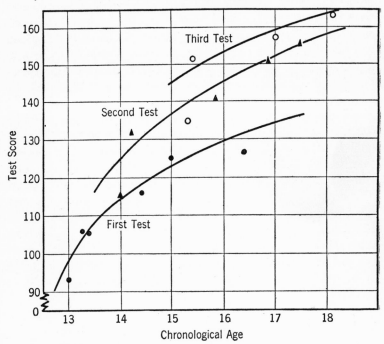

Fig. 25.—Three successive testings of the same population.

Dorothy Adkins[7] has recently published a study of data collected at Mooseheart. Successive testings at approximately one-year
intervals were available for several different grade levels and with
several different tests.

The results for the Otis group test are in Figure 25. The solid
circles represent the results of a testing program initiated in 1930.
For all the children involved, this was the first time this intelligence
test had been given. We have drawn a solid line, the lowest,

[7] Dorothy C. Adkins, "The Effects of Practice on Intelligence Test Scores,"
Journal of Educational Psychology, 1937, 28, 222-31.

through these data. It is drawn in a way that seems fairly to represent the trend of the small circles.

Approximately a year later the data shown by the small triangles were collected. The general level of the scores this time is clearly above the first administration of the test. The youngest group, now 14, comes very close to scoring in exactly the same place that we would have predicted it would if practice had had no effect (shown by the small ▲ at 14 very close to the solid line). This one point is an exception to the remainder of the data, however; hence this time we draw our solid line to represent the second testing distinctly above the first one. A third testing gave the results shown by the small open circles. Here we do not have as many experimental points to use in determining our trend so that the location of the topmost line is more arbitrary.

The conclusion is clear-cut. *Successive practices, even as much as a year apart, do affect intelligence test scores.* If we confine our attention to age 16, we see that a first testing gives an average score of about 130. But if that group of children had first been tested at 15, their average performance at 16 would have been raised to about 145, and if two administrations had preceded the attainment of age 16, the average would have been raised to 152. The effect is different at the different ages and, of course, differs in amount with different tests. We cannot generalize more precisely than that there is an effect. Whether practice raises scores 1 per cent or 100 per cent depends on so many factors that to generalize is out of the question.

Summary of the chapter.—We have shown how the "intelligence test" grew out of the practical necessity for predicting progress in school before it actually was accomplished. In selecting the items for the tests Binet introduced the method of comparing the test scores of the scholastically successful and the unsuccessful. Once selected, by further experiment, these tests were modified and arranged in the form of an age scale. In order to define precisely how an individual stood he was to be compared with others his own age by means of an index known as the I.Q. When one tests "intelligence" he is not testing an inherited segment of behavior. Inherited structures probably help to determine what an intelligence test score will be, but they are not the only determiners. Successive practices, even as much as a year apart, have their effect. Just how much effect they will have depends on the nature of the test, the age of the subjects and probably upon other factors besides. Just what some of these "other factors" are is the main topic of our next chapter.

VII

THE MEANING OF INTELLIGENCE
TEST SCORES

THE difference in scores for children brought up under urban and rural conditions has been observed from time to time and is undoubtedly a fact. Figure 26 shows the difference between the I.Q. of urban and rural populations as determined by the earlier Stanford-Binet test. It was shown most recently by the 1937 revision of that test. But why the difference? Do intelligent people leave the country and take their children with them, or are rural children at a distinct disadvantage in taking the test? In order to answer the second part of the question we might examine the separate items of the tests to find if there is any reason why these subtests should be easier for city children. Then we shall examine the evidence that offers an answer for the first part of the question.

1. LACK OF OPPORTUNITY

Jones, Conrad, and Blanchard have studied the items of the Binet test from this point of view. They write:

Among the urban four-year-olds a pencil is not uncommonly used as a plaything, whereas among our rural sample the preschool children obtain very little practice in paper-and-pencil behavior—partly because of the predominance of out-of-door interests, and partly because the use of pencils tends to be reserved for older children and adults. By the seventh year this handicap no longer obtains, and the test of copying a diamond presents a rural-urban difference of a more moderate and probably more valid character.

In naming coins, rural children are handicapped by relatively few opportunities to handle coins or to make purchases at stores, and, in addition, probably by less training at home in the specific task. This may be reflected further in the penny-counting tests, which show a marked separation in the early years; at four years, 33 per cent of the urban children and none of the rural children pass the test of counting 13 pennies. At a later age, however, school training and other experience have removed this handicap; in the test of making change the rural retardation is very slight.

The comprehension questions at year VI are specifically difficult, and somewhat unfair, for a rural group. The child is asked, "What is the thing for you to do,

(a) If it is raining when you start to school,
(b) If you find that your house is on fire,
(c) If you are going some place and miss your car (or trolley, or bus, according to local usage)?"

The city child is much more likely to have experienced a definite regime in connection with the first question; experience with fires and fire engines is more common in the city, as is also experience with electric cars. These rural children are all familiar with automobiles, but many of them have never heard of cars or busses traveling as common carriers. . . .

The extraordinary difficulty of the date test for rural children is to a large extent due to differences in the rural and urban manner of living. A daily newspaper is rarely seen, and (particularly during vacations, when these tests were given) the schedule of activities goes on with slight attention to the calendar. . . .

In view of its rural setting, it is perhaps surprising to find the rural children inferior in the ball-and-field test. The difference is reliable at ages 6, 7, and 8, but is insignificant at 9, and at 10 the rural children pull slightly ahead. We may interpret this as due to a change in the actual character of the test, with increasing mental age. The instructions for this test are wordy and complicated; it is reasonable to suppose that in the earlier ages the rural children do poorly, because of a comprehension and memory span difficulty, in reacting to detailed and possibly confusing verbal directions; at the later ages, individual differences may be a function of the task itself rather than of an understanding of instructions.

Rural children suffer a handicap in the vocabulary tests (and in abstract words) owing to the fact that their environment is less "literary" than that of urban children; except for words in colloquial use, they have a relatively limited opportunity for acquiring verbal information. This handicap does not extend to the definitions test at year V, which deals with such homely everyday words as spoon, chair, horse, etc. . . .

But this does not imply that an intelligence scale made up of non-verbal elements would wholly eliminate the difference between rural and urban children. If it did, we should be justified in suspecting the validity of such a scale. In the present scale, we find that such non-verbal tests as the divided rectangles, the memory span for digits, and the digits reversed are, without evident basis in a language handicap, very effective in discriminating between the urban and rural children. . . .

So far as the urban superiority may arise from environmental advantage, this is due not to the verbalness of the tests as such, but rather to the opportunities for special training regardless of the verbal or non-verbal nature of the material. . . .

As a further step it would be possible to consider in similar detail the remaining tests of the Stanford Revision. The foregoing discussion, however, is no doubt sufficient to bring out the following points, which are presented as hypotheses or as tentative conclusions:

(1) The rural inferiority in I.Q. is due partly, although not wholly, to environmental factors;
(2) The environmental handicap is specific rather than general;
(3) Specific handicaps are those which relate to limitations in the material environment, to lack of adaptability to certain arbitrary test requirements (as in speed tests), and to lack of language information.[1]

If these hypotheses are true, it would appear at first glance as though the difference in I.Q. at the successive chronological ages should become increasingly large. The earlier in life these children are tested, the smaller should be the influence of a restricted environment. In Figure 26 a set of data collected from rural New England homes is compared with the urban population that served to standardize the Stanford Revision of the Binet test. The fact that

[1] H. E. Jones, H. S. Conrad, and M. B. Blanchard, "Environmental Handicap in Mental Test Performance," *University of California Publications in Psychology,* 1932, 5, 80-83.

the trend for both the populations shows a downward direction as age increases should be neglected. It is harder to obtain high I.Q.'s at the higher ages. The fact that we want to observe is that there is no divergence of the two trends. The differences that are present at

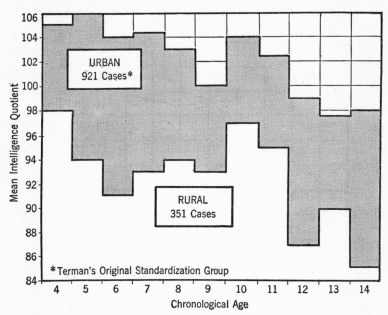

Fig. 26.—A comparison between urban and rural children in intelligence test score.

12, 13, and 14 are also present at 4, 5, and 6. It has been suggested that "the retardation of the rural children is to some extent halted when they enter school and thus begin to share in an environment which has more points of similarity than that furnished by rural and urban homes." We shall have to look further; we shall have to find other groups that are more isolated than rural children in most sections of America if we want to show more clearly that lack of opportunity affects intelligence test scores.

2. CITY LIFE

In a series of studies on the effect of city life on intelligence test scores, Klineberg [2] has presented evidence showing definite increases in scores as a result of having moved to the city. All of

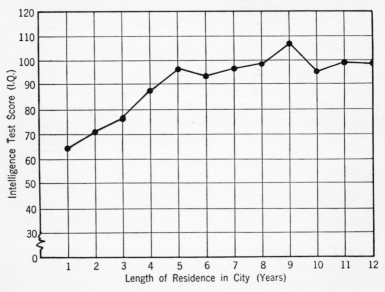

Fig. 27.—The relation between intelligence test score and length of residence in the city.

the subjects in this study were Southern-born Negroes who had migrated to Harlem. Selected so that they would be of the same sex and age, all were twelve-year-old girls. In the large group of children available it was possible to find a limited number who, although Southern-born, had been in the city only one year, some two, three, and so on up to twelve; the latter group, of course, were Harlem-born. In all, 619 of these twelve-year-olds were tested by means of the National Intelligence Test—one of the better tests —in February and May, 1932.

[2] Otto Klineberg, *Negro Intelligence and Selective Migration,* Columbia University Press, New York, 1935.

The results are shown in Figure 27. There were 30 girls who had been in the city only one year; their average score was about 63 points. There were 28 who had been in the city two years; their average score was about 70 points. For a nine-year residence there were only 14 cases and for ten years', only 15, so that the irregularity in the curve at this point is probably due to the small number of cases available. The twelve-year group was Northern-born. Since there were 359 of them, more weight should be given to this point on the graph than to the others. The trend of the averages is perfectly clear, however, and has been substantiated by eight other studies which show approximately the same thing. *It should be perfectly clear that if the more intelligent people move to the city, then there should be no dependence of intelligence-test score on length of urban residence as is shown by this study.*

3. ISOLATED LIFE

Further indication of environmental handicaps is to be found in intelligence test measurements which have been made on people living in remote parts of the United States where the ordinary advantages of public schooling are not present to give a certain uniformity to the lives of both the urban and rural populations. In a section of Virginia within a short distance of the national capital the topography of the country has provided a natural experimental setting for studying this factor. Five "hollows" in which the penetration of civilizing influences was varied have been discovered.

(1) One hollow, Colvin, consists of a few scattered families living the most primitive life without school, church, or other social organization. No one there can read or write. There is no road to the outside world.

(2) A second community, Needles Hollow, connects with the outer world by a rocky mountain trail. A few men can read and write. There is a combined church-school where meetings are held occasionally.

(3) Oakton Hollow is accessible to the skilled driver of an automobile. Agriculture is organized. There is some shipment of

agricultural products to the outside world as well as the beginning of a small fruit-drying industry. There is a church-school, and two religious denominations are represented. One-room cabins have given way to three- and four-room houses. Every home has a mail order catalogue from which most of the buying is done. There is a general store with its post office.

(4) In Rigby Hollow mail can be received daily. There is a fair road connecting with the state highway system. The people generally have more money, bigger houses, better sanitation than in the other hollows. School is in session seven months a year. About three-quarters of the people are literate. They read and understand the newspapers.

(5) The fifth community is a small village, Briarsville, through which a hard-surfaced road runs. It is typical of the small towns through which everybody has passed in rural districts. There is a modern school and church. Newspapers, magazines, automobiles, and radios are familiar to everyone.

The restricted environment in the four communities affected the intelligence test scores to a very marked degree, even in the parts of the tests where the language handicap would not, at first glance, seem to be a factor. For Colvin and Needles Hollow children many of the tests were, for all practical purposes, in a foreign language.

As an example of how the environment restricts the mental test performance, we quote from Sherman and Henry's *The Hollow Folk*.[3]

The children were asked to define "postoffice." The majority of those who tried to define this word said that a postoffice was a place with baskets of apples in front of it. Some added further details, such as "and some men sitting at the door." They had seen the postoffice in Oakton Hollow which is in the general store. Not one directly associated mail with the definition of postoffice, probably because mail rarely comes into Colvin Hollow.

[3] Mandel Sherman and Thomas R. Henry, *The Hollow Folk*, Thomas Y. Crowell, New York, 1933. The student will find that a perusal of the entire volume will repay him. Many students have never come into contact with the complete lack of opportunity described in this book.

The road to Briarsville

The road to Needles Hollow

FIG. 28

(From Sherman and Henry, *The Hollow Folk*. Courtesy of
Thomas Y. Crowell Company, publishers.)

A Colvin Hollow group

A group of Briarsville children

Fig. 29
(From Sherman and Henry, *The Hollow Folk*. Courtesy of
Thomas Y. Crowell Company, publishers.)

. . . One test item consists of a circle with an opening drawn on a sheet of paper and the child is told that it represents a closed field in which a ball has been lost. The child is instructed to trace with a pencil the path he would take to find the ball in the best way possible. The correct solution obviously is to circle the field in a systematic manner until the lost object is located. In the majority of cases this test resulted in failure. Despite patient explanations, the children did not seem able to visualize a field as a comparatively level, treeless, enclosed space. There are "fields" in the mountains planted with corn but they are more nearly vertical than horizontal. One boy made a curious effort. First he corrected the picture in accordance with his idea of what a field should be, by placing pencil marks in the enclosed space. These represented trees. Thus oriented, he proceeded to "find the ball" by hunting around the bottom of each tree.

Fig. 30.—One boy's solution to the "ball and field problem."

This solution, of course, was a failure according to the standard directions for scoring the test. But this child had been presented with a problem every element of which was new to his experience. The makers of the test had not considered a child who did not know the meaning of "field." Furthermore the idea of a lost ball, so familiar to most children, was hard for these youngsters to comprehend. Playing with a ball, until very recently at least, had been foreign to their experience. They had never hunted for a lost ball. They could not understand why anyone should attach any significance to such a situation. . . .

Ability to make specific space and time differentiations also was quite undeveloped. When a boy nineteen years old was asked where the next family lived, he replied: "Over thar a piece."

He didn't know what was meant when asked whether the distance was a mile or a hundred yards. Asked where another family lived, he again replied: "Over thar a piece."

One of these families lived a mile and the other about a quarter of a mile away. He could not differentiate distance in definite terms. The nearest any child came to making such a differentiation was that one family lived "not a far piece over the hill" and that the other lived "a good piece through the woods."

The children of Briarsville, *of the same racial stocks* as those of Colvin and Needles and the intermediate communities, were not much inferior to the California children who served to standardize the test originally. The poor performance of these isolated children cannot be attributed to "poor heredity." *Environmental restriction was the only variable and on the psychological tests the children arranged themselves in order of the opportunities and lack of them that go with the description of the way they live.*

The canal-boat children.—This same retardation in relation to age has been observed in the case of a study of canal-boat children in England.[4] Throughout most of their lives these children are isolated from the contacts that ordinary children have; for instance, they go to school only one or two consecutive half days each month. As a consequence of this fact, with increasing age the retardation, which is barely evident at the earlier ages where the environment fits the needs of the maturing organism, becomes most marked as the children master their environment to the extent that no further demands are made upon them. As a matter of fact, the mental age is almost constant while, of course, the chronological age varies. This makes the younger children score between 90 and 100 I.Q. points, while the older children are definitely "feeble-minded." Gordon also reports these same findings for Gypsy children, who, like the canal-boat children, are isolated from ordinary childhood contacts.

In order to evaluate the significance of a mental test performance, it must be kept clearly in mind that *the Binet scales and others derived from them have as their criterion how well a child can progress in school.* The good students in a school system have been used as criterion groups, as we have seen (page 110). *The significance of a high or low intelligence test score, then, is determined by the value that the cultural group places upon the classroom skills*

[4] H. Gordon, "Mental and Scholastic Tests among Retarded Children," London, Board of Education, Pamphlet No. 44, 1923.

of being able to read and to write and to handle abstractions with ease and with promptness. As we have seen, *in those communities and in those social groups where these skills are not important for existence, the concept of intelligence as measured by these skills simply does not apply.*

4. PRIMITIVE PEOPLE

This latter generalization is substantiated by studies of primitive people, particularly where comparisons are to be made. A set of values, of which intelligence is an example, is entirely incommensurate with another set or system under the demands of a totally different way of living. Porteus, a psychologist who has lived among the Australian aborigines and the African Bushmen, says:

I am quite ready to admit, on the basis of my experience, that, in his own environment, under his own cultural conditions, the African native or the Australian aboriginal is not only equal, but superior, to the white man. He is a better animal—and that is saying a lot in his favor. He can endure the pains of existence with a fortitude of which I am utterly incapable. Anyone who has witnessed the victim's hardihood when suffering a circumcision or subincision operation by means of a stone knife will not doubt the stark courage of the native.

If humor be defined, not as the ability to see a subtle joke, but as the ability to keep a cheery spirit in the face of the most depressing circumstances of poverty and injustice, then the African has a decidedly superior sense of humor—and humor, after all, is the saving social grace.

If also the ability to support the rigors of a terrifying environment is everyday courage, then the Australian aboriginal is much braver than I. If the assurance that life is essentially worth living under any circumstances is more firmly set in the African native's mind than in mine, then I must give him credit for a more effective foresight and hindsight than I possess. There may be many other ways in which the black man may be considered superior and his contributions on the credit side of living should be freely acknowledged. But when it comes to his ability to cope with the white man's environment, which by reason of so-called progress, or of the turn of circumstances, has been thrust upon Negro and aboriginal alike, then I cannot but question their adaptability, especially that of the Australian. The latter, in his natural surroundings, is so far superior to the white man that if he were even equal to the white man in the latter's environment it would be most surprising. If that were the case he would soon inherit the earth.[5]

Another psychologist, Margaret Wooster Curti, has had an opportunity to study the test scores of a limited group of Jamaican children.[6] She had available data collected in 1929 by geneticists, interested principally in race crossing.[7] There were only sixty-eight infants examined in all, but these three-year-old children were distributed about equally within each year of the first three. If this number appears inadequate it can be contrasted with that of the children with whom they were compared who numbered only fifty at each of these three levels.[8]

The infants were tested at the Kingston City Day Nursery, an institution which takes care of the babies of working mothers during the day. The mothers work at hard menial tasks at very low pay—about 62 cents a week. The homes are crowded and sanitary conditions are bad. A bed, for instance, is constructed of boards supported by empty boxes; the bedclothes consist of rags, a sheet, and a pillow stuffed with straw. Such a bed is occupied by the whole family.

The cultural background of these Jamaican children is totally different from that of the New Haven children. Manners and customs differ—children, for instance, are not taught to play; houses are built differently; different stoves and different cooking and agri-

[5] S. D. Porteus, *Primitive Intelligence and Environment,* The Macmillan Company, New York, 1937.
[6] Margaret W. Curti, Francis Botkin Marshal, and Morris Steggerda, "The Gesell Schedules Applied to One-, Two-, and Three-Year-Old Negro Children of Jamaica, B.W.I.," *Journal of Comparative Psychology,* 1935, 20, 125-126.
[7] C. B. Davenport and M. Steggerda, *Race Crossing in Jamaica,* Carnegie Institution of Washington, 1929, pp. 516.
[8] Jamaican children were given the developmental tests described by Arnold Gesell in *The Mental Growth of the Preschool Child,* 1926, pp. 447. The New England children used to standardize these tests consequently determine the standards with which the more primitive West Indian children were compared.

cultural implements are used. Pencils and paper and books are rare and play materials almost nonexistent. In tests where pencils were required they were sometimes used like spoons. A rubber ball used in some of the tests was completely new to the child and in some instances he seemed to have been afraid of it. No attention is given to counting in Jamaica, so that not one of the sixty-eight children was able to count four pennies. All of these factors combine to depress the test scores. As a group the children were decidedly retarded in their development, but there were certain tests in which they either more nearly approached the white norms or actually exceeded them.

No consistent effort is made in Jamaica to train the eliminative functions; even so, the native children were not markedly different from the white children in New Haven. Since no other bodily function ever receives the careful training that the eliminative functions do in America, these results raise the question of wasted labor in our culture. The suggestion is that the processes of elimination are so markedly dependent on the maturation of the controlling muscles and nerves that to try to impose training too early is a waste of time and energy.

In two other tests for the three-year-olds—"putting on shoes" and "running errands"—the Jamaican children are definitely superior as they are in the age at which they first stand and walk. This result suggests that the absence of intimate care of the young may make for self-sufficiency at earlier ages than is characteristic of American children.

5. THE FEEBLE-MINDED

The question often arises as to what becomes of the children who do not get along well in school. Is there a place for them in our social scheme? What kinds of lives do they lead once they leave the school system? There have been several surveys of a limited kind which have had as their object the study of this problem, but there have been few controlled investigations made in which an equal number of children who had not been classified as subnormal have also been followed up later to find out how they turned out. A complete study of this latter kind is available in the work of Baller.[9] The students who had been in the special classes of the public school system of Lincoln, Nebraska, and an equal number of Lincoln students who had not been in the special classes were the subjects in the study. Of the nine items especially investigated, seven concern us here:

(1) The aspects of the home background which particularly characterized these individuals.

(2) The kind and amount of schooling.

(3) The marital status.

(4) The extent to which the subjects had been successful in regulating their conduct so as to conform to the laws and social customs of the community.

(5) The occupational choice and permanence of employment.

(6) The degree of economic self-sufficiency or dependence.

(7) The respects in which mentally subnormal individuals who succeeded in making reasonably satisfactory social adjustments differ from those who failed.

The experimental and control groups.—There were 206 individuals in the subnormal group, of which 126 were men and 80 were women. None of them had had I.Q.'s of more than 70 when they were tested in the elementary schools, and all of them were more than 21 years of age at the time this study was completed. These 206 people were paired one at a time with a normal group, on the basis of age, sex, and nationality but the I.Q.'s of the normal group were between 100 and 120 so that we have equal groups differing only in respect to I.Q. What is called normal here is actually somewhat above normal. The range was chosen in order to obtain clearly contrasting groups.

Locating the subjects.—The reason why more of this work has not been done will be evident when we consider the difficulties in-

[9] Warren Robert Baller, "A Study of the Present Social Status of a Group of Adults, Who, When They Were in Elementary Schools, Were Classified as Mentally Deficient," *Genetic Psychology Monographs,* 1936, 28, 80.

volved in following up groups of this size after they have been out of school a few years. The first step was to look up the names of the subjects in the city directory and in the telephone book. When the names did not appear in these places, the names of the subjects were submitted to various agencies, such as the Child Welfare Bureau, police courts, penitentiaries, reform schools, and institutions for the insane and feeble-minded. Letters to employers, ministers, lawyers, relatives, and friends were used in the hope of turning up a lead that would prove profitable. For one case fifteen separate and distinct leads had to be followed and it took 318 different leads to locate 196 of the subjects.

General description.—After the subjects were located, an attempt was made to interview each one of them, to visit the home, to get acquainted with the relatives, to observe the living conditions in the neighborhood, and so forth. After a good deal of work, 196 of the 206 subnormals and 202 of the control subjects were located and complete information was obtained about them. It turned out that 7 per cent of the subnormal group and 1 per cent of the normal group were deceased. Six and one-half per cent of the subnormal group and none of the control group were in institutions for the feeble-minded. One person from each group was in a hospital for the insane. State reformatories and county jails accounted for two of the subnormal group, but for none of the control group. Fifty-nine per cent of the subnormal group were still living in Lincoln. Fifty-five per cent of the control group were still in the same town. Only 12.25 per cent of the subnormal group had moved to other states, but almost twice as many of the control subjects had moved out of Nebraska. Although the migratory tendencies of the subnormal group are thus demonstrated to be somewhat limited with respect to the states that they live in, within the town of Lincoln they change their addresses much more frequently than the control subjects do.

Family background.—The family background records showed that the subnormal subjects come largely from the lower occupational levels and have practically no representation in the higher professions. In larger proportions, moreover, they have either one or both parents deceased, parents divorced, and families listed with relief agencies before the subject's twenty-first birthday, and more criminal and disorderly conduct records on the part of the parents.

Educational record.—The educational achievement of the subnormal group is expressed in the average of $4\frac{1}{2}$ grades completed for both the boys and the girls. But what is probably more significant is the fact that 23 boys and 10 girls completed the 8 grades of work and that one boy and 2 girls finished high school. The work of a number of these people who got as high as junior high school was of a very special type, however. There was one pupil of the subnormal group who finally finished almost one year of college, but she was 22 years of age when she was graduated from the high school. The control subjects, on the other hand, on the average completed the 12 grades of school, and about half of the 51 boys entering college were graduated. Of these, three took M.A. degrees, one an M.D. degree, and one a Ph.D. degree. Thirty-one of the girls went to college, 9 of them were graduated in four years, but none received a higher degree. As we could have predicted at the start on the basis of intelligence test scores, there is a clear-cut difference between school performance for these two groups.

Marital status.—Almost 60 per cent of both the subnormal and normal women married, and about 50 per cent of the normal men were married, but a significantly smaller percentage (about 33 per cent) of the subnormal men were married. These data show that feeble-mindedness is not a preventative factor in marriage in women, but since more than 50 per cent of the normal men and only 33 per cent of the subnormal men married, feeble-mindedness is a deterrent, probably for economic reasons, among men. There are also more children among the feeble-minded than among the controls, and the feeble-minded women are married at a significantly younger age. *But notice that the great difference between the groups which was evident in the scholastic attainments no longer obtains in marital status.*

Social adjustment.—There are consistent and significant differences between the conduct records as revealed by the juvenile police courts, county and city jails, reformatories, and penitentiaries for both groups of subjects. Twenty-five per cent of the subnormal subjects have appeared in juvenile court, while only 4 per cent of the control subjects have appeared there. For the police court about 18 per cent of the subnormal subjects, as compared with 6 per cent of the normal subjects, have records. About 19 per cent of the subnormal subjects have been in either the county jail, city jail, reformatory, or penitentiary, while only 3 per cent of the control subjects have been committed to these institutions. These commitments were for the comparatively serious offenses, including wife desertion, destruction of property, driving while intoxicated, and assault and battery. If violation of the traffic ordinances had been considered, then the court appearances of the normal subjects would have been doubled.

Occupational adjustment.—The occupational record of the two groups shows a clear-cut superiority for the normal group with reference to both temporary and permanent employment, and the kinds of occupations represented in the two groups also indicate a higher type of adjustment. The degree of independence is shown by the fact that about 83 per cent of the subnormal subjects are either wholly or partially self-supporting, whereas 99 per cent of the control are wholly or partially self-supporting. The percentage of subjects who were aided by relief agencies is about 40 in the subnormal and about 16 in the control subjects. These figures do not tell the whole story if we consider that the per capita cost for the subnormal group was greatly in excess of that for the normal group. The fact that 83 per cent of the subnormals have been to some extent self-supporting, the amount varying from the income derived for tasks such as mowing lawns and occasional work in the homes of acquaintances to a regular income from permanent employment, is rather striking in view of their distinct abnormality on the intelligence tests. Taken together, all of these results seem to indicate that these deficient people have fared better in the task

INDUSTRIAL POSSIBILITIES OF THE FEEBLE-MINDED WITHIN AN INSTITUTION [10]

MENTAL AGE 3 OR BELOW

Boys

1. Picking up and piling stones.
2. Picking up and piling wood.
3. Putting stones in cart.
4. Using grub hoe, shovel, rake. (Rough work with no accuracy.)
5. Floor polishing with rope rubber.
6. Sandpapering. Flat surfaces.

Girls

1. Floor and table polishing.
2. Picking up and carrying to proper receptacle paper, rags, etc.
3. Carrying dirty clothes to laundry bags and clean clothes to ward.
4. Moving tables, chairs, etc., in house cleaning.
5. Carrying metal dishes from dining room to side room for washing.
6. Picking up and piling stones.

MENTAL AGE OF 5

1. Sandpapering of furniture preparatory to varnishing.
2. Harvesting vegetables not requiring judgment, such as pulling up whole field of mature beets, carrots, or turnips.
3. Cutting rags with scissors into accurate strips.
4. Sorting palmetto and tampico bristles for brushes.

1. Vegetable paring.
2. Crocheting (chain stitch).
3. Knitting (simple stitch for wash cloths).
4. Bed making.
5. Dishwashing.
6. Vegetable paring.

MENTAL AGE OF 6

1. Mowing lawns.
2. All-round kitchen helper.
3. Cement mixing and mason's helper.
4. Waxing, sweeping, and all-round ward helper.
5. Weeding (coarse work).

1. Rag-rug weaving with pattern.
2. Knitting and purling.
3. Crocheting (open mesh).
4. Embroidery (lazy-daisy and blanket stitch).
5. All-round ward helper.
6. Hanging up and taking down clothes from drying bars.

MENTAL AGE OF 7

1. Painting (farm tools, etc.); no fine work.
2. Shoe repairing except trimming and burnishing.
3. Harvesting garden vegetables except table corn, tomatoes, peas and other vegetables needing more mature judgment.
4. Plowing, harrowing, and cultivating.
5. Felling trees with axe.
6. Carpenter work. (Simple repairs, such as vegetable boxes, brush backs, etc.)

1. Operating household sewing machine.
2. Harvesting garden vegetables except table corn, tomatoes, peas and other vegetables requiring more mature judgment.
3. Hoeing and thinning vegetables.

[10] Adapted from C. S. Raymond, "Industrial Possibilities of the Feeble-Minded within an Institution," *Proceedings* of the American Association for the Study of the Feeble-Minded, 1926, 50, 28-39.

The occupations listed under the mental age of eight and upwards represent the types of work often performed by the boys and girls who have left the school on parole and are working for wages.

MENTAL AGE OF 8

Boys

1. Operating engineer's helper: handling coal and ashes, cleaning tubes, and assisting in repairs.
2. Waiter for employees.
3. Meat cutter's helper: chopping and trimming bones; cutting meat for stews.
4. Hair cutting and shaving.
5. Carpenter's helper.
6. Cane seating.

Girls

1. Knitting (sweater, caps and neck scarfs).
2. Embroidery: French knots, buttonhole stitch and cross stitch through canvas.
3. Making hooked rugs.
4. Making dresses cut out by others.
5. Laundry: plain ironing.
6. All-round kitchen helper.

MENTAL AGE OF 9

1. Broom making.
2. High-class woodwork where accuracy in following design is necessary.
3. Furniture repairing.
4. Painting toys, games, window sashes (fine work).
5. Shoe repairing. (Whole process, including operation of burnishing machine.)
6. Harvesting all kinds of garden vegetables and fruits.
7. Gardener's helper: wheel hoe and scuffle hoe cultivating of small garden vegetables.

1. Basketry (advanced patterns).
2. Cloth toy making: stuffing and finishing.
3. Operating jig saw: picture puzzles, toys, etc. Power sewing machines.
4. Pottery.
5. Cutting out and making dresses.
6. Laundry: fancy ironing, running washing machine.
7. Plain cooking or waiting table.
8. Orchestra: viola, drums.

MENTAL AGE OF 10

1. Printing: setting and sorting type.
2. Sign painting.
3. Gardener's helper.
4. Electrician's helper.
5. Steamfitter's helper: cutting and threading pipe.
6. Form making for cement walls and floors.
7. Shellacking and varnishing.
8. Band: cornet, bass.

1. Basketry: raffia and reed work with patterns.
2. Laundry: starching and polishing; sorting clean clothes for distribution.
3. Fancy cooking: frosted cakes, candy, etc.
4. Orchestra: second violin, cornet, saxophone, bass.
5. Canning plant; slicing machine.

MENTAL AGE OF 11

1. Band: trombone.
2. Janitor work: care of employees' cottage boilers with very little supervision.

1. Folding, checking from slips and bundling employees' laundry.
2. Pastry and all-round family cook.
3. Orchestra: first violin, cello, flute and clarinet.
4. Canning plant; power sealer.

of providing a living for themselves and in getting along with their fellow men than the earlier prognoses indicated.[11]

Baller concludes:

That it is possible for many of them [the feeble-minded] to remain law-abiding and useful citizens is suggested by the altogether satisfactory status of a considerable number of the group. *The notion that deficient mentality practically precludes social usefulness and a chance for happiness on the part of the individual is certainly not supported by the results of the present study.* That even a greater number of mentally deficient individuals may come to be well adjusted and better able to enjoy life as our program for their training in school and supervision after school is improved can hardly be doubted when their possibilities are carefully and sympathetically examined.

6. TRAINING THE FEEBLE-MINDED

Experiments at the State School for the Feeble-Minded at Letchworth Village, New York,[12] show that even the very lowest grades of the feeble-minded can be trained to be more useful than they ordinarily are. In most feeble-minded institutions the imbeciles and the idiots who can neither dress nor undress are playing around without purpose, creating all kinds of disturbance and generally making complete nuisances of themselves.

Since dressing and undressing were most troublesome, the children were given special training that finally resulted in fifty-one out of fifty-seven acquiring some considerable skill in these operations. A week of intensive training was required. They were taught to lace and to tie their shoe laces by merely giving very special at-

[11] One generally thinks of commitment to a feeble-minded institution as a final disposal of the committed person: he is doomed to remain an inmate the rest of his life. But that a feeble-minded institution can be an instrument of preparation for life outside its walls is a newer notion that is just developing. Cf. E. A. Doll and S. Geraldine Longwell, "Social Competence of the Feeble-Minded under Extra-Institutional Care," *Psychiatric Quarterly,* 1937, 11, 450-64.

[12] George J. Veith, "Training the Idiot and the Imbecile," *Proceedings* of the American Association for the Study of the Feeble-Minded, 1927, 51, 148-68.

tention to these processes which are picked up without special training by the normal. It required five months of practice before forty-
seven of them were able to select their own names in the labels on
dresses, shoes, and nightgowns. By intensive training, these very
low-grade people were taught to become fairly independent and
socially useful within the institution where they had previously been
entirely dependent and troublesome in their conduct. Boundless
patience alone is required to teach them the simple things that are
learned by more competent people without special training.

Summary of chapter.—Lack of opportunity in a rural environment affects specific items of the Binet test that would help to account for the observed difference between the rural and urban
populations. That the observed difference is not greater than it is
can be ascribed to the effects of school on rural children which helps
to equate the environments of the two groups. City life, on the other
hand, is associated with progressively higher intelligence scores as
the length of city residence increases. Isolated life in remote sections makes the use of a standard   intelligence test impossible
because of the extreme dearth of experiences in common with
those of the standardizing groups. This is particularly true for
primitive people whose sets of values differ so radically from our
own. Whenever there is any particular value placed on a function
which happens to be part of our concept of intelligent behavior,
then primitive people do not fare so poorly on the test and even
may exceed the white American norms. Children who have been
classed as feeble-minded while they were in school, when compared
with a superior group do not fail so miserably to make an adjustment in the world as we might expect they would. As we learn
better how to teach them the things they need to know it is possible
that the outlook will be even more favorable.

VIII

PHYSIOLOGICAL CONDITIONS

A PERSON'S physiological condition at the time an act occurs is a major determinant of the kind of behavior that will take place, but it is not the *only* determinant. That heredity and maturation are important we have seen. The cultural level of the group in which he grows up is of major importance, as the last chapter has shown. For the present we shall concern ourselves with the physiological conditions which are important in determining what a person will do when any kind of a situation demands an adjustive activity on his part. These would include, among others, any new thing he has to learn; any old thing he must remember; any situation to which he has to react promptly, skillfully, without fumbling or groping; any situation requiring a discrimination between things that are very nearly alike.

Among the factors which produce identifiable physiological conditions are fatigue; stimulants like caffeine; depressants like nicotine and alcohol and a host of less well-known drugs; deprivation of food or some of the accessory food factors like the vitamins; deprivation of oxygen as that incurred in flying to great heights; toxic substances absorbed through the skin or inhaled as illustrated in some occupational hazards; toxic substances manufactured in the body as in an infected or abscessed tooth or diseased tonsils; and finally, chemical substances manufactured in the body as a result of the functioning of some gland of internal secretion, like the thyroid, the pituitary, the adrenals, or the sex glands. These chemical and toxic substances either may or may not have an observable effect on behavior.

It is clear that with all these possible factors, and this is only a partial list, it would be necessary to devote the remainder of this book to their interrelations if we examined them in detail. In order to have time for other things equally important, we will have to select from the available material that which finds more immediate application in everyday life. A person frequently comes into contact with alcohol and tobacco; he infrequently meets with morphine, or heroin and hashish. We shall confine our interest in drugs to the two mentioned first and as an example of a toxic condition we shall examine the effect of tonsil infection on intelligence. Finally, because of the present interest in the results, we shall discuss the influence of a lack of oxygen on psychological events.

Psychological precautions.—If one were to investigate the influence of any of the drugs on behavior, he must take special precautions to guard against two effects. First, the subjects will almost all have some preconceived bias with respect to the effect that any well-known drugs may have upon them; for instance, it is hard to convince some people that coffee won't keep them awake. Some observations have been made that indicate that a person can be slightly more influenced by the anticipation of a cocktail than he is after drinking one, i.e., he may be slightly more intoxicated before drinking a cocktail than afterward. Testimonials of the kind appearing in patent-medicine advertisements can be obtained after treatment with the most innocuous substances which can have no possible relation to recovery from colds, hay fever, or any other troublesome malady. The drug trade, in fact, supplies a variety of substances which are designed to satisfy people who demand unnecessary prescriptions from their physicians. Second, the method of administering some drugs may be more potent in influencing a person's behavior than the effects of the drug itself. Any drug that has to be administered by a hypodermic needle may produce a prompt recovery in a functional disorder because the administration is so unpleasant. One glandular substance (pituitrin), which has to be administered this way, is recommended for persistent enuresis in children. We might suppose that the same kind of painful administration of a perfectly neutral saline solution would also produce some recoveries. The rhythmical breathing required to pull on a pipe or cigarette is known to produce an effect on heart rate and possibly on blood pressure, in the entire absence of any tobacco at all. Both these effects will produce certain changes in behavior, changes which will mistakenly be attributed to the action of the drug or the toxin if controls are not used.

1. THE EFFECTS OF TOBACCO

Most of the work done on the influence of tobacco is perfectly useless since neither the bias of the subjects nor the incidental accompaniments of the administration were taken into account. In 1917 a committee for the study of the tobacco problem initiated an investigation finally published in 1924 in which all these factors were to be considered. The committee depended on Clark Hull,[1] then the director of the psychological laboratory at the University of Wisconsin, for expert technical guidance in the problem. Hull saw clearly that the principal difficulty would be in the administration of a control dose of tobacco that would present all of the features of the actual smoking except one—the tobacco itself must not be given. He had heard that in the dark, habitual smokers frequently allowed their pipes to go out without being aware of the fact. Pipe smoking is as much, or more, a matter of watching the smoke as it is of smelling and of sensing warm air on the tongue. With this observation as a cue, he invented a pipe through which the subject could draw warm moist air but no tobacco smoke. In the dark it produced an illusory effect that satisfied even inveterate smokers. The experimenter himself smoked in the same room so that the subjects could smell the smoke, but in this way they got so little actual tobacco that the effects observed in the experiment were not made dubious.

Method.—For the duration of the experiment the subjects must never be given any notion that a control pipe exists. To this end, it was necessary to mislead them as to the real nature of the procedure. They were told in two preliminary periods that the effects

[1] Clark Hull, "The Influence of Tobacco Smoking on Mental and Motor Efficiency," *Psychological Monographs,* 1924, 33, 161.

of tobacco smoking were to be studied by tests before and after smoking; there was never a hint that part of the time they wouldn't actually be smoking. They must, they were told, give their conscientious application to the tests throughout the entire experimental period. A solemn promise was exacted from them to keep up a maximum effort every day.

The subjects were, in this way, prepared for a rather elaborate technique. They consequently showed no surprise, either when they were blindfolded for the smoking session or when the experimenter always handled the pipe, whether it actually contained tobacco or whether it was the control. It was necessary for the experimenter to handle both pipes to keep the subject from detecting the difference between them. To the lips they felt the same, but to allow the subject to

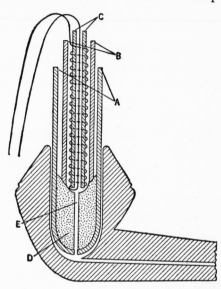

Fig. 31.—A drawing of the experimental pipe. (From Jenkins, *Psychology in Business and Industry,* p. 138. By permission of the publishers, John Wiley & Sons, Inc.)

touch them would have been to give the whole thing away. To regulate the amount of tobacco, the subject was permitted three puffs every twenty seconds for twenty-five minutes.

When the subject took his usual place in the laboratory, he saw the regular pipe. The experimenter elaborately cleaned it before him. After he was blindfolded he would hear the experimenter tapping on the tin and striking the match, and he would smell the odor of the freshly lighted pipe. After the blindfold was removed he would see the burned-out ash in the pipe. The usual pauses made by the experimenter in securing the special pipe from its hiding place and preparing it for the subject were as scrupulously maintained on the days when the subject actually did smoke as on the days when he didn't.

The illusion provided by this method was so perfect that one man insisted on blowing smoke rings on the days when there wasn't any smoke just as realistically as he was able to do when he was really smoking. One subject's results had to be discarded because he peeped one day, saw the control pipe and couldn't be fooled again. Some of the reports of the other subjects are shown

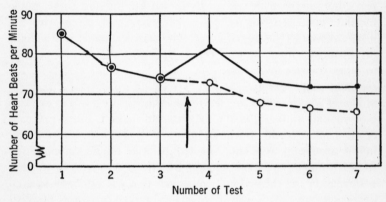

FIG. 32.—The heart rate curve.

on page 154. If one examines these reports in detail he must conclude that to smoke warm air in the absence of visual cues seems, on the whole, to be as satisfactory as to smoke tobacco.

In this experiment for the first time we see the introduction of a new experimental method. There is no need for separate "control" and "experimental" groups. Each person serves as his own control in the sense that half the time he is inhaling tobacco and the other half he is inhaling moist, warm air. In the various curves shown here the results of several subjects are exhibited by their average performance on "tobacco nights" compared with "no-tobacco nights."

Subjects.—There were nine nonsmokers and ten habitual smokers in the group; it was one of the nonsmokers who was eliminated because he accidentally caught sight of the "fake" pipe.

The routine of the habitual smokers was not disturbed except that they were not to smoke for three hours immediately preceding the experiment. We shall show only a few of the principal findings. The heart-rate curves in Figure 32 indicate a gradual reduction in the pulse rates from an average of about eighty-five to about seventy-eight in the course of sitting quietly in the laboratory for fifteen minutes. Between the third and fourth time that the pulse was taken on the "tobacco nights," as indicated in the chart, the tobacco was administered with the results shown by the solid curve, while for the "no-tobacco nights" the control dose was given with the results shown in the dotted curve. The dotted curve shows a slight disturbance in its downward trend due to the puffing and perhaps to other features of the situation, *but where all these features are the same except for the tobacco there is an unmistakable increase of almost 10 per cent in the heart rate.* This effect persists in decreasing amounts throughout the experimental period. Forty per cent of the increase is still present an hour and three-quarters after smoking. These results were obtained with habitual smokers alone. Pulse records were not obtained on enough of the nonsmokers to warrant a conclusion for them. Hull points out that the effect of tobacco on people who don't use it presents a rather academic problem anyway.

Steadiness.—Two charts (Fig. 33) show the effects of smoking on steadiness. Steadiness was measured by having the subjects insert a stylus into a hole only slightly larger than the diameter of the stylus. If they were "shaky" they made more contacts with the sides of the hole. These contacts were automatically counted by an electrical arrangement. *Tobacco has more effect in producing tremor in the habitual smokers than in nonsmokers.* The habitual smokers were also more unsteady at the beginning of the experimental period.

Speed of adding.—The task given to the subject was to add, as quickly as he could, a single integer starting with 6 to any two-place number the experimenter gave him. He continued to add successively 7 and 8. If the experimenter gave him 36, he would add 6 and call out 42; then he would add 7 to this total and say 49;

The Nightly Schedule of the Nineteen Subjects

A subject finished his evening meal at about 6:25 and reported at the laboratory at 6:50 P.M.:

6:50 Pulse taken after which subject sat quietly for about 15 minutes.

7:05 Complete series of tests given requiring 30 minutes. The tests began with counting the pulse beats. *This is the normal of the day.*

7:35 Pulse taken after which eight minutes were consumed in preparation for the smoking.

7:45 Began either smoking or taking the control dose, which lasted 25 minutes.

8:10 Experimenter puts away tobacco.

8:12 Complete series of tests repeated.

8:42 Subject rested for 5 minutes.

8:47 Complete series of tests repeated.

9:17 Subject rested for 5 minutes.

9:22 Complete series of tests repeated.

9:52 Pulse taken.

9:55 Subject excused.

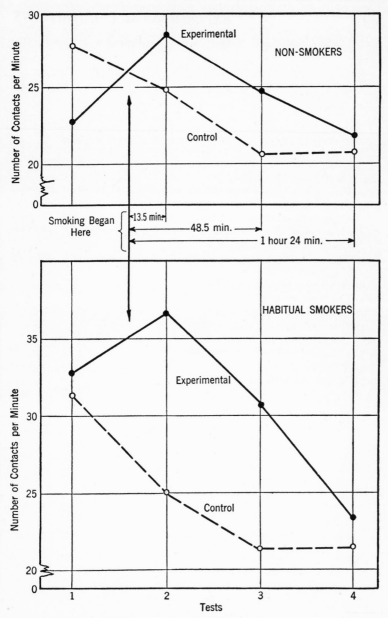

FIG. 33.—The effect of tobacco on tremor.

then 8 and say 57. He then returned to 6, added it to the new total, getting 63; then 7 would make 70, and 8 would make 78. This process of adding 6, 7 and 8 was continued until the experimenter gave him a new two-place number at the end of thirty seconds. The test as a whole continued for ten minutes so that ten sets of

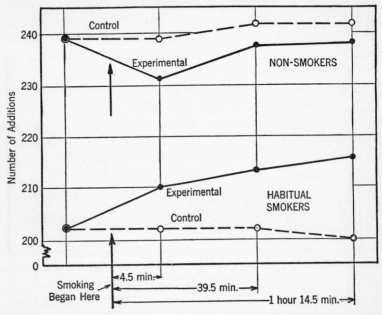

Fig. 34.—The effect of tobacco on the speed of adding.

additions were obtained. The score was the total number of correct additions in five minutes. The results are shown separately for the habitual smokers and the nonsmokers. The first postsmoking test came at 4.5 minutes after the smoking period; the second came at 39.5 minutes; the last at 1 hour 14.5 minutes after.

The effect of the tobacco is exactly reversed for the two groups.

(1) The nonsmokers show a consistent decrement lasting throughout the period of an hour and a quarter.

(2) The tobacco causes the habitual smokers to add a little quicker.

In neither case is the effect very much, about 3 per cent average decrease and 5 per cent average increase, but since every single subject in each group showed the effect, the result is highly reliable, even though small.

Rate of learning.—The task which sampled the simple learning ability of the subjects was similar to that which would be involved in learning a foreign language, where five new words would constitute each test. In order to be sure that none of the subjects started

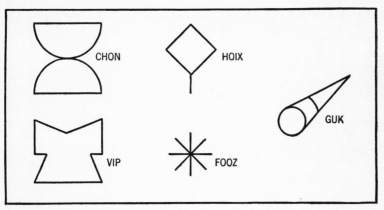

Fig. 35.—Five of the geometric characters used in the experiment. The names pronounced by the experimenter are shown to the right.

with an advantage and in order to have available a considerable body of test material of equal difficulty, none of the existing foreign languages could be used. Artificial tasks which resemble the learning of new words have been worked out in various psychological experiments. In this one, geometrical forms which had no ordinary name were given one-syllable nonsense names. Five of these are shown in Figure 35.

Details of method.—The forms were presented one at a time at a small window by a machine built for the purpose. The subject never saw the one-syllable names; he heard them only when they were pronounced by the experimenter at the middle of the five-second interval that the exposure device provided. The first time through the five cards the subject would have to be prompted every

DETAILS OF TWO SUBJECTS' REPORTS

A. M. G., one of the subjects, thinks that if he inhaled the smoke there wouldn't have been any difference in the laboratory from ordinary pipe smoking. As it was, the only way he could tell he was smoking was by the gradual increase in the strength of the smoke and the bite on his tongue. He sometimes could tell that he was smoking by the smell but he was able to tell at all times that he was smoking. There were several times that he could not tell whether the pipe was going or not. Such periods were for three or four puffs. He was always sure he was smoking most of the time on every evening. *There was never any evening when he could have been persuaded that he had not been smoking at least ninety-five per cent of the time.* He thought that some nights there was little or no stinging on the tongue. On such nights he told by the flavor. The last night of the experiment (a tobacco night) it was so strong he did not like it. It bit his tongue and it was an effort to take another pull. The night before, however (a control night), it was fairly good. It didn't bite the tongue to any great extent, not enough to bother much. *It would be an easy matter for him to break off smoking if it were always like the last night.* He enjoyed it the night before. It wasn't strong at all. It tasted fairly well and took the place of not being able to inhale. *He thinks it would be pretty hard to quit under such (control) conditions.*

G. W. M., another subject, always felt rather hungry for a smoke when he first came to the laboratory. *But after the smoke in the laboratory he was always satisfied.* He says that he did not enjoy the smoking, though, when it was going on. This, he feels, was probably because he couldn't see or handle the pipe. It was given to him more slowly than he was accustomed to taking it. He thinks it very difficult to tell while blindfolded whether he is smoking or not. He has wondered lots of times whether the pipe wasn't pretty near out. These periods were for three or four minutes. But this can't be true because he heard the experimenter light the pipe. *There was never any night when he was in doubt as to whether the pipe was lit throughout the evening as a whole.* He thinks that on one evening one might have persuaded him that the pipe was not lit. He never wondered about the matter except this one night.

These comments were taken after the experiment was finished. They show clearly that these subjects were entirely unaware that half the total number of nights they were "smoking" warm, moist air, without any tobacco at all.

time, since he wouldn't know any of the names that had been arbitrarily assigned. The second time, when the cards were presented in a different order, he might be able to anticipate a name before it was spoken by the experimenter. If he did, he got credit for a correct anticipation. If not, a minus sign was recorded by the ex-

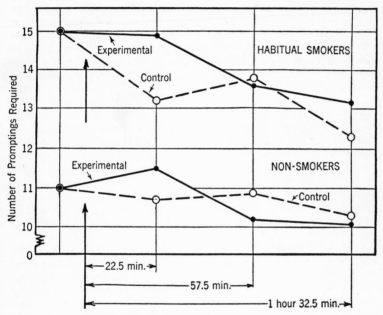

Fig. 36.—The effect of tobacco on learning names.

perimenter on a prepared blank. After several presentations of the five forms, each in a different order, the subject would finally be able to anticipate the experimenter's prompting each time. The number of promptings he required before he could anticipate correctly each time would be a measure of how quickly he could learn this kind of material. The results for this experiment are presented in terms of the number of promptings required.

No single series was learned twice by the same subject. For each new test five new forms and five new syllables were used. Each point on the graph represents an average of eight to ten separate experiments for each of the nineteen people concerned (nine nonsmokers and ten habitual smokers). This would make about 190 separate learning tasks if each person were tested only once each night, but since there were four tests each night the actual number of series represented is more than 750.

We go into this detail only to show how much labor can be represented in one of the graphs shown in this book. The appearance of the graphs is simple, but one should not be misled by the appearance of simplicity.

Results.—These curves show that the habitual smokers do not learn quite as promptly as the nonsmokers at any time. Since the curves show the number of promptings, the higher the number the more inadequate the performance. A drop in the curve means a more adequate performance. Both groups show this drop on the control days. The effect of tobacco seems to be to retard this drop slightly. In any event, since the curves cross and recross, *we must conclude that there has been no definite lasting effect on either group as we have seen in the case of heart rate, tremor, and speed of adding.*

Summary.—There is a small but certain increase in heart rate; a small but consistent increase in tremor for both smokers and nonsmokers. For speed of adding, the effect is reversed in the two groups: nonsmokers are made slower, smokers faster, the differences being between 3 and 5 per cent. There is no consistent effect on rate of learning as measured here.

A practical application.—If a dean of students wanted to find out whether tobacco smoking had a detrimental influence on college grades, he would probably select two groups of students, smokers and nonsmokers. After he had looked up their grades he would probably find that the nonsmokers had higher grades than the smokers, and he would be inclined to conclude that tobacco smoking *causes* lower grades. There can be no doubt but that smoking *is* associated with lower grades, but to go a step further and attribute the cause to the tobacco is not justified, either in the light of Hull's results or according to the rules of ordinary logic. The fact that low grades and smoking are related is no proof in itself that one causes the other. Both may be caused by another hidden factor.

Among the hidden factors which *might* be effective is that of sociability. Those that are more active socially in college may be the smokers because smoking is essentially a social pastime. That studiousness and extreme sociability do not ordinarily go together is obvious. If this hypothesis were true, it would account for the fact that smokers, as a group, are poorer students. At present we don't know whether it is true, but *we do know that a positive statement to the effect that smoking is harmful to grades and to learning efficiency generally is not justified.*

2. THE EFFECTS OF ALCOHOL

The greatest stumbling block in finding out what effects alcohol has on human behavior lies in the lack of a control dose. Beverages which contain alcohol in even small amounts are readily detected through taste and smell from nonalcoholic mixtures. Most experimenters have made no effort at all to control this important feature of the experiment; consequently their results are of doubtful significance. The dire effect of alcohol on animals that we hear about frequently has been the result of dosing, starting with infancy, in quantities far in excess of most human inclinations or capacities.

Alcohol a depressant.—Among the better-known experiments with people the researches of Dodge and Benedict [2] take first rank from the technical standpoint. They did not use control doses, but the generalization that we can draw from their experiments does not depend upon this omission. They found that, contrary to the popular belief, *alcohol does not affect the "higher mental processes" like "judgment" and "reasoning" first and the simpler reflex acts last.* The effect of the alcohol was first detected in a change in the simpler motor co-ordinations and reflexes. Since this generalization involves the relative effects of alcohol on two functions, the lack of the control dose does not vitiate the conclusion. An experimenter, using instruments of precision, can detect the effects long before an

[2] Raymond Dodge and F. G. Benedict, *Psychological Effects of Alcohol,* Carnegie Institution of Washington, Publication No. 232, Washington, D. C., 1915.

observer who does not have measuring instruments available notices any change in behavior. A further generalization from these studies, and one in which all experimenters in this field concur, is that *the effect of alcohol is always depressing, never stimulating*. Again, this is contrary to the popular opinion, which has it that alcohol in small amounts, at least, is a stimulant. The popular notion is based on two kinds of observations: the subjective report, which does not often agree with objective measures of organic condition or production; and the observation of several physiological changes which superficially *appear* to mean stimulating rather than narcotizing or depressing influences. The principal physiological change so observed is that alcohol, like tobacco, increases the heart rate. To interpret an increase in heart rate as a stimulating effect is to display ignorance of the heart-rate mechanism.

Normal heart rate for a given set of conditions is dependent upon what might be considered a balance between the impulses of two sets of nerves. One nerve, the vagus, tends to slow the heart rate. Whenever impulses from this nerve are interfered with, the heart increases its rate automatically. For some unknown reason, alcohol produces more blocking in the vagus nerve than it does on the sympathetic, so that heart rate increases, not as a result of a stimulating effect but as the result of a blocking of normally inhibiting impulses.

Another observation which has been held to demonstrate the stimulating effect of alcohol is the feeling of warmth which follows alcoholic consumption. This observation is caused by the easy circulation of warm blood in the skin, but ease of circulation is accomplished by a relaxation of the walls of the blood vessels, a depressant effect. The feeling of warmth is illusory, however. This mechanism allows heat to radiate from the body more easily, and hence the body temperature, carefully measured, is actually less than it is when one doesn't feel so warm.

Hollingworth's experiment.—The experiments of Hollingworth [3] are among the better-known ones which have principally

---

[3] H. L. Hollingworth, "The Influence of Alcohol," *Journal of Abnormal and Social Psychology*, 1923, 18, 204-37; 311-33.

been concerned with psychological rather than physiological effects. He used six subjects who ranged from total abstainers to moderate drinkers. Under experimental conditions, they drank 2.75 per cent beer in varying doses and a control beer of exactly the same manufacture but from which the alcohol had been removed by the brewer. Ordinary drinking water and lemonade were also used as controls in some parts of the experiment. The subjects reported that the 2.75 beer was weak; the dealcoholized beer was reported even weaker. This device, two beers of little and no alcoholic content, is the nearest approach to an experimental and a control dose that has yet been used. Even these weak beers produced measurable effects, as we shall see.

Eight different psychological tests and a count of pulse rate constituted the nine segments of behavior sampled in the experiment.

The testing schedule.—The subjects reported at the laboratory at 9:00 each day, where they remained until 4:00. Each experimenter, stationed in a different room, gave two tests to two people. The subjects shifted from room to room until at the end of a half hour all the tests had been administered to them. Then they began all over again, continuing the routine until 12:00.

At 12:00 they ate and drank variously as the schedule (page 160) required and at 1:00 returned to the tests which were administered continuously until 4:00. There were, then, six forenoon measures on each test and six in the afternoon.

The subjects did not know the purpose of the experiment beyond that they were to be tested after drinking different amounts and different kinds of beer. They did not know that on some days they actually drank no *alcohol* when they were drinking beer.

Preliminary practice.—There were three days of preliminary testing to perfect the details of the routine and to make certain that the men had reached the peak of their performance uninfluenced by the special conditions which were to come later. They were also accustomed to drinking fairly large quantities of liquid—on these days either water or lemonade.

PLAN OF THE EXPERIMENT

Friday, June 6: First Practice day, employed in learning the method of the tests, standardizing the routine and technique. Each subject did each test six times. At lunch hour tried drinking as much water as possible, along with three small sandwiches.

Saturday, June 7: Second Practice day, each man made ten rounds of all the tests, and at lunch hour drank three or four bottles of lemonade along with three thin slices of bread spread with peanut butter.

Monday, June 9: First Blank day, twelve rounds of all tests were made. At lunch hour each man had three thin slices of bread and one small orange, and was allowed to drink as much of one bottle of water as he cared for.

Tuesday, June 10: First Control day, each man drank five bottles, each containing 12.5 ounces, of the Control beer, no food whatever being taken this day.

Wednesday, June 11: First Beer day, each man drank, during the noon hour six 12.5 ounce bottles of the Standard beer, no food being allowed this day.

Thursday, June 12: Second Blank day, each man had the three thin slices of bread, an orange or banana, and as much of one bottle of water as he cared for.

Friday, June 13: Second Beer day, each man drank four bottles of beer, taking one bottle each fifteen-minute period, along with three thin slices of bread, spread with peanut butter.

Saturday, June 14: Second Control day, each man had two thin slices of bread spread with peanut butter, and, except for No. 2, drank six bottles of Control beer during the noon hour. No. 2 was made sick and vomited after the third bottle, and continued to vomit thereafter, so he was allowed to quit drinking after the contents of the fifth bottle had been swallowed.

Monday, June 16: Third Beer day, each man had three thin slices of bread spread with peanut butter, and drank, except for No. 2, five bottles of the Standard beer during the noon hour. No. 2, who had been uniformly made sick by more than three bottles, was again made sick, and was allowed to take only three bottles.

Tuesday, June 17: Fourth Beer day, each man had, during the noon hour, four to six crackers and a bit of cheese, and three bottles of the Standard beer during the noon hour.

Wednesday, June 18: Last Beer day; after making three rounds of all the tests, a halt was made for a few minutes while each man drank one bottle of the Standard beer, at 10:45 A.M. After another round of tests, each man drank a second bottle at 11:15 A.M. After another round of tests each man drank a third bottle, at 11:50 A.M. and then made another round of the tests. At 12:30, a halt was made for the regular noon hour. During the previous drinking, the six men had eaten, along with the beer, three or four crackers each. At the noon hour, each man was allowed the three thin slices of bread and peanut butter, and drank as much beer as he could during the hour, in addition to the three bottles already drunk since 10:45 A.M.

Thursday, June 19: Dinner day; instead of drinking Beer or Control, or carrying on a Blank day, this day a special six-course dinner was set, at which all the subjects ate as much as they cared for, had a small black coffee, and smoked one cigar or several cigarettes if they wished. No alcohol was included in the meal, the idea being to determine the influence of a hearty meal on the process being measured. Immediately after the meal, the tests were continued in the usual way, and as they had been also on the morning of that day.

The tests included:

(1) *Steadiness:* The number of contacts was counted which the subject made when he attempted to hold a stylus in a hole only slightly larger than the stylus. This is a standard test for steadiness. It was also used in the tobacco study.

(2) *Eye-hand co-ordination:* A triangular plate with a metallic contact at the bottom of a small hole served as a target for a stylus held by the subject. An electric counter kept a record of the number of hits as the subject progressed in a clockwise direction around the triangle. One minute was allowed for the test. Any disturbance of co-ordination showed in a reduced score as the subject fumbled, missed the target, and tried again and again to make contact.

(3) *Control of speech mechanism:* The stammering, fumbling, and blocking of the speech mechanism was measured by the Woodworth-Wells Color Naming Test. Five colors occurred twenty times in random order. To name these colors as they occur at random required a high degree of speech control. Each time the subject made a mistake, the experimenter called "No," whereupon the subject had to give the correct name before proceeding. Time thus becomes a measure of the degree of speech control.

(4) *Adding:* Fifty two-place numbers were presented on a card in two vertical columns. The subject was required to add seventeen to the first number, then seventeen to the next, and so on. If the answer was wrong, the experimenter said "No," and the subject was required to correct himself before going on. The time required for fifty additions was the measure of production.

(5) *Logical relations:* Fifty adjectives were presented on cards. The subject was instructed to speak aloud the antonym of the word he had seen. Again, if he did not give the exact opposite, the experimenter said "No." A satisfactory opposite was required before proceeding.

(6) *Learning:* The quickness with which the subject could substitute letters for the geometrical forms of the Woodworth-Wells substitution test constituted a measure of the learning speed.

(7) *The pulse record:* The pulse was counted as physicians usually do it.

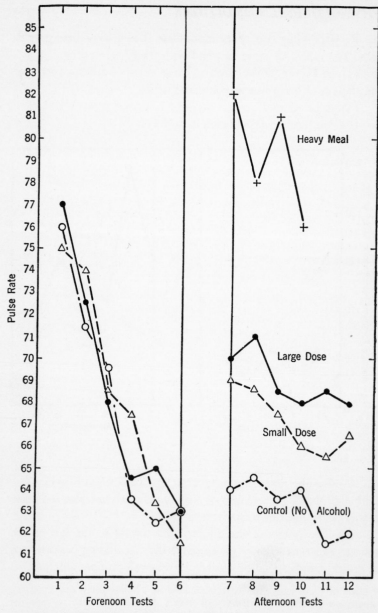

Fig. 37.—The effect of alcohol in small and large doses on afternoon pulse compared with the effect of a heavy meal. There is also a small rise in the control experiment.

Results.—Only two of the results are shown, and these graphically. The others all agree in trend with these.[4]

(1) In Figure 37 the effect of large doses of alcohol (three or four bottles of beer) can be compared with

(a) A heavy meal

(b) No alcohol, light lunch (control)

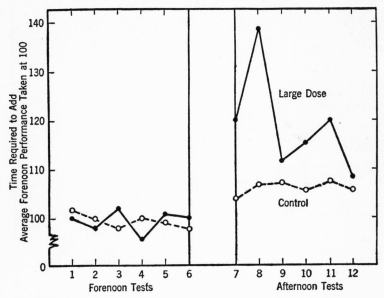

Fig. 38.—The effect of alcohol on the speed of adding. A rise in the curve means poorer performance.

(c) Smaller doses of alcohol (one or two bottles of beer)

Although the larger amounts of alcohol definitely increase the pulse rate, a heavy meal increases it even more.

(2) The results of the adding test, similar to the test in the tobacco experiment, show conclusively that the adding performance is greatly handicapped by alcohol in relatively minute amounts.

---

[4] Many of these same tests have been used by Hollingworth and others in studies on the effects of caffeine. All studies show that caffeine has just the opposite effect that is shown here for alcohol. There are wide individual differences in the effect, and as in the case of alcohol, a tolerance for the drug seems to develop.

General conclusions.—Both the pulse-rate results and results from the adding test indicate that *alcohol has a definitely depressing effect on the organism*. That the heart rate is increased merely means that inhibitory effects on its rate have been removed by alcoholic blocking.

We could generalize then that *a person who drinks even minute quantities of alcohol in the face of any kind of a problem that he has to solve, is making a psychological mistake. Although he may feel more competent, and to himself may seem cleverer and quicker, actual measurement shows the opposite to be true.*

Practical application.—In the same way that mere association of two factors has been confused with causal efficacy, as we have seen in the case of tobacco, so also has alcohol been held responsible for just about everything that can happen to a person. Insanity of a kind has been attibuted to alcohol as well as inefficiencies and minor eccentricities. There is no clear-cut evidence that the various insanities and eccentricities would not have occurred without the alcohol. No really controlled observations have ever been made in this field so far as I have been able to discover. Again, in the absence of positive evidence, we must suspend judgment.

Professor Miles concludes a summary on the psychological effects of alcohol with these words:

When an individual has had the experience of promptly securing the comfort and joy of psychological escape simply by the drinking of alcoholic beverages, he readily adopts this procedure and follows it unless checked by social pressure or by an unusual degree of self-criticism. For the well-integrated individual, the moderate use of alcohol may be a habit or custom under control whose chief and perhaps only real damage is in substituting effortless escape for the learning and use of strategy and skill in meeting life's difficulties. Such an individual limits his use of alcohol, both in amount and also in frequency, by partaking only on the occasions when he desires a self-acting substitute for mental adjustment. He carries on without noticeable interference in the working-day accomplishment. If, however, tension becomes too great and he is hard pressed and fatigued, he may find it natural to drink more heavily, perhaps to the disadvantage of both work and morale. The weaker individual who is conspired against by circumstances has great difficulty in keeping himself from turning often to this ready means for personal relief. With psychological escape so accessible, the discouraged and the baffled find more and more difficulties and annoyances from which they feel justified in seeking refuge. For abnormal and unstable personalities, notwithstanding that they may have thought of it as the most divinely beneficent thing in the world, alcohol has been and still is a veritable millstone.

Miles's entire chapter in *Alcohol and Man*,[5] from which this quotation is taken, is well worth careful reading. Other sections of the book cover the effects of alcohol in its physiological, hereditary, toxicological, medical, and psychiatric aspects. They, too, are well worth reading.

The experimenters in both these studies secured positive results, i.e., *both* tobacco and alcohol showed some effect on behavior. Other experimenters working in this same general field have not enjoyed this success, and as a result their task has been much harder. Let us suppose for an instant that no effect had been demonstrable in these measurements. Would that have meant that neither alcohol nor tobacco had any effect at all on behavior? Obviously not, because of all the possible conditions that could have been investigated, only a few were used in these experiments. The tests themselves lasted only a few minutes at the most so that a subject might have been able to hold himself to a task by exerting greater energy for a short time, collapsing as soon as the experimental period was over. This has been a troublesome detail in experiments involving the use of short tests.

3. HIGH ALTITUDES

Essentially the effect of flying or mountain climbing at high altitudes is produced by a lack of oxygen. Although the proportion of oxygen in rarefied air at high altitudes is the same as at sea

[5] Haven Emerson, ed., *Alcohol and Man,* The Macmillan Company, New York, 1933.

level—21 per cent—nevertheless, the absolute amount of oxygen available in each breath becomes less with every foot of ascent. On the top of Mt. Blanc at about 16,000 feet, one would have to breathe twice as often to get the same amount of oxygen as at sea level, while on Mt. Everest, at about 30,000 feet, one would have to breathe three times as fast. Curiously enough there is an adaptation at high altitudes. In the Chilean Andes [6] people do live and work at altitudes as high as 19,000 feet but they do not consider their lot an easy one, and, in spite of high wages, the labor turnover is high. At 14,000 feet, however, the native Indians produced their magnificent Inca civilization.

It was proved [7] as long ago as 1878 that decreasing air pressure *as such* produced no untoward physiological effects. More recent experiments show that subjects suffer no discomfort, at least until 30,000 feet, if they are supplied with oxygen. This situation is quite unlike that of increasing pressure, where nitrogen bubbles forming in the blood give rise to the painful "bends" experienced by divers and tunnel workers. This fact enables experimenters working at sea level to simulate the effects of various altitudes by decreasing the concentration of oxygen available. Thus they can undertake studies that would be impractical if the apparatus and the subjects had to be taken to great heights.

In one series of investigations with pilots of the Cambridge University Air Squadron [8] simulated heights from sea level to 22,000 feet were studied. The pilots were given tests of simple reaction time, where a single stimulus had to be reacted to as quickly as possible; of choice reaction time, where four different colored lights required different reactions which had to be made promptly; of memory; of judgment; and of emotional control. The effects of the lack of oxygen (anoxemia) became noticeably apparent after altitudes of 14,000–16,000 feet.

[6] Ross A. McFarland, "Psycho-Physiological Studies at High Altitudes in the Andes, IV. Sensory and Circulatory Responses of the Andean Residents at 17,500 Feet," *Journal of Comparative Psychology,* 1937, 24, 189-220.
[7] Paul Bert, *La Pression Barométrique,* Masson, Paris, 1878.
[8] Ross A. McFarland, "The Psychological Effects of Oxygen Deprivation [anoxemia] on Human Behavior," Archives of Psychology, No. 145, 1932, Columbia University.

Not only was there a loss of judgment in relation to their own behavior and impairment of memory of recent events, but there was also a complete distortion of emotional control simulating many of the characteristics of certain mentally abnormal patients and of those suffering from excessive amounts of alcohol or narcotics. In the more acute experiments with 9 per cent oxygen (22,000 feet), the pilots would frequently lose the capacity for sane judgment and for self-criticism. Some of the pilots responded with great hilarity and uncontrollable laughter, while others became very angry and destructive.

Samples of handwriting and choice reaction times were secured in a number of the pilots during a period of one hour while the oxygen was gradually depleted. At a simulated altitude of 20,000 feet, for example, one subject appeared to be quite pleased with himself and became highly amused at the slightest provocation. At 23,000 feet (8.5 per cent oxygen) he began to omit letters from common words and his writing became quite illegible. He complained of his feet feeling a long way off and of his inability to orient other parts of his body. At 26,000 feet (7.4 per cent oxygen) he was greatly incapacitated and yet he appeared to be cheerful and very pleased with his performance. He became quite annoyed when he was removed from the apparatus and insisted that he could go much higher. He was convinced of his marked deterioration only after seeing his handwriting. In the choice reaction-time experiments, there was marked impairment above 20,000 feet. The mental and emotional abnormalities of the subjects in poor physical condition were very striking at simulated altitudes as low as 14,000 feet.

One subject in a low oxygen chamber containing 8.5 per cent oxygen was unable to make the movements necessary to complete a simple form board test. His eyes were fixated on the blocks, but his movements were too jerky and his arms and fingers too rigid to put the blocks in their proper places. He knew where they should be placed, but his motor reactions were too impaired to carry out the test. These reactions tend to disappear immediately upon the administration of oxygen.

The similarity between the behavior of the subjects who suffered from anoxemia and that resulting from intoxication was striking. As a matter of fact, it has been suggested that the effect of alcohol is to interfere with the normal use of oxygen by the individual body cells, particularly those of the nervous system.

If the ascent is abrupt, then the effects are more pronounced than if it is gradual. A scientific expedition that spent several months in the Andes collected data that indicated an impairment in all the behavior studied, but in general it was not so pronounced as in more rapid changes of altitude. They did find that the ten members

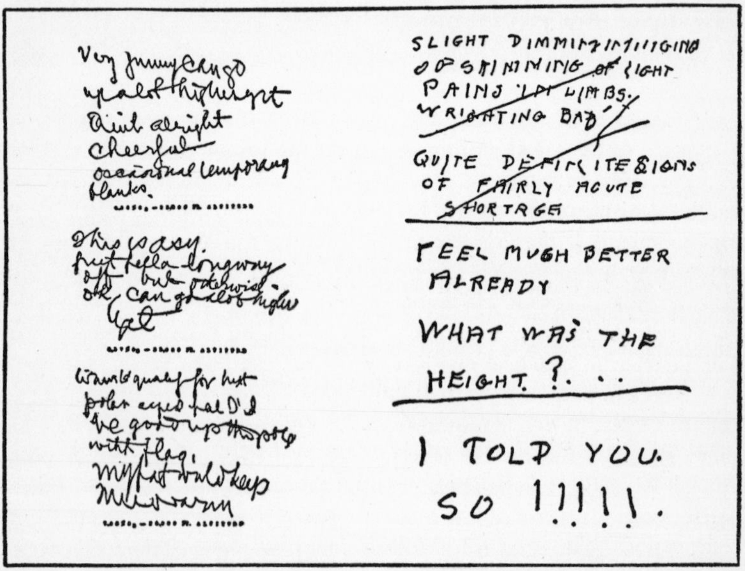

Fig. 39.—Handwriting samples under various degrees of anoxemia. On the left the amount of oxygen obtained corresponded to heights of 22,000, 25,000, and 28,000 feet; on the right, recovery is shown upon the administration of oxygen at 37,000 feet. Each column shows one subject's writing. (After McFarland.)

of the party complained of a greater effort required to carry out tasks, of a more critical attitude toward other people, of "mental laziness," of heightened sensory irritability, of being touchy on various subjects, of disliking being told how to do things, of difficulty in concentration, of slowness in reasoning, of frequently recurring ideas, and of difficulty in remembering.[9]

In studies made of transcontinental and transpacific runs (in

[9] Ross A. McFarland, "Psycho-Physiological Studies at High Altitudes in the Andes, III. Mental and Psycho-Somatic Responses During Gradual Adaptation," *Journal of Comparative Psychology,* 1937, 24, 147-188.

the latter the average altitude is 9,500, and 12,000 is not at all uncommon), the effect on the passengers if flight is smooth is not at all marked if they sit quietly and if the ascent has required an hour or more. The tests previously mentioned, however, indicate an impairment of from 6 to 10 per cent.[10] The pilots and crew seem to become truly acclimated to the altitude.[11] These altitudes are just below those in which impairment becomes acute so that if planes are to be flown higher, oxygen will have to be supplied.

4. DISEASED TONSILS AND ADENOIDS

Several hundred New York City school children who had diseased tonsils were compared with an approximately equal number who did not have infected tonsils.[12] The results are shown in Figure 40. It is perfectly obvious that there is no difference in the two distributions. The average of both is 95; they both have the same range. If there were a difference in intelligence between the children who have diseased tonsils and those who do not, the open circles would form an entirely different distribution from the solid circles, and two curves, rather than one, would be required to represent their distribution.

Twenty-eight children whose tonsils were infected were matched in intelligence with twenty-eight other children who also had bad tonsils. The first group of twenty-eight constituted an experimental group whose diseased tonsils were removed immediately after the first test was given. The other group constituted a control; their tonsils were not operated. Six months later both groups were retested and again at twelve months, but by this time, one or the other of seven of the pairs had moved or for some other reason

[10] Ross A. McFarland, "The Effects of Oxygen Deprivation [high altitude] on the Human Organism," Bureau of Air Commerce, Department of Commerce, Report 13, May, 1938.
[11] Ross A. McFarland and H. T. Edwards, "The Effects of Prolonged Exposures to Altitudes of 8,000 to 12,000 Feet During Trans-Pacific Flights," *Journal of Aviation Medicine,* 1937, 8, 4.
[12] M. C. Rogers, "Adenoids and Diseased Tonsils: Their Effect on General Intelligence," *Archives of Psychology,* 1922, No. 50, pp. 1-70.

failed to take the test. This reduced the twenty-eight pairs to only twenty-one. The results of three administrations of a standard intelligence test are shown in the table. The units are I.Q.'s in which notation 100 is normal.

	N-28		N-21
	First Test	*Retest 6 Mos.*	*Retest 12 Mos.*
Experimental (Tonsils removed).....	92	94	95
Control (Tonsils not removed) .	93	96	98
Gain.................	1	2	3

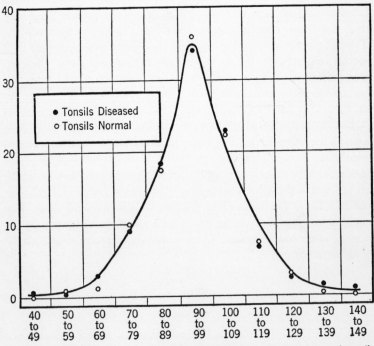

Fig. 40.—Distribution curve for intelligence of children who have diseased tonsils and those who do not.

The average gain in intelligence was actually a little more for the nonoperated group than for those whose tonsils had been removed. The amounts of change are insignificant, of course. Our generalization based on these two different approaches to the problem is that *removing diseased tonsils and adenoids does not produce a change in intelligence test score,* however important the operation may be for the preservation of health. The practical significance of this finding is obvious because tonsils have been removed in the hope of increasing the intelligence of dull children, just as infected teeth were, a few years ago, extracted wholesale in institutions for the insane in the futile hope of restoring hundreds of patients to sanity.

Summary of the chapter.—Among the factors which influence a person's behavior, the physiological condition at the moment has received wide attention. This condition is modified by common depressants, alcohol and tobacco, as well as a host of other conditions that make up what has been called the "internal environment." Typical experiments demonstrating these effects were reviewed with special emphasis on the methods used to find out about these effects. The question of method is important in this connection because so many reformers have blamed nearly all our human ills on these two handmaidens of vice. One widespread misconception —that alcohol in small amounts is a stimulant—has also been dealt with. The effects of high altitude were shown to be due really to anoxemia, and it was suggested that intoxication was also due fundamentally to lack of oxygen. Other physiological factors which do not attack the nervous system so directly do not produce the expected effects. The toxin from diseased tonsils is one of these. The intelligence test was used here only as a sample of behavior. There may be other considerations which would indicate that tonsils ought to be removed.

IX

DRIVES AND MOTIVES

IN addition to the physiological conditions that we have described in the preceding chapter, there is another group of a similar kind that is important enough to be dealt with separately. There are certain master tissues in the body which exert a great control over the activity of the whole body. The stomach is one of these. When food has not been taken for some time the walls of the stomach start a series of vigorous contractions which result in stimuli that give rise to activity. Any movements that a person executes at this time are definitely more vigorous. If one's strength of grip is measured before he has eaten it is found to be greater than it is after a meal; his intelligence test score is also somewhat higher.[1] Although in most people these stomach contractions result in "hunger pangs," which are recognized for what they are, there are others who cannot report these pangs but experience only a heightened tension and a tendency to be irritable; in childhood this is typically true. Very young children do not know when they are hungry; they are aware only of discomfort and find that things do not go right with them. It has been found in nursery schools that a mid-morning lunch definitely reduces conflicts between children. Muscular tensions are generally heightened before a meal so that smaller stimuli produce larger reactions. When a person becomes older he actively seeks food, or foods of certain kinds, and is even critical of the way in which food is prepared and served, and demands certain implements with which to eat it. The particular combination of preparation and implementation which he demands depends upon the way in which he was brought up—particularly

[1] Tomi Wada, "An Experimental Study of Hunger in Its Relation to Activity," *Archives of Psychology*, No. 57, 1922, pp. 65.

the culture to which he belongs. That the Chinese get on very well with chopsticks is a trite example.

In these cases a real change has taken place in the fundamental and mechanical process of stopping the hunger contractions. *Fundamentally,* the problem is that of getting so many calories, so much bulk, and so many vitamins and minerals into the body, but this end is accomplished under a variety of circumstances in different families within a given culture and with ever greater diversification as one proceeds from one culture to another. This fact is recognized in the literature on the subject, which uses the word "drive" when the simple mechanical facts are to be emphasized. Thus we employ the term "hunger drive" or say a person or an animal is "hunger driven" when we want to emphasize the energetic character of the response and imply that it is directed toward no special end. When we want to express the importance of the cultural, familial, or individual overlay, then we use the term "motive"; we would then speak of the "hunger motive" or say a person is "motivated by hunger." The latter expression implies that specific kinds of food and ritual are demanded, depending on individual habits, while the former term implies that any food will suffice. So many authors are careless in the use of the terms, however, that we frequently have to depend on the context for precise meanings.

More definitions.—There are still other terms which are employed in this field and which demand some explanation. *Incentive* is one of these. An *incentive* and a *goal* are the same thing according to most usage—either term can be used to signify the food whether "food in general" is meant or whether some specific food is to be designated. Because most motivated activity involves a variety of preliminary adjustments, the final act by which the goal is attained is important enough to have a name of its own: it is called the *consummatory response.* This term has caused some trouble to beginning students in the past—it does not have its origin in "consume," which means "to use up" or "to destroy"; rather its roots are in another Latin word which means "to bring to completion," "carried to the utmost," "complete," or "perfect."

What has been said regarding *hunger* as an example could also be said for other tissue conditions within the body—thirst, sex, certain conditions of temperature liberation through the skin, and tensions resulting from the distention of eliminative organs. A discussion of the precise mechanisms resulting in drive behavior is a matter for the physiologist. The psychologist is more interested in the fact that *goals are generated which seem to have not the slightest connection with any of these tissue needs, but which exert just as powerful an influence on human destiny as though they themselves were biologically determined needs.* The need for companionship, or privacy; the need for recognition; and the need for social approval are common examples. Some of these will be discussed in our next chapter, but in the meantime our appreciation of the concepts of *drive, motive, incentive, frustration,* and *satiation* can be enriched by the considerations that follow here.

1. PHYSIOLOGICAL DRIVES

Scientists everywhere find they must measure whatever it is they are trying to study. In the natural sciences this requirement led to the perfection of methods of measuring weight, extent, and duration in terms of grams, centimeters, and seconds. A scientific heritage so precise impels modern psychologists to attempt to measure the strength of seemingly abstract concepts like "drive" and "motive." In the process of measurement these concepts are made less abstract because if one wants to count something he has to be very certain that he is counting.

Although there was no way of measuring drives directly, it occurred to one psychologist [2] that a barrier of some kind imposed in the path of a hungry animal on the way to food might make possible the measurement of the drive by the measurement of the height of the barrier. One such barrier could be an electric shock. If one animal could be prevented from reaching food by a weak

[2] F. A. Moss, "A Study of Animal Drives," *Journal of Experimental Psychology,* 1924, 7, 165-185.

shock and another would endure the shock or a greater one in order to perform the consummatory response, then the second animal could be said to be behaving under the influence of a stronger drive.

To a beginner this may seem a roundabout way to go after a problem, but to a laboratory scientist it is a perfectly natural way to proceed. A few years ago there was no way of measuring the light that falls on a reflecting surface except by an indirect process. The central portion of the reflecting surface was made translucent (at first by the very ordinary method of putting a spot of grease on it). A source of illumination placed behind this surface was arranged so that it could be moved back and forth. When it was close to the surface the translucent part appeared lighter than the surroundings, when it was distant from the surface the grease spot was darker. There was one point at which a balance occurred and the grease spot could not be seen; this was the point at which the light falling on the surface from the front just equaled the light transmitted through the grease spot. The transmitted light could be calculated, so that the unknown amount reflected from a source in the opposite direction could also be determined. Nothing is more roundabout, and at the same time nothing is more simple.

This is only one example of the devious ways in which scientific problems are handled. In fact, some such training as this was what made Moss think of measuring the strength of the hunger drive by measuring the magnitude of an obstruction which, paradoxically enough, would keep the animal from getting food.

Moss's method.—An apparatus was arranged in which a common laboratory animal, the white rat, could be put at one end. This was called the starting compartment. In the opposite end, and within sight and smell of the rat, some food could be placed. This was called the incentive compartment. In between was a narrow passageway containing an electric grill in the floor over which the rat would have to go in order to get to the incentive compartment. The voltage impressed on the grill could be varied at the will of the experimenter.

This method has since come to be known as the "variable-voltage obstruction method." The strength of the drive is assumed to be proportional to the voltage which serves as a complete obstruction to the animal. Among many technical reasons why this is probably not true, one simple fact is immediately obvious. A voltage of, say, 10 does not mean that every animal gets the same shock. How much shock he will get depends on the resistance of his body, and since body resistance varies over a wide range, the shock individual rats get must be different. This must mean that the actual obstruction is not what the experimenter thinks it is when he reads the voltmeter. All in all, the method is not a good one, but it is important because it was the first experiment which was ever made that attempted to measure a drive. First attempts, even if they prove to be failures, always blaze new trails.

Warden's method.—A modification of Moss's variable-voltage obstruction has been worked out by Warden and his co-workers at Columbia University. They redesigned the apparatus, improving it in many ways, but the most significant change they made was in keeping the voltage constant. They used a very high voltage with a very high resistance in series with it. The reason that this is an important change is made clear in the next paragraph.

Let us suppose that one rat has a body resistance of 25,000 ohms and another a resistance of 15,000. This is a ratio of 5 : 3 and with any voltage whatsoever, these animals would be receiving shocks in this proportion. But suppose that in series with the animal's body resistance there was a high external resistance of, say, 2,000,000 ohms. Then the proportion is 2,025,000 : 2,015,000, or about 1.005 : 1.000, about ½ of one per cent difference in the two shocks, whatever the voltage.

The other change in method that they made involved counting the number of times an animal crossed the charged grill in a chosen time interval. They assumed that the strength of the drive was proportional to the activity of the animal in overcoming a *fixed* obstruction, rather than proportional to the greatest magnitude of the obstruction he would surmount as the magnitude was varied.

Typical results are shown in Figure 42 for the hunger drive. The abscissa shows the days since the animal has eaten and the ordinates show the average number of crossings that a standard group of 20 rats made. The two curves display the results for the males and the females separately. The results are shown in this way because the maximum strength of the drive seems to come fully two days earlier for the females, although if we compare the magnitude of the maxima we find them to be the same.

These results may be somewhat contrary to what we might have expected. We might be inclined uncritically to suppose that the strength of the drive would continue to increase indefinitely.

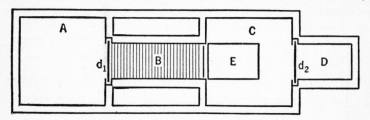

FIG. 41.—The obstruction apparatus used in measuring the relative strength of physiological drives.

The animal to be tested is placed in compartment *A*. The door, d_1, is raised so that the animal has access to the obstruction chamber *B*. The floor of *B* is covered by an electric grill, making it possible to give the animal a standard shock of low intensity. If the obstruction is crossed, and the animal gets to *E*, door d_2 is opened automatically. The incentive compartment contains food, water, or an animal of the opposite sex, depending on whether the hunger, thirst, or sex drive is being studied. It contains a newly-born litter if the maternal drive is being measured. Sometimes, however, compartment *D* is made much larger, contains posts and sawdust, and presents in general a "situation-to-be-explored," a device aimed at a measurement of the "exploratory" drive.

There was no way of knowing before these measurements were made that it typically increases rapidly at first and then gradually decreases. Persons who have fasted for long periods have reported that the first several days were the hardest. After this interval, the thought and odor of food may actually become distasteful. These results with rats seem to substantiate the reports from human beings but by an entirely different approach.

When the rats are rendered thirsty and allowed all the dry food they will eat, the same apparatus can be used to measure the strength of the thirst drive. In this case, water is substituted for food as the incentive, but all other conditions remain the same. The total range of deprivation is less than for starvation because the rats do not live as long without water. The maximum appears on the first day and it is higher than for the hunger drive. We could conclude, then, that *comparing the maxima, the thirst drive is stronger than the hunger drive. But if the comparison is to be made later than the first day, then the hunger drive is stronger.* This conclu-

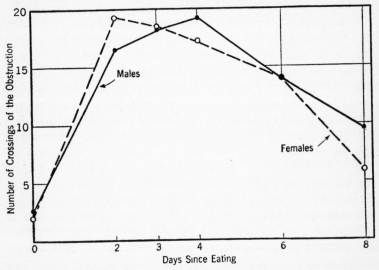

F IG. 42.—The average number of times rats will cross the grill in twenty minutes.

sion is applicable only to this method of measuring these drives in these animals. It is conceivable that this relation is not universal.

In a similar way, the sex drives in both males and females have been studied. The male sex drive follows the typical pattern of rapid ascent [3] following a short period of sex deprivation; as with hunger, the drive does not build up indefinitely but rather falls off following longer periods of deprivation. The picture of the female sex drive is totally different. It does not depend upon the period of deprivation at all, but rather on the phase of the oestrous cycle

[3] This statement assumes an intact animal. The activity pattern is completely changed by castration. Cf. R. G. Hoskins, "Studies on Vigor: II, The Effect of Castration on Voluntary Activity," *American Journal of Physiology,* 1925, 72, 324-30.

under examination. The oestrous cycle is a little less than five days in the rat, so that approximately every five days we find a period of intense activity where the peak slightly exceeds that of the male at its highest point. This periodicity is completely lacking in the male unless the two are kept in adjoining cages, in which case the general activity of the male falls into the same general pattern as that of the female.

In addition to the hunger, thirst, and sex drives, the exploratory and maternal drives have been studied in the same way. By comparing the maxima in each instance we arrive at an order for the strength of these drives: (1) maternal, (2) thirst, (3) hunger, (4) sex, (5) exploratory. The incentive for the maternal drive is the newborn litter of a female; for the exploratory drive a special compartment which allows for complete exploration constitutes the goal. For the other drives the incentives are obvious. It must be remembered, though, that this order is probably not universal. It depends upon the fact that groups of rats were used in each instance and upon the use of a twenty-minute test period. Even changing so simple an element as the length of the test period would probably change the order that we have given here. To argue that the order would remain the same for different species is probably unsound. What we know of the differences between individuals within a species, in the absence of any positive evidence to the contrary, would lead us to believe that the order might consistently be different for different individuals.

A further complicating feature is found in the fact that no animal ever behaves as a result of only one drive. In these experiments on the hunger drive, the effects of the sex drive were rendered as inconsequential as they could be by using males who had undergone a long period of deprivation and only females in the dioestrum, but even this leaves a host of other possible conditions which could affect hunger. As far as purely biological factors are concerned, the situation is complicated enough, but when we add the modifications that can occur as a result of learning we find a truly puzzling array of facts. When we study the behavior of human beings we find that, under certain sets of conditions, people can go on hunger strikes to the detriment of biological impulses.

Hence we may hastily conclude that psychological or learned modes of behaving have definite "right-of-way"; but on the other hand, there are instances, and perhaps more of them, which demonstrate a clear-cut dominance of fundamental drives. Whichever is true in a given case depends upon the relative strengths of drive and motive.

2. HUNGER DRIVE AND RATE OF LEARNING

Aside from the more distinctly physiological methods of studying persistent behavior which we have already seen, drives can be studied in still another way. *If groups of animals of equal abilities are compared in the quickness with which they learn a new thing, then the group showing the quickest learning could be said to be the most highly driven or motivated.* The Warden method of studying drives and the learning method are similar in that both involve the use of an obstruction. In the learning method the maze pathway constitutes the obstruction, and in mastering it the animal is thrown upon its resourcefulness in a way that is impossible when the electric shock is used. Ingenuity rather than brute strength is the important factor in getting to the incentive quickly.

The learning method has been used with rats again as subjects.[4] There were twenty animals in each of three groups who were put into a maze after having been without food for six, twelve, and twenty-one hours, respectively. The performance of the animals was measured by the length of time they took to find their way through the maze to the food box. On the first trial all the groups required about 1,500 seconds on the average. By the end of the fifth trial, three definite trends were observed: the animals without food for 21 hours required less time than those which had been without food for 12 hours. But instead of the 6-hour group requiring even more time than the 12-hour group, they actually required less, falling, as the succeeding trials showed more clearly, between the 21- and the 12-hour group. There is other evidence

[4] E. M. Ligon, "A Comparative Study of Certain Incentives in Learning in the White Rat," *Comparative Psychology Monographs,* 1929, pp. 1-95.

which indicates that at about 6 hours after feeding there is an increase in activity corresponding with this more rapid learning. We can conclude with Ligon that, in addition to the hunger drive, there

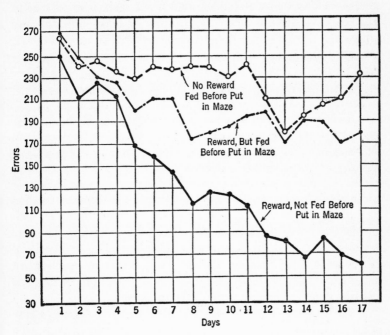

FIG. 43.—Error records of rats running a maze under three different incentive conditions. (After Tolman and Honzik, University of California Publications in Psychology, 1930, 4, 241-256.)

is a further "feeling of well-being" which at certain times after feeding complicates the simple relation between deprivation and performance.

3. INCENTIVE AND LEARNING IN RATS

The dependence of performance in learning upon the incentive is shown nicely in the data exhibited in Figure 43. Here the experimenters placed one group of 36 rats in a standard maze and gave the full daily ration in the food box at the end of the run. Only one trial was given each day. Another group of 36 rats received the same amount of food at the end, but these rats were also fed between times so that presumably they were not as hungry. The hungry group learned the maze promptly, while with the same number of trials the less hungry rats reduced their errors by only a small amount. For still another group which was not hungry there was no food at all in the food box. The performance of these rats was the worst of all. We can interpret these data to mean that *there is a pronounced effect on the learning of a new act by the incentive which is furnished by the situation in which the learning takes place.* Experiments of this kind have led to the generalization that animals generally are motivated to learn in proportion to the magnitude of the incentive.

4. CHANGE OF INCENTIVE

The way in which a given incentive becomes part and parcel of a habit is shown in an experiment on changing the reward during the course of learning.[5] Two groups of animals learned a standard maze pattern, one group being rewarded with sunflower seed, the other with bran mash. The group running for the bran mash made better scores consistently throughout the first few days. On the eleventh and succeeding days this group was also rewarded with sunflower seed. The figure shows what happened. The errors immediately rose at first to equal the poorer performance of the sunflower-seed group and later to become even greater. The effect is not temporary. This experiment shows that these rats were not just running the maze because they were hungry but because they were rewarded in a specific way. The experimental plan could have been improved by including another group of rats which would have been changed from sunflower seed to bran mash at the same time the alternative change was made.

[5] M. H. Elliott, "The Effect of Change of Reward on Maze Performance in Rats," *University of California Publications in Psychology,* 1928, 4, 19-30.

5. SUBSTITUTE INCENTIVES

As we shall see in the next chapter, people work for prizes and ribbons or for a word of commendation. Although these things have little or no intrinsic reward value, they serve as effective substi-

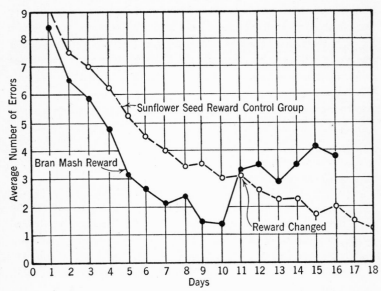

Fig. 44.—Effect of change of reward on maze performance.

tutes for more directly satisfying rewards. In the simplest cases they have become symbols of food, water, and more truly biological incentives. How this comes about has not been demonstrated in experiments involving human beings; hence for the most part we shall have to fall back on discursive arguments to make the point.

There are two experiments in the animal field that serve as models for the kind of experiments needed with human beings. One of these involves rats; the other, chimpanzees.

Rats learned a simple association of "white" with food.[6] They

[6] K. A. Williams, "The Reward Value of a Conditioned Stimulus," *University of California Publications in Psychology,* 1929, 4, 31-55.

were always fed in the white compartment of a simple discrimination box. Such a box allows the experimenter to change the reward and the associated stimulus from one side to the other at will. It is generally used in experiments where the sensory capacity of the animal to make fine discrimination is under investigation. In such cases the stimulus patches would be made very nearly alike, two shades of gray, for instance. But in this case one of the compartments was always white, the other always black. No food was ever given in the black compartment. In time "white" thus became the *symbol* for food in the sense that the animal commenced to make anticipatory feeding movements for "white" as well as for food. This is quite analogous to a variety of things that human beings learn. Paper money is symbolic in this way. So is a school color, a song, a flag, a word, or a gesture. People go to great lengths to accumulate money, while a lack of reverence for a school color or for a flag has been subject to great penalties. Certain words and gestures are so pregnant with meaning that, as Owen Wister's Virginian remarked: "When you call me that, *smile!*"

Once learned, can the symbol "white," which seems to provoke the same anticipation that food itself does, be substituted for food at the end of the maze? In this case no food at all would be offered; only the sight of the color white would reward the animal. That is the problem which K. A. Williams studied. The experimental plan involved the use of a control group that learned the maze in the usual way with a food reward. The comparison group was at first put into the maze without either food or the symbol for it. Even under these conditions some learning took place, presumably because being taken out at the end of the maze, though otherwise unrewarded, constituted an incentive. On the ninth day, however, the symbol white was introduced to the experimental group. Immediately the errors dropped to the level of the "food-rewarded" animals. *Hence we can conclude that even for a white rat a symbol is effective as an incentive.* It did not remain effective for long, however. By the fifteenth day from the beginning, or the sixth "synthetic day," there was a definite trend away from the comparison performance of the "food-rewarded" animals and by the twentieth day from the beginning, the performance of the experimental rats was no better than it would have been had no symbol been used. This latter fact was demonstrated by the use of another control group which from the very beginning had had neither food nor the symbol for food presented to it in the maze.

The decay of the incentive value of the symbol seen in this experiment is quite commonly observed in learning experiments. In the basic conditioned response experiment, for instance, a dog can be caused to salivate at the signal of the bell. This is accomplished by presenting food and the bell together a great number of times. The salivary response to the sight and the smell of food becomes conditioned to the sound of the bell, so that now the bell alone, which was formerly indifferent as a stimulus, causes almost as much saliva to flow as the food did originally; but not indefinitely. If the bell stimulus is not occasionally *reinforced* with food given at the same time, it becomes as ineffective in producing salivation as it was originally. This phenomenon is known technically as *experimental extinction.* Something analogous to experimental extinction is involved in the lapse in efficacy of the white symbol in Williams's experiment. Another example occurs in classical mythology where a shepherd boy called "wolf" too often.

Another experiment involving symbols, but with chimpanzees as subjects, was made by another investigator.[7] He first taught the chimpanzees that poker chips could be used to operate a "vending machine" which could be made to supply either food or water. This corresponds to the simple discrimination problem for the rats, and at this stage "chip" or "token" could not be considered a substitute incentive. Presumably, the placing of a token in the slot of the machine is no more symbolic of the final incentive than the pulling of the lever which delivered the food. However, when the chip was used as the only reward which the animal got for the performance of some other task, then it became truly a symbol of the final incentive. One of these tasks which was thus rewarded involved pulling a heavy weight. In this experiment the bars of an

[7] J. B. Wolfe, "Effectiveness of Token-Rewards for Chimpanzees," *Psychological Monographs,* 1936, 12, 72.

experimental cage kept the animal from getting the reward directly. Within his reach, however, was a rope attached to a box. The ape could see the experimenter place the reward in the box. He could then pull the box toward himself and obtain the reward. The measure of the strength of his motive, or what is the same thing— the attractiveness of the reward—is the weight in pounds which he will pull. In these preliminary studies it was shown that several chimpanzees would pull heavier weights for actual food than for a poker chip which could be used indirectly to obtain food. This is a reasonable state of affairs—the food itself has slightly more incentive value than the token. Other tokens—brass discs—had no value; i.e., the animal could not use them for anything. They elicited even less pulling.

In a more extended study [8] it was shown that the chips would even be collected, several at successive trials, saved or hoarded and at a later time and in a different place used for food rewards from vending machines. This latter finding makes it even more certain that the token was a real substitute incentive, and suggests that something analogous to this takes place when human beings learn the value of symbolic rewards. On the animal level these symbols are definitely limited in significance because animals lack language. Among human beings the elaboration of substitute on substitute produces situations difficult to untangle.

Summary of the chapter.—In this chapter we have traced the elaboration of a relatively simple drive into a more complex motive, and, because there are no experiments on human beings which enable us to accomplish this end, we have had to refer to the experiments on animal subjects to illustrate the mechanism involved. The first experiment showed how it is possible to measure a physiological drive by counting the number of times a hungry rat will surmount a barrier which is placed in the direct avenue to food. This fact makes the concept of drive less mystical than it appeared before measurements were made. Measurements have also been made on a variety of drives resulting in data which per-

[8] John T. Cowles, "Food-Tokens as Incentives for Learning by Chimpanzees," *Comparative Psychology Monographs,* 1937–38, 14, 96.

mit comparisons to be made between the strength of various drives. The hierarchy thus established should be limited to the particular animals, apparatus, and method used in the experiments. There are observations which we have not examined that lead us to conclude that these results can not be generalized beyond the precise conditions under which they were obtained. The second experiment showed that it is also possible to measure the strength of a drive by comparing the rates with which animals learn a maze. The point was made that the maze pattern constitutes a barrier which utilizes the modifiability of the animal rather than being concerned principally with the energetics of behavior. The third experiment shows how groups of animals learn at different rates depending upon the intensity of the drive. That we are dealing not alone with a pure drive situation is shown by the fourth experiment, where it appears that the specific nature of the reward is inextricably bound up with the performance—change the reward and performance is profoundly modified. The fifth experiment shows how the incidental features which are uniformly present when an animal is fed can themselves serve as substitute rewards. The sixth experiment shows how certain objects (tokens) can serve as symbols of distinctive reward values.

X

MOTIVES AND INCENTIVES

IN this chapter we shall show how human beings react to a great variety of rewards which have little intrinsic value. As a result of having grown up in our culture, many people learn to respond to symbols which serve as incentives so that behavior can be motivated by the use of a symbol almost as effectively as though more direct means were used to satisfy physiological drive conditions.

1. MOTIVATION IN SCHOOL

Twenty years ago, thirty-two pupils of the 5B grade in a Cleveland Public School [1] acted as subjects for an experiment by Western Reserve professors to test the efficacy of certain incentives of a different type from what we have seen before. By the time children are in the fifth grade there are all kinds of social conditions which serve as incentives. It is no longer necessary to reward with food—social approval is as effective.

Method.—On the basis of preliminary tests, two groups of sixteen students each were selected for the experiment. The experimental plan here, as before, would require the use of two groups, one of which is especially motivated, the other of which is provided with no special motivating devices. The tests were of simple addition, geared to fifth-grade ability, and a substitution test in which geometrical figures were to be substituted for numerals given. The better a key had been learned, the less frequently a pupil would have to refer to it, and consequently the more substitutions he

[1] J. C. Chapman and R. B. Feder, "The Effect of External Incentives on Improvement," *Journal of Educational Psychology,* 1917, 8, 469-74.

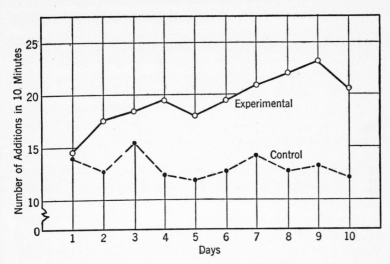

FIG. 45.—The effect of motivation on addition.

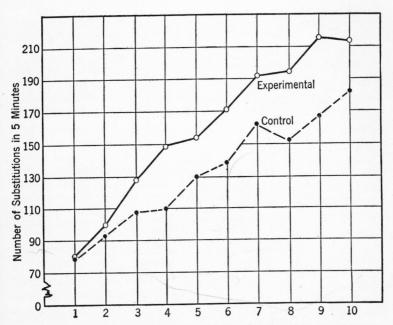

FIG. 46.—The effect of motivation on substitution.

could make in the time allowed. The time limits were ten minutes for the addition and five minutes for the substitution.

Both groups were motivated, of course; both knew what scores they were making. As we shall see, knowledge of how we are progressing is a powerful incentive. But in addition to this ordinary motivation there were four other ways in which the experimental group was especially motivated:

(1) Each individual's results were posted.

(2) The point that the subject had reached on the previous day was marked with a blue pencil on the fresh sheets for each day's work.

(3) The general improvement of the whole group was presented in a graph each day.

(4) Stars were given to those in the top half of the group each day. It was understood that those having the most stars at the end of ten days would receive a prize.

Results.—The results are shown in two figures. In arithmetic addition, the control group actually goes down hill. In substitution both groups improve, but the experimental group as a whole improves more than the control group. It is to be understood that these are average results. There were some *individuals* in the control group who were better than some *individuals* in the experimental group, but the group trends are, in all likelihood, real. *Additional motivation in the form of prizes, knowledge of results, and competition with oneself improve performance in learning over what it would have been had these incentives not been operating.*

If we refer to the curves shown in Figures 11, 21, 31, and 37, we see that the typical pattern of these curves is something like that of the generalized forms shown in Figure 47. A theoretical limiting performance seems to exist which the actual performance appears to be ever approaching but never reaching, however long practice is continued. This limit has been called the "physiological limit" because it is supposed that there is an ultimate limit imposed by the anatomical structures themselves upon whatever behavior is under consideration. The speed with which a nervous impulse can pass from sense organ to muscle and the time required for the selection of the proper response is certainly not zero. *A person's structure, then, limits his performance.* But has this ultimate limit actually been closely approached in the experiments that we have seen heretofore? There is no way of knowing because they have all been accomplished under constant motivating circumstances. If we could increase motivation beyond the levels ordinarily employed in psychological experiments, would the physiological limits change correspondingly?

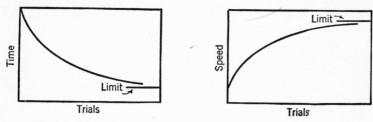

FIG. 47.—Theoretical learning curves showing the physiological limit.

2. BONUSES

A partial answer to the question of physiological limits is found in the records of forty hand compositors [2] in a Chicago printing establishment. These men had had ten years' experience before entering this particular plant, but even so for the first twenty weeks, their production showed, on the average, a decided increase even after all these years as supposed masters of their trade. The secret of their heightened production rate *probably* lies in the way that they were paid. The output of expert compositors as determined in a preliminary study was called 100. Seventy-five per cent of this amount was called a fair day's work, and every worker was paid a flat rate based on this amount whether he actually accomplished it or not. But for every point on the scale in excess of 75, he was paid ⅔ of 1 per cent of his base rate. This means that if he

[2] H. D. Kitson, "A Study of the Output of Workers under a Particular Wage Incentive," *University Journal of Business*, 1922, 1, 54-68.

attained 100—the output of the expert—he would earn a bonus of 16.5 per cent in excess of his flat rate. The average results for the forty compositors are shown in Figure 48.

In several respects these records fail to meet the criteria of a planned experiment and as a consequence leave us somewhat un-

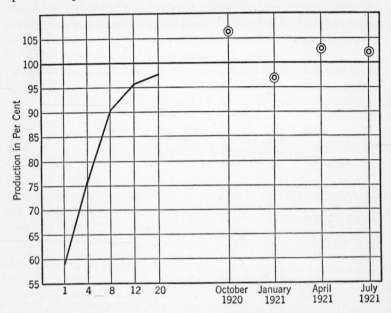

Fig. 48.—Increase in production under a bonus system.

certain as to the true explanation of the results. The observations were put together from the records the company kept. The forty men did not constitute a newly formed squad who entered the employment of the company at the same time for the purpose of making this experiment. They entered upon employment at different times and during the first twenty weeks improved their production perhaps partly because of the arrangement of the materials, the illumination, the stimulus of new surroundings, and so on. After twenty weeks their production leveled off, and later spot checks at the dates given indicate that the level was maintained. But why did the new level assert itself? Why didn't production keep on climbing? There are several possibilities: men who earn too much are not popular with their fellow workers; men usually fear that the base rate will be changed if they produce too much; there are probably many other factors which tend to depress production, so that we cannot conclude that the new level is determined by structural limitation. The generalization still remains, however, that *even after long experience, production can be markedly improved.* It is interesting to surmise what would have happened had it been possible to increase the incentive somewhat once this new level had been reached. What are the final limits of human improvability? Production cannot increase indefinitely because of the structural limits imposed by nerve and muscle.

3. INCREASING THE INCENTIVE

An experiment made in England by Flügel [3] contributes to this problem but does not finally answer it. As a matter of fact, Flügel was mainly interested in an entirely different set of facts, but he did use an increasing money reward which operated in this wise: The task involved adding numbers from a sheet provided and the work was done each school day under carefully controlled conditions. Each subject received a small flat rate as long as the experiment continued. In addition to the flat rate, the experimenter also provided a system of special prizes and bonuses. At the beginning of the first day's work, it was understood that there would be three prizes of 1s., 9d., and 6d. (24 cents; 18 cents; 12 cents), respectively, for the best performances on that day. Then the subjects were told that every time they exceeded their previous record, they would receive a special bonus. This bonus was to be gradually increased as the experiment progressed. During the first week each person who exceeded his previous record was to get 2 cents every time. The second week every time the previous record was broken, the reward for excellence was to be 3 cents. The third week the bonus was to be 4 cents, and so on, increasing at the rate of 1 cent a week

[3] J. C. Flügel, "Practice, Fatigue and Oscillation," *British Journal Psychology Monograph Supplement,* 1928, No. 13.

through the 10 weeks the experiment was to run. In the last week, the bonus would be 11 cents a day, or 55 cents a week. This would be a considerable money reward for the 9- to 13-year-old school-girls who served as subjects, particularly when we consider that the purchasing power of the British money, of which we have given the United States equivalents, was almost twice as great as ours. Also it would have been quite expensive to the experimenter if all of the forty-six girls who made up the group received bonuses on each of the forty-six days that the experiment lasted. This, by the way, is the principal reason why experiments like this one have not been made more frequently. An incidental result supplies another reason why such experiments are not made more often: The forty-six girls working furiously for a total of fifteen and one half hours in the whole experiment produced more than two million combinations. The labor involved in checking each one of these additions for accuracy is tremendous. If one clerk could check one combination per second, 3,600 every hour for eight long hours a day, about seventy consecutive days would be required to complete the job.

The money reward system was not the only way in which the girls were motivated. They kept individual progress records; they had complete knowledge of their results and those of others; they worked in a group, a fact which in itself is known to have motivating power. When the school physician thought he detected signs of an infectious disease in two subjects and was sending them home, they rebelled because they were "test girls," set apart, they thought, from the other students, and not subject to trivial rules of quarantine. When public health measures prevailed, they left the school in tears.

The incentive, then, in this case was a complicated one, consisting of no one knows how many factors. All of them had been used before with the exception of the gradually increasing money reward with no particularly striking results. Flügel therefore attributes the unique results in this experiment to the unusual nature of his bonus system. He observes that *a reward once attained is not as attractive as it is before having been experienced, and the only*

*way to keep motivation at a high level throughout an experiment
like this is to increase the bonus constantly,* as he did.

Results.—The results of this system are shown in the graph.
The total number of additions in each 20-minute work period for
the 46 girls is plotted against the 46 experimental days. The striking

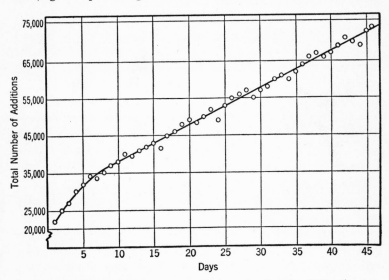

Fig. 49.—Production under a constantly increasing incentive. Notice the complete lack of any limit. Mondays are always the low points in the week with two
exceptions. One of them occurs at the beginning of the learning. The other with
Tuesday was a holiday. Wednesday of that week is the low point.

thing about the graph is the fact that there is absolutely no indication of any flattening off—any physiological limit.

This experiment is weak at one point: there is no control group
with which to compare the highly motivated group. But the weakness is a result of our particular point of view. All Flügel needed
for his problem was a highly motivated group. He was not interested in comparing the relative merits of several different kinds
of motivation. From other experiments that are similar to his—that
seem to differ principally in the fact that the money reward was
not increased, Flügel infers that there would have been little in-

crease in score after the first 10 or 12 days had he not used the increasing bonus system.

We can conclude then, that a *gradually increasing reward for performance that becomes more and more difficult is effective in producing performances that greatly exceed ordinary everyday accomplishments.* Just how broadly this generalization applies in *all* cases we cannot say until more experimenters have examined the multiple relations that must be important here.

4. PUNISHMENT AND KNOWLEDGE OF RESULTS

Reward for relatively complicated learning performances is not the only way that responses can be modified. Punishment is an effective motivating agent. The relative effect of punishment and incentive in the form of knowledge of results on the time required to make a simple finger movement to an auditory signal has been studied by Johanson,[4] who employed three different conditions under which the reactions were obtained:

(1) A normal series in which each reaction was obtained in the usual fashion, i.e., without any knowledge of whether a response was fast or slow and without any encouragement or punishment. The subject was instructed to react by pressing a key as quickly as he could after an auditory signal. This stimulus was preceded by a ready signal which could come from one to several seconds before the auditory stimulus. The subject never knew whether the interval after the ready signal was going to be long or short; if he had known, or if the interval had been constant, he would have soon commenced to "jump the gun" by anticipating the auditory stimulus.

(2) An incentive series in which the subjects were told what their last reaction time had been. This procedure is known to have an effect on more complex learning processes, but it had never been studied in connection with reaction time before Johanson's experiment.

[4] A. M. Johanson, "The Influence of Incentive and Punishment upon Reaction Time," *Archives of Psychology,* 1922, No. 54, pp. 53.

(3) A punishment series in which the subjects were automatically given a slight shock to the fingers if they started to slow down. This, again, was new. It had been supposed that since the subjects were instructed to react as quickly as they could, they were doing the best they could do anyhow.

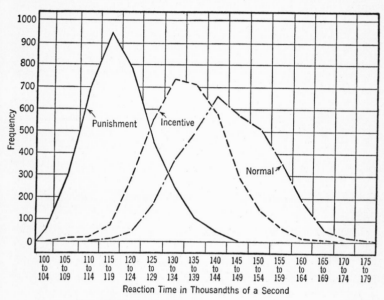

Fig. 50.—The effect of motivation on reaction time.

The different series were rotated in the usual way, so that all the measurements were not made in the order stated here. Obviously, had this control not been instituted, it would have been impossible to determine whether the effects that were observed were due to the incentive and the punishment, or whether they were due to practice, or fatigue, or ennui. *boredom*

Results.—The results for the three conditions are shown in the graph. There are about 3,600 individual reactions for each one of the curves. These are the total responses for three different individuals. We cannot tell from the curves which response belongs to which person, but we are more interested in a comparison of the three different conditions. The average of the normal series is 143.9 milliseconds; for the incentive, 135.0; for the punishment, 122.3. This is a reduction of about 6 per cent for the incentive and about 15 per cent for the punishment series.

So here we find that a little punishment is more effective than a knowledge of results. But of course *we are not justified in generalizing that punishment always gives the best results.* As a matter of fact, it may not. It is even questionable whether the use of the word "punishment" is appropriate to this situation. The small electric shock that was used may have served primarily as a very effective informant. In any event it is worth while to point out that the shock came as an outcome of the situation, precisely, inevitably, and automatically.

The word "punishment" ordinarily refers to situations in which some human being detects an infringement of some rule and since he is not present at all times to judge, or his standards differ at different times, a defection is not uniformly followed by a painful stimulus. Situations of this kind have been shown to produce neuroses (Chapters XI and XII). Then, too, "punishment" seldom follows *immediately* upon the mode of behavior which the "punisher" seeks to control; as a consequence its value in influencing behavior is small (Chapter XVI). All of these considerations lead to the conclusion that punishment is a poor mode of behavior control in everyday life, even though on the surface this experiment seems to show that it is effective in the laboratory. This does not mean that the laboratory experiment is useless, but only that laboratory conditions seldom obtain in our everyday relations with other people.

5. PRAISE AND REPROOF

An experiment by Hurlock [5] seeks to compare the relative effectiveness of two kinds of incentive that are used every day from

[5] Elizabeth B. Hurlock, "The Value of Praise and Reproof as Incentives for Children," *Archives of Psychology*, 1924, No. 71.

kindergarten to graduate school in the thousands of schoolrooms the world over.

One of these incentives involves reproving the pupils for a performance. To a great many people, who conceive it as a substitute for actually slapping either children's fingers or more extensive parts of their anatomy, it is related to the "punishment" in the preceding experiment. The expression "tongue lashing" is descriptive of this view. People who scold others expect thereby to improve the performance of the one who is reproved. But another widely used method—praise of an inferior performance in the hope of improving it—has, to casual observation, been found sometimes as effective as reproof. Now, since these two methods are so unlike in the reactions they induce in the person who submits to them, it would be somewhat puzzling if both were equally effective in producing an improvement.

In addition to the two experimental groups required to make a study of the relative effectiveness of these two methods, Hurlock added a control group and what she called an "ignored" group. Just what happened to the four groups is shown in the next paragraph.

Method.—On the basis of preliminary tests, the personnel of the four groups was chosen so that the members were of the same age and had the same ability to solve the arithmetic problems that were to serve as the experimental materials. There were 30 problems to be solved in the fifteen minutes allowed. The experiment lasted five days and a different group of 30 problems was used each day. Previous work had shown these problems to be of equal difficulty.

(1) The reproved group was told how poorly it had done before the whole class. The pupils in it had actually an average of 11.8 problems, but they didn't know how well they had done; the experimenter merely told them they had done poorly.

(2) The praised group was told how well it had done before the whole class. The members of this group, too, actually had solved an average of 11.8 problems. But beyond the fact that they were praised for how well they had done, they had no actual knowledge of their results.

(3) The ignored group heard the praise and the reproof administered to the others but its members were entirely ignored. They had also solved 11.8 problems on the average.

(4) The control group, after the first day, was taken to another room so that it never heard either the praise or the reproof admin-

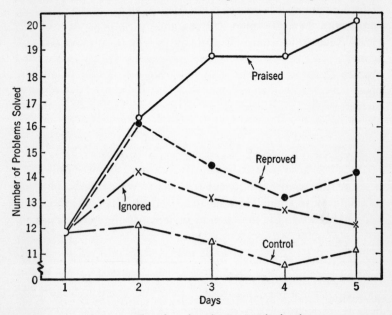

FIG. 51.—The effect of motivation in schoolwork.

istered to the others. The members were given no information at all on their progress. For five days they worked in total ignorance of how well they were doing. This is not an artificial situation. Pupils frequently go more than five days completely unaware of their progress.

Results.—The results for the four groups are shown in the figure. The control group serves as a standard against which the effects of the other conditions can be judged. The general trend for the control group is slightly downward. The small rises and falls which give a ragged appearance to the line are probably due in part to the greater or lesser difficulty of the problems from day to day.

All three of the special motivating conditions give rise to more production. Even the ignored group shows some improvement, but it becomes progressively less as the experiment progresses. There is little to choose between praise and reproof on the second day, but after that time the reproved group steadily loses its initial gain. The trend for the praised group, on the other hand, is entirely different; throughout the 5-day interval it continues to improve.

We would conclude, then, that with children, anyway, *praise is much more effective as a motivating agent than reproof.* In the absence of actual evidence to the contrary, there seems to be no good reason why this generalization should not be extended to include adults.

6. HABITS OF WORK AS MOTIVATORS

The story is told of a newspaper man who became a syndicated columnist of some note and successful enough financially to have a study in his home. He confessed to his most intimate friends that he had a study just because people expected him to have it. It was all front. His years of experience in newspaper work had so habituated him to noise and to confusion that he couldn't work where it was quiet. Reversing the commonplace, he retreated from his quiet study and sought a nice, noisy newspaper editorial room when he had a bit of heavy thinking to do.

Everybody has some notion of whether he can do his best work in the presence of a hubbub or in a peaceful quiet. Some feel that excitement surrounding them stimulates them to more accomplishment; others are just as certain that noise makes good work impossible. It may well be that the kind of task determines which condition will be true, but if it is, psychological experiments have not yet succeeded in demonstrating this truth. As a matter of fact, experiments have been peculiarly contradictory in this field. Now when experiments present contradictory evidence—when one experimenter gets one result and another person gets a different result, or when there is no clear-cut difference in result between what appear to be entirely different procedures—one possible explanation is that the experimenters have had more factors affecting the results of their experiments than they were aware of.

After reading all the published literature on the question of the effect of noise on the speed and accuracy with which a person could work, and making some preliminary experiments of his own, Baker [6] conceived the notion that the attitude of the subject was a probable factor which had been overlooked when the experimenters had said that "all the factors were constant except the noise." An answer to this question is of tremendous practical importance, because if noise does have a deleterious effect on production, then we should make more use of soundproofing materials than we do now and our efforts at the reduction of city noises, elevateds, automobile horns, garbage pails, and traffic noises generally, should be more consistent programs than the spasmodic noise abatement drives that we have seen heretofore.

In a typical experiment in which production under noise was to be compared with production in the same kind of task when no noise was used, Baker proposed to examine the extent to which an attitude that was imposed upon a subject could influence the results.

Method.—The problem was a simple one that has been used in numerous psychological experiments. The subject was given a two-place number and he was to add successively 6, 7, 8, 9, calling each subtotal. That is, he was given 27, he added 6 and called 33; then 7 and said 40; then 8 and said 48; then 9 and said 57; then 6 again, repeating the series until stopped by the experimenter at the end of 30 seconds; whereupon he was given a new two-place number. He did not use pencil or paper. A record of his sums was kept by the experimenter so that the time required to solve the number of correct combinations he made might be computed. This is the same method that Hull used in his study on the psychological effects of tobacco (cf. page 149).

The noise or music was supplied from a transcribed source by means of a loud-speaker. Each day was divided into two parts, a noise period and a quiet period. There were ten experimental days

[6] Kenneth H. Baker, "Pre-experimental Set in Distraction Experiments," *Journal of General Psychology*, 1937, 16, 471-88.

in all, and for half these days, the noise or music came first and in the other half the quiet period came first. If the noise is called condition A and the quiet condition B, then what is known to experimenters as the A B B A order was used. This control is necessary because if the noise always came first, then whatever results were obtained might be due to the fact that the task was performed first, and not to the fact that it was performed in the presence of noise.

The subjects were divided into groups of ten men.

Group A was called a control group because there was no attempt made to institute a special set or attitude in its members. This statement does not mean that they did not have any notion of whether they could do better under the one condition than under the other, but the experimenter at least did not try to change their attitude as he did in the experimental group. The subject was told each day what his *total* performance was, but he wasn't told whether he did better under one condition than another.

In *Group B* each person was told that he was going to serve as a subject in an experiment to determine the effects of distraction. Other work, he was told, had been done and this experiment was to be a check on the previous work. What purported to be the results of a previous experiment were shown in a graph which contained two curves, one red and one black. The red curve was labeled "with distraction." It showed that in this imaginary experiment which all the subjects believed was a real one, noise had facilitated the performance so that there was a clear difference between the red and black curves. The curves remained in the experimental room posted in full view of the subject throughout the experiment.

Group C was composed of other men who were shown a curve in which the red and black lines were interchanged so that their inevitable interpretation was that noise interfered with this kind of performance.

Group D was shown a curve in which the red and black lines crossed in such a way that they interpreted the graph to mean that for the first few days noise had an inhibiting or distracting effect, but became less and less a distracter and finally clearly facilitated performance.

All the subjects accepted the charts as representing bona fide experiments and did not question the results.

Results.—For Group A the performance curves cross and re-cross so that we conclude there is no consistent difference in production when no effort is made to impose an attitude either favorable or unfavorable to either one of the conditions. This conclusion is opposed to that of some other studies in that consistent differences have been found. A possible explanation for this difference in results becomes apparent when we examine the results for the other groups.

Each of the other groups reproduced the condition which had been suggested to it by word and by chart. This is even true of the last group which was told that there would be interference at first, facilitation later. There were *individuals* in all groups who resisted the suggestion, but they were not numerous enough to change the group response from the imposed set.

Summary.—The general inference from this experiment is that experimenters who have obtained results showing how music or noise facilitates—together with their fellow experimenters who obtained just the opposite results—are really guilty of inadvertently communicating to the subjects the results they hoped to get. This does not necessarily mean that these experimenters were dishonest; they may merely have been enthusiastic and perhaps careless. Many undergraduates will be certain that they were not dishonest because the issues here are not significant enough for people to misrepresent them. But consider for a moment the position of a manufacturer of sound-deadening materials, whose sales will depend in theory on the outcome of an experiment like this. Or think of an educational expert whose reputation will depend upon children's learning more under one set of conditions than another. A teacher might be so convinced that one educational method was superior to another that his enthusiasm for the method would so influence the subjects that they would actually do much better under it than under its competitor. But another educator could easily be so sincerely convinced of the superiority of the rival method that he in turn could prove his method to be the better one. Now which really is the better method?

The relation of the process of motivation to Baker's experiment may not be perfectly obvious. The point in introducing it here is to show that the production of a subject does not depend entirely on the circumstances which surround him. He can either convince himself through observing or reading that a certain condition ought to produce a certain result, or be convinced by others, so that he will produce in amounts consistent with his conviction. From a practical standpoint, where production is the only consideration, as in comparing one method of instruction with another, it makes little difference whether the increase is due to one factor or to another. But if we are really interested in understanding human behavior, we will not overlook the potency of a personal conviction in explaining the results in experiments of this kind.

7. INDUSTRIAL MOTIVATION

We have shown previously how printers of ten years' experience raised their production rate during the first twenty weeks in a new shop and how they maintained it after that time at a new high level (page 191). Some doubt was expressed as to whether the bonus system alone brought about this result—a doubt which is increased by a study [7] conducted at the Hawthorne plant of the Western Electric Company in Chicago. This study, which has since become a minor classic, started out as a continuation of studies made during World War I in England and in the United States. They were devoted to finding out more about fatigue and monotony. It had been observed that production was heightened in munitions factories and in other industries if rest periods were allowed and if hours of work were shortened.

At the Hawthorne plant five girls who assembled small electrical relays were transferred from their usual locations in the

[7] Elton Mayo, *Human Problems of an Industrial Civilization,* The Macmillan Company, New York, 1934.

Excerpt from an Observer's Notes

In this department, anyone who exceeded the group's standard (which was low) was looked upon with disfavor, and various tactics were used to bring such people into line. In the following account, W6 was one of the faster workers and W8 one of the slower ones:

W8 (to W6): "Why don't you quit work? Let's see, this is your thirty-fifth row today. What are you going to do with them all?"

W6: "What do you care? It's to your advantage if I work, isn't it?"

W8: "Yeah, but the way you're working you'll get stuck with them." (Meaning that W6 would have to refrain from reporting all the work he did.)

W6: "Don't worry about that. I'll take care of it. You're getting paid by the sets I turn out. That's all you should worry about."

W8: "If you don't quit work I'll bing you." W8 struck W6 and finally chased him around the room.

Observer (a few minutes later): "What's the matter, W6, won't he let you work?"

W6: "No. I'm all through, though. I've got enough done."

W6 then went over and helped another wireman. This practice was sanctioned by the group.

factory to an experimental room where it would be possible to vary certain surroundings. Records of their production were carefully kept and the effects of different degrees of illumination, ventilation, rest periods, mid-morning lunches, and so on were observed. They generally worked under a given set of conditions for two weeks, sometimes even longer, and since thirteen different conditions of work were examined, the experiment extended over several years. The result was that in spite of several supposedly adverse working conditions which were introduced, *their production records throughout the whole period kept climbing to entirely new levels.*

This curious outcome, which was as surprising to the girls as it was to the officers in charge of the experiment, can be accounted for by the social background in which the experiment took place. *Social conditions were, then, more important in determining the outcome of this experiment than the experimental surroundings, which were varied.*

The key to the whole situation seems to lie in the transfer of these girls to a special room and the treatment accorded them there. We have already noted incidentally that in Flügel's experiment the British schoolgirls considered that participation in his experiment was a definite social distinction (page 194). This same recognition plus the further fact that the girls were interviewed frequently and that they were consulted before changes were instituted in the experiment all had the effect of imposing a sense of responsibility on them. They did not feel that they were lost in a big impersonal machine. Their attitude toward their supervisor changed, they ceased to think of him as a taskmaster. They gained confidence in him and expressed themselves freely. They reported that they felt "happier" and "freer"; that they felt no restraint. The work, they thought, was easier; they had no sense of working faster, although the production record showed that they were.

Since the relationship between the superior and the employee changed so much in this experiment it was decided to put special emphasis on problems of personnel in training the supervisors for the plant as a whole. Supervisors are the link between management and labor through whom the policies of management are explained to the employees and through whom the grievances of labor find their way to management. A survey showed that actually there was great variation in relationships that, on paper in the offices of the executives, appeared to be the same. In some instances the supervisor sided with the men and, although his control of them became more certain, he found that he had to conceal certain information from his superiors. In other cases the supervisor was essentially an outsider who imposed conditions upon the men and who as a consequence was cordially disliked. To describe this condition further would take us too far afield; the student will find the published report on the experiment interesting reading.[8]

All this work extends over a period of twelve years and consists of several experiments, aside from the one mentioned, as well as of personal interviews with 20,000 employees. Yet a generalization on it may be made somewhat as follows: Management can not arbitrarily impose new work conditions upon workers and expect them to be accepted, even though they may ultimately benefit the employee. Men are not simply selling their services to employers. They continue to live during the time they are employed, and when groups of them work together in a single department, social organizations spring up. These organizations really control production, usually by slowing it up. They are more effective in regulating production than are physical surroundings. They can be made effective agents in greater production if as much time and energy is put into studying and understanding them as is spent in studying and testing the raw materials of the industry.

Summary.—The first experiment in this chapter shows how school children react in providing learning curves that are analogous to those obtained when rats are used as subjects. With children of this age it is no longer necessary to use food as an incentive, a knowledge of results serving as an incentive for human beings, just as do bonuses, gold stars, and ribbons which express recognition. The third experiment shows how by increasing the incentive throughout the period of learning the point ordinarily

[8] F. J. Roethlesberger and W. J. Dickson, *Management and the Worker,* Harvard University Press, Cambridge, Mass., 1939.

thought of as the physiological limit is greatly exceeded. That behavior can also be controlled by what is called punishment is shown in the fourth experiment; but in the discussion of this experiment it is important to remember that the word "punishment" can mean several different things. Generally speaking, as demonstrated by the fifth experiment, praise is much more effective than reproof in controlling human behavior. The sixth experiment suggests that the conditions under which a person learns to work and the attitude he has towards these conditions serve as incentives for the accomplishment of the work, whatever it is. The last section shows that social organization is much more important than the physical surroundings in controlling the production in an industrial organization.

XI

FRUSTRATION[1]

IF a young child in the process of pulling a toy wagon across a room gets it securely wedged behind the leg of a table, a temper tantrum is likely to ensue. It is a situation to which the child is unable to react any more adequately than he does. A more intelligent response, we assume, is beyond this child's understanding of the relations which obtain between the toy and the table leg. This situation can be conceived as a simple illustration of a variety of conditions in which we figuratively get our toys caught—if we look at it this way. The child is engaged in an activity pleasing to him; persistence in the activity can be regarded as a goal. The activity would have continued until a more attractive incentive presented itself had the table leg not intervened to cut it short. The table leg can be conceived as a barrier to the activity; the temper tantrum, a natural outcome of the frustrating circumstance. The barrier does not have to be in the form of a table leg. It could have been the command of an adult to come to dinner; the activity, playing with blocks. In older children it may be a picnic interfered with by a thunderstorm. For an adolescent, a date forbidden by parental authority. But whatever the specific situation, an interference with the activity results in an emotional display (cf. page 251).

This display is generally, but not always, of the explosive variety that we have been accustomed to call emotional. It might be a rather quiet withdrawal from the situation. The German psychologist Lewin has used the term *aus-dem-Felde-gehen*—"going out of the field"—to describe figuratively this latter kind of behavior.

That two so seemingly dissimilar kinds of behavior are really caused in different people by the same external circumstance seems

[1] To understand the full significance of the material in this chapter it will be necessary first to master the content of our chapters on emotion and motivation. Chapter XII especially should be read in connection with this material.

incredible, but it has been demonstrated to be fact by experiments with animals.

1. EXPERIMENTAL NEUROSIS

Pavlov,[2] a Russian physiologist who is both famous and infamous among psychologists because of his invention of the term "conditioned reflex," was among the first to observe that animals could be made as tense and high-strung as human beings are to whom we apply the same designations. We say tense people given to childish displays of temper are "neurotics." Pavlov applied the same appellation to his dogs who bit and scratched their attendants and had doggish temper tantrums. He conceived the basic mechanisms in human beings and in dogs to be the same and pointed out similarities in the ways in which dogs and men become neurotics. We will discuss the case of the dogs first.

In the conditioned reflex experiments a dog is required to be harnessed in a rather complicated apparatus designed to keep him as quiet as possible so that the registration of his responses can proceed without interference. In one set of conditions, a stimulus, say a light, is presented and at the same time the foreleg of one of the dogs receives a slight shock. The shock causes him to raise his foreleg and after several, or in some cases several hundred, presentations of the light and the shock together, whenever the light is shown alone, the dog lifts his leg in the absence of the shock. All this seems very trivial. But the importance of the conditioned reflex technique to those interested in dogs can be seen when the notion is developed further.

Suppose we are interested in how sensitive a dog's ears are. If we substitute some sound for the light in the illustration above, it is clear that the intensity of such a sound could be gradually reduced. As long as the dog kept raising his paw for very weak sounds, we could infer that he was still hearing them, *even if they were so weak that the most sensitive human ears could hear noth-*

[2] I. P. Pavlov, *Conditioned Reflexes*, Oxford University Press, London, 1927, p. 430.

ing at all. Such experiments have been made and have proved that dogs in general do have more sensitive ears than those of people. We say this only because it is a fact that may have some general interest, for we are not now interested in this phase of conditioning.

It is in a related problem that we find our main interest. Suppose we wanted to know whether a dog could discriminate an ellipse from a circle of the same area as well as a man can. We would start with an ellipse whose major axis was clearly longer than its minor, and present it alternately with a circle in some haphazard order. The dog would be taught to make one response to one of the figures and some other response to the other. Then we would gradually change the ellipse until to the dog it would be indistinguishable from the circle. But all does not go so smoothly in actual practice. When the two forms approach each other in appearance the dog commences to "go to pieces." It either becomes excited with a good deal of loud barking, biting, scratching, and throwing itself about, or it is depressed, stuporous, lethargic, or sleepy and may even refuse to eat. At first these responses are observed only in the experimental room, but if the experiment is continued, they become generalized—observable not only in the experimental room but outside as well. All of the effects of the previous training are lost and the experiment has to be started all over again from the beginning.

Pavlov also reports that the usual prescriptions for human neurotics—resting in the country, quiet surroundings, the use of some mild sedatives—are about as effective with dogs as they are with people.

The generalization that we can draw from these experiments when considered in the light of clinical observations on human beings is that *difficult problems, problems that have no solution, problems beyond the capacity of the organism to discriminate or to perceive, result in one of two types of behavior, hyperexcitability or lethargy.* Which it will be we cannot with any certainty predict.[3]

[3] H. S. Liddell and his associates at Cornell University are continuing this work in this country. "The Development of Experimental Neurasthenia in Sheep during the Formation of Conditioned Reflexes," *American Journal of Physiology,* 1927, 81, 49.

There is some evidence that constitutional factors like basal metabolic rate may be the effective determinants.

It has been shown that inconsistency in the handling of children is productive of more anger displays than are observed in other children whose social environment is more uniform, and, according to our interpretation, Pavlov's observations on dogs is related to this fact (cf. page 252). Suppose that a child jumps up and down on a davenport with perfect safety when there are no guests, and suppose that when there is company he is scolded. The two situations may be quite beyond his childish ability to discriminate. At one time he is punished for doing what to him is exactly the same thing that another time goes unnoticed. That one is supposed, in some families, to act differently before guests means nothing to him. He may be in exactly the same dilemma that confronted Pavlov's dogs when they were unable to discriminate between a circle and an ellipse. The consequences in both cases mean neurosis.

The same conditions obtain when parents or teachers are too strict. "Being strict" means that adult standards are imposed on childish abilities to conform. "Being strict" sometimes means expecting kinds of behavior from children that one really doesn't expect from himself or his adult associates. In either case, extremely difficult problems, beyond the capacity of children to solve or even appreciate, are presented to them. Only hypertension or extreme lethargy can result.

2. NEUROSIS IN ADULTS

Liddell has suggested that, aside from the difficulty of the problem presented to them, another possible reason [4] why Pavlov's dogs became neurotic was that there was no possibility of escape. The dogs were held securely in a kind of stanchion which allowed them no latitude of movement.

In wartime, men are not harnessed to stanchions of any real kind, but the social harness holds them as securely as though they were actually strapped as immobile as Pavlov's dogs or Liddell's sheep. Having no real reason to fight, never having actually been

[4] This possibility is supported by experimental evidence.

SHELL SHOCK

B was evacuated from the Front because of tremor following pro-longed bombardment. He was an artist who for long months had cheer-fully borne the hard life of the trenches, but there came a day when, after a particularly heavy firing, "the machine got out of order," to use his own expression. He began to tremble.

He himself writes: "For nearly four months, ever since I was evac-uated from the Front, my nervous state, which I thought would last barely a fortnight, still persists, although slightly ameliorated. There is no doubt that I am calmer. My heart does not beat as it used to do, neither do my hands perspire so profusely upon the occasion of the slightest emotion or effort.

"At first the slightest shock would make me tremble uncontrol-lably. I can master the tremor for a few minutes but no longer. On a tram, or in the Metro, I feel that people are looking at me, and it makes me miserable. The tremor is arrested by the noise of the doors of the Metropolitan, a wavering light, the whistle of a locomotive, the yap-ping of a dog, a childish peevishness. The theater, music, the reading of poetry, a religious ceremony, have exactly the same effect. I went lately to see a flag placed in the Invalides, and before the moving spec-tacle, I fancied myself cured. Then all of a sudden, I began to tremble, and to such an extent that I was obliged to sit on the ground and cry like a child. Sometimes the tremor came on suddenly without cause. For instance, I went to a shop with my wife to do some shopping. The crowd, the lights, the rustling of silks, the colors of materials were all a delightful contrast to our life of misery in the trenches. I chattered and was as happy as a schoolboy on holiday. Then, suddenly, without any reason, I felt my strength going. I stopped talking, I had a pain in my back, I felt my cheeks become drawn, my gaze became fixed and the tremor returned, and with it a feeling of great physical discomfort. At such times, if I can lean up against something, sit down, or especially lie on my back, the tremor diminishes or even stops pretty quickly.[5]

[5] Tom A. Williams, "Tremor Following Explosions," *Journal of Abnormal Psychology,* 1920, 14, 393-405.

harmed by the enemy, it is hard for them to see why it is necessary to let someone else shoot at them. One solution to the problem is to run away—to desert. Armies have for so long been plagued with wholesale desertions that severe penalties, including death, have been inflicted on people who run away. Aside from fear of the death penalty, there is a social pressure that keeps men in the ranks when there are many other places where they would rather be. As a matter of fact, social pressure operates in the fear of the death penalty. It is not a fear of death so much as a fear of disgrace—a social factor—which operates here. In a situation of this kind there are honorable ways of escaping social condemnation. One method is to be wounded and sent home; another is to be too ill to engage in active fighting. Self-inflicted wounds are not uncommon, but the penalty for using this way out is almost as severe as that for desertion. A person can be paralyzed, blinded or nauseated, or have headaches, and in this way achieve escape by being counted unfortunately ill. This latter method of solution was used by hundreds in the World War, who recovered miraculously as soon as the Armistice was signed.[6]

These methods of adjusting are important to us because they do not occur only in wartime: we have people who use them every day to escape responsibility. These people complain of inability to sleep; what sleep they get they say is disturbed by nightmares; their hearts palpitate and they have sensations of falling just before they do drop into a fitful sleep. In the morning they are not rested, they feel suffocated, their eyes pain them, dizziness and headaches are not uncommon; during the day they are easily flustered, they blush or stutter, they have queer unpleasant feelings in various parts of the body, they lack energy and feel tired most of the time. They may feel that people are watching them, following them, or plotting against them.

[6] An author who had been in Spain during the recent Spanish Civil War and who was sympathetic to the Loyalist cause said that there was far less of this kind of escape among Loyalist troops than in the Allied Armies in World War I. Whether his observations were accurate there is no way of knowing now, but they are reasonable psychologically. When motivated highly, as Loyalist troops probably were, people do not try to escape. When they are *forced* to fight for reasons they can not comprehend, they do try to escape.

Not every person who is poorly adjusted to the demands of his life has all these symptoms. As a matter of fact, we are not very certain that any of them are either absolutely necessary to indicate maladjustment, or do indicate maladjustment when they are present. They have been observed in those cases where a maladjustment has been serious enough to warrant psychological treatment. But there are doubtless many people perfectly normal in their adjustment who, for various reasons, exhibit some of these peculiarities in specific situations.

3. THE PREDICTION OF BREAKDOWN

During wartime it is necessary that the army be able to select those who can stand the strain of wartime existence without breaking down.[7] During World War I Woodworth of Columbia and some of his colleagues were given the problem of finding a method of eliminating potential neurotics that could be applied to large numbers of men called for service. Those that we are about to describe may not be the best methods. A skillful clinical psychologist might be able to do better, but he would require so much time that the war would be over before he could really get under way.

Woodworth and his committee had available a mass of poorly systematized observations on the symptoms that we have described above. Most of them were contained in a book by MacCurdy called *The War Neuroses*. A typical case history from another

[7] It has been suggested that constitutional factors determine whether or not dogs become neurotic. With people at least, there is also the possibility that the training a person has had is an important factor. Not only is cultural background important in determining whether or not a breakdown will occur, but it may determine the exact nature of the symptoms if breakdown does occur. British officers, recruited more exclusively from the upper classes, were less likely to complain of bodily symptoms than the men. In the American Army, where there was less class distinction, there was less difference in symptoms between officers and men. Social factors may also be important in determining the frequency of the withdrawal adjustment. Cf. Robert E. L. Faris, "Cultural Isolation and the Schizophrenic Personality," *American Journal of Sociology*, 1934, 40, 115, and Ruth Landes, "The Abnormal among the Ojibwa Indians," *Journal of Abnormal and Social Psychology*, 1938, 32, 14-33.

source is to be found on page 214. The committee selected about two hundred of these symptoms that seemed to have some relation to becoming neurotic under stress. Naturally one wouldn't expect all of these symptoms to be equally important in revealing a neurosis. Just which ones were and which were not, no one at that time knew. The war did not last long enough for the selection of the items that finally was made to have any practical significance, but all the work of this type that has been done since 1918 has its roots in the work of this wartime committee.

Method of selection.—The original list of two hundred items was given to Columbia University students. The exact nature of the information the Woodworth committee hoped to obtain was concealed by labeling the test a "Personal Data Sheet." The items were printed on a page. Each was followed by a T and an F, meaning "True" and "False." If a person felt that generally "his sleep was disturbed" (this was one of the items) he would circle the T. According to the information then available, this would mean that he possessed one item of behavior which indicated a neurotic make-up. Not all the "neurotic" items were stated in the positive; sometimes neurotic make-up was indicated by circling the F. This procedure follows good practice in questionnaire construction.

Out of the 200 items in his original collection, Woodworth retained 116 as a result of some preliminary experimenting. The items can be classified as follows: [8]

Physical symptoms, pains, etc.	28
Adjustment questions	20
Fears and worries	16
Unhappiness and antisocial conduct	16
Dreams and restless sleep	10
Reactions to alcohol, tobacco, drugs, sex	7
Mental symptoms	6
Vacillations	5
Compulsions	4
Questions about family	4
	116

[8] P. M. Symonds, *Diagnosing Personality and Conduct,* D. Appleton-Century Company, New York, 1931, p. 178.

LIST OF MOST DIFFERENTIATING QUESTIONS IN THE PERSONALITY
SCHEDULE

Do you get stage fright?
Do you have difficulty in starting a conversation with a stranger?
Do you worry too long over humiliating experiences?
Do you often feel lonesome, even when you are with other people?
Do you consider yourself a rather nervous person?
Are your feelings easily hurt?
Do you keep in the background on social occasions?
Do ideas often run through your head so that you cannot sleep?
Are you frequently burdened by a sense of remorse?
Do you worry over possible misfortunes?
Do your feelings alternate between happiness and sadness without apparent reason?
Are you troubled with shyness?
Do you daydream frequently?
Have you ever had spells of dizziness?
Do you get discouraged easily?
Do your interests change quickly?
Are you easily moved to tears?
Does it bother you to have people watch you at work even when you do it well?
Can you stand criticism without feeling hurt?
Do you have difficulty in making friends?
Are you troubled with the idea that people are watching you on the street?
Does your mind often wander badly so that you lose track of what you are doing?
Have you ever been depressed because of low marks in school?
Are you touchy on various subjects?
Are you often in a state of excitement?
Do you frequently feel grouchy?
Do you feel self-conscious when you recite in class?
Do you often feel just miserable?
Does some particular useless thought keep coming into your mind to bother you?
Do you hesitate to volunteer in a class recitation?
Are you frequently in low spirits?
Do you often experience periods of loneliness?
Do you often feel self-conscious in the presence of superiors?
Do you lack self-confidence?
Do you find it difficult to speak in public?
Do you often feel self-conscious because of your personal appearance?
If you see an accident are you quick to take an active part in giving help?
Do you feel you must do a thing over several times before you leave it?
Are you troubled with feelings of inferiority?
Do you often find that you cannot make up your mind until the time for action has passed?
Do you have ups and downs in mood without apparent cause?
Are you in general self-confident about your abilities?

In 1928 the Thurstones[9] gave 223 items of this type to 694 entering freshmen at the University of Chicago. The items contained all of Woodworth's questions and many more taken from other sources. Besides the "Yes" and "No" which followed the item there was also a "?" which allowed for a doubtful answer to each question. From their knowledge of psychology the Thurstones arbitrarily decided whether a neurotic person would select the "Yes" or the "No" or the "?" After the papers were scored and arranged in order, the 50 most neurotic and the 50 least neurotic students were selected on the basis of their total score. Each item was then examined to see whether there was any difference in the way the extremes marked it. An item which all 50 of the most neurotic and none of the least neurotic marked would be very discriminating. There was no item that was quite this clearly differentiating but the following are nearly so.

	Neurotic Answer	No. of Most Neurotic	No. of Least Neurotic
Do you often feel self-conscious in the presence of superiors?	Yes	45	4
Do you often feel lonesome even when you are with other people?	Yes	42	1
Do you worry too long over humiliating experiences?	Yes	40	1
Do you consider yourself a rather nervous person?	Yes	32	0

There were some items that failed to differentiate adequately between the groups.

	Neurotic Answer	No. of Most Neurotic	No. of Least Neurotic
Has any of your family had a drug habit?	Yes	0	0
Do you ever walk in your sleep?	Yes	1	0
Are you often in a state of excitement?	Yes	1	0
Has any member of your family been insane, epileptic, or feeble-minded?	Yes	2	0
Have your employers generally treated you right?	No	3	0

[9] L. L. Thurstone and Thelma Gwinn Thurstone, "A Neurotic Inventory," *Journal of Social Psychology*, 1930, 1, 3-30.

From the samples we have given it would appear that the neurotic answer is almost wholly "Yes," but this is not the case: only about three-quarters of them necessitated an affirmative answer to confirm a neurosis and proper editing would have reduced this number.

Now it is clear that had the Thurstones made a mistake in their arbitrary assignment of a "Yes" or a "No" on their original key it would have shown up at this point. The 50 least neurotic would have shown higher frequencies than the high group, and the scoring of that particular item would have had to be revised in order to make it consistent with the others. That there was only one item of this kind discovered speaks well for the psychological insight of the experimenters.

The validity of the schedule.—In the last paragraph we have been skirting a problem which is discussed in technical literature under the title "Validity" (cf. page 45 and page 110). It will be recalled that the determination of validity is a matter of observing how well the test scores agree with the criterion.

In personality schedules or neurotic inventories, there is no well-established criterion. The best that a test technician can do at the present time is to depend primarily on the judgment of experts in clinical psychology who try to see what the common elements are that run through all their hundreds of cases similar to the one shown on page 214. That is what MacCurdy, McDougall, Hollingworth, and others who worked with the war neuroses tried to do.[10] This method gives us a list of items that can be used as a paper and pencil test. Applied to these items, the technique of the Thurstones tries to get rid of the "deadwood"—items that do not discriminate between the extremes in score. When the Thurstones finally select the best 40 or 50 items out of 200 or 300, they haven't added anything the test didn't have in the first place; they have merely refined it, selected the best, thrown away the worst, reduced

[10] One of the first generalizations which would occur to a person making an investigation of this kind is that explosions and long bombardments resulted in a large number of breakdowns. This notion is incorporated in the word "shell shock" which was used to describe these sufferers. By actual count only about one-half of all shell-shocked patients had actually experienced bombardment; some of them never got overseas. Like the "nervous breakdown," "shell shock" is a layman's term used to conceal a multitude of sins.

its size. *In tests where the validity can be determined, it has been shown that a procedure of this kind can improve the validity of a test,* that is, show a closer relationship to a criterion. By inference, when we can't determine the real validity, the same conclusion holds.

The table on page 223 shows the best arrangement that the Thurstones could use, with the data they had available, to prove that their inventory selected the best-adjusted and most poorly adjusted from a college population. Fraternity men, as a group, are probably better adjusted than all the freshman men. There are many individual exceptions, but if a neurotic inventory didn't show this simple group-fact, it wouldn't be very valuable. The table shows a distinct difference between these two populations.

More recently two other investigators [11] using the same kind of questions as those contained in the Thurstones' list (although derived independently from a study of clinical records), have succeeded in demonstrating the validity of the schedule by another, more direct method. They submitted the questions to 250 neurotic outpatients of the Psychiatric and Neurological Institute of Columbia Medical Center in New York City. These patients were carefully selected in that in no case was there any known organic involvement. The normal subjects were college students for the most part. Four random samples from these groups made widely different average scores. The differences were highly reliable in the statistical sense.

From the forty-two most differentiating items given on page 218 we can infer that a *neurotic is one who responds in a disorganized emotional way to situations where there is no adequate emotional stimulus. He has learned to react emotionally to a variety of situations which are not conducive to emotion in the people he associates with. He makes inadequate social reactions to people and to the situations in which people are ordinarily met.*[12]

[11] Ross A. McFarland and Clifford P. Seitz, "A Psycho-Somatic Inventory," *Journal of Applied Psychology,* 1938, 22, 327-339. Students interested in the complete history of attempts to validate these questionnaires will find C. I. Mosier's "On the Validity of Neurotic Questionnaires," *Journal of Social Psychology,* 1938, 3-16, of considerable interest.
[12] Ralph Stogdill, "Neurosis as Learned Behavior," *Psychological Review,* 1934, 41, 497-507.

REGRESSION

M. B., an Australian twenty-two years old, had spent several months at the Front. He was sent to the hospital following a heavy bombardment. When I saw him shortly after his arrival in the ward he was in a completely childish condition. He sat in bed alert and lively, like a young child taking a keen interest in new surroundings. He childishly displayed his few bits of property and pointed inquiringly toward various objects. He showed no trace of comprehension of spoken or written language and uttered no sounds other than "Oh-sis-sis-sis"; this was frequently repeated and used partly as an emotional expression; partly to call our attention to the objects of his curiosity. Given a pencil he made no attempt to write; he seemed to have little or no understanding of the use of ordinary objects and utensils, most of which he examined with mingled expressions of curiosity and timidity.

All his motor functions seemed to be intact, save that when put on his feet he walked jerkily, with short hurried steps, the feet planted far apart. As soon as allowed to do so he slipped down upon the floor and crawled about on his buttocks with the aid of his hand, as some young children prefer to crawl. This peculiar and childish gait and preference for crawling to walking persisted for many weeks.

He could not or would not feed himself and was fed with a spoon by the nurse who, he insisted by gesture, had to taste each spoonful before he would take it, quite in the manner of some "spoilt" infants. He played in a childish manner with various objects, making toys of them, and he quickly adopted and became very devoted to a small doll kept as a mascot by a neighbor in the ward.

There were four exceptions to the generally infantile way in which he acted.

1. When offered a lighted cigarette, smoked it and stuck lighted stub behind ear. Subsequently would light cigarette and throw burning match on bed.

2. Showed some slight command of finger lnaguage.

3. Shown a picture of steeplechase, he became excited and straddled chair and made as though riding horse.

4. Several weeks later, when he had made some progress, but still walked like a child, he was taken to a swimming pool. He stripped off his clothes, dove in and swam.[13]

[13] William McDougall, "Four Cases of Regression in Soldiers," *Journal of Abnormal Psychology*, 1920, 15, 136-56.

FREQUENCY DISTRIBUTIONS FOR THE PERSONALITY SCHEDULE

	PERSONALITY SCORE	FRESHMEN			FRESHMAN FRATERNITY MEMBERS		
		Men	Women	Total	Men	Women	Total
Unusually well-adjusted	0	8	3	11	3		3
	5	18	7	25	3		3
	10	20	13	33	3	2	5
Well-adjusted	15	40	14	54	13	3	16
	20	43	26	69	14	4	18
	25	40	31	71	8	5	13
	30	51	31	82	16	4	20
	35	26	22	48	4	1	5
	40	22	26	48	1	3	7
Average	45	21	27	48	3	7	10
	50	22	23	45	2	4	6
	55	22	19	41	4	3	7
	60	11	15	26	1	2	3
Emotionally maladjusted	65	7	9	16	2	1	3
	70	8	9	17	1		1
	75	6	11	17	2	1	3
	80	8	4	12		1	1
Definitely in need of emotional readjustment	85	3	2	5	1		1
	90	3	6	9			
	95	3	4	7			
	100	2	2	4			
	105		3	3			
	110						
	115						
	120	2		2			
	125						
	130						
	135	1		1			
		387	307	694	84	41	125

As far as we know, anybody at all who has had one or more unfortunate experiences can be made neurotic. All of us have exhibited neurotic behavior on occasion, but as long as this behavior is appropriate to the situation according to the judgment of our associates, we are not called neurotic. A neurotic's behavior is ordinary behavior appropriate to some specific situation which has become generalized. *It appears to be abnormal to us because we are not sufficiently well acquainted with the personal biography of the neurotic person to see that his behavior is perfectly normal for him.*

Precisely herein lies the most important advantage in the use of animals in the study of human neuroses. We can make certain that a cage of white rats has had a completely controlled life history. A human neurotic is usually not seen by a psychologist until after his symptoms have become so troublesome to himself and his associates that he finally decides to do something about them. No clinician has ever seen a neurosis develop; he has had to reconstruct its genesis out of what the patient tells him. And surprisingly enough, most patients, or even most normal people, are not able to recall the really significant features of their behavior biographies.

4. REGRESSION

In emotional situations the most recently acquired behavior is lost temporarily and the individual is reduced to a more primitive stage in his development. Inability to speak is very frequently observed in severe emotional disturbances and stuttering is quite common (page 259). Inability to think of anything to say in a slightly disturbing circumstance is quite commonly reported. In these cases the demands of the situation generally do not extend beyond a few minutes; hence the regression is only temporary. When a child is prevented from getting an attractive toy by a gate that he cannot unfasten, it has been observed that one method that is used in adjustment is to become temporarily more childlike, as evidenced by his motor control.[14]

[14] R. Barker, T. Dembo, and K. Lewin, "Experiments on Frustration and Regression in Children," *Psychological Bulletin,* 1937, 34, 754-755.

The same phenomenon is more lasting if the situation is less transitory. In such cases if regression is adopted as a relatively permanent solution to the problem, we have a serious case of maladjustment to contend with. A new baby in the home is a frequent situation of this kind for a first-born. The child finds it difficult to make an adjustment to the new member of the household and to the attendant circumstances which alter completely his own status. Sometimes, but not always, he adjusts by becoming more infantile himself. Because the new infant is a permanent fixture in the family, this kind of adjustment under certain circumstances persists. The normal development, or progression of, a child who adjusts in this way is critically interrupted. He loses control of bladder and bowel functions, refuses to talk or else simply vocalizes in an infantile way, loses the motor control that has enabled him to walk and feed himself and in all other ways becomes an infant again.

More or less permanent regression is not confined to childhood by any means. McDougall's description of regression in the Australian soldier (page 222) is an example of a persisting maladjustment in wartime which can be multiplied many times. But people also meet situations in ordinary everyday life which may result in regression (see page 230). Nor is regression observed alone in human beings; animals may regress. It is particularly fortunate that they should, because that fact will enable us to make experiments in this field which would be impossible with human subjects and which would throw some light upon an area which now is largely speculative.

People regress under the most unexpected conditions. A child that has been carefully prepared for the expected arrival of a younger member of the household sometimes regresses. A child who has had no preparation at all frequently does not. The best generalization that can be made at the present time is that *whether or not a regression becomes permanent depends upon the consequences of the adjustment.* If the person who regresses "gets his way," i.e., *if the solution is adequate for him—gets him what he wants—it will continue.* But we do not now know with any precision what the facts are that lead to regression on the one hand and continued development, or progression, on the other. Experiments with animals should help us to find some explanatory principles here as they have in other fields.

A beginning on this problem has already been made. The immediately preceding paragraph expressed some uncertainty regarding the conditions under which regression occurs. The previous discussion had implied that regression means going back to childish habits, just because we are childish, but some recent experiments on animals throw some doubt on this interpretation.[15] They leave the impression that *a habit returns in the face of frustration,* not because it is more infantile, but *because it is more firmly fixed in the behavior repertoire than the habit it displaces*. It is true that in most instances a fixed habit is acquired at an earlier age and can therefore be said to be more childlike, but to attribute its return to its childish character is to misinterpret the true nature of regression even though this explanation may suffice as a rough approximation. This notion can be best elucidated by recounting the experimental plans of several animal studies.

A habit—it makes little difference what—can be established in a group of white rats. In one experiment [16] this habit consisted of turning always to the left in a simple T-shaped maze. At a later date another distinctive and incompatible habit was taught; in this experiment the second habit was to turn to the right. Hamilton and Krechevsky called the first habit "A" and the second "B"—names which are still used in regression experiments to designate habits of this kind. After habit B was partly learned it was disturbed by the application of an electric shock just before the animals got to the point where the choice must be made. Under this additional stimulation, which tended to disrupt the more recently acquired habit B, eleven out of eighteen animals regressed to the older and more completely learned left-turning habit A. Why all of the ani-

[15] O. H. Mowrer, "An Experimental Analogue of 'Regression' with Incidental Observations on 'Reaction Formation,'" *Journal of Abnormal and Social Psychology,* 1940, 35, 56-87.
[16] J. A. Hamilton and I. Krechevsky, "Studies in the Effect of Shock upon Behavior Plasticity in the Rat," *Journal of Comparative Psychology,* 1933, 16, 237-253.

mals did not regress we do not know. As a matter of fact, this experiment raises more questions than it answers. It is well known that rats have distinct preferences in turning either right or left; i.e., for a given animal it seems to be easier or more natural to make a turn to the left than to the right and conversely for still another animal. Whether the rats were falling back on a *more firmly fixed habit A*—fixed because of their previous experience—or on a *more natural, biologically determined habit A* is not clear from this experiment.

In a repetition of this experiment under somewhat different circumstances at a later date by another experimenter [17] it was shown that *all* of the rats would regress if habit A were the "naturally preferred" route as well as the route fixed by the experience of the animal, but, unfortunately, the group of animals used was not large, so that we are in no position to say that this result will *uniformly* obtain. The experiment does show clearly, however, that the function of the electric shock is not that of an emotionally disorganizing stimulus, because when the animals were shocked or otherwise emotionally disturbed *before* they were put into the maze, no regression occurred. Apparently habit B has to be disrupted when *it is in process or very shortly before.*

The most recent experiment [18] (Mowrer's) employs an interesting new technique in the study of regression. The rats were placed one at a time in a small box, the floor of which was built of small metal bars insulated in such a way that they served as an electric grill. The apparatus was arranged so that voltage automatically built up from zero to some maximum intensity in a period of two and a quarter minutes. It would stay at this maximum value until the current was shut off by the experimenter at the end of fifteen minutes. The rats soon learned that by sitting quietly on their hind legs and holding their forepaws well off the grill they received a minimum shock. This sitting posture constitutes habit A. At the end of six days all of the five rats used had learned this

[17] Marjorie J. Sanders, "An Experimental Demonstration of Regression in the Rat," *Journal of Experimental Psychology,* 1937, 21, 493-510.
[18] *Op. cit.,* 62-67.

habit. In the second part of the experiment a pedal inside the cage which had been covered by a screen in situation A was now made available by taking the screen away. When the rat depressed this pedal the current was shut off, but the voltage began to build up again immediately under automatic control, so that the whole sequence was repeated. For about the first minute under this condition the rats did not appear to feel the shock, but there

. . . then appeared minor signs of agitation, such as sniffing at the grill, lifting of individual feet, "sitting up," moving the head to and fro, and so forth. As the current became stronger, the agitation became progressively more violent, culminating in jumping, squealing, biting at the grill, clawing at the walls, and random running about. Under these circumstances the average rat would, through chance, hit the pedal and thereby turn off the shock within three to six minutes after its onset. This first, wholly fortuitous escape from shock created a noticeable tendency [on the part of] the animal to stay at the pedal end of the apparatus; and when the shock next became liminal, the resulting agitation consequently occurred primarily in this vicinity. On the second trial, the animal usually hit the pedal within two to four minutes, and very commonly "froze" as soon as it did so, in precisely the position that it happened to be in at the instant when the shock went off (reminding one of the game of "Statue" played by children). On the third presentation of the shock, the amount of random movement that occurred before the pedal was pressed and the shock terminated, was relatively limited. Learning, in other words, was fairly precipitous. By the time an animal had had ten presentations of shock, random agitation had virtually disappeared and the pedal-pressing reaction had become prompt and specific. . . .

This quotation constitutes a description of habit B.

It will be recalled that all five rats learned habit A in six days, and that on the seventh day the screen was removed from the pedal so that the conditions under which habit B could be learned were made available to the rats for the first time. Within ten minutes some of the animals pressed the pedal in the course of their random activity, but for the remainder habit A—sitting quietly on the haunches—had to be disrupted by pinching the animals' toes with a slender rod.[19] This additional stimulation served to start the random activity again so that the pedal-pushing habit B was eventually learned. Habit B was presumably preferred to habit A because it resulted in a complete cessation of the shock, while A only made it less intense. *A control group of five rats learned only habit B.*

Thus we have two groups of rats that present objectively exactly the same reaction when put on the grill: their responses are indistinguishable from one another; all of them uniformly depress the pedal when the shock becomes perceptible. But there is this difference—one of the groups has experienced the prior habit A which it has had to abandon before progressing to B and the other has not had an opportunity to learn any other adjustment.

In the third and critical part of the experiment, the pedal itself was wired in such a way that it now produced a shock when the animal touched it. The situation is now conceptually the same as those previously described (cf. page 226)—when habit B is in the process of execution an obstruction in the form of an electric shock interposes a barrier to its straightforward accomplishment. The results were that the animals in the control group continued to perform habit B in spite of the obstruction, whereas four of the five animals in the experimental group regressed to habit A.

Upon first encountering a given form of noxious stimulation (grill shock), the rats in the Experimental Group in the present study made a characteristic adjustment to it (Habit A). This adjustment represented a *first fixation*. It was not, however, an entirely adequate solution to the problem, and when a new, more completely satisfactory type of adjustment was made available, the animals (in some instances with a little prodding) fairly quickly *progressed* to it (Habit B). This new adjustment constituted a *second fixation*. Now, however, when an "external obstacle" (shock on pedal) was placed in the way of this latter type of behavior, i.e., when a *frustration* was introduced the impulse to terminate the grill shock by means of Habit B was thrown into *conflict* with the impulse to avoid the pedal shock. Since the margin of advan-

[19] This fact is well worth remembering because it is an example of the way in which fixed habits have to be disturbed in order to bring about an adjustment that is ultimately more satisfactory.

Regression in Domestic Life

. . . The subject is a beautiful young woman who for years had been caressed and loved by her parents. The parents were wealthy and had consistently showered gifts and attentions upon their only child; they placed her upon a pedestal, believing their daughter to be nearly perfect. At the age of twenty-two she married a brilliant, industrious young lawyer. From him she expected to receive all the loving attentions, gifts, and flattery that early training had taught her to accept as her due. The husband, however, turned out to be much less demonstrative than she had anticipated; in fact, he expected his wife to be somewhat aggressive in showing love for him. The immediate consequence of the marriage was unhappiness and maladjustment. The young couple talked things over frankly and finally decided to live apart for a few months, in the hope that they would grow to miss each other and could then renew married life with devotion. As a result the girl stayed on a ranch with friends for several months; but after returning to her husband the maladjustment was fully as severe as before. Instead of trying to make herself more attractive to the husband and being demonstrative with him, she spent many hours in crying and complaining that her husband did not love her. At about this time she started to pay long visits to her parents, who resided in a distant city. They were always delighted to see her, treated her like their little child, showering fur coats and other gifts upon her, all the while making affectionate demonstrations. Each time when she returned to her husband after a visit at home she missed more and more keenly the love and attention which her parents gave. The husband became restrained and preoccupied with his work, finding it unnatural to make the expected display of attentions. At this time the young woman frequently unburdened her troubles to an intimate friend, saying, "All I long for is a little love." The visits to her parents' home became increasingly frequent and of longer duration; she showed less and less concern for the husband and displayed a weakening determination to work out a satisfactory love life with him. After a few years they were divorced; and the young woman made a permanent home with the parents, resuming her childhood relationship to them.[20]

[20] P. T. Young, *Motivation of Behavior,* John Wiley and Sons, Inc., New York, 1936.

tage that Habit B had previously had over Habit A was not eliminated (in four of the five animals), Habit A became the preferable (less "painful") mode of adjustment and was reverted to. . . .

. . . The first major point to be emphasized in the present connection is that the regressive behavior here reported was *historically* determined. Since the animals in the Control Group did not abandon Habit B when its previously unhampered execution was interfered with, it follows that the animals in the Experimental Group did so, under externally identical circumstances, solely for the reason that their *past experiences* had been different. In other words, because they had first learned, and later abandoned, a given type of adjustment (Habit A), they were *predisposed* to return to it, in a way that the animals in the Control Group were not, when the subsequently acquired adjustment (Habit B) was interfered with. . . .

Summary.—In the process of growing up an individual learns a great many habits which later have to be abandoned as a result of new demands made upon him by his parents, teachers, and associates. The fact that he himself is becoming larger and more mature also introduces factors causing progressive changes in his habits. All of these habits may be regarded as having a certain stability or fixity of character, so that they offer resistance to change even though a new adaptation to the surroundings would be ultimately more satisfactory. *For this reason some people never really grow up. Habit fixation* of this kind results in many inadequate adult personalities. In addition to the phenomena of *progression* and *fixation,* there is still a third possibility—habits may *regress* from a later to an earlier mode of dealing with situations. The experiments in this section offer examples of each of these phenomena in the field of animal experimentation. Animals rather than clinical material from human beings are used because the principles—which are the same —can be more clearly presented. Obviously a great deal more work needs to be done. For example, in all of the experiments made to date there are only two possibilities: the rat either regresses or he does not. We need experiments which will allow several different possibilities in regression. When a habit is frustrated there should be available and appropriate to the situation several different habits which were learned under a variety of conditions. One simple factor which could be examined would be the relative availability for regression of a habit learned early in life and one learned in maturity. The earlier habit is assumed not to have been used for some little time. Under such conditions would the earlier habit or the later one be more dominant?

Summary of the chapter.—When activity directed toward some goal [21] is frustrated, one of several things can happen, depending on the strength of the goal-directed activity and the effectiveness of the barrier. If the frustration is temporary, the condition fulfills the requirements for a display of temper, as we shall see in Chapter XII. When the frustration is more permanent, when no escape is possible, whatever the subject does, either one of two things happens: the subject becomes hypertense,[22] or lethargic. There is evidence for the assertion that both the constitutional and the cultural factors can determine which reaction will occur.

Sometimes older habits which are usually more childlike or even infantile are sometimes employed. Unfortunately at the present time we do not know enough about all these interrelations to be able to predict with certainty just what will happen in frustrated behavior.

[21] All activity is directed toward some goal. But the phrase is used here to emphasize that the more important the goal, the more severe the ensuing behavior. This fact is observed clinically, but has not yet been demonstrated experimentally.

[22] Considerable progress can be made in treating hypertension by training the subject to relax. Cf. Edmund Jacobson, *You Must Relax,* McGraw-Hill Book Company, Inc., New York, 1934, pp. 201.

XII

THE DEVELOPMENT OF EMOTIONAL BEHAVIOR

BY the time most of us are adults, our fear reactions to snakes, and sometimes to frogs and fish and worms and spiders, are so definitely fixed that it is hard to believe that there ever was a time when we didn't have them. It seems impossible that this paralyzing effect is really a learned thing. It is so intense, and so uncontrollable, that we feel there must be some basis in the notion that the fear of snakes, anyway, must be inherited.

1. FEAR OF SNAKES

Harold Ellis Jones and his wife, Mary Cover Jones, put this hypothesis to actual test by confronting infants, adolescents, and adults with harmless but vigorous snakes.[1] The idea had been tested before, but not with the care nor with the number of subjects that these investigators employed.

Method.—A pen, eight by ten feet by six inches high, was built in the nursery floor. Within the pen, a number of blocks and toys were scattered. There were also two black suitcases. One contained a mechanical toy and the other a six-foot snake (*Spilotes carais*). The snake was a vigorous active specimen. A mechanical arrangement allowed the concealed observer to open the suitcase containing the snake if the child himself did not do so after a reasonable time.

Results.—The results are in the form of protocols, five of which are reproduced on page 236.

[1] H. E. Jones and M. C. Jones, "Fear," *Childhood Education*, 1928, 5, 136-43.

Of fifteen children aged between fourteen months and six and one half years, seven showed absolutely no fear that could be detected. The other eight showed various degrees of withdrawal; among them were two cases that could be definitely interpreted as fear reactions. One of those fear reactions was made by a twenty-six-month-old child. Since this observation was the only withdrawal observed up to three years, it leads us to believe that there is a greater frequency of fear responses in the older age groups.

Tests with older children.—To test this result further, the experiment was repeated with thirty-six school children ranging from six to ten years.

The children were sitting on low chairs in a circle about twenty feet in diameter. The experimenter placed the suitcase containing the snake in the middle of the circle, asking, "Who wants to open the suitcase?" Harry, eight years of age, opened it, and took the snake out when requested. The snake glided about the floor, passing between the feet of one of the boys; no disturbance was shown. The experimenter now asked, "Who wants to touch the snake?" holding the snake's head so that children had to reach past it, and walking slowly around the inside of the circle. The first eleven children touched the snake with no hesitancy. Four boys about ten years of age hesitated, one withdrawing markedly, another falling over backward in his chair. . . . Two girls refused to touch the snake, but jumped up and ran around behind the circle, following the experimenter and watching closely. An undercurrent of reassurance was constantly heard, "He won't let it hurt you. Go ahead, touch it, it won't bite."

Result.—Only nine of the twenty-six children showed definitely resistive behavior, and these were chiefly the oldest in the group.

Tests with adults.—In order to make a comparison with the behavior of adults, the experiment was repeated under somewhat different conditions with about a hundred college students.

In several classes of undergraduate and graduate students, the snake was introduced as "a perfectly harmless animal; the skin of this reptile has a smooth and pleasant feeling, and we guarantee that in touching him no one runs the slightest risk." In some classes the same reptile was used as in the preceding experiments; in others the snake was a boa constrictor, somewhat smaller and of a less "dangerous" appearance than the Spilotes. Of about ninety students nearly a third refused to have the snake brought near; a third touched him, with obvious hesitation and dislike, while the remainder (including as many women as men) reached forward with apparently complete freedom from any emotional disturbance. Several of the women obviously regarded the presence of a snake in the room as an almost unbearable ordeal, and several of the men solved the problem of emotional conflict by retiring to a neighboring room until the experiment was concluded.

Summary.—The whole study on fifty-one children showed that up to the age of two there was no fear apparent; by three or three and a half, there was some hesitation and caution. Definite fear responses occurred more frequently after four. The adults showed more definite fear responses than the children. The girls were no more fearful than the boys; the young women no more than the young men.

These results can be explained by regarding fear as a response to a change in the total situation: *Any change which requires a sudden adjustment that the individual is not prepared to make results in a series of responses that we call "fear."* With a very young infant, the number of different kinds of changes is limited, but as he grows older, more kinds of new things are effective as stimuli. *Fear arises when we know enough to recognize the potential danger in a stimulus, but have not advanced to the point of a complete comprehension and control of the changing situation.*

2. CHILDREN'S FEARS

Jersild and Holmes [2] have reported on an extensive study of fear by an entirely different method. They did not make an experiment like the Joneses'; in the part of their study reported here they merely counted the instances of fear and made a record of what the situation was in which the fear appeared.

[2] A. T. Jersild and Frances B. Holmes, "Children's Fears," *Child Development Monograph,* 1935, pp. 360.

FROM THE PROTOCOLS

Subject 1. Irving, age 1 year, 3 months. Irving sat in the pen, playing idly with the ball and blocks. After being released, the snake glided slowly towards Irving, shipping up his head and deflecting his course when within twelve inches of the infant. Irving watched unconcerned, fixating the snake's head or the middle of his body, and letting his gaze wander frequently to other objects in the pen. The snake furnished only a mild incentive to his attention.

Subject 3. Enid, age 1 year, 7 months. Enid sat passively in the pen, playing with blocks in an unsystematic fashion. The snake was released and moved fairly rapidly about the pen. Enid showed no interest, giving the snake only casual glances and continuing to play with her blocks when it was within two feet of her. When (later) the snake was held by the observer directly in front of her face, she showed no changes in facial expression, but presently reached out her hand and grasped the snake tightly about the neck.

Subject 8. Sol, age 2 years, 3 months. When the snake began moving about the pen, Sol watched closely, holding his ground when the snake came near, but making no effort to touch it. He resisted when an attempt was made to have him pick up the snake (this was the same guarded reaction that he had shown previously with the rabbit and the white rat). He stood unmoved when the snake was thrust toward him, and showed no overt response, save an attempt to follow visually, when the head of the animal was swung in front and in back of him, neck writhing and tongue darting. After the snake was returned to the suitcase, he went to it again and lifted the lid, looked within and then closed it in a business-like manner.

Subject 11. Laurel, age 3 years, 8 months. Laurel opened the suitcase, picking out two blocks which were lying against the snake's body. The snake was immobile and she evidently had no differential reaction to it. The snake was taken out. Laurel: "I don't want it." Avertive reactions, moved off, then stood up and started to leave the pen, although without apparent stir or excitement. Experimenter: "Let's put him back in the box." Laurel: "I don't want it." Experimenter: "Come and help me put him back." After slight urging, she came over and assisted, using both hands in picking up the snake and dropping him quickly when she reached the suitcase.

Subject 12. Edward, age 4 years, 2 months. Edward sat down in the pen and began playing constructively with the blocks. At sight of the snake he asked: "Can it drink water?" Experimenter: "Do you know what it is?" Edward: "It's a fish." He puckered his brows and made slight avertive reactions when the snake was swung within a foot of him, but this was overcome through adaptation in three trials. When encouraged to touch the snake he did so, tentatively, but soon grasped it without hesitation at the neck and body.

Method.—There are four distinct parts of their study in which we are now interested: data collected (1) by observing children less than two years old; (2) by observing children between 4 and 5 inclusive;[3] (3) from children 5 to 12 who were interviewed; and (4) from adults who wrote their recollection of childhood fears.

Groups 1 and 2, comprising 105 children, were observed by adults, generally a member of the family who offered to co-operate in the study. The period of observation lasted 21 days and in special cases even longer. The observers for the most part were not trained, but they were given specific directions on how to write exactly what they observed and were provided with blanks.

The following instances taken from the blanks give some idea of how the records appeared when they were returned to the experimenter.

A child aged 2 years exhibited for a period of several months a marked fear of the noise of rattling window shades. However, he showed no fear of a variety of other noises, including loud claps of thunder during storms.

At the age of 20 months, a girl who had previously often ridden in elevators began to insist that she had to be careful in stepping over the crack between the elevator and the floor. Even though the open space was only an inch wide, it seemed to trouble her. She would hesitate, draw back, look at the crack, and would ask to hold her mother's hand.

A girl, aged 3 years, was very much frightened while in the cellar of her home by a colored porter who released a rat trap which snapped with a loud noise. She subsequently showed no fear of the cellar (a response we would expect), but for some time she continued to claim that she did not "like" the colored porter.

At the age of 2 years, Albert showed extreme fright when he was taken to a lake and saw several people swimming and diving. He cried and refused to go near the water. An effort was made at once to combat this fear. The visits to the lake were repeated and the swimmers co-operated by showing signs of pleasure in going into the water, laughing when they came up after a dive, throwing sticks out to him from the water, going into the water slowly after preliminary play with him. He

---

[3] There was another group in the original study between 2 and 4, but we have not considered it here.

Form Used by Parents in Recording Fears

Name of Child _____ Time When Observation Began _____
Name of Observer _____ Time When Observation Ended _____
Date _____ When Recorded:
                        (1) At time of observation? _____
                        (2) How long afterward? _____

If no fear occurs, simply indicate with a check mark here _____
Use a new blank to describe each fear and a new blank for each period
of observation, even when no fear occurred. Use back of sheet if more
space is needed.

If during the day any of these or other conditions occurred outside of
the child's regular routine, please underline or specify: Child taken visiting, shopping, riding in automobile, to doctor or dentist, etc. Child came
in contact with strange children, adults, or animals inside or outside of
home. Child missed usual daytime nap, had less than usual amount of
sleep last night, had meals at irregular hours, etc.

Underline or specify as to physical condition: normal, lack of appetite,
slight cold, heavy cold, fever, digestive upset, other unusual physical
conditions.

Situation in which child gave signs of being afraid (place, time, what
child was doing at time, persons present, apparent cause of fear, etc.):

Behavior of Child (words spoken, cries, other vocalizations, jumping,
starting, withdrawing, running away, and other physical activity, etc.):

was enticed to put his toes into the water, following a game in which he had been induced to chase a stick. After some play with the stick, the adult threw it to a place where the child could reach it only if he went into the water a few inches. After several repetitions of this technique, the child seemed unafraid of going into the water up to his waist. Traces of fear remained for a long time, however. The following year he again showed extreme fright when he saw someone swimming in rough water. It developed that the fear was due in part to his belief that his mother was among the swimmers. When he discovered that she was not in the water, his signs of fear disappeared. (But he did not then enter the water himself.)

After these records were collected, the fears had to be classified, because one could not read through several hundred specific instances of this kind and arrive at any understanding of them without classification of some kind.

From these data two important tallies were made: (1) describing the situation; (2) describing the behavior of the child.

Procedure with the older children.—The children from 5 to 12 were asked in an interview to "tell me about the things that scare you, things that frighten you. Tell me what makes you afraid . . . Tell me more about that . . . What else makes you afraid? . . . What else?"

There were 398 of these interviews with 398 different children. The questions on fears were preceded by others on wishes, ambitions, likes, dislikes, and so on,[4] so that the children were not suddenly confronted with the necessity of revealing an emotional episode. Had they been required to do so they might not have talked freely about their fears. The slightly less than 900 fears expressed by the 398 children were classified according to the situation.

Procedure with adults.—The adults were asked to recall their childhood fears in answering a questionnaire which covered four specific points (page 242).

The problem of classification was no easy one. The 23 principal

[4] A. T. Jersild, F. V. Markey, and C. L. Jersild, "Children's Fears, Dreams, Wishes, Daydreams, Likes, Dislikes, Pleasant and Unpleasant Memories," *Child Development Monograph,* 1933, No. 12.

topics required to cover all of the cases did not include the numerous subtopics and were as follows:

1. Animals
2. Specific objects or events
3. Sudden movements
4. Lights and flashes
5. Sudden disappearance of persons
6. Rapidly approaching object
7. Sudden or rapid motion plus noise
8. Noises
9. Falling, danger of falling
10. Pain and painful treatment
11. Strange objects or situations
12. Strange persons
13. Danger of threat of bodily injury

14. Warnings
15. Signs of fear in others
16. Loss of property
17. Dreams
18. Failure and ridicule
19. Robbers, kidnappers
20. Dark and being alone in dark
21. Being alone apart from darkness
22. Dark plus mention of imaginary creature
23. Imaginary and supernatural creatures

Each one of these categories was developed until a small manual of classification was required in order to arrive at a placement. We reproduce the subtopics and category 10, *Pain and Painful Treatment,* on page 244.

Results: Classification of situations.—The most important results from the standpoint of our interest are shown in the table on page 241. The various categories are combined in different ways according to the description at the left of the table. The per cent that this combination is of all fears is shown separately for infants, preschool children, elementary school children, and adults. Noises and noisy things, and pain and painful treatment account for almost 50 per cent of infants' fear responses, but as the children become older these things are reacted to in more adequate ways. Animals gain in fear-producing potency as do threats of bodily injury, illness, and death. Imaginary creatures and criminal characters of an imaginary kind introduced through stories, books, and movies become more significant. The adults' recollections of childhood fears agree fairly well with the actually reported fears of later childhood.[5] It is significant that about one-third of the fears that they recollect are still persistent problems for them.

The fears of infancy are related to concrete situations of a rather transitory nature, but as a person becomes older these are replaced by fears of an anticipatory or imaginary character.

THE PER CENT OF EACH GROUP FEARFUL IN VARIOUS SITUATIONS

	Months 0-23	Months 48-71	Years 5-12	Adults
Number of subjects	58	47	398	303
Number of fears		127	886	1,112
Animals	6.7	17.3	20.4	18.8
Sudden unexpected movements, lights, shadows, reflections, flashes	5.6	3.1	2.4	1.6
Noises and agents of noise	25.4	9.4	3.4	3.1
Falling, loss of support, danger of falling, high places	12.7	4.7	1.4	4.8
Pain, medical treatment, etc.	17.9	8.7	3.0	5.6
Strange objects and persons	24.2	7.8	2.7	4.5
Threat of bodily injury, illness, dying	0.0	14.2	11.5	17.2
Criminal characters, burglars, kidnappers	0.0	0.8	9.4	4.0
Being alone in dark	3.4	12.6	7.9	12.9
Imaginary creatures (not including mention of darkness)	1.1	6.3	11.1	5.0

Classification of responses.—It was also possible to classify the responses made by the younger children. In making this tabulation, the given response was entered only once, even if the child exhibited it several times in the 21 days he was under observation. If a child in a given situation dodged, stepped aside, and then ran, a single tally was placed in the category that contained all of these

[5] This generalization is not as clearly supported as it might be in the data shown here. In the original, the years 11 and 12 are separated from the 5-to-12 range with the result that the agreement between the adults' recollections and the fears of early adolescence is more marked.

FORM GIVEN TO INDIVIDUALS WHO WERE ASKED TO SUBMIT WRITTEN
ANONYMOUS REPORTS OF FEARS RECALLED FROM CHILDHOOD

We should like to ask your help in obtaining data in a study of fears. At present we are getting material from several sources.

We should like to get descriptions of fears remembered by adults from their own childhood. We are interested in reports on the following questions:

1. What is the earliest fear you remember? (Age when it occurred; apparent cause; history of the fear; time when it was overcome; if overcome, how, etc.) Were you living in city or country?
2. What was the most intense fear of your childhood? (Age, cause, history, effect on behavior, etc.)
3. Name other fears which were also quite intense. (Origin, history, effect, how overcome, etc.)
4. What other fears occurred during your childhood? (Describe in specific detail as many as possible.)

As far as possible, give information also on such questions as: Was any fear a major source of unhappiness during childhood? At what age? What was the original occasion or cause of the fear? What were the chief causes of fear, the chief helps in overcoming fear? What fears from childhood have persisted into adult years?

The reports need not bear any signature other than Male or Female, but should give present age.

We shall be grateful for your help.

criteria; three tallies in three separate categories would be misleading.

From this table it appears that as children grow older, their reactions to "fearful" situations are somewhat modified. There is less crying and screaming and more whimpering and protesting; there is less clinging to adults and more active avoidance and hiding. *Children learn to deal with situations in different and generally more adequate ways as they grow older.*

Whether or not a child becomes more or less fearful is dependent upon the way he is reared. The kinds of things his associates do when the child once becomes afraid determine whether or not he will be afraid of the same thing a second and a third time.

3. ELIMINATION OF CHILDREN'S FEARS

In another study [6] the parents of forty-seven preschool children were interviewed to find out how they handled the fear reactions of their children. The results are certainly not typical of what the whole population does, because these people were all well educated and lived in urban localities in or near New York City. The most popular methods among these forty-seven people turned out to be:

1. Verbal reassurance and explanation.
2. Verbal explanation, and reassurance plus a demonstration.
3. Use of an example of fearlessness in others.
4. Attempt to cause the feared object or event to occur simultaneously with an interesting unfeared event.
5. Enforced contact with the feared situation.
6. Provision of opportunities for the child to become acquainted with the feared situation of his own accord.
7. Graded introduction of feared stimulus by easy degrees.
8. Specific attempt to promote skills that will allow the child to deal actively with the feared situation.
9. Refusal to take notice of the fear, especially when the child seems afraid.
10. Removal of the cause of the fear by steering the child away from the feared situation.

[6] A. T. Jersild and Frances B. Holmes, "Methods of Overcoming Children's Fears," *Journal of Psychology,* 1, 1934, 75-104.

Pain, Painful Treatment, Painful Situations

Persons inflicting pain, objects inflicting pain, fears arising as result of previous infliction of pain, also tactual shocks.

Persons inflicting pain (other than medical) or corporal punishment with actual specific blows (as distinct from harm such as threatening to shoot, throw into water, etc.) or who by specific word or gesture are immediately threatening to hit, inflict pain or corporal punishment: boy who was slapping child; boy who strikes with fist at child's eye; older boy who claws at child's face; sister who strikes at child; older child who scratches child.

Persons previously associated with pain or previously inflicting pain (as above) but not at the moment active or threatening (other than medical). Person who previously spanked; fear of child who previously hit.

Fear of medical situation, of doctor's office and its surroundings and contents, occurring when child is brought to the situation or told that he will be brought, and appearing in response to the situation as a whole before doctor or nurses begin to approach or to apply treatment or wield any instruments: immediate fear on approach to health station; fear on approach to doctor's office; nurse's office at nursery school.

Fear in medical situation arising only when doctor or nurse begins to perform (*Note:* If child has already shown fear in response to situation as a whole, do not tally here.); presence of surgeon who previously performed tonsillectomy (*ex.:* doctor approaching father).

Fear in medical situation apparent only when specific instrument or piece of apparatus is introduced (*Note:* If child has already shown fear in response to situation as a whole or in response to doctor or nurse, do not tally here.): sight of hypodermic needle; doctor brings out stethoscope; clinical thermometer.

Painful experience or tactual sensory shock, not including medical situation or pain inflicted by persons (*Note:* Count response as fear only if reaction is described as containing an element of fear, including such elements as prolonged crying, clinging, running to mother, trembling, etc., distinct from immediate cry or withdrawal in response to the impact of pain as such.): sprinkle of cold water in bathing; rush of air against child's face through mouthpiece of balloon; fear persisting following a violent coughing attack; hysterical crying and trembling for more than an hour and withdrawal following slipping against hot radiator; electric shock on contact with a transformer (*ex.:* older brother pushes blade of knife across his hand; brother hits mother and mother pretends to cry; older sister hits younger sister; fear when mother approaches to touch hot objects).

Object or event previously inflicting or associated with physical pain or tactual shock: towel child had previously sat on when hot; brush with stiff bristles that previously pricked; fear of plant following previous experience of being pricked by thorns of another plant and fear of leaf of raw spinach apparently for same reason; fear of potato following previous contact with hot potato; electric light bulbs after previous contact with hot bulb; radiators after previous contact with hot radiator; bathtub in which child had hurt her elbow; water basin after previous scald; steam after previous scald; hot-water bags; iron objects after a burn.

Painful situation other than medical and distinct from reaction limited to specific person: fear of basin and preparations to wash child's head; fear of clipping and scissors during haircut; having head washed.

Situations previously associated with pain as in above. Barber shop where part of child's ear had previously been clipped off.

The best methods.—According to the results in this study, the most effective single method was that which attempted to promote skill in handling the situation. The method was used with considerable success in treating the fears of imaginary creatures as well as the more tangible objects and events. This is particularly fortunate because a technique that could be used in overcoming a fear for a real rabbit (introducing the rabbit by degrees at mealtime) would hardly work with a spook. What is meant by competence in handling a particular situation is best illustrated by means of an example.

One child was much afraid of an imaginary dog. Instead of observing the more commonplace procedure of giving the child an academic explanation of the groundlessness of her fear, the mother tried to help the child to outsmart the dangerous creature. She entered into make-believe play with the child and brought the imaginary dog into the play. Through such games the child was helped, so to speak, to acquire skill in dealing with this spectral dog, to manipulate the dog for her own purposes as a character in her own imaginative activities. According to all indications, the child's fear of the imaginary creature completely vanished through this treatment.

Other instances in which the promotion of skills was effective in dealing with fears that apparently had a large imaginative element include fears of the dark or of specific dark places. One mother made a dark and much-feared closet the center of games with her child, thereby leading the child to explore the closet and to incorporate it into her own activities. One mother encouraged her child's interest in doing small errands about the house, and capitalized upon the child's enthusiasm for such activities by sending her occasionally on errands into a much-feared dark bedroom. After some time the child showed no more fear of the bedroom even when no attractive errands were in progress. In both of these instances the child was not dealing directly with the imaginary features that underlay the fear, but in making actual contacts with and coping with the abode of the imagined danger; in gaining competence in dealing with tangible features of the feared situation, the child lost his fear of hidden dangers.

When one considers the multitude of similar fears that affect children, and often persist into adult years, one cannot help wondering at

Frequency (in Per Cent) of Various Forms of Behavior Exhibited by Persons When Described as Being Afraid

	0-11	60 and over
Age		
Total	96	49
I. Vocal expressions		
A. Cries, screams	28.1	22.4
B. Yells, "makes loud noises"	2.1	0.0
C. Calls or cries for help	1.0	0.0
D. Whimpers, exclaims, "fusses," makes frightened noises, protests, "voices apprehension," "catches breath audibly"	4.2	16.3
II. Avoids, withdraws, retreats, seeks help		
A. Withdraws		
1. Runs away, withdraws, retreats, dodges, shrinks	12.5	24.5
2. Stops play, "becomes very quiet," drops toys, "hesitates," stops eating, watches, inspects, paralysis	2.1	2.0
B. Avoids feared event, goes out of way, changes direction, "steers clear," hides	2.1	10.2
C. Seeks help or protection		
1. Runs to parent or other adult	0.0	4.1
2. Looks to adult, turns to adult	1.0	0.0
3. Clings to adult, clutches, reaches for adult, reaches for help	11.5	2.0
III. Aggressive protective reactions: struggles, hits, resists, kicks, pushes, guards another, scratches, etc.	3.1	2.0
IV. Other motor expressive reactions		
A. Trembles, shivers, shudders	0.0	0.0
B. Starts, jumps, "jerks"	12.5	4.1
C. Facial expressions: puckers, "screws face," "scared expression," eyes widen, eyes dilate, "downcast expressions," turns pale, flushes	11.5	6.1
D. Gestures, throws out arms, waves hands, throws up hands, becomes rigid, stiffens, shakes head, "nervous movements," "fidgets," restless movements, covers face, covers head, uneasy, excited, panicky	6.3	6.1
V. Autonomic		
A. Voids self, regurgitates	1.0	0.0
B. Sneezes	1.0	0.0

the number of situations in which techniques similar to those above might be effective. In daily life there are many opportunities for helping the child to face and to master the dangers that lurk in cellars and closets, old trunks and boxes, dark hallways, lonely rooms, haylofts, mysterious houses—to mention only a few of the places which the imaginative child peoples with sinister influences.

The next most successful methods are probably (1) the provision of opportunities for the child to grow acquainted with the feared situation of his own accord by making it accessible to him in his daily environment. The success of this method is probably contingent on the use of no compulsion at all. (2) The graded introduction of the feared stimulus. (3) Verbal explanation accompanied by reassurance.

The poorest method.—The least successful methods are (1) steering the child away from the contacts with the feared situation, comforting and helping him when he is afraid. (2) Ignoring the fear: changing the subject when he mentions a feared situation. (3) Enforced contact with a feared situation, verbal pressure, ridicule and invidious comparison. *Following the use of any of these methods, as a general rule the child is just as fearful as he was before, and in some cases his fears increase in number and intensity.* Sometimes, however, one observes that a child overcomes a fear even where these methods—poor in principle—are used. These exceptions to the generalization can only mean that we do not know all the factors that are operating.

4. ANGER

Goodenough [7] has studied forty-five children's anger responses in very much the same way Jersild studied the fear responses. She depended on parents' observation in the same way and furnished the parent-observer with the same kind of guidance in instructions

[7] Florence Goodenough, *Anger in Young Children,* University of Minnesota Press, Minneapolis, 1931, pp. 278.

and blanks upon which to write the observations. Both of these experimenters recognize that a better method would be to put a psychologically trained observer in each home to record any kind of emotional response, but they both point out that such a method would be so costly that it would be prohibitive.

We may doubt whether these untrained observers could distinguish between fear and anger responses in a great many instances; they also probably based their discrimination on the emotions that they themselves would have in similar situations. What shall we do with the child who kicks, screams, struggles, and finally bites the dentist's hand when he is first brought to a dentist's office? Is he angry or is he afraid? There is really no way of knowing. The important thing is to get a description of the exact behavior. What it means in terms of adult reactions, assuming that we know what they are, is another story.

The responses of kicking; stamping; jumping up and down; striking; throwing self on the floor; holding the breath; stiffening of the body; making the body limp; refusing to budge; pulling away; struggling; running for help; turning away the body, the head, or tightly closing the mouth; refusing to swallow; pouting; frowning; pulling and pushing; throwing objects; running away and running toward the offender; reaching or grabbing; pinching or biting; crying or screaming; inarticulate vocalization; verbal refusal; threatening and calling names; arguing and insisting; are all reported in varying percentages. Most of these things indicate an active dealing with the situation which is absent in the descriptions of fear. *The fear responses involve, in most cases, a withdrawal by a child from an active participation in a situation. Anger responses, on the other hand, involve an active though inadequate participation in the situation.*

Some of the responses assumed popularly to be part and parcel of anger are actually observed only in a few instances. Holding the breath, for instance, occurred only 4 times in the 1,878 emotional outbursts which were reported for the 45 children, in periods varying from 6 to 133 days for the various children. These children were under observation 22,716 hours.

The cause of anger.—The specific and immediate causes of anger, as the table shows, change with age. Outbursts during the first year are mainly associated with bathing, dressing, and handling; during the second year problems of self-help and conflict with authority become more pronounced. From the descriptions of the situations given at the left of the table, it is clear that aside from physical discomfort, the large majority of *anger responses come when a child is somehow blocked in the activity he is engaged in or is about to become engaged in.* This blocking or *frustration* may come from the physical relations in the situation, as when the child gets a toy that he is pulling by a string caught under the rocker of a chair or behind the leg of a table. The frustration may come when an adult or another child interferes by robbing him of a toy or breaking in on an interesting activity with a call to dinner or to bed. However it comes about, there is in most of these cases interference with what to the child is an absorbing activity.

Methods used in coping with anger.—Goodenough provided a list of the methods commonly used by parents in controlling a child once a temper tantrum is under way. This list follows. It is intended to include all things parents do, not just what they *should* do.

Scolding	Appeal to self-esteem or humor
Reasoning	Spanking or slapping
Threatening	Other methods of corporal punishment
Frightening	Deprival of privileges
Coaxing	Putting in a chair
Bribery	Deprival of food
Praise	Isolation in separate room or closet
Soothing	Diversion of child's attention
Ridicule	Removal of source of trouble
Ignoring attitude	Social approval or disapproval
Putting to bed	

The parent was required to write the name of the method, or the successive methods, used in handling the situation and also to indicate the outcome—whether or not the child eventually had his own way. Aside from instances in which the child got his own way because the issue was yielded, we can distinguish instances in which

	Less than 1 Year	1 Year	2 Years	3 Years	4 Years & Older
No. of children	2	9	13	10	11
No. of outbursts	144	426	490	479	339
Routine physical habits					
Going to toilet or to bed, coming to meals, objections to specific kinds of food, washing face, bathing, combing hair, brushing teeth and dressing	27.1	28.4	20.4	16.9	19.7
Changes in routine or change in some minor habit or custom	3.5	1.9	7.6	1.4	1.2
Direct conflict with authority (other than that involved in physical habits and self-help)	0.0	26.6	21.2	16.2	15.1
Self-help					
Refusal of help in some task; refusal to put away toys; unsuccessful attempt to do something alone; assistance forced when child did not invite it	4.2	7.7	11.3	4.8	12.9
Social situations					
Desire for attention; inability to make desires understood; unwillingness to share possessions, and so forth	27.1	19.7	19.9	44.2	28.4
Minor physical discomfort					
Desire for food between meals; wet, soiled, cold; medicine administration; fear or startle change to anger	23.0	3.8	5.8	9.0	4.5
Miscellaneous					
Objection to some particular article of clothing; impatience in the face of some coming event; mother's impatience at child's slowness	8.9	6.8	8.8	9.4	17.0

the child yielded, either voluntarily or involuntarily; various compromises in which the issue was yielded in part; and finally, instances in which the issue remained unsettled because of some interruption which intervened before a conclusion could be reached. Unfortunately, there were so many diverse ways of handling the various situations which arose that the number of cases wasn't large enough to permit clear-cut decisions as to which method is best. It was clear, though, that the *methods used by parents had some effect in determining both the frequency and severity of the anger behavior.*

A child was undressing herself. She got into difficulties and did not want help. She threw herself on the floor, screamed, and kicked, and the mother finally undressed her by force. A somewhat similar example is the case of a girl of three years, for whom the issue is yielded or a satisfactory compromise offered in almost 50 per cent of all outbursts recorded for her. A single instance will serve as illustration. The child had been put to bed for her nap. After the mother left the room, the child moved her bed so that she could climb out of it into the bed of her sister, who slept in the same room. The mother heard her doing so, came in, and replaced the bed. The child jumped up and down, screamed, and refused to go to sleep. The mother first threatened to spank her, then did so, then "appealed to self-esteem," then ignored her for fifteen minutes, and finally allowed her to have her bed where she wanted it.

The poorest methods of dealing with anger.—Soothing, coaxing, and petting seem to be ineffective in terminating anger, and these methods, together with instances where the child is allowed to have his way, were used more frequently by the parents of the children who had more than their share of the outbursts.

A two-year-old girl was taken to her grandmother's for a visit of several days. The mother notes at this time: "Unable to get the child to go to bed either at night or for daytime nap without lying down with her—a very lengthy process." On their return home, the child continued to demand company on going to bed. On the first night the record recounts that the child was willing to go to bed, but wanted mother or father to go with her. When they refused, she screamed for two hours.

The parents tried coaxing and ignoring her screaming, but after two hours, the father finally lay down with her.

On the following night the behavior was repeated. This time the outburst lasted for three hours before the issue was yielded. Again the father finally went to bed with her. On the third night the same behavior recurred. This time the child was spanked, but at the end of one and a half hours she was taken into the parents' room. On the fourth night the child went to sleep at the end of nearly two hours of screaming. The following night the parents went out at the child's usual bedtime, leaving her in the care of the maid. Although the usual outburst followed, it lasted for only fifteen minutes, after which the child went to sleep.

Thereafter the issue appears to have been forced through. However, there are sporadic recurrences of the behavior on several occasions both at night and at nap time, with outbursts lasting from fifteen minutes to an hour and a half. In this child's record there are a number of other instances in which the issue is yielded at the end of a prolonged outburst most frequently caused by the child's wanting the mother instead of the maid to do something for her. If the protest is sufficiently violent and prolonged, the child usually succeeds in getting her own way about it.

Inconsistency of treatment was responsible for a large number of anger responses.

A boy of four and a half was "wandering around looking for trouble." When his mother told him to put his blocks away, he refused, called his mother names, and "was sent to bed until he changed his mind." After a few minutes he was allowed to get up, and his mother "picked up most of the blocks for him." It may be noted here that this mother makes a greater use of threats than any other parent in our group. In many instances these threats appear to be made without any intention of carrying them out. They include a number of threats to tell Santa Claus, to tell Daddy, to put his toys in the attic in case he refused to pick them up, to go visiting without him, and the like.

Picking up toys is a frequent source of controversy between a girl of four and a half and her mother. This report occurs a number of times with no essential difference in the methods employed. The child refuses to pick up her toys, she is isolated, and then the mother offers to let her come out if she will help to pick them up. (Note that in the original request no mention of help is made.) The mother then reports that she picks up most of them for the child. On one occasion this child was playing with her younger brother. She kept teasing him and snatching his toys. The mother shut her in the vestibule. The child screamed and kicked the door, whereupon she was taken out, spanked, and put to bed for a time. The mother reports that upon getting up, the original behavior was resumed, but there is no indication of further punishment. On another occasion the child was in bed for her nap when her father came home. She wanted to go down to see him. The mother at first refused to let her go. The child cried and pleaded and the mother scolded her, but as the behavior continued she was finally permitted to go down.

Typical reactions to frustration can be produced if the child is reared in a general atmosphere of disapproval. If every adjustment he makes is subject to criticism, more than the usual number of outbursts will be recorded. The following case shows how a mother is continually harping on her private "Peck's Bad Boy."

One gets the impression of an overanxious and somewhat self-righteous type of mother who continually irritates the child by a sirupy type of nagging. In the records of her own methods of control, self-congratulatory adjectives continually recur: "I spoke to him *gently*"; "I inquired *casually* why he was so late"; "reminded him *courteously* that lunch would soon be ready," and so on. The following verbatim report is an example:

"The child was eating his cereal at breakfast and complained that it was too hot. He habitually complains about his food. Was told *gently* that it had not been dished up before [the food for] the rest of the family, that mother had been too busy dampening extra clothes to iron for him to make up for the ones he got muddy in puddles last week."

The child's response commands our sympathy. He kicked, snarled, and screamed at his mother, "Don't talk, don't talk!"

The margins of the sheets are written full of accounts of the child's misdemeanors that have no direct bearing on the records. These accounts describe the child's dislike of school, his unkindness to his little sister, his untidiness, his blustering and boasting, and so forth. Apparently the child is being reared in an atmosphere of constant disapproval.

The best methods of dealing with anger.—Diverting the children's attention, ignoring the outbursts, and isolating or reasoning with the child when outbursts do unavoidably occur seem to result in fewer anger displays.

Perhaps the most outstanding tendency that appears in the disciplinary methods used by parents of children who have few outbursts as compared to those used by parents of children who have frequent outbursts is an attempt to avert difficulties before they actually occur or to bring them to a prompt end by diverting the child's attention or by making the original difficulty seem trivial. Although our evidence with regard to the control of anger by prevention as opposed to the attempt to handle it purely by correction is obviously incomplete, since our records as a rule show only those instances in which the preventive method proved unsuccessful and anger resulted, there is nevertheless sufficient indirect evidence in the records to make it fairly certain that such preventive methods were used to a far greater extent by certain parents than by others. In the records of the children who have few outbursts we find occasional notes such as this: "Both children seemed fretful today, but by keeping them occupied at different kinds of things was able to prevent any actual occurrences of anger." When preventive methods fail, we find these parents employing very prompt and ingenious methods of diverting the child's attention before the difficulty becomes serious. The following example will illustrate.

A child of twenty months was pouring water in the sink and getting himself very wet. In an attempt to stop the objectionable activity without raising an issue the mother suggested that he do something else in another room. However, this time the scheme did not work. The child screamed, kicked, and refused to leave the sink. The mother ignored the behavior, went into the next room, and started an activity there in which she knew he would be much interested. This brought the outburst to a close, and the child left the sink in less than a minute. On another occasion the same child was playing with a favorite toy when bedtime came. He refused to go to bed, kicked, jumped up and down, and cried. The mother first diverted his attention away from the original activity by playing the piano for him to dance and after this he went to bed cheerfully. The entire performance occupied three minutes. It may be noted that this child has very few outbursts occasioned by difficulties over the routine habits of going to bed, meals, toilet, and so on, in spite of the fact that he is at an age when training in habits of this kind usually constitutes a real problem in child management.

Summary of the chapter.—*Fears of specific things like snakes and the dark are not inherited, they are learned.* Fear reactions do arise naturally with little of a learned nature in them when any situation is presented to which the child cannot adjust. His inability to adjust may be due to his immaturity and his consequent inability to control the situation. The number of situations of this kind for the very young is extremely limited, but unpleasant experiences of many kinds with doctors, barbers, nurses, and attendants soon result in a remarkable elaboration. As these situations are reacted to more adequately, a greater frequency of imaginary and impossible or unlikely fears develops. *The best method of eliminating any fear is to allow the child an opportunity to master the situation by attaining some skill in connection with it.* Presumably the same technique would be effective for older people. Without such treatment, the fears acquired in childhood are frequently the source of a good deal of unhappiness in adult life.

Anger is differentiated from fear chiefly in that it is an active attack on a situation rather than a retreat from it. The explosive outburst is directed at the destruction of the situation and is not an escape from it. Anger results when the activity of the child is interfered with. It can be avoided by making substitute goals more attractive than the one which is engaging the child's attention at the time when it is necessary to interrupt him. Of course, where one succeeds in doing this, the child isn't really interrupted. In many homes children are needlessly interrupted and interfered with, corrected and curbed, nagged and restrained. In these homes and in others they are treated inconsistently. Both conditions lead to increased frequency in anger seizures. We should also remember that if a temper tantrum results in a child's getting his way, then it is not an inadequate way of dealing with a situation. Under these conditions, it may become a favorite way of meeting any problem even in adult life.[8]

[8] For an interesting account of anger reactions in college students see H. Meltzer, "Students' Adjustments in Anger," *The Journal of Social Psychology*, 1933, 4, 285-309.

XIII

EMOTION IN ADULTS

THE director of the Scripps Institution for Oceanography was sitting alone reading a newspaper before a fireplace in the dining room of his home in La Jolla, California, on the morning of February 3, 1922. It was just before breakfast. His niece, Alice, came downstairs ahead of the rest of the family and stood with her back to the fireplace while she prattled in six-year-old conversation with her uncle. Over her night clothes she wore a dressing gown of flannelette, a soft nap-covered cotton material. Suddenly the whole back of this garment ignited from being too close to the fireplace.

Here we have a situation which contains all the essentials of a typical emotion-producing incident: it is presented suddenly and it is a situation for which one is hardly prepared.

Research on emotion has been hampered because it is ordinarily impossible to reproduce in the laboratory a situation which is as real—as demanding of adjustment—as those that occur in everyday experience. When one tries to frighten or anger subjects, they realize that "nothing really is going to happen" to them, or that "after all this is an experiment"; hence it is difficult to get them really stirred up.

1. DR. RITTER'S REPORT

The instances in which someone has recorded, on the same day, his retrospective description of his own behavior during an emotion are consequently valuable. Dr. Ritter did just that. Later on the same day he wrote the account of his actions as we give them below.

Director Ritter [1] continues his observations on what he did when Alice's clothes were flaming.

Alice was within easy arm's reach of me and my first recognition of what was going on consisted in seeing the flame over her shoulder and hearing a little outcry by her. At the very instant, so far as I can tell, of my awareness of what was happening, there was before my mind the case of a terrible burning of one of my own sisters which occurred while I was an infant, and concerning which I consequently had only indirect knowledge. The burn left my sister badly scarred for life and the event was epochal for the entire family. "The summer Ella was burned" was a more or less cardinal date of reference for many of the incidents in the family history.

Along with this memory-picture stood the picture of the little B. girl. This case happened in La Jolla some six or seven years ago and, although outside my own family connections, it was within my circle of acquaintances and I had considerable knowledge about it. The little girl, considerably younger than Alice, was clothed in much the same way, at least so far as the outer garment was concerned. The fire caught, in her case, from the flame of a coal-oil stove, but the spread of it was apparently much like that which I was here witnessing. The clear proof in these two cases of the high inflammability of cotton flannel gave me a feeling of condemnation for garments of this sort for children, at least.

The B. child was horribly burned. The hands were nearly burned off, the throat and face were made almost unrecognizable, and the little patient hovered between life and death for weeks. However, she recovered, but so disfigured as to make her a distressing object to look upon, and almost helpless. The realization that dear little Alice was in imminent danger of such a calamity was a large part of my "content of consciousness" from the very first instant.

But with all the rest there was the automatic impulse to action. To throw down the paper I was reading, to spring to my feet, and to grasp the girl with both hands were acts quite independent, so far as I can tell, of thought directed to them. But thought as to what course to pursue came almost simultaneously with the initial perception and actions. Four main alternative possibilities presented themselves together, so far as I can tell: smother the flame within the garment itself; smother

[1] Dr. Ritter's account was turned over to his friend, Stratton, who added some interpretive comment and published it under the title, "The Functions of Emotion as Shown Particularly in Excitement," *Psychological Review,* 1928, 35, 351-66.

it in a blanket or something similar; pull off the garment; or flood the whole with water.

As to the choice between these four courses, smothering the flame within the garment, being the most immediate possibility, was tried at first. But an instant of effort showed its futility. No blanket or anything suitable for smothering was available without leaving the room (the possibility of using a small floor rug that was within reach did not occur to me until later, but it seems now that the stiffness and heaviness of the rug and its inadequacy in size would probably have made this alternative less effective than the one pursued). As for extinguishment with water, the chances, though something, were so remote that it was given no great consideration. The only chance was a faucet in the kitchen which meant passing through a door and carrying Alice at the same time, as there was no one to open the door; and obviously the flame was doing its deadly work so rapidly that there was little promise in this direction.

Consequently, the fourth alternative, that of stripping off the flaming garment, was settled upon as offering the greatest chance of success. Alice's outcry and effort to protect her face by throwing up her arms and diving her face down on her chest and under her arms was an instantaneous reminder of the danger of inhaling the flame. Consequently to help her instinctive action in this was part and parcel of the task in hand. My whole action-system operated to the twofold end of keeping the flame from her face and getting the garment off by stripping it over her head. Such a thing as unbuttoning and removing it in the usual fashion was obviously out of the question. To strip it over the head and by main force pull it loose from the body was the only thing. This was accomplished with, however, more hard jerking and hauling than were really necessary. The flaming garment was torn off and thrown into the fireplace to prevent its setting the house on fire, with no burns on Alice except some singeing of her hair. This fortunate outcome was undoubtedly largely due to the fact that she had on a woolen union-suit under her gown. Except for this, the body would have certainly been severely burned. The immunity of the face and mouth was attributed mainly to her own instinctive protective responses, but partly to my effort to keep the front of the garment, which was less enveloped in flame, as close as possible to her face while pulling it off.

But in connection with this part of the situation, a new and terrible thought came to me. Alice's outcries largely subsided toward the end of the struggle; and the query, "Has she actually breathed in the deadly flame?" gave me an instant of dreadful suspense. But this was only momentary, for she scrambled to her feet from the floor where my hard treatment had thrown her, and was ready to run to mother and father— clearly unhurt. The sense of relief at such an issue of such an event is great indeed!

My vocalization was, I am aware, fairly vigorous but almost involuntary and aimless. Whether I uttered any definite call words I am unable to say positively. My impression is that I did not.

The thought of help certainly came into my mind—particularly help in the way of holding Alice so that I might have something to pull against in tearing off the garment. The father naturally came forward most distinctly in this connection, but the mother and Mrs. Ritter were also dimly present in my thought, as were the two members of the household in the kitchen preparing breakfast.

I am quite sure now, as I think back over the affair, that the rapid spread of the flame and the distance away of father and mother, with closed doors intervening, influenced me against spending time or effort trying to get help. Vaguely my thought was, essentially, "yourself alone or disaster."

The organization of these observations came after the incident was over. It is most unlikely that the four alternatives were considered in the order named or that they had any order at all. But for words on paper to have meaning for us we demand organization. Had this material been put down in the way the events actually took place, instead of this neatly organized account, we would have an impressionistic jumble more like a foreign movie with its quick change of camera angle and position and its piling of scene on scene simultaneously that leaves one wondering what it is all about. As it is, there is evidence of considerable disorganization in the rough handling of the child and the aimless but vigorous vocalization of Dr. Ritter.

The usual way to interpret a situation like this is to say that the emotion is valuable to the person who has it. It makes him stronger and helps him meet the situation. Had he been calm he would not have thought of so many different things to do. The more things he can think of doing, the greater the likelihood that, before it is too late, he will hit on one that solves the problem. But there is another way to look at instances like this one. We grant that a solution was accomplished here, but at what damage to Alice? Had Dr. Ritter been accustomed to saving little girls from burning every morning before breakfast, wouldn't he have gone about it more efficiently? Alice might have been less singed than she was and she might have had fewer bruises.

The physiological changes that take place in a person who is excited, angry, or afraid do make him stronger, but they fit him for survival in a rough-and-tumble, devil-take-the-hindmost kind of living that is entirely inappropriate since man dispersed from Central Asia.

2. A LABORATORY EXPERIMENT

A method used in the experimental laboratory to produce a sudden and unexpected stimulus causes the subject to drop backward.[2] Blatz [3] provided a chair for his subjects, the back of which would drop when released by a trigger mechanism. The main group of eighteen subjects had no notion concerning what would actually happen when they first agreed to take part in the experiment. The first time the chair dropped backward gave them as much of a shock as it would anyone in a similar circumstance. Their responses were compared with those of three other subjects who were told what to expect. In the second part of the experiment the chair was dropped for a second time. The subjects were in a condition of heightened expectancy during the interval between the first and second fall because they did not know the exact instant when the chair would give way.

Blatz sought to measure the changes that took place in the breathing and heart action of his disconcerted subjects. His interest in these two aspects of behavior which result from this kind of stimulation was doubtless engendered by the common observation that when a person is taken unaware—when figuratively his chair

---

[2] Other investigators have had their subjects watch the experimenter decapitate live frogs with a dull knife, put their hands in a bucket containing live frogs, and so on.

[3] W. E. Blatz, "The Cardiac, Respiratory and Electrical Phenomena in the Emotion of Fear," *Journal of Experimental Psychology*, 1925, 8, 109-32.

falls from under him—his heart rate increases and his breathing rate quickens.

A considerable amount of preparation is required in order to demonstrate these simple facts in the laboratory. A rather complicated setup was used to record the heart rate and breathing changes. The record finally obtained resembled that shown in Figure 52. Periods of inspiration are plainly shown at the lower edge of the plate. Alternating with these, the expiration periods are shown at

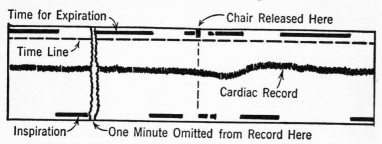

FIG. 52.—A tracing from one of Blatz's figures. Inspiration at lower edge; expiration at top. The cardiac record is in the center. (From Blatz, *Journal of Experimental Psychology*, p. 112.)

the top. The cardiac record runs through the center. The change in the cardiac record at the point where the chair was released shows a change in the vigor and rate of the heart-muscle contraction, but the picture is somewhat complicated because other muscles also contracted and resulted in additional electrical effects which were also recorded.

Blatz's principal interest in this experiment was to find out whether an objective record like this could be used to find out whether a person has experienced a "fear." If the subject reports that he was afraid when the chair was released, can one find any reliable indicator of the "fear" in the heart and breathing records? He concluded that it was possible. *The subjects who said they were afraid showed more profound changes than those who reported that they were not afraid.* And we must remember that Blatz was recording only a small part of the total number of internal changes that must have taken place.

When his control subjects' records were compared with the

naïve subjects' records, he was able to show that the effects were less marked with those people who had an insight into what would happen to them. This observation supports a generalization that was made earlier: *An emotional response takes place when a situation is presented for which the subject is unprepared*. This experiment shows that it can be made less intense if the subject is prepared beforehand for what will happen to him.

3. LIE DETECTION

If these changes in breathing and heart rate follow harsh stimuli like Blatz used, could sensitive instruments record similar changes that would presumably be present when the subject wasn't treated quite so roughly? That there are internal changes of this type is evident to anyone who has ever lied to his roommate or to his girl friend. We hope that the other person won't notice these internal changes which are perfectly obvious to us even though they are principally inside us and consequently hidden to a casual observer.

The question of lie detection has intrigued criminologists since the days of Lombroso [4] (about 1880), the enthusiasts in the field expecting to find a particular pattern in the pulse, blood-pressure, and breathing changes that would indicate whether a person was lying. But a careful study of numerous records by many competent psychologists over almost half a century has shown that *there are no special changes in a whole array of internal responses that would serve to distinguish any one emotional response from any other one*.

Lying, like being afraid, being angry, or being surprised, results in internal changes which cannot be distinguished from one another or from a whole host of other special conditions that we have names for. Precisely speaking, there is no lie detector. There is no instrument which, when attached to a person, rings a bell or

[4] A famous Italian criminologist, most of whose work has been discredited. He believed that there were "criminal types" of men who could be recognized by certain "stigmata of degeneracy" like low foreheads and eyes set too close together.

lights up a red lamp when he lies. But there are instruments that have been called "lie detectors" that are simply special arrangements of standard laboratory equipment. Particular attention is given in their construction to the features of portability, compactness, and ruggedness.

One of the most popular of these instruments depends entirely upon registering breathing, pulse, and changes in blood pressure. A pneumograph is placed around the subject's chest. As he breathes, movements of his chest wall are faithfully reproduced on a moving tape by means of a writing lever. A rubber bag such as a physician uses to measure blood pressure is wound around the subject's arm just above the elbow. Unlike the physician, who inflates this bag with air so that sufficient pressure is created to stop entirely the flow of blood in the arm, the experimenter in this instance only partially inflates the bag. This technique allows a continuous registration of the pulse, and changes in level of the record give some indication of blood pressure changes, although not precisely.

Expert opinion required.—Typical data may be found in Larson's book,[5] a record of actual police cases. It must not be assumed that such records are so clear that anyone can identify the points at which lying took place. Long experience is required, not only in identifying the significant changes but also in formulating the procedure in each new case, and few police officers have the necessary background to plan or to administer the technique.

Objections to the technique.—Not all psychologists, by any means, are agreed on the usefulness of lie detection as a practical technique in criminology. Some hold that the whole procedure is in an experimental stage and that it should be withheld from the public until we are more certain of our results. Some of these objectors hope eventually, however, that the method will replace the usual "third degree." The proponents of lie detection hold that even now the method is more accurate than the usual grilling of suspects in which confessions can be wrung from innocent suspects by long hours of questions, suggestions and accusations. Indeed, it is pos-

[5] J. A. Larson, *Lying and Its Detection,* University of Chicago Press, Chicago, 1932, p. 295.

sible for a person to become so confused that he comes to believe he has committed a crime of which he is actually innocent.

Another objection involves more strictly technical considerations. As we have seen, *lying cannot be distinguished from a number of other conditions of which fear is one.* What would happen if an innocent person became afraid? Would he be counted guilty just because he was afraid? The proponents of the technique point out a fear of this kind is manifest throughout the record, while a guilty person shows these same changes only in response to significant questions about the crime. After the confession, as we have seen, a repetition of the same questions produces no observable disturbance. When a person meets the critical situation in which he is being questioned as a suspect of a crime actually committed by some offender and realizes the seriousness of the situation, to reply to a question which he does not wish to answer involves a conflict between telling the truth and telling a falsehood. Whether this is a stimulus which arouses an emotional response of fear, anger, confusion or tension matters little in this instance. The important thing is not what name to apply to the response but the fact that a change in breathing, heart action, or some other organic change actually occurs at significant points.

4. GALVANIC SKIN RESPONSES

As part of a course called "psychobiology" in the medical school of Johns Hopkins University, Adolph Meyer regularly requires the students to write autobiographies. These are rather frank statements for the most part in which the students try seriously to write on paper a great many of their likes and dislikes, emotional responses, feelings, hopes, ambitions and wishes of a domestic, cultural, educational, and vocational kind. Some of these papers are, according to direction, marked "Personal" and are intended for the information of Dr. Meyer alone. Others, perhaps not so intimate, are not so marked and as a consequence are available for other people to study.

Syz [6] has made use of some of these in a study of the galvanic skin responses. These responses are observed when a sensitive galvanometer is connected to the body, and apparently occur in response to various stimuli but more markedly perhaps to those that would be called "emotional" or affective.

Syz examined sixty-four medical students in all, administering four classes of stimuli to which reactions on the galvanometer were obtained. First, a list of fifty-five words was read at intervals of from eight to twelve seconds. Some of these related to family, sex, social standing, success, money, religion, moral standards, and self-esteem, all of which would be likely to produce emotional responses. There were included in the fifty-five, at intervals, other words like *book, green, window, basket,* which ordinarily are reported to be neutral.

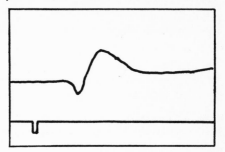

FIG. 53.—A single galvanometric deflection. This is a tracing of one of Syz's photographs.

After the words were read, a pin prick on the right forearm and one on the neck were administered. Then there was a threat of a pin prick on the left forearm, and after the threat—which itself could produce an emotional response—the subject actually was pricked slightly. The words were then read again.

The subject was to remain seated in a quiet semidark room, shut off from a view of the apparatus and the experimenters except when the sensory stimuli were applied. He was asked not to speak and to remain as relaxed as he could.

In addition to the galvanic response, which was registered on photographically sensitive paper, the way the subject breathed was also registered on the same tape. There was also a time line and a stimulus line. Figure 53 shows how the record looked after the sensitive paper was developed. After the stimulus word was spoken, there occurred typically a single deflection of the galvanometer as shown in the displacement of the *GSR* line. Not all of the curves look like the one shown. There are various irregularities and secondary effects which complicate the picture. There are even some curves that have no plausible relation to the stimulus at all. The number of responses that could be directly attributed to the verbal stimuli varied from seventy-one to none for the different subjects. The average frequency for the entire group was thirty-four for the one hundred and ten words.

Syz analyzed the responses aside from their frequency, in terms of their shape, their time relations to the stimulus, and their amplitude.

Relation to the autobiographies.—The autobiographies enter the picture when the experimenter tried to find some distinguishing characteristics in them which would account for the wide range in the number of direct responses shown by the galvanometer. The smallest number of responses were zero, six, and eight for the one hundred and ten words. Evaluations of the autobiographies for these three subjects follow:

1. *No response.* Generally cheerful. Likes everybody; says that he never disagrees with anybody; socially well adapted; has no special problems. Describes his temperament as happy, foolish, joking, childlike. Emotions of others stir him but little.

2. *Six reactions.* Enthusiastic. Accepts things always as they are; not hard to please. Time filled with actual tasks; constant in his work and much interested in everything he does. Says he has no imagination. Conventional; no difficulties of adaptation.

3. *Eight reactions.* Interested in things. Clocklike regularity in daily activities. Says he reacts to things with calmness and composure. Ambitious, and activities well adapted in a self-confident and conventional way.

There were four people who showed an extremely high number of reactions, seventy-one, seventy, sixty-seven, and sixty-six. Summaries of their autobiographies follow:

1. *Seventy-one reactions.* Timid and overmodest. Many interests; more complex character than the average. Describes temperament as

outgoing, active, happy, but oversensitive. Stirred deeply by moods of others.

2. *Seventy reactions.* Of meditating nature, musical. Difficulty in mixing; shy with girls. Easily embarrassed and influenced by slight disturbances. Overconscientious. Says he is very emotional, moody, self-centered, acting on the impulse of the moment.

3. *Sixty-seven reactions.* Cheerful. Inclination to hot temper but controlled. Uneasy with strangers. Easily homesick and "blue"; does not always get over discouragement quickly.

4. *Sixty-six reactions.* Generally in good spirits but bashful. Complains of feelings of inferiority; at times retiring. Activity in spurts. Says he is influenced to a great extent by the esteem of others, that he is diffident and self-depreciating. Tendency to sarcasm.

It seems reasonable to conclude tentatively that nervous, easily worried, easily embarrassed persons give relatively large numbers of galvanic skin responses, and that, on the other hand, the emotionally stable give few. There are certain reservations to the conclusion that we will treat later.

From other observations which Syz made it appears that the *magnitude* of the response is not important in discriminating between the emotional and the nonemotional. A big deflection indicates the relative importance of a stimulus word to the subject, but that importance is specific, not general; a person who gives few responses may occasionally give big ones and still not be "emotional" as revealed by his autobiography. *There was no evidence that the different kinds of emotional responses could be identified in any characteristic of the deflections.*

This experiment is no more than a beginning in this extremely important field. The method suffers because the sixty-four casual autobiographies cannot be arranged in order like the galvanic responses, and no precise comparisons can be made. When we work with the extreme cases only we can't be certain how many of those between these extremes will violate the generalizations that we draw. When we commence to select only a few extreme cases, as this experimenter has done, it sometimes happens that we shut our eyes to all the exceptions.

The autobiographies themselves are likely to contain only the socially acceptable information about their authors. People report about themselves in stereotypic ways following conventional patterns laid down by the novels and biographies they have read and the movies they have seen. They may not be willing to report all of

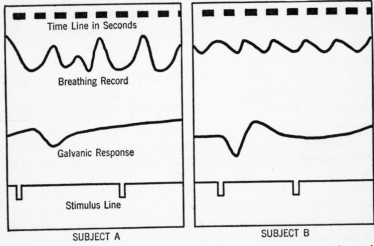

Fig. 54.—Both subjects said that there was no emotional response to the words "misspent youth," both said that there was a response to the word "Father." The objective records show just the opposite condition to obtain. "Misspent youth" was given simultaneously with the first depression of the stimulus line; "Father," at the second.

the private emotional episodes that they have experienced. As a matter of fact, there is some suggestion that this might be true from Syz's own work. He found that his subjects frequently reported some emotional disturbance for words like "father" when no galvanic response was present. On the other hand, a phrase like "misspent youth" actually resulted in some cases in marked deflections, but the subjects denied that there was any emotional response at all. *Most of them reported fewer than one-quarter of all the responses that could be identified in the galvanic records.*

5. EMOTION AND THE MOVIES

Ever since movies became popular there has been a controversy concerning their effect upon young children. Some critics believe that the vivid portrayal of tragedy, crime, and romantic love has a degrading effect upon the young. The producers have argued that such pictures always teach a moral, and therefore the exposure to dramatic and erotic pictures is elevating, but others more disinterested claim that, though we may overlook the moral aspect, such pictures overtax young children by creating an undue amount of emotional excitement. It is only recently that this problem has been attacked by the application of scientific psychological methods.

One such study is the investigation by Dysinger and Ruckmick.[7] In one of their experiments, motion pictures were shown in the laboratory. The pictures used—"Hop to It, Bellhop," a slapstick comedy, and "The Feast of Ishtar"—presented many scenes characterized as portraying danger and conflict and love episodes. Another series of experiments was conducted in a theater. Here the pictures were selected at random, with no effort to get extreme results from more frightful pictures. Results were obtained from "Charlie Chan's Chance," "The Yellow Ticket," "The Road to Singapore" and "His Woman."

Though pulse and breathing records were obtained, chief reliance was placed in the records of changes in electrical skin resistance as obtained by the "psychogalvanograph," a sensitive galvanometer similar to the one Syz used in his study (page 265). In the theater, the equipment, the experimenter, and the subject were given a space in the gallery or back row of the main floor slightly removed from the main body of the audience. After the film had been shown the subject was asked merely, "What were the exciting parts?" After pictures displaying romantic or erotic scenes a second question was sometimes asked, "How did you like the love scenes?" In general no other questions were asked nor reference made to any detail.

[7] W. S. Dysinger and C. A. Ruckmick, *The Emotional Responses of Children to the Motion Picture Situation,* The Macmillan Company, New York, 1933.

The subjects may be classified into the three average age-groups of nine, sixteen, and twenty-two years respectively, though some were near the six-year level and a few were as old as fifty years. In general, the reactions, as indicated by the degree of galvanic response, were as follows: To danger and conflict the twenty-two-year-olds reacted least and the nine-year-olds reacted most. To erotic scenes the youngest group exhibited the least reaction and the sixteen-year-olds the greatest, with the oldest group falling in between.

Method of handling data.—A summary of the results taken with the first part of "The Feast of Ishtar" will make clearer the procedure in dealing with data of this kind. In this case the subjects were divided into the age-groups 6-11, 12-13, 14-15, and 16-18 years. The numbers given in the synopsis of the film designate the specific scenes which the experimenters wished to investigate.

(4) This scene was classed as erotic because of the scanty clothing. Among the seven subjects under eleven years a substantial average was found because of the strong reactions of three girls and one boy. Among those of eleven and twelve years the average was much lower. The 13-15 year group averaged much higher. The 16-18 year group gave a still higher average.

(7) Another erotic scene. The groups 6-10 and 11-12 gave small responses. About half of them were zero readings. The 13-15 group responded with a significant but not extreme average of deflection.

(12) The same erotic elements. The two younger groups show small increases over (7). The 13-15 group gave a small but consistent deflection. Among the 16-18 group there was a larger deflection.

(14) A close-up. There was a considerable response from the 6-10 group. The 11-12 group gave a much smaller average. The 13-15 group gave a significantly larger response and the 16-18 group still larger. Those older than 18 gave a smaller average.

(25) Unambiguously erotic. There were small responses in the two younger groups, increasing responses in the 13-15 and 16-18 groups with a decreased deflection in the adult group.

(29) This scene is ambiguous. The kiss is erotic but the servant

peering through the drawn curtains was interpreted by youthful subjects and possibly by some adults as presaging danger.

(32) Unambiguous love scene. The index of deflection of the 6-10 group was small with five out of eleven cases giving zero readings. The 11-12 group much higher deflection. A small increase was given by the 13-15 group. The 16-18 group showed a decrease in average with only one zero reading.

(34) Tisha in Jether's arms. The 6-10 group showed a definite response, especially among the girls. The 11-12 group gave a larger response, one of the girls giving a very large reaction. The 13-15 group gave a much smaller response with a very large deflection from one of the boys. The 16-18 group gave a greatly increased average.

(51) Conflict and eroticism (57 and 58). These scenes gave small deflections in the 6-10 group, larger deflections, especially at 58, for the 11-12 group, increased response in the 13-15 group, increased response in the 16-18 group and a sharp decrease for adults, especially at 57. Similar comparisons appear at 61.

Conclusions.—When the results with the different age groups from all the pictures were compared with their verbal reports, it was found first of all that *a child's reactions can not be predicted upon the basis of an adult's judgment.* The adult perceives the artificiality of the pictorial story; he judges the excellence of the performance and, in effect, remains aloof from the scene. The child, on the other hand, perceives specific situations, but not as they are interpreted by the adult, and he frequently fails to grasp the meaning of the whole story. Thus, the erotic scene (29) in the early part of "The Feast of Ishtar" was interpreted as "danger," and the final scenes portraying the destruction of the temple are variously described as "a storm," "a fire," "an earthquake." That they were destroyed because they were wicked is entirely overlooked.

Scenes of pseudo tragedy, danger, and conflict incited the greatest intensity of response in the age-groups under twelve years of age, somewhat less intense near the age of sixteen, and much less among those over nineteen years. In scenes of love and scenes suggestive of sex, most children below the age of nine years gave very

THE FEAST OF ISHTAR

The picture opens with a view of the feet of the dancing priestess, Tisha, followed by a full-length view. (4) After the dance she lies on a divan (7) and her maids fan her. A youth enters and kneels before her announcing the arrival of an expected visitor. She dismisses him, rises, and calls her maids to prepare the beauty aids. She lies down again (12) and in a close-up stretches her arms above her (14).

Jether, a country youth of wealth, is introduced. He enters the palace with awe and is admitted through luxurious curtains to the presence of Tisha. He approaches bashfully as Tisha responds boldly. He slowly comes nearer to her. She reaches out with her foot, touching him on the hand (25). He takes her extended hand and walks nearer to her, sitting beside her. A servant peers through the curtains. She guides his lips to hers (29) and then turns her scantily clad back. After hesitation he kisses her back and she reclines in his arms (32), where he kisses her lips (34). Another scene shows her displaying her wiles as she reclines on the idol, Ishtar (41).

At a later time Jether enters the palace and sits on a divan. Tisha is engaged with an unseen lover who gives her a ring from behind a curtain, receiving a kiss as a reward. She approaches Jether, who kisses her hand, noting the new ring. They quarrel over the ring (51). A jewel merchant tries to sell Jether jewelry for Tisha. Jether refuses to buy in spite of Tisha's plain request. The conflict reaches a climax as she throws the wanted jewelry on the floor.

A large hall is shown into which Pharis, a sea captain, comes. Dancing girls are seen upon the stage. As a part of the act, they discard their capes (57) and then their skirts (58). They come onto the hall floor and dance around Pharis (61). Tisha's servant offers to introduce Pharis to Tisha. Pharis enters Tisha's palace, receives a welcome from her and drinks with her. Tisha's servant extends his hand in mute request for a reward from Pharis for the introduction but Pharis in answer spurts wine over his hand. The servant leaves as Pharis and Tisha drink.

little response. As age increased, the number responding increased, with the greatest responses at the sixteen-year level.

Summary.—In general we may say that these investigations show that scenes of danger, or those thus interpreted, are most stimulating to children under twelve years, but love and erotic scenes do not begin to be affective until about the twelfth year, except in a few cases. Finally, the judgment of adults is inadequate in predicting what will stimulate the child.

Summary of the chapter.—The first section gives one of the few accounts we have of a person's actions as they were recorded closely following an incident that everyone would agree is emotion-producing. The characteristic behavior seems to be a disorganization in which the individual is rendered less capable, albeit stronger and more vigorous. His movements are poorly co-ordinated and he loses his most recently acquired behavior (both ontogenetically and phylogenetically). The second section shows how conditions resembling this one are attempted in the laboratory. The principal reason for making these physiological studies of breathing and cardiac response was to find if there was a typical pattern in breathing or in any other physiological variable which would serve to differentiate fear from rage, from love, from anger, and so on. In the literally hundreds of experiments that have been made, of which this one is only a sample, no differentiae have been uniformly found. The third section discusses one of the more popular "lie detectors" and points out that the instrument is misnamed. Although there is some question about the interpretation of the results, it is concluded with some reservation that the method will prove a useful one in the hands of experts. The fourth section points out a fundamental weakness in Syz's conclusion regarding the relation between "nervousness" and the *GSR,* but the experimenter deserves credit for a pioneer experiment in an important field. The last section shows how the *GSR* apparatus can be used in a practical situation.

XIV

SUGGESTIBILITY AND HYPNOSIS

IN previous chapters we have shown how human behavior can be controlled by setting up various conditions of motivation. There was the implication that very frequently words, gestures, and symbols of other kinds were as effective in controlling behavior as the more strictly biological rewards. It is this theme which is continued in the present chapter.

When a person develops a set of symptoms for a disease after hearing them described or when he recovers from a headache after taking a harmless placebo, he is said to be suggestible. A woman recently said that when she was talking over the telephone to a particular male friend she could always smell his pipe. She was convinced that odor stimuli could be transmitted over telephone wires. We know that they can not be, but we can accept the woman's statement as true, because the effect is easily explainable in the same terms we use for accounting for any learned effect. It could be said that this woman was suggestible to the extent that she had learned to associate the sound of a particular voice with the odor of a pipe. If that is true, then we are all suggestible, and I suspect we are, in different degrees and to sets of stimuli that are extensive in some cases and more restricted in others. Suggestibility, then, is not the unique property of a few people.

1. SUGGESTIBILITY

Suggestibility merely means that people respond to the indirection in a given situation. In the example given above, although no odor stimuli were present, the woman definitely did experience an odor of a pipe. The same result could possibly be obtained if one had commanded her to sniff and described for her the odor of burning tobacco, but in such an instance the suggestion would have bordered on a command rather and would not have fallen into a classification of suggestion.

The late E. E. Slosson,[1] a chemist, is responsible for an experiment which has been used frequently in class demonstrations of suggestibility. One day he brought to his lecture hall a bottle of what he said was a new compound having a particularly penetrating odor and he wanted to find out how quickly its odor was diffused to those in the room. Would the students please hold up their hands when they smelled the odor? Soon those in the front row were holding up their hands, then those in the second, and so forth until practically everybody was sure he had smelled something. Then it turned out that the bottle contained perfectly odorless distilled water. There have been many variations of this demonstration made. If the odor is described to be like peppermint or lemons, more people seem to smell it than if the supposed odor is not exactly specified. One experimenter made a colored grade-school pupil so sick from smelling distilled water that she had to be dismissed from school for the remainder of the day. All the experimenter did was to hold her head away from the distilled water as she poured it on a piece of cotton, all the while making a face as though the nonexistent odor were nauseous.

Another factor seems to be the prestige of the person who is doing the suggesting. We are more inclined to be impressed if one person tells us a thing than if another lesser light tells us the same thing. Slosson had more prestige than Slosson's assistant would have had. It is common to distinguish between prestige suggestion in which a person is involved and nonprestige suggestion in which the nonpersonal factors are effective in producing the effect.

Prestige suggestion.—One of the simplest examples of an experiment in which the effectiveness of prestige suggestion has been measured is contained in the pioneer investigations of the French-

[1] E. E. Slosson, "A Lecture Experiment in Hallucinations," *Psychological Review,* 1899, 6, 407-8.

"Place beside each name a figure indicating the order of preference you have for the following authors. Make your judgment solely on the grounds of subjective liking for the words of the writer. If you have no feeling of like or dislike for a certain author, you may omit his name. Place the figure (1) beside the name of the writer whose work you like best, (2) beside the next, and so on until you have arranged all with whom you are acquainted."

Sir James Barrie
Joseph Conrad
James Fenimore Cooper
Charles Dickens
Thomas Hardy
Nathaniel Hawthorne
Rudyard Kipling
Edgar Allan Poe

John Ruskin
Sir Walter Scott
Robert Louis Stevenson
William Makepeace Thackeray
Tolstoy
Mark Twain
Walt Whitman
Thornton Wilder

men, Binet and Henri.[2] They had a schoolmaster show a group of his pupils a five-centimeter line and ask the students to reproduce it from memory a few minutes later. He then showed them a line only four centimeters long but told them that it was *longer* than the first line they had seen. They were then asked to reproduce the second one from memory. Only nine of the eighty-six children were able to resist the statement of the teacher and actually reproduce the second line as it actually was—shorter. This experiment tells us nothing about the basis of prestige suggestion but merely quantifies the susceptibility of the young children to statements of a teacher when the statement is contrary to the facts. We might reasonably infer that most children go through a process of learning that most of what adults, particularly teachers, tell them is true and as a consequence any statement of an adult is likely to be accepted without questioning.

A demonstration of a more subtle kind of suggestion is found in an experiment reported by Sherif.[3] The experiment was conducted in two parts. In Part I, which was preliminary to the really important part of the experiment, the names of sixteen well-known authors were presented to the subjects in approximately the form shown on page 276. This process resulted in a series of preferences which were used in the second part of the experiment.

One month later the same subjects were given sixteen slips of paper on each of which was a short selection of three or four lines. Three judges had previously agreed that these excerpts were about equal in literary merit. Each selection was attributed to one of the sixteen authors mentioned on page 276 by placing his name under it. Actually, however, they were all from a single author—Robert Louis Stevenson. The subjects were asked to assign a number to each selection as in Part I, but this time they were to make their judgments solely on the grounds of liking or disliking the passages.

A comparison of the two orders from Parts I and II of this

[2] A. Binet and V. Henri, *La Suggestibilité*, 1900.
[3] Muzafer Sherif, "A Study of Some Social Factors in Perception," *Archives of Psychology*, 1935, No. 187.

experiment showed that *the subjects were strongly influenced in their judgments of literary merit by the prestige of the author in question*. There were several subjects who ignored the authors' names and in these cases the relation was low. Again we find that prestige is no mysterious quality that some people carry around with them. The preference for the authors in the first place was obviously determined by an evaluation of their work arrived at either independently by each person as a result of reading, or through hearsay evidence accepted from others.

Nonprestige suggestion.—In the nonprestige field we have Williams's experiment [4] which, in turn, is based on several older ones.

A coil of wire on a table was connected conspicuously to a battery through a knife switch. Closing the switch would cause the coil to become heated slightly. But current could not pass from the battery to the coil, even when the knife switch was closed, unless a button out of sight of the observer was covertly pressed by the experimenter's knee. The directions to the subject were:

The purpose of this experiment is to determine the smallest amount of heat that you can feel with your finger.

When the experimenter says "ready" you are to place your finger on the coil and hold it there until you can *just barely* feel the warmth. *At the instant* you feel any warmth whatsoever remove your finger sharply from the coil. Then wait until the experimenter tells you to replace your finger on the coil.

The experimenter simultaneously called "ready" and closed the knife switch. For the first four trials he also pressed the push button so that the coil actually did warm up. The following six trials were made by closing the knife switch alone. The subject continued to touch the coil for thirty seconds even if he did not feel the warmth. The experimenter then said, "All right, you did not feel it this time," and the subject was allowed to remove his finger. Exactly the same pause followed the last six trials as the first four, ostensibly

[4] G. W. Williams, "Suggestibility in the Normal and Hypnotic States," *Archives of Psychology,* 1930, No. 122.

to allow the coil to cool. Exactly the same procedure was followed whether the subject accepted the suggestion or not.

All the subjects accepted the suggestion some of the time and some accepted it every time. The average for eight subjects in twelve opportunities was approximately eight acceptances. Prestige factors are not entirely eliminated in this study, but the use of all this equipment doubtless enhanced the acceptance of the suggestions. The various pieces of apparatus helped to add verisimilitude to the situation because of the previous experience of the subjects with like pieces of equipment.

Another older experiment is more clearly a matter of non-prestige factors and shows an additional feature of true suggestibility that is important. Daniel Starch [5] gave 106 people passages which they were told to copy in their own handwriting. There were four different samples, one typewritten and the other three written with various degrees of letter width and slant. He found that the great majority of the subjects modified their handwriting either in slant or letter width or both to conform to the model from which they were copying. *The subjects were entirely unaware of having accepted the nonprestige suggestion offered by the model.* This latter point is important because it helps to distinguish between true suggestion and conscious copying or imitation, which is a different phenomenon altogether.

The techniques of advertising and propaganda make wide use of suggestion in bringing about changes in attitude and action favorable to the particular wares of the promotional source. All of the methods employed make use of the principles of prestige and nonprestige suggestion.

[5] Daniel Starch, "Unconscious Imitation of Handwriting," *Psychological Review,* 1911, 18, 173-181.

2. SLEEP AND HYPNOSIS [6]

In all of the common methods of inducing hypnosis the word
sleep is used. "Now you are going into a sound, sound sleep. You
will not wake up until you are told . . ." Not only in the directions
for accomplishing the trance, but also in the theory concerning it,
there has been frequent mention of sleep. How alike or how differ-

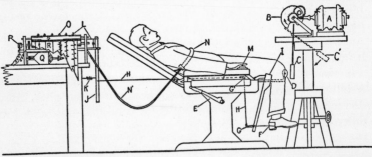

FIG. 55.—The arrangement of the apparatus and the subject in Bass's experiment.

ent these two states are was the problem which Milton Bass [7] set
out to solve.

Criterion of sleep.—He conceived the solution to depend upon
finding some bit of behavior or some reliable physiological sign of
sleep which could be used to distinguish between sleeping and
waking. The hypnotic trance could then be examined for the presence or absence of the sign of sleep. If the sign of sleep was present
in hypnosis, then there would be some justification for asserting that
there was at least some connection between the two states.

A sign or criterion of this kind has long been known to exist

[6] This chapter is written on the assumption that the student has read enough
about hypnosis to know what is meant by the usual hypnotic phenomena,
e.g., catalepsy, anesthesia, amnesia, posthypnotic amnesia, positive and negative hallucinations and posthypnotic suggestion. If a demonstration is planned
it should precede the reading of this chapter; if a demonstration does not appear feasible, the motion-picture film, *Hypnosis,* by Lester Beck may be used.
[7] Milton Bass, "The Differentiation of the Hypnotic Trance from Normal
Sleep," *Journal of Experimental Psychology,* 1931, 5, 382-89.

in the patellar reflex. In sleep the extent of leg movement to patellar stimulation is considerably diminished or in some cases abolished altogether. Regular hammer blows to the patella which are necessary to follow the course of the decrement in the knee jerk as sleep ensues, instead of preventing a person from going to sleep, have been shown by several investigators to be actually sleep-conducive.

Method.—The subject lay supine in a modified barber's chair. His legs hung freely beyond the knees so that the extent of leg movement could be recorded. An automatic device raised a hammer and let it fall through a known distance. The instant in which the hammer made contact with the leg was recorded automatically on a moving tape which also carried the record of the leg movements resulting from the striking hammer. The stimulus was given every 9.68 seconds. This much of the apparatus is all that was needed to differentiate between sleeping and waking.

Criterion of hypnosis.—Now to differentiate between sleeping and hypnosis. It is well known that a hypnotic subject will continue to react to any intermittent stimulus if he is commanded to do so. During sleep these responses cease. They are present, of course, when the subject is awake. The choice of stimulus was a bell which was caused to sound with a single soft but clearly audible tap every 90 seconds. These stimuli were recorded on the tape together with the resultant response, which was secured by means of a button on the right chair arm to be actuated by the index finger of the subject. A breathing record was also obtained. Since it did not prove of any value in differentiating between any of the states, it will not be mentioned again.

More details of method.—There were seven practiced subjects used. Each was given one hundred strokes on the patellar tendon in each of the three states, awake W, asleep S, and hypnotized T. To avoid practice or adapatation effects, the records were taken in the six possible combinations:

WST	TSW	SWT
WTS	TWS	STW

In all there were forty-three experimental periods in which about 1,300 patellar stimuli were recorded.

In the WST period, one hundred stimulations would be given when the subject was awake. This operation would require about fifteen minutes. At the end of that time the subjects would be asked to try to go to sleep. At the end of the next hundred stimulations the subject was awakened. He was then put into a trance, and again one hundred stimulations were given.

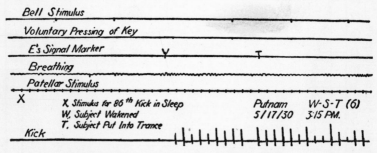

FIG. 56.—A sample of the record obtained.

Results.—The record shown in Figure 56 shows the end of a sleep period. There was no voluntary response to the bell stimuli and to the eighteen patellar stimuli shown there was not a single kick. But when the subject was awakened at the point marked W, the kicks begin as do the responses to the bell. Both of these latter continue when after about two minutes the subject is placed in a trance. A practiced subject like this one can be hypnotized almost instantly.

Figure 57 shows a summary of the patellar data for all subjects and for all experimental periods. The ordinates show the amplitude of the kicks as measured in millimeters on the tape. The abscissa-units show the number of kicks, or—what is the same thing—the time from the onset of the three states. Each five kicks are averaged for amplitude so that there are twenty abscissa-units instead of one hundred.

All three curves show some tendency to fall. This can be interpreted to mean that the subjects became more and more relaxed in each of the states as time went on. The sleep curve, however, follows an entirely different course from the other two. For the first minute the amplitudes of the kicks during sleep are almost as high as for awake and trance, but this effect can be expected since it is reasonable to suppose the sleep did not ensue instantaneously.

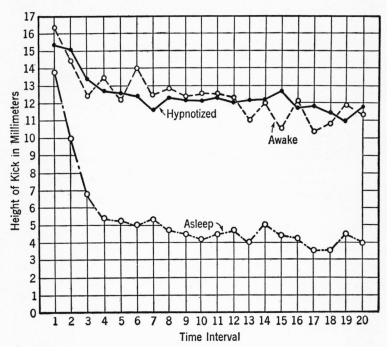

Fig. 57.—The amplitude of the patellar reflexes in sleeping, waking, and hypnosis.

The per cent of voluntary responses to the bell can also be plotted in exactly the same way. The curves are not shown here because in appearance and interpretation they are the same as those shown for the knee jerk. The per cent of responses was clearly lower in sleep, while for hypnosis and waking there was hardly any difference at all.

Conclusion.—A reasonable interpretation of the appearance of the whole graph is that in so far as the amplitude of the patellar reflex is an index of the condition of the organism, *being asleep is entirely different from both waking and hypnosis.* Being hypnotized is not a physiological condition or state like being asleep, however much the behavior of a person hypnotized superficially resembles his behavior asleep. If there is any difference between being awake and being hypnotized this technique does not exhibit it. Of course, there is a difference. Just what this difference is will be set forth as well as it is now understood in the following sections.

3. AMNESIA

Not only does a hypnotized subject sometimes act as if he were asleep, but very frequently he disclaims any knowledge of what has happened to him while he was hypnotized. Like the sleeping person, time passes rapidly for him and movements that he makes he does not remember. This is known as *posthypnotic amnesia.* The question that arises is: Is this effect a fundamental one involving a basic physiological process or is it simply a matter of temporary inability to recall similar to that which overtakes us all on occasions of emotional inhibition or blocking due to fatigue?

Hypothesis.—If the amnesia were a complete process which involved the basic physiological processes as well as the language mechanism, then a subject who had been practicing something would show no effect of an interlude during which he practiced the same task while hypnotized. He should start, subsequent to his hypnotized practice, at the same level he left off prior to hypnosis.

Method.—This hypothesis has been subjected to experimental test by Patten at Miami University.[8] He used fourteen subjects in all; seven hypnotized for a time, and seven who were never hypnotized. The task was to add successively 6, 7, 8, and 9 to a two-place number given between 10 and 99 (see page 149).

There was absolutely no difference between the procedures for the control and the experimental groups for the first six days. But on the seventh day, and the following ones including the twelfth,

[8] E. F. Patten, "Does Post-Hypnotic Amnesia Apply to Practice Effects?" *Journal of General Psychology,* 1932, 7, 196-201.

the experimental group was hypnotized and made to perform the additions in the trance. On the thirteenth day and subsequently it again practiced while awake. Uniformly the hypnotized subjects asked at the end of the hypnotic periods, "Aren't you going to have me add today?" This is the kind of evidence that is normally required to prove the existence of amnesia and it demonstrates that the subjects were satisfying the ordinarily imposed criteria for amnesia. There is no question but that they were hypnotized and that they were amnesic.

Results.—The results of Patten's experiment are shown in two figures. Although the control subjects were always inferior to the experimental group in the number of additions they could accomplish in five minutes, this does not spoil the experiment. The comparison that we are interested in is the comparison of trial six and its predecessors with trial thirteen and its followers. Trial thirteen is not the continuation of trial six. Even if the intervening trials were not on the graph, our first inference would have to be that some practice took place in the hypnotized interval. The general appearance of the curve for the experimental and the control groups is exactly the same. Figure 59 shows this better than does Figure 58. In the former the initial performance of the control group is taken as 100 and the subsequent trials of both groups are compared to it as a base, an operation which compensates for the difference of the two groups in ability. This treatment of the data is legitimate because we are not interested in the differences in ability between the two groups. We want to be rid of it because it obscures the effects we are interested in.

Conclusion.—The solid circles, showing the performance of the hypnotized group, fit into the general trend nicely. They have to be there to explain what follows. This can only mean that *the amnesia of hypnotized subjects is entirely independent of the course of learning during hypnosis.* That the subjects honestly deny remembering what happens does not mean that they are in a state of suspended animation in which ordinary experiences leave no effect.

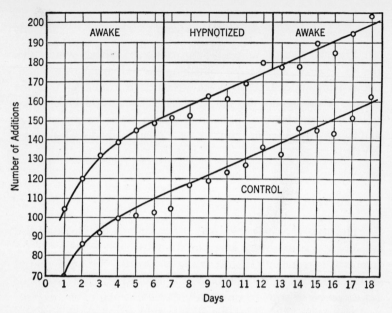

FIG. 58.—Learning curves for addition: hypnotized and control groups.

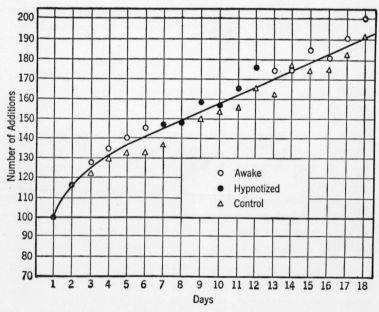

FIG. 59.—Same data as shown in Figure 58. The lower curve of Figure 58 is moved up to adjust for the difference in initial ability.

We infer that the amnesia of a hypnotized subject is more like that of a person who knows something "as well as his own name" but is temporarily blocked when it comes to exhibiting what he knows. These results are not necessarily contradictory. It is not unusual in psychology to obtain a certain result by one method and an entirely different result by some other method. (Cf. Chapter XVIII.)

4. RAPPORT

Hypnosis is naïvely described as the conquest of a weak-willed person by one of strong will. On the stage and in literature the hypnotist is represented as exercising an unusual degree of control over the actions of the person he has hypnotized even when the consequences of such action are clearly detrimental to the interests and well-being of the hypnotized. Scientific men have been misled by the *apparent* willingness of the subject to carry out trivial suggestions until they, too, in some instances, have described hypnosis as a peculiar relationship between subject and operator which they call *rapport*.

Whether or not rapport is essential to hypnosis has been tried in a series of observations by Paul Campbell Young,[9] who asked himself several questions which he later subjected to a test.

Can a subject annul rapport?—Two subjects who had previously been hypnotized several times were used. They were asked to write on a piece of paper the suggestions they would resist. A list of ten different things had been provided which would make suitable material for testing the resistance. The experimenter did not know which one of the things had been chosen, so he ran through the whole list each time the subject was hypnotized, redoubling his efforts to produce the effect if there appeared to be any resistance at all. The subjects were not told whether they would be successful in resisting or not. They were merely told that this was a point

[9] Paul Campbell Young, "Is *Rapport* an Essential Characteristic of Hypnosis?" *Journal of Abnormal and Social Psychology,* 1927, 22, 130-39.

Samples from the Experimenter's Notebook

April 16, 10:00 A.M.; Subject H. During the period all suggestions were carried out with the exception of those pertaining to analgesia.

When the experimenter stuck the subject as usual with a sharp skewer, the subject winced considerably. On repetition of the suggestion and renewed pricking, the painful expression became more pronounced. When challenged as usual, "Do you feel anything?" the subject said, "It hurts." After being awakened, the subject wrote the following report: "I have no definite remembrance of anything after being put in the chair. I have a vague remembrance I was told that I was not to feel it, but was fighting that order and was straining my senses to feel it. The object seemed like a pencil point, rather used and blunted. It was not painful in the least."

In this experiment it is to be noted that not only did the subject react strongly in hypnosis, contrary to the idea of rapport, but the only memory left of a long séance was the one concerning his autosuggestion, remembered despite the experimenter's orders.

The signed statement of the subject handed to the experimenter after waking was as follows: "While in a state of hypnosis I will obey all commands except that of becoming insensible to pain."

April 16, 3:30 P.M.; Subject H. As usual, the experimenter did not know what autosuggestion the subject had given himself until after the session was over, and consequently was somewhat surprised to see that every command was obeyed without any show of resistance. After the session was over, however, the operator was even more surprised to find that the subject remembered everything that had occurred during the whole time. The subject's written report after waking covered two pages and cannot be given in full here. Excerpts are as follows: "Everything in this sitting seemed clear after being wakened, whereas I can scarcely remember anything of the one just previous to it (which had taken place during the forenoon) . . . I was pricked with a pin on both hands, being ordered to move the hand touched. I could not move the 'dead' hand, although I could feel the pin-prick (it did not hurt in the least) . . . I was told that I was one-armed and that my arm had been torn off. I had a terrible sensation of pain at that time in my shoulder where it seemed that the arm had been unjointed when you 'pulled it off.' "

The subject's written instruction to himself was: "While in a hypnotic state I will obey any and all commands except that I won't forget everything or anything that goes on."

In this experiment we note that the self-suggested attitude to remember, assumed in defiance of the direct commands of the experimenter, given in this sitting as well as in all sessions, modified the kind of rapport in hypnosis and frustrated the command to forget all the events after awaking.

upon which some experiments would be made. The account of the sitting, as Dr. Young reports it, is shown on page 288.

Conclusion.—From these two instances we can conclude that it is possible for a subject to "make up his mind" that he will not do a certain thing when the experimenter commands him to do so. *His behavior follows closely his own instruction in spite of anything the hypnotizer can do.* In these cases the subject does not necessarily "wake up." Sometimes he does wake, however, still contrary to the suggestions given him.

Emerson Hall, Cambridge, Mass., Dec. 24, 1922, Subject M. Just before sitting in the chair to be hypnotized one morning this somnambulistic subject asked the experimenter to be sure to bring the experiment to a close at 12:00. The experimenter assured the subject that he would be awakened before 12:00. At 11:55 the experimenter, noticing that the tests would be incomplete at the time agreed upon, tried to prolong the session by suggesting to the subject that his sleep would become deeper and deeper, and that he would not awake until ten minutes had passed. *In spite of the means thus employed, the subject began to toss restlessly, and at the striking of Memorial Hall clock awoke.* As soon as he was fully conscious, and had understood the nature of the case, the subject composed himself to be hypnotized again. But in spite of his apparent co-operation and his avowed purpose, the subject, who had always been very easily inducted into the somnambulistic state, and often two or three times in one sitting, could not at this time be re-hypnotized. After three vain attempts to go to sleep again, he confessed that, fearing he might be kept at this session so long as to miss a luncheon engagement at 12:30, he had before coming to the room given himself the suggestion to awaken at the sounding of twelve o'clock.

In this experiment we see that decisions made by the subject prior to hypnosis can break up the rapport of the hypnotic session and even prevent its being re-established.

These generalizations have recently been challenged by Professor Wesley Raymond Wells,[10] who has repeated Young's experi-

[10] Wesley Raymond Wells, "Ability to Resist Artificially Induced Dissociation," *Journal of Abnormal and Social Psychology,* 1940, 35, 261-272. Also see W. R. Wells, "The Extent and Duration of Post-Hypnotic Amnesia," *Journal of Psychology,* 1940, 9, 137-151.

ments. He used, in all, sixteen subjects who had been hypnotized from one to four times before the session in which they were to attempt to resist certain commands. These items were the same as Young used: not being able to open the eyes; not being able to unclasp the hands; not being able to recall one's own name; not being able to hear anything except the hypnotist's voice; not being able to raise the feet from the floor; not being able to walk; not being able to feel pain (analgesia); having visual hallucinations; completing posthypnotic suggestions; posthypnotic amnesia. The subjects drew by lot one of the ten items which were written on cards and, according to the experimental plan, agreed to try to resist this item when it was offered with others in the test. The subjects were required (in some instances) to write their expectation of the outcome of their attempted resistance in advance of the experiment. The experimenter did not know in any instance which of the ten commands the subject had determined to resist.

Contrary to Young's results, all sixteen of these subjects were unable to resist the commands of the hypnotist. Ten of them expected in advance to be able to resist the commands but were unsuccessful in doing so. In eleven of the cases the experimenter could not tell which item the subject was trying to resist. Professor Wells's criterion of hypnosis involves this factor of helplessness. He would simply say that those who were able to resist were not completely hypnotized. As he himself points out, if he had got these results on only one subject his argument would have been just as cogent because then these failures could have been attributed to the failure to obtain complete hypnosis in the other cases.

Neither one of these experiments is a good one, although both are valuable to us in making this point: *A good experiment would have varied the conditions leading up to the acceptance or the nonacceptance of the commands.* The variations in prior events should be of such magnitude and diversity that given such-and-such a subject with such-and-such a preconception, influenced in subtle ways by the prestige of the hypnotist, the outcome would be predictable.

Can a subject be hypnotized and then change this rapport to someone else?—To test this question it is necessary that the person to be hypnotized make prearrangements with a third person present during the trance. The hypnotizer must not know what the previous arrangements between his subject and the third person have been. It was under these conditions that the following events took place in one of Young's experiments.

May 4, 4:00 P.M.; Subject R. Professor A. present. What happened in this experiment is forecast in the prior autosuggestion, which the operator at the time knew nothing about: "I will submit to hypnosis. When fully hypnotized I will not respond to suggestions from the experimenter, but will respond to A. as follows: when A. says one, relax right arm. When A. says three, I will stand. When A. says four, I will about-face. When A. says five, I will sit down. I will awake when three taps are given by A."

And so the experiment actually went, in spite of the strenuous efforts of the hypnotist to make the subject obey. There was no resistance to the experimenter's suggestions; they were simply ignored entirely.

After hypnosis, the subject remembered nothing that the experimenter had said after talking to him about relaxing, but he did remember having heard A.'s voice. He described his procedure during hypnosis in the following words: when he came into the room, he "just had the suggestion I had given myself on my mind, and kept it on my mind during the hypnosis; I did not have to think of it during the hypnosis—I was not thinking of anything. I had no difficulty in knowing what the signals meant."

Conclusion.—Here, apparently, we have a genuine hypnosis void of rapport with the one doing the hypnotizing, but showing rapport with one who had been previously selected by the subject.

Professor Young considers the subjects whose records are given above as completely hypnotized as any he has ever worked with. If they were, then the conclusion must be: *An experimenter can hypnotize a subject who thereupon can be out of rapport with the experimenter and come back into rapport only if, as, and when he has determined to do so before being hypnotized.*

5. POSTHYPNOTIC SUGGESTION

It is well known that the hypnotist can make an appointment with a hypnotized subject during a trance. Upon waking the subject does not recall the date, but he generally turns up at the time appointed, especially if the appointment is made within the next few days. With some subjects, it is reported, private arrangements have been made in advance to have them involved in some interesting occupation or diversion; but still the appointments are almost invariably kept. The conditions under which observations of this kind have been made are uncontrolled. We are not certain how much a hypnotist has been impressed by the instances in which appointments have been kept and how many instances have been forgotten where the subject is somehow prevented from appearing. Perhaps in many instances the apparently attractive diversion was not a diversion at all. It may have irked the subject to an extent that an excuse for discontinuing the activity was a welcome escape. Our only answers to these questions must come from the laboratory where control over these factors can be exercised.

Patten [11] again has contributed to our knowledge of hypnosis here. He gave a posthypnotic suggestion to eighteen totally amnesic subjects. His testing schedule follows:

2 were tested immediately	2 were tested after 15 days
2 were tested after 1 day	2 were tested after 20 days
2 were tested after 3 days	2 were tested after 25 days
2 were tested after 5 days	1 was tested after 30 days
2 were tested after 10 days	1 was tested after 33 days

This procedure leaves much to be desired in that the sampling error must be considerable, only one or two subjects being used after each interval. A better plan would have been to divide the subjects into two or three groups of six or nine subjects each. But it will remain for some other experimenter to rid this experiment of the sampling error. There are other features of Patten's experiment that make it

[11] E. F. Patten, "The Duration of Post-Hypnotic Suggestion," *Journal of Abnormal and Social Psychology,* 1930, 25, 319-34.

valuable even if we are not quite certain that a repetition of it would show *precisely* the same result.

Control group.—The same suggestion was given to a group of sixteen subjects who were never hypnotized at any time during the course of the experiment. They constitute the control group without which it would be impossible to interpret the findings based on the hypnotized subjects alone. These subjects were spaced like the experimental group at the various periods up to thirty-three days. None was tested immediately, since there were only sixteen in the control group.

Method.—The suggestion given was most cleverly conceived. All of the subjects were shown thirty words. The words were exposed by means of an automatic device which ensured that each item in the list would be in view for the same length of time. The subject's attention was maintained during the exposure of the list by informing him, while he was awake, that one word would be repeated. He was expected to report on the word repeated at the conclusion of the experimental sitting. The repeated word was always near the end of the list, its predecessor was always near the beginning, so that for the important part of the experiment, the subject was actively looking for something in the words that were exposed.

But now the clever part. In the list, between the first and second occurrence of the word that was repeated, were the names of three animals. In the trance which preceded all of this, the experimental group was told that each time the name of an animal appeared, they would depress the index finger of the right hand without being aware that they were doing so. The finger was placed in a small loop connected by means of strings and levers to a kymograph so that its slightest movement would be recorded. The whole hand was screened from the subject. It should be remembered that the subjects were awake when they saw the list of words. The suggestion had been given in a hypnotic trance preceding the whole affair; thirty-three days previously in the case of one subject and at the intervals shown above for the others.

For the control group the procedure was the same except that this group was never hypnotized; hence the finger depression would be susceptible to the ordinary laws of forgetting.

The strength of the obedience to the suggestion was assumed

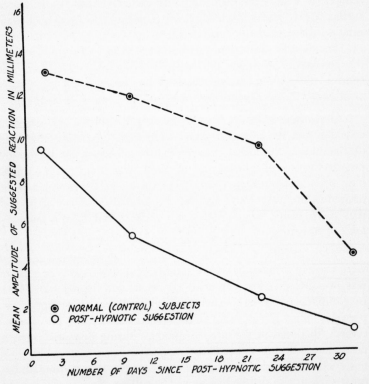

FIG. 60.—The duration of posthypnotic suggestion. (After Hull, Courtesy of D. Appleton-Century Company.)

to be proportional to the extent of the finger movement. This movement was measured in millimeters from the kymograph tape.

Results.—The mean reaction in millimeters for each subject for each day was found. The means of the two subjects at each interval were averaged for the dependent variable. Because so few subjects were used, the original curves are very erratic. But Clark Hull [12] has shown how it is possible to pool the results for days 0, 1, and 3, which are plotted at day 1; days 5, 10 and 15 plotted at 10; days 20, 25 plotted at 23; and days 30 and 33 plotted at 31, into a composite for 6 subjects rather than 2 at each plotted point. This graphically reduces the data to the form suggested earlier—larger groups spaced further apart—and it compensates in a measure for a lack of planning on the part of the experimenter.

The results show that there is a clear-cut difference between the amplitude of finger movement for the hypnotized and the control subjects, but the *posthypnotic suggestion is not as effective as ordinary waking instruction in producing a finger movement.*

Conclusion.—On the basis of this experiment we are forced to conclude that the reports relating to subjects who invariably, and on the minute, keep appointments that have been made days ahead even in the face of difficult and, at times, frustrating circumstances, have been grossly exaggerated. The experiment leaves much to be desired in the way of subjects tested at each interval, but it is clear that *posthypnotic suggestion is not independent of the ordinary laws of forgetting.*

Summary.—Bass's experiment showed that hypnosis and sleep were entirely different phenomena, but it did not show that there was any difference between a subject awake and hypnotized. There is a difference. Patten's experiment showed that the amnesia reported is only a fact in so far as the subject's ability to report is concerned. Measured in the effect of practice during hypnosis, there is no amnesia. Young showed that rapport was not essential to hypnosis. His observations also show that amnesia is not essential, because subjects can still be hypnotized according to other criteria and remember perfectly what has happened during the trance. Patten also showed, in another experiment, that posthypnotic suggestions are forgotten as things are normally forgotten. Other experiments not cited here show that catalepsy is not essential to hypnosis. In a word, none of the usual phenomena that are said to differentiate hypnosis are actually necessary. As a result of an extended analysis

[12] Clark Hull, *Hypnosis and Suggestibility,* D. Appleton-Century Company, New York, 1933, p. 163.

of all the experimental literature on the subject, Hull concludes that *there is not a single item which is characteristic of hypnosis that can not to some extent be produced in the waking state.* When the experimenter's suggestions and commands are accepted uncritically by the subject, he is hypnotized. People who are the most suggestible [13] while awake are not always the best hypnotic subjects, however. The subject's own preconceived notions of hypnosis enter the picture in a way that is not entirely clear at the present time.

6. ANESTHESIA

The fact that hypnotized people can be made to feel too warm or too cold at ordinary room temperatures or to writhe with pain when an imaginary cigarette is "burning" their fingers brings up a troublesome question in both waking suggestion and hypnosis. Does the subject really sense the warmth or is he just a good fellow who agrees with the experimenter because it is too much trouble to be negative? It is not beyond the bounds of probability that a verbal stimulus can actually cause an individual to sense a warmth where there is none that can be measured by a thermometer. If we instruct a subject to imagine a blue cube on the desk in front of him, there are some people who can imagine the cube so well that it has all the characteristics of a real cube and actually can be manipulated in certain ways. All the time they are wide-awake, of course. It has been reported that electricians whose screw drivers slip sometimes feel a shock where no actual shock was possible; the same thing has been reported in conditioning experiments where the sound of a buzzer actually caused the subject to feel a shock even when there was no shock administered.

But how about the reverse of these phenomena? Is a tactual stimulus administered under the suggestion of anesthesia in an arm or leg actually felt, or does the subject just deny having felt it?

[13] As a matter of fact, there probably is no general waking suggestibility. People who are extremely suggestible under one set of conditions may be only faintly suggestible under another.

An old parlor trick which everyone must have seen at one time or another helps to give one answer to this question. If an individual extends his two hands in front of him with both thumbs pointing down—i.e. with the backs of the hands together—and one arm is crossed over the other at the wrist so that the palms can be made to come in contact and the fingers are intertwined, then if the arms are brought back to the body and the hands still locked together are rotated so that the thumbs are uppermost, it is extremely difficult to tell whether a given finger belongs to the right or to the left hand. If one hand were to be anesthetized by hypnotic suggestion, then it would be hard for the subject to fool either the experimenter or himself when the fingers were touched in haphazard order. If the hands were simply placed side by side, it would be easy for the subject simply to act as though he did not feel any touch made on the supposedly anesthetized hand. Professor Pattie [14] has made the "position of the Japanese illusion," as it is called, serve a useful scientific end in a study of the genuineness of hypnotically produced anesthesia. If he had simply touched the hypnotized subject's fingers when they were in the confusion position and then asked for a report on whether the touch had been sensed, it would have been relatively easy for the subject to have made incipient movements of the fingers, finally hitting on the one just touched and by that means arriving at a judgment of right or left; from that he could infer that he should say "felt" or nothing at all. But Professor Pattie had a method by which he could completely disconcert such too co-operative subjects. He had them count the number of stimulations they sensed. In a series of touches, which came at the rate of about two a second, he kept them so completely occupied that they didn't have time to cheat. If the "anesthesia" were genuine then they would be able to count only the contacts on the unanesthetized hand; but if they simply failed to report on what they thought was the anesthetized hand, the confusion position would ensure their making an appreciable number of errors.

The procedure used with the hypnotized subject was as follows:

[14] Frank A. Pattie, Jr., "The Genuineness of Hypnotically Produced Anaesthesia of the Skin," *American Journal of Psychology,* 1937, 59, 435-443.

An anesthesia of the right hand and arm was suggested, and the sensitivity was tested by pinching, pressing, and pricking the subject's hand. If he declared that he sensed nothing, he was then blindfolded by tying a thick newspaper around his head. The subject's hands were then put into the position of the Japanese illusion, and the following instructions were given:

You can feel nothing with your right hand. You will now receive a number of touches, and since you can feel nothing with your right hand, they will be felt only on the fingers of the left hand. Count the touches received by the fingers of your left and report the number as soon as they cease. No finger will be touched twice in succession. Do not estimate, but count as well as you can.

The touches were delivered by the experimenter, who touched the fingers of the left hand, and an assistant, who touched the fingers of the right hand. The stimulators were pieces of rubber taken from ordinary large rubber erasers and with dimensions of 1.5 × 0.5 (the surface applied to the skin) × 2 cm. They were attached to thin strips of brass (11 × 1.5 × 0.03 cm.), which in turn were fastened to wooden sticks of a size convenient for the hand. The brass strips projected over the end of the wooden stick 3.5 cm. A wire fixed above the brass strip marked the amount of bending of the strip necessary to produce a pressure of 75 grams. Care was taken to insure that the experimenter's and the assistant's touches were equally intense. The experimenter's touches were applied at a variable rate, which did not exceed 2 a second. A stop watch was used to time the touches so that the maximum rate might not be exceeded. . . .

Ten series of touches were applied to each subject. Each series consisted of 20 sets of stimulations ranging in number from 11 to 30 applications on the critical hand. The order of these 20 stimulations was determined by chance (numbered cards were used and shuffled before each series was made up). Five series were given in the first hour of experimenting, and five in the second hour, which came after two or three days. To be sure that the subject knew what he was to do, he was first given 11 or 12 touches on the left hand, while the assistant also was touching him. His report on this first stimulation was not recorded.

Subjects were scored thus. The errors made in each of the 20 reports in a series were added without regard to sign (e.g., the error was 4 if the subject called 11 touches either 7 or 15). If the subject said that he lost count, the particular number on which he lost count was repeated at the end of the series. Losing count was infrequent.

There were five hypnotized subjects and in the first series they made 44 errors on the average. Their results are shown by the solid curve in Figure 61. Of course these data are useless unless we have a comparison group; hence the whole experiment was repeated with fifteen subjects who were awake, but in other re-

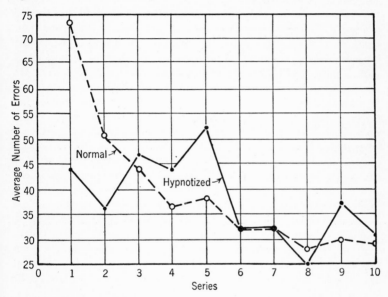

FIG. 61.—Comparison between number of errors of identification made by hypnotized and nonhypnotized subjects when the hands are in the confusion position.

spects comparable to the hypnotized group. Their results are shown by the broken curve in Figure 61. It is perfectly obvious that, taken as a whole, there is no basis for the conclusion that the suggestion actually made the one hand as anesthetized as some drug would have done. In contrast, Pattie found that when the hands were clearly separated the subjects made practically no errors. As a matter of fact, the hand which had been anesthetized by the suggestion employed, could be pricked or slapped or pinched and still the subject gave no overt evidence of having sensed the stimulus. But are the various implicit signs of painful stimulation, such as heart rate and galvanic skin response, inhibited?

Sears[15] has made an experiment which answers these specific questions.

On numerous occasions he produced anesthesia in one leg of seven different subjects. There were 101 experimental sessions with the seven subjects. The other leg of the subject was stimulated without suggestion of anesthesia and constituted a control. The painful stimulus was the prick of a needle administered in a special way so

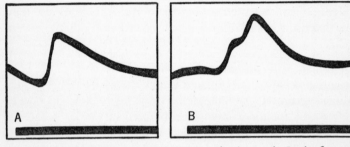

Fig. 62.—A tracing of one of Levine's galvanic records. In the figure to the left there was no suggestion of anesthesia as the skin was punctured with a needle at A. In the record to the right with suggested anesthesia, there is still a response when the same stimulus is applied at B. (After Levine, *Bulletin* of Johns Hopkins Hospital, 1930, 46, 333.)

that the exact time and vigor of the stimulations could be recorded pneumatically on a kymograph tape. (See Chapter XIII.)

The facial grimace of the subject in the region of the eyes was recorded if it occurred. This operation was accomplished by attaching a lever by means of adhesive tape to the left cheek, just below the eye. The lever actuated a Marey tambour, another tambour reconverted the resulting air pressure variations to mechanical movements which were recorded by means of a stylus. Breathing records and records of the galvanic skin response and pulse were also recorded. (See Chapter XIII.)

We have, then, the verbal response of the subject and, correlated with this record, the automatically recorded grimace, breathing, pulse and galvanic skin reflex, including some items under

[15] R. R. Sears, "An Experimental Study of Hypnotic Anesthesia," *Journal of Experimental Psychology*, 1932, 15, 1-22.

voluntary control and some which are not, although they differ in the degree to which they can be kept under control.

Results.—In general, considerably more reduction was observed in the voluntary than in the involuntary segments of behavior examined (verbal reports of pain and facial grimace were practically eliminated), but even in the galvanic skin reflex there was a suppression of the effect in about 20 per cent of the stimulations. In waking, none of these things could be modified to any extent. There is evidence, then, that the reactions to painful stimuli are not only modified verbally but are also changed somewhat in other segments as well.

Summary of the chapter.—The intent of this chapter has been to show that behavior can be controlled by the use of verbal stimuli and other forms of communication involving gesturing. Totally aside from the specific words which are used in various situations, the person who gives the suggestion is important in determining the outcome. A schoolteacher, for instance, has greater prestige with school children than another child or even a stranger. In all social situations these prestige factors seem to operate, as, for example, in the field of literature, where we showed there was a relationship between the prestige of an author and the rating of a literary passage which was falsely attributed to him. It is also important to distinguish between prestige suggestion of the kind we have been talking about and nonprestige suggestion in which another person is not involved but where a situation indirectly leads to a certain result as was demonstrated in Williams's experiment. The ultimate effectiveness of suggestion is found in the phenomenon known as hypnosis. As Bass's experiment shows, the states of being hypnotized and being asleep are totally different from each other as both are different from being awake. The next experiment shows that, although it is possible to produce amnesia in a hypnotized subject, one does not actually at that time eliminate what he has learned from wherever it happens to be located deep in his organism. Posthypnotic amnesia is a blocking phenomenon. The next section on *rapport* shows that there is nothing mysterious at all about the peculiar relationship that exists between the hypnotizer and the one hypnotized, and in connection with the work of other authors who have obtained different results we conclude that additional information is needed in this field. One puzzling phenomenon has to do with the production of anesthesia under hypnosis. The question has always been: How is it possible to burn or to lacerate tissue while a person is hypnotized and still have him report that he feels no pain? Sears's experiment shows that physiological effects over which the subject has no voluntary control actually do take place although they are suppressed, and that hypnotic anesthesia is therefore not the same thing as an anesthesia produced by drugs, where it is actually a blocking of the nervous impulses.

Thus we are left with the generalization that hypnosis is a special kind of suggestion phenomenon. Nonprestige suggestion is probably not related to hypnosis at all, and prestige suggestion is not related to it in any *precise* way that has yet been discovered.[16] The subject's own preconceived notions regarding hypnosis profoundly influence his reactions. Persons are not equally susceptible to different kinds of suggestion. It is not possible, therefore, to speak of a general suggestibility nor of a general hypnotizability, and the relation between them. Hypnosis is different from waking only in the heightened susceptibility to prestige suggestion, but no point can be undisputably located on one side of which we could say that a person is hypnotized and on the other side of which we could say he was awake. Hypnosis is not unique among psychological phenomena in this respect.

[16] Waking suggestions to the effect that the subject will fall in a certain direction may be an exception to this generalization. Hull reports that practically all subjects who exhibit an acceptance of a suggestion to fall are good hypnotics.

XV

PERCEPTUAL BEHAVIOR

BECAUSE the lens of the eye is a simple optical system, the image of any object is actually upside down on the retina, and reversed in the right-left direction. Suppose that by some curious accident of genetics, a person were born with a more complex lens system in his eyes so that this normal reversal were rectified. Would he *see* things any differently from the rest of us, or would the directions "up" and "down" have the same significance for him that they have for us? When one works with a microscope, with the ground glass of a camera, or with a transit for any length of time, he adjusts to the "upside-downness" so that it doesn't appear strange at all any more. He might even have to stop to consider the question if someone asked him if the images he saw were upside down.

1. STRATTON'S EXPERIMENT

It remained for Stratton, whom we have met before, actually to wear an auxiliary lens system that reversed everything he saw. When he looked up he saw the floor and his feet, when he looked down he saw the ceiling, when he looked right he saw what was on his left, and when he looked left he saw what was on his right. He wore the lenses about ten days all told. During the whole time, when he rested or retired, his eyes were kept closed until an assistant could carefully bind them so that he could not see.

Wearing an arrangement of this kind is not as easy as putting on a pair of spectacles. The lenses cannot be like spectacle lenses. The whole apparatus forms a tube about eight inches long. Stratton used only one eye, his right, and in it the visual field was greatly restricted by the tube. A plaster cast of his upper face helped to hold the lens through the hole made in it over the right eye where the tube was inserted. The left eye was kept completely covered by the plaster cast. This arrangement only partly fulfills ideal requirements. The lenses, for example, do not move when the eye does. Ideally, they should be attached directly to the eye so that they would move with it, but an arrangement of this kind is patently impossible in view of the optical necessities.

The following excerpts from Stratton's published record of his experiences while wearing this apparatus make interesting and instructive reading.

First Day. The entire scene appeared upside down. When I moved my head or body so that my sight swept over the scene, the movement was not felt to be solely in the observer, as in normal vision, but was referred both to the observer and to objects beyond.

Almost all movements performed under the direct guidance of sight were laborious and embarrassed. Inappropriate movements were constantly made; for instance, in order to move my hand from a place in the visual field to some other place which I had selected, the muscular contraction which would have accomplished this if the normal visual arrangement had existed, now carried my hand to an entirely different place. The movement was then checked, started off in another direction, and finally, by a series of approximations and corrections, brought to the chosen point. At the table the simplest acts of serving myself had to be cautiously worked out. The wrong hand was constantly used to seize anything that lay to one side. In pouring some milk into a glass, I must by careful trial and correction bring the surface of the milk to the spout of the pitcher, and then see to it that the surface of the milk in the glass remained everywhere equally distant from the glass's rim.

Whether as a result of the embarrassment under which nearly all visually guided movements were performed, or as a consequence of the swinging of the scene, described above, there were signs of nervous disturbance, of which perhaps the most marked was a feeling of depression in the upper abdominal region, akin to mild nausea. This disappeared, however, toward evening; so that by half-past seven it was no longer perceptible.

Second Day. This feeling of nervous depression, just mentioned, returned the next forenoon. Movements, though, had in many respects grown less laborious, and were performed more on the basis of the actual sight-experiences, and less by excluding these as a means of guidance. Once, at least, in the afternoon, I noticed that in washing my hands I had given myself up completely to the actual scene; but at the next instant inappropriate movements occurred, and with the consciousness that I had thus given myself up the old pre-experimental translation of things returned.

As to the uprightness or inversion of things, the general feeling was that the seen room was upside down; the body of the observer, represented in pre-experimental terms, was felt as standard and as having an upright position. But different circumstances produced a different shade of feeling. When I looked out over a wide landscape, the position in which I felt my body to be and the position of the scene before me were surely discordant and unnatural. Yet I could not, as I had the day before, take either the one or the other unreservedly as standard. It seemed as if an abnormal position of my body in viewing things might just as well account for the facts as would an inversion of the scene. But even when, indoors, the view was almost completely filled with the dining table and its furnishings, there was no striking and obvious feeling that the scene was upside down.

During a rather long walk in the evening I was unable to recognize my surroundings most of the time, although normally they were quite familiar. Recognition evidently depended largely on external relations of position and direction, and with a disturbance of these, the objects themselves seemed strange.

On being blindfolded for the night, there was an immediate and involuntary recurrence to the older way of picturing things. Only rarely could anything be represented in terms of the later sight.

Third Day. I was now beginning to feel more at home in the new experience. At no time during the day did any signs of nervous distress appear, and the hours passed more rapidly than on either of the preceding days.

Contacts in walking past objects had hitherto for the most part been surprising, because the contact was felt in a different place from the one anticipated. But today I noticed that expectation was coming more into harmony with the actual experience. It was also evident that this expectation, when joined with a vivid representation of the region of the body in question, had a perceptible influence upon the direction in which the contact was actually felt. If, for example, I walked up to a low railing which came against my abdomen, the sensations of pressure seemed to come from the new visual position of the abdomen if I called up a vivid image of this part of my body in its new position and expected the sensations to come from there. But the unexpected contact of the railing with my arms (then out of sight), which had not been represented in their new position, was referred only in the old way, until these too were distinctly imaged as the abdomen had been. But even when the localization was in accord with the new visual experience, there was still a subordinate background localization after the old manner.

Fourth Day. By the fourth day the new experience had become even less trying. There was no sign of bodily discomfort, and for the first time during the experiment, when nine o'clock in the evening came I preferred to keep the glasses on rather than sit blindfolded—which had hitherto been chosen as a welcome relief.

During the day, actions appropriate to the new visual perceptions frequently occurred without any conflict or apparent tendency to react by a misinterpretation of visual positions. My hands, in washing, often moved to the soap or to the proper position in the basin, without premeditation or any need of correcting the movement.

Fifth Day. At the thought of putting on the lenses, in the morning, there was an influx of ideas in the new visual form. I even noticed in many cases that there was a reconstruction in the new terms of objects which I had just before been thinking of in the old way.

At breakfast, with the lenses on, the inappropriate hand was rarely used to pick up something to one side. The movement itself also was easier and less wayward; seldom was it in an entirely wrong direction. When hand and object were both in sight I did not, as a rule, have to calculate or try to find the direction and extent of movement necessary to reach the object, but merely fixed my attention on the thing, and the hand was laid upon it without more ado, except for an occasional slight correction of the direction.

In walking I did not so often run into obstacles in the very effort to avoid them. I usually took the right direction without reflecting and without the need any longer of constantly watching my feet. When the doors were open I could walk through the entire house by visual guidance alone, without holding out my hands in front of me to warn in case of a misinterpretation of the sight-perception. For the first time I dared to turn and sit down on a chair without beforehand assuring myself with my hands that I had placed myself aright. My movements were of course still cautious and awkward. An evidence of the growing ease with which simple movements were coming to be done is given by the fact that I took a sheet of my notes and laid it upon a shelf in another part of the room, all the while intent on something entirely foreign to the matter in hand.

Localization in cases of unseen contact often went astray, mainly in that the wrong visual side was first suggested, but corrected before I turned my eyes on the thing touching me. Localization of sounds was various, and at times gave a sudden and surprising turn to the experience. Thus, as I sat in the garden, a friend who was talking with me began to throw some pebbles into the distance to one side of my actual view. The sound of the stones striking the ground came, oddly enough, from the opposite direction from that in which I had seen them pass out of my sight, and from which I involuntarily expected to catch the sound. I unhesitatingly accepted the visual directions of throwing and of the stones' movement, but the auditory spatial suggestion was in complete discord with these.

. . . .

Eighth Day. Localization of sounds varied, being different when the source of sound was in sight from what it was when this was out of sight, and also in the latter case differing with different directions of attention, or with different suggestions as to the direction from which the sound came. The fire, for instance, sputtered where I saw it. The tapping of my pencil on the arm of my chair seemed without question to issue from the visible pencil.[1]

Summary.—It is clear from these notes that:

(1) At first the visual field appears to be inverted.

(2) Unlike the normal condition, when the head moves, the whole visual field seems to be rotating or swinging.

(3) Vertigo and nausea are the result of the readjustment required.

(4) During the period of eight days there is a rapid readjustment until most daily tasks can be done with a minimum of annoyance.

(5) There were some confusions that remained in the tactual and auditory fields, particularly if the sound or touch sources were not in the visual field.

[1] G. M. Stratton, "Vision without Inversion of the Retinal Image," *Psychological Review,* 1897, 4, 341-60; 463-81.

Experience upon removing the lenses. When the time came for removing the glasses at the close of the experiment, I thought it best to preserve as nearly as possible the size of visual field to which I had now grown accustomed; so that any results observed might be clearly due solely to the reversion of my visual objects and not to a sudden widening of the visual field. Instead, therefore, of removing the plaster cast from my face, I closed my eyes and had an assistant slip out the brass tube which held the lenses, and insert in its place an empty black-lined paper tube that gave about the same range of vision. On opening my eyes, the scene had a strange familiarity. The visual arrangement was immediately recognized as the old one of pre-experimental days; yet the reversal of everything from the order to which I had grown accustomed during the past week, gave the scene a surprising, bewildering air which lasted for several hours. It was hardly the feeling, though, that things were upside down.

Movements which would have been appropriate to the visual arrangement during the experiment were now repeatedly performed after this arrangement had been reversed. In walking toward some obstacle on the floor of the room—a chair, for instance—I turned the wrong way in trying to avoid it; so that I frequently either ran into things in the very effort to go around them, or else hesitated, for the moment, bewildered what I should do. I found myself more than once at a loss which hand I ought to use to grasp the door handle at my side. And of two doors, side by side, leading to different rooms, I was on the point of opening the wrong one, when a difference in the metal work of the locks made me aware of my mistake. On approaching the stairs, I stepped up when I was nearly a foot too far away. And in writing my notes at this time, I continually made the wrong movement of my head in attempting to keep the center of my visual field somewhere near the point where I was writing. I moved my head upward when it should have gone downward; I moved it to the left when it should have gone to the right. And this to such a degree as to be a serious disturbance. While walking, there were distinct signs of vertigo and also the depression in the upper abdominal region, noticed during the earlier days of the experiment. The feeling that the floor and other visual objects were swaying, in addition to the symptoms just mentioned, made my walking seem giddy and uncontrollable. No distinct errors in localizing parts of my body occurred; I was more than once surprised, however, to see my hands enter the visual field from the old lower side.

Interpretation.—These observations all show that a person can quickly learn to adjust to the uninverted retinal image. Although it is true that from the physical standpoint the image is ordinarily upside down on the retina, being upside down has no purely visual significance. Any other arrangement, sidewise if you will, or any other intermediate position would do just as well.[2] If the relation is constant, the tactual and kinesthetic experiences that one has with objects will soon bring the visual patterns into integration with the other sense avenues so that the field appears perfectly normal.

2. AUDITORY REVERSAL

"Suppose," writes Paul Thomas Young, "a master surgeon could transplant the right inner ear to the left side of the head." Suppose that the auditory nerve could be stretched so that none of the neural connections would be disturbed. And suppose that at the same time the left ear were in the same manner transferred to the right side. Now an operation of this kind is entirely out of question, but just as Stratton reversed the visual field, so Young proposed to reverse the auditory field by means of an instrument called a *reversing pseudophone*. Two trumpets for the hard-of-hearing were modified in such a way that they constituted a soundproof extension of the auditory canal from one side of the head to the other.

The following quotation is an excerpt from Dr. Young's notes made while wearing the pseudophone for the first time.

While writing in my notebook the creaking of a door was heard directly behind and then a laboratory assistant was seen entering the door immediately in front (180° reversal). A few minutes later this same assistant stood beside his desk on my left and dictated a letter. His voice seemed louder than normal and it had an unfamiliar timbre. When I looked at him the localization of his voice was entirely normal. The same door opened a second time. At first the creaking sounds were

[2] This has been tried out experimentally. The field at first appears to be slanting, but finally this effect is less noticeable, although complete adjustment is not attained in a week. Cf. W. Brown, "Perception of Depth with Disoriented Vision," *British Journal of Psychology*, 1928, 19, 117-46.

Plan of the Experiment

During the experiment the pseudophone was worn for a period of eighteen consecutive days. For the first nine days the pseudophone was worn an hour daily (11 to 12 A.M., June 10-18). For the following six days the period was lengthened to two hours (10 to 12 A.M., June 19-24). Most of this time was spent upon the streets of Berlin in the region of the *Kurfürstendamm,* observing the localization of various street sounds. Finally the pseudophone was worn continuously for three complete days. At night during the latter period the pseudophone was removed and the ears were plugged with *Ohropax* (a commercial product) and vaseline. The time (June 25-27) was spent on the street, in the house under everyday conditions, and in the psychological laboratory. During the main experiment the pseudophone was worn for a total of fifty-eight hours. From first to last in the present investigation the writer observed with the pseudophone approximately eighty-five hours.

Excerpt from Notebook on Eighth Day

"I have learned that when I hear a sound on the left it is necessary to look to the right in order to see the source, and vice versa. Consequently I sometimes look deliberately in the *wrong* direction and this generally brings the expected source into view. The most natural thing to do is to look towards the place where the sound is heard. Sometimes I follow the auditory cue and sometimes I reinterpret the cue and deliberately look in the opposite direction. I do not mean to imply that I always look or start to look when I localize; this is not the case. In most cases the localization is immediate; it is made before there is any observed bodily movement; the sound is initially heard *there;* movements may be absent or unobserved."

heard in the rear but when I looked at the man entering the room the localization of these sounds changed to front.

The noise of rain pattering on the windowpane across the room at my left was distinctly localized off to the right and at the same time a watch seen on a table on my right was heard ticking at the left (double simultaneous reversal). The assistant who stood in front of the window spoke and his voice was normally localized but at the same time the rain pattering on the window was heard on the opposite side (simultaneous normal and reversed localization).[3]

Two days later the account continues:

On May 14 I stood before an open window of the Institute[4] and listened to the street sounds in front and a few feet below. The tread of horses on the pavement, auto horns, streetcar bells, the hum of motors, etc., seemed to be normally localized. Once a horse came from the left to the median plane. The sound of the tread was normal in localization. When the horse reached the median plane I closed my eyes. Then the horse was distinctly heard to recede in the direction from which he came. A moment later the eyes were opened and when the horse was again seen the localization of the tread quickly became normal.

While walking along the sidewalk I heard the voices of two ladies and their steps approaching and overtaking me from behind on the right. Quite automatically I stepped to the left, making more room for them to pass. I looked back and found that I had stepped directly in front of them. My automatic reaction as well as the localization was reversed.

There were repeated cases in which I would expect a truck, horse, streetcar or something else to appear in the left (or right) portion of the visual field but, contrary to expectation, the object would appear on the opposite side. In some of these cases I noticed a gross bodily adjustment towards the position of the expected source.

I found myself deliberately correcting known reversals. I heard a pedestrian overtaking me from behind on the right. Knowing that the person was actually on the left, I stepped aside to the right to let him pass. Once I heard a team of horses drawing near on a side street to my right. Deliberately I looked to the left and saw the team there, and at the same time the localization of the sound shifted.

[3] Paul Thomas Young, "Auditory Localization with Acoustical Transposition of the Ears," *Journal of Experimental Psychology,* 11, 1928, 399.
[4] The Psychological Institute in Berlin.

I heard a pedestrian overtaking me on the left. As the sounds came nearer I expected the person to pass on the right but the sounds were still heard left. For a moment there was an interplay between sensory expectation (left) and intellectual expectation (right). Then I *heard* the pedestrian on the right at the moment he appeared there in indirect vision.

The effect of habituation. Throughout the main experiment, when a sound came suddenly, unexpectedly or from an unknown position, the localization was reversed. When, in other words, localization was made on a purely auditory basis, reversal was the usual thing at the close of the habituation period.

The case is different when the influence of vision is considered. At the very start of the experiment localizations were occasionally normal when the source was seen or when its position was attentively fixated. This was reported by every one of the nine control subjects, who, incidentally, gave reversed localization when tested with closed eyes.

As the experiment progressed a casual glance at an object was sufficient to check up the fact that its sound was normally localized. With habituation, all of the sounds in a complex situation were normally localized without any thought about the matter. On a busy street, for example, with a streetcar *here* and a man talking *there* and an auto passing *yonder,* etc., all sounds were normally localized and the total visual-auditory experience was as it is in everyday life without the pseudophone. And not only this! When a source passed out of view its localization remained normal when I paid any attention to the matter. In other words, at the start vision sometimes determined the localization, and with habituation there was increasing dominance of vision until finally a stage was reached indistinguishable from normal. There was increasing and finally complete visual dominance in determining sound localizations but, as noted above, this did not extend to auditory localizations lacking a visual cue.

In everyday life one does not have to search far to find situations in which vision dominates in determining sound localization. The ventriloquist speaks consistently in one voice when he moves puppet A and in another voice when he moves puppet B. The onlooker becomes gradually adjusted to the situation and then gets the well-known ventriloquist's illusion. The talking motion pictures gives a further illustration of the same principle. The voice of a speaker in an auditorium may be indefinitely localized but fixation upon the speaker makes the localization more definite. Here are cases of visual-auditory localization!

Conclusion.—The present experiment has made it clear *that sound localization is not merely a function of the ear. It is an accomplishment of the organism as a whole involving muscle systems common to both eye and ear.*

Other features of perception do not lend themselves to a treatment of the kind comprising this volume. For that reason we leave this chapter with a feeling that the topic is unfinished as, indeed, it is. Laboratory demonstrations with visual and auditory materials will serve to make significant the principles of "closure," "figure and ground," and *Prägnanz* in a way that cannot be accomplished by our method of treatment.

Summary of the chapter.—The two experiments show that no precise relations need obtain between the various sense departments. Any relation, after a period of readjustment, is as satisfactory as its predecessor. All this points to the fundamental integrity of the *whole* organism as the reacting mechanism.

XVI

CONDITIONING

ARLY in this century an American psychologist[1] was study-ing the knee jerk. A system of apparatus had been arranged to give uniform light hammer blows to the leg just below the patella, and measurements on the extent of the reflex in response to constant stimulation were being made for the first time. As an entirely incidental matter this author observed that when some-thing went wrong with the apparatus and a blow was *not* deliv-ered to the kneecap, the leg kicked anyway. He made some re-marks about the "association of ideas" and thereby missed the opportunity to become the accredited discoverer of a phenomenon which has since come to be called the "conditioned reflex."

1. PAVLOV'S DISCOVERY

It remained for the Russian physiologist, Ivan Pavlov, to see the significance of these "conditioned reflexes." He stumbled upon the phenomenon in the course of a series of studies on the digestive processes in dogs, an endeavor which later earned for him the Nobel Prize in Physiology. What he observed was very simple: that if an incidental stimulating condition is uniformly present at the time dogs are fed, that condition becomes the stimulus for reac-tions previously associated only with food. Anybody who has called "Kitty, Kitty!" or whistled for a dog at mealtime has observed as much. Pavlov's principal contribution was a quantification of this observation plus an insight into its significance.

His animals were prepared by operation so that the ducts of

[1] E. B. Twitmeyer, *A Study of the Knee-Jerk,* University of Pennsylvania, Philadelphia, 1902, pp. 36.

the salivary glands were led to the outside of the dog's cheek. Under these conditions it was possible to observe the magnitude of the dog's salivary response to food. The unconditioned reflexes caused by the chemical and mechanical properties of food on the dog's tongue were precise and predictable, but the "learned reflexes"—anticipatory feeding reactions occasioned by the sound of the footsteps of an attendant who fed the dogs—appeared to be capricious, variable, totally unreliable, and not really worthy of scientific attention. Enough apparatus was eventually fastened to the dog so that precise measurements of as little as a tenth of a drop of saliva could be made. At the same time the dogs were kept in soundproof rooms far removed from the usual sources of stimulation. The experimenter even manipulated the apparatus mechanically and remotely from another room. The measurements finally became so precise that the buzzing of an insignificant fly accidentally admitted to the experimental room was enough to upset the experiment.

The essential findings of Pavlov have been described and used in explanations previously. (See pages 211-212.) For the purposes of this chapter, however, we must recall that whenever a consummatory response is made, whatever conditions are present at the same time become associated with it to the extent that they serve as substitutes for the normal stimulus eliciting the consummatory response.

In the simplest case we may think of the responses uniformly present when food is placed directly on a dog's tongue. Aside from gulping and swallowing, copious salivation occurs. If some indifferent stimulus occurs at the same time—a stimulus which does not originally result in this response—after several presentations this stimulus alone will cause the dog to salivate. Pavlov called this *acquired* salivation a "psychic reflex" to distinguish it from an ordinary reflex, which was presumed not to be a matter of personal biography but rather a matter of inherited structure.

It soon became apparent, however, that many conditions which were thought of as inborn traits were actually learned. The "sight of food" elicited anticipatory responses in dogs that were practically indistinguishable from the consummatory responses accompanying food placed directly on the tongue. Because of their association with food, odors are known to be particularly efficacious in releasing salivation, and among human beings *words* like "lemon" produce these responses. Obviously the efficacy of a word like "lemon" depends on the experiences that a person has had with this particular auditory or visual pattern—the equivalent word in a foreign language would not produce a flow of saliva or any other identifiable response. Today we use the term "conditioned response" to imply any response which is conditioned upon a particular training, while "unconditioned" means a natural or unlearned response which is independent of the training of a particular person or animal. As usual, there are borderline cases difficult to classify. For instance, the visual stimulus caused by the rapid approach of an object toward the eye will not, in the newborn, cause a protective blinking of the eyelid. Nevertheless, in an older child or in an adult, such stimuli release responses as appropriate to the occasion as an actual contact with the cornea. As implied in the description, not only the approach reactions characteristic of eating may serve as the source of conditioned responses, but also any withdrawal response which is ordinarily made to noxious stimuli can serve as the basis for a wide range of withdrawals to stimuli originally ineffective in this respect.

Higher order conditioning.—These learned or "conditioned responses" can actually be used in the production of other conditioned responses as though they were inborn or natural. Thus the sound of a bell, which has, in a certain animal, resulted in salivation, can be employed as though it were an unlearned response in the production of a new conditioned response to a visual stimulus. These responses are called conditioned reflexes of the second order. Such reflexes have been established to several higher orders, but eventually there is a limit beyond which further training is ineffective. Just what these limits are for human beings has not yet been determined.

Experimental extinction.—Even conditioned responses of the first order will not forever continue to be displayed. If the sound of a bell is not *occasionally* followed by a reinforcement, the actual consummatory response, the sound will gradually and finally become as ineffective as it was at first. This phenomenon, when it occurs under the eyes of an animal psychologist, is known as "experimental extinction," but it happens every day as, for example, when a child fails to find the approbation he has experienced before upon the consummation of a difficult task. We have had occasion to use the concept of experimental extinction previously. (See pages 184-185.) If a conditioned response is extinguished as a result of unrewarded (unreinforced) trials given at one time, the next day it will have reappeared. The extinction process has to be repeated. This routine may have to be repeated on several occasions before final extinction takes place.

2. TIME RELATIONS

Still another finding of the experimentalists secures confirmation in everyday experience, but, unfortunately, few people have had the observational training to distinguish between the time relations involved. It has been shown that, for effective learning, *the unconditioned stimulus must come either simultaneously with or slightly after the conditioned stimulus*. In other words, the bell must be rung either slightly before or simultaneously with the eating response if a connection between the two is to be established. To give the reward before an act is performed is to violate every appropriate finding in psychology or physiology; still we find that mode of behavior control exerted in numerous interpersonal situations, as, for example, when we say to a child, "I will give you a lollypop *now*, if you will (on such-and-such later occasion) run an errand for me."

Helen Morrill Wolfle [2] has examined the relation between the unconditioned stimulus and the conditioned stimulus as it relates to the magnitude of the conditioned response so established. She used the withdrawal of a finger, ordinarily the consequence of a slight electric shock, as the unconditioned stimulus. The condi-

[2] Helen Morrill Wolfle, "Conditioning as a Function of the Interval between the Conditioned and the Original Stimulus," *Journal of General Psychology*, 1932, 7, 80-103.

tioned stimulus was produced by an electrical device which threw a plunger against a metal plate, thus producing a short, sharp sound.

The stimuli were administered in pairs, either simultaneously or with known amounts of time separating them. As demanded by the experimental plan, some of the time the shock came before the sound and part of the time the reverse was true.

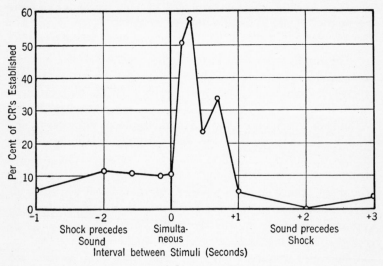

FIG. 63.—Relation between interval separating stimuli and frequency of conditioned responses established.

Seventy-two students in elementary psychology comprised the experimental group; none of these had previous information as to the nature of the experiment. Each subject was given a demonstration of the correct method of placing his hand and finger on the electrodes, and was instructed to lift his finger when shocked, and to replace it after the shock was over. No subject was used for more than one interval.

Practice periods for each subject were forty minutes in length; thus two hundred pairs of stimuli were presented during each period. The subjects came from three to six times, and sometimes even more frequently. The conditioned stimulus was never presented alone during the first twenty minutes of any practice period, and only ten times at irregular intervals during the last twenty minutes. Thus, 30 per cent of conditioning for one practice period would mean that the subject lifted his finger three of the ten times on which he was tested.

The unconditioned stimulus (shock) was constant for each subject in the sense that its intensity was just sufficient to cause a withdrawal movement; however, the absolute intensity varied from subject to subject, and in general was gradually increased throughout each forty-minute period.

The subject sat in a room by himself, the only apparatus in it being the electric hammer and the device for administering the shock. The interval timer and recording apparatus were in an adjoining room.

The results are shown in the figure, where the time intervals between the stimuli are the abscissa units. In this curve the percentage of conditioning for simultaneity between the stimuli is shown on the ordinate marked "zero." As we proceed to the left we find the unconditioned stimulus coming first, with greater and greater separation between the two until the maximum of two seconds is encountered. All of these time relations result in only about 10 per cent conditioning. As we proceed to the right there is a sharp upturn in the proportion of conditioned responses observed but a maximum is reached in less than half a second. At even one second's delay after the sound before the shock is given, conditioning is not so successful as it would have been had the unconditioned stimulus come first. Greater delays up to three seconds simply confirm this fact.

3. SENSORY PRECONDITIONING

In the experiments presented thus far the fact that the conditioned response is developed can be accounted for by observing that the development takes place in the presence of either strong approach or strong avoidance reactions. The incentive value of both noxious and more attractive stimuli has already been elaborated (Chapter X), but there are instances in which an incentive does not seem to be a necessary factor in conditioning. In such cases the mere simultaneity of two stimuli without regard to motivation may be enough to cause a connection between them. This phenomenon is perhaps most clearly shown in an experiment by W. J. Brogden [3] involving dogs. Brogden used eight dogs who were subjected daily for ten days to a pair of stimuli—one a light, the other a sound—twenty different times a day. There was no feeding or withdrawing for either of the two stimuli—they simply were presented together for two seconds, a short wait, then two seconds of sound and light together again. Since this part of the experiment lasted ten days, there were two hundred combinations of these two stimuli during this period.

The group of eight dogs was then arbitrarily divided into two subgroups of four animals each. One of these groups was conditioned in the ordinary manner to withdraw the foot when a bell was rung, the unconditioned stimulus in this case being a slight shock to the left foreleg. Twenty times each day the bell would be sounded, to be followed a short time later by a shock which could be avoided if the animal raised its left forepaw. The second subgroup was conditioned to a light stimulus in the same manner. The results of this conditioning are shown in the table. The numbers in the column on the extreme left are the numbers of the experimental days. On each of these days twenty combinations of either bell and electric shock (BE) or light and electric shock (LE) were given. Since dog 1 avoided the shock twice in the twenty opportunities on the first day, a score of 10 per cent conditioning was entered for him. In the next two days, however, he failed to avoid the shock at any time and as a consequence got two scores of zero. After that the percentage of correct responses gradually increased until by the tenth day he was completely conditioned. The other dogs show about the same picture in the acquisition of the conditioned response, but in some instances more time was required to reach the criterion of always anticipating the shock.

The third part of the experiment consisted in giving only the light to the subgroup that had previously been conditioned to the bell and vice versa. These results are shown at the bottom of page 322. Dog 1, for instance, *reacted to the light as though it were the signal for an impending shock in 55 per cent of the cases on the*

[3] W. J. Brogden, "Sensory Pre-Conditioning," *Journal of Experimental Psychology*, 1939, 25, 323-332.

first day. It was as though this dog had been conditioned before to the light. In the preliminary experiment he had experienced two hundred combinations of the light and bell but it could not be said that he was conditioned to either one because neither had been reinforced. Two of the eight dogs showed no influence of the preliminary association, but the others reacted to either the light or the bell in varying percentages from 10 to 40.

Control.—In order to show that the preliminary association is the effective agent in determining these results, the whole experiment must be repeated with a different group of dogs in which the preliminary training is omitted. Brogden made this control experiment. Had he not done so he could never have been certain that the preliminary training was at all effective, for, as other experiments have shown, the phenomenon of *generalization* could have accounted for his findings. *Generalization* is a name given to the fact that, at least in the early stages of the acquisition of a new conditioned response, almost any stimulus will release the conditioning. If a bell has been used in training, almost any sound can cause withdrawal. At a later stage the response becomes specific to the particular stimulus used in training.

The results of Brogden's control experiment will not be given in detail. Suffice it to say that seven of eight other dogs gave zero withdrawals when the preliminary training was omitted. The other dog gave 20 per cent withdrawals the first day, but none the second.

We may conclude, then, that *the simple association of two stimuli when neither is reinforced can result in the establishment of some connection between them.* It can not be said that these stimuli are completely interchangeable because in the critical experiment the highest percentage of responses was 55 and in two instances there was no sensory preconditioning.

This finding is important because it has been asserted that all learning has to be motivated in some way. On the basis of this and other experiments, a better generalization would be that *although learning can take place without identifiable incentives, it is uniformly more prompt and more complete when some incentive condition is present.*

Results Obtained from the Experimental Animals

The scores in the table represent *in percentages* the number of times conditioned flexion occurred to the conditioned stimulus. Twenty stimulus-presentations were given during each test period.

Bell and light given in combination for 2 seconds, 20 times per day for 10 days.

Experimental Day	Group BE				Group LE			
	Bell and Shock to Left Forepaw				Light and Shock to Left Forepaw			
	No. 1 Score	No. 2 Score	No. 3 Score	No. 4 Score	No. 5 Score	No. 6 Score	No. 7 Score	No. 8 Score
1	10	0	0	15	0	0	10	0
2	0	0	0	20	0	0	0	15
3	0	50	0	20	20	35	15	10
4	35	85	50	30	20	25	0	0
5	90	85	75	40	75	15	0	0
6	95	95	90	75	50	20	35	0
7	95	95	95	85	55	30	70	15
8	90	95	75	75	65	10	55	10
9	90	95	95	70	95	55	75	40
10	100	95	95	80	100	60	90	60
11		100	90	95		30	90	75
12			95	90		65	85	90
13			100	95		70	100	85
14				100		95		90
15						90		90
16						85		100
17						90		
18						100		

Critical Tests

Experimental Day	Light Alone				Bell Alone			
1	55	0	15	0	40	25	10	20
2	30		10		5	0	0	20
3	10		10		5			45
4	5		0		0			20
5	0							30
6								25
7								10
8								0

4. SUBSTITUTE RESPONSES?

For historical reasons that we can not go into here, many psychologists have been inclined to believe that the conditioned response is the same response as the unconditioned reaction. The familiar diagram found in so many texts—

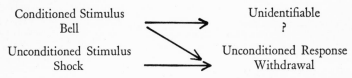

Conditioned Stimulus	Unidentifiable
Bell	?
Unconditioned Stimulus	Unconditioned Response
Shock	Withdrawal

oversimplifies the true situation because it implies that the reaction to a conditioned stimulus is simply transferred from one stimulus to another. This interpretation has been criticized by several writers, Bechterev, for example, showing that if a dog was prevented from making a conditioned response in the right leg, he would make it with the left, although the left leg had never been trained. A result of this kind is totally unpredictable from the diagram. A psychologist or a physiologist of some insight might expect the dog to react this way, but he would be using other sources of information in arriving at his prediction.

Wickens[4] has set up a situation that gives experimental support to the notion that stimulus substitution is an utterly inadequate concept. He used eighteen subjects who were conditioned to withdraw one of their fingers from an electrode, using a buzzer as the conditioning stimulus. The details of the experiment are so nearly like those of Wolfle's that we shall not repeat them here. The principal difference was that in the original training the subject's hand was strapped, palm down, in such a position that in order to avoid the shock he must raise one of his fingers, a movement which involves a contraction of the extensor muscles and a relaxation of the flexors. After the conditioned response was thoroughly established the hand was turned over so that in order to avoid the shock the

[4] Delos D. Wickens, "The Transference of Conditioned Excitation and Conditioned Inhibition from One Muscle Group to the Antagonistic Muscle Group," *Journal of Experimental Psychology,* 1938, 22, 101-123.

flexors had to contract and the extensors relax. These are totally incompatible movements.

After the hand was turned over the buzzer alone was presented. Ten of the eighteen subjects immediately withdrew their fingers from the electrodes, although a group of muscles that had not been trained in contraction had to be used to accomplish this result. In the case of the other subjects, there simply was no response to the first presentation of the buzzer in the new situation. *They did not make the inappropriate response of pushing their fingers harder against the electrode,* a reaction that would have occurred had they simply been behaving according to the demands of their previous training.

Summary of the chapter.—This chapter in a sense only recapitulates the principles already employed in other chapters and is therefore a summary in and of itself. It is valuable to the structure of this book because it serves to systematize previously scattered references. It is not systematic with respect to the entire field of conditioning because it mentions only a few of the literally thousands of experiments that have been made.

XVII

LEARNING

ONE of the central problems in psychology today concerns the manner in which a person learns something. Considerable progress has been made in the direction of solving the problem, but scientific explanations frequently do not satisfy people who are looking for final causes. We find people impressed with the fact that "scientists can't tell us what electricity is," for instance. Much is made, in their thinking and talking, of the inability of the scientist to tell them what electricity is so that they can understand it. They grant that physicists and engineers and, for that matter, housewives and power station attendants, can control electricity, but they regard as a fundamental failure the incomplete understanding of the nature of the phenomenon. Exactly the same kind of criticism, if it is a criticism, can be leveled against the psychologist's explanation of learning. It consists of descriptions of the way learning rates vary under different conditions. Situations can be set in which no modification of behavior at all will result; there are others in which the modification comes about with varying degrees of promptness and permanence. The relation between the individuals who are to learn and the innumerable factors of the situation which can change the extent and nature of the modification of the learner's behavior is the problem of learning. A *description* of these relations is a scientific *explanation* of learning.

1. KNOWLEDGE OF RESULTS

We have already pointed out (Chapter X) that a knowledge of results is one factor which modifies the rate of learning. To emphasize this important point we look at another experiment on the same topic.

One hundred twenty-four juniors and seniors in psychology classes at Indiana University[1] took part in four different learning experiments which involved between forty-five and seventy-five practice periods each. Since the results in all four experiments, in-

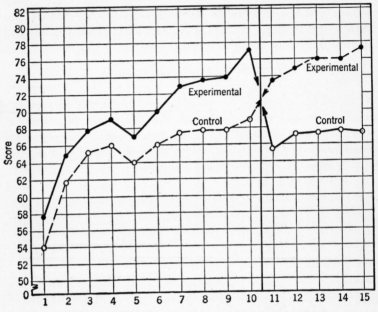

FIG. 64.—The effect of knowledge of results on performance.

volving different kinds of activity, were uniform, we confine our attention to just one simple task—that of making legibly as many written *a*'s as could be accomplished in thirty seconds. This is not a task in which we would expect beforehand that college students would show very much improvement. But as a matter of fact, they improved markedly, even without a knowledge of results.

Method.—In the usual way two groups were formed. For the first ten days, for fifty practice periods, five each day, one of these groups was kept in comparative ignorance of how well it performed

[1] William F. Book and Lee Norvell, "The Will to Learn," *Pedagogical Seminary*, 1922, 29, 303-62.

by having every person fold over the paper on which the *a*'s had just been made, so that no accurate record of the score could be made. The experimental group, on the other hand, counted its *a*'s and each person wrote his score in a prominent place on his paper. After fifty practice periods the control and experimental groups were reversed, so that for the last twenty-five practice periods each person worked under exactly the opposite set of conditions that had been used for him in the first part.

Results.—The results are shown in Figure 64.

The experimental group, with knowledge of results, from the first was clearly superior to the control group. After the change was instituted at the end of the fiftieth trial, there was an immediate effect on both groups. *The lower group, now working with knowledge of results, became clearly superior to the group that up to this time had exceeded it in performance.*

The fact that the control group made any improvement at all can be attributed to either one or the other of two causes, or perhaps to both of them. The subjects were not likely to be *completely* in the dark regarding their progress. The fact that no special precaution was taken to ensure that they knew how they were getting along would not keep some of them, or all of them, from keeping a private record however inaccurate or casual. Moreover, there may have been other factors besides knowledge of results which operated to produce some increase in score from practice to practice.

2. PRACTICE

In view of the old adage that "practice makes perfect," it should be true that the fifty practice periods themselves could account for part of the learning. But the efficacy of sheer practice is doubtful. Thorndike [2] asks us to consider the following experiment.

You sit at your desk with a large pad of paper and a pencil, close your eyes and say, "Draw a four-inch line with one quick movement,"

[2] E. L. Thorndike, *Human Learning,* D. Appleton-Century Company, New York, 1931, pp. 8-9.

Distribution of Responses

Frequencies in Sittings 1 to 12

Length of Line Made	1	2	3	4	5	6	7	8	9	10	11	12
3.70-3.79				1								
3.80-3.89					2							
3.90-3.99												
4.00-4.09				3						3		
4.10-4.19	2			3	1				1	4		
4.20-4.29	1	2	1	6	3		1			8	4	
4.30-4.39	4		3	5	4				1	9	3	
4.40-4.49	3	4	2	12	4	3			6	12	13	
4.50-4.59	11	7	8	14	15	3	7	2	14	18	18	3
4.60-4.69	11	14	8	14	13	8	7	3	23	23	20	
4.70-4.79	21	14	9	13	25	16	14	11	22	14	20	6
4.80-4.89	26	19	15	18	16	17	27	14	18	15	22	6
4.90-4.99	30	18	10	16	21	18	28	22	24	24	17	13
5.00-5.09	20	19	24	14	25	29	21	26	24	16	20	25
5.10-5.19	22	31	22	14	15	14	32	25	12	16	10	27
5.20-5.29	16	28	18	16	25	23	21	24	12	8	11	24
5.30-5.39	12	16	18	18	8	17	13	21	11	2	8	30
5.40-5.49	7	7	12	12	8	7	10	10	8	2	4	17
5.50-5.59	3	4	13	10	8	7	8	13	4		1	12
5.60-5.69	2	2	5	4	1	4	7	4	2			7
5.70-5.79	1	3	4	6	2	5	2	4	1			3
5.80-5.89			2		1			1				
5.90-5.99		2	1					1				1
6.00-6.09												
6.10-6.19				1								
6.20-6.29						1						1
Total	192	190	175	200	192	172	198	181	183	174	171	175

and again and again draw with one quick shove a line intended to be four inches long. You keep your eyes closed throughout. Day after day you do this until you have drawn 3,000 lines, no one of which you have ever seen.

If one were persevering enough to do an experiment of this kind, he would be testing the effects of dogged drill without the interference of other factors which can accompany repetition and he would be conducting the test in just about as ideal a fashion as any experimenter could hope to get. Thorndike has made this experiment, with the results shown in the table on page 328.

On the first day, the longest line made was 5.7 inches, the shortest 4.1; most of them were 4.9. In the whole experiment, the shortest was 3.7 and the longest 6.2 inches. The interval which contains the median is indicated in italics. If a line were drawn across the table to connect these italicized numerals (in effect this is what we do when we draw a learning curve), we would see that there is not the remotest resemblance to a learning curve in the resultant trend. *The 3,000 repetitions caused no learning at all.*

3. FREQUENCY AND RECENCY

The ineffectiveness of practice alone in explaining the learning process has been shown in still another way by means of an instrument called a mental maze.[3] When the principle upon which this maze is constructed is once revealed, the problem is so very simple that the progress of learning cannot be observed. But when a person is thrown on his own resources and has to discover for himself the correct way through the maze, the problem appears to be very complicated and, as in the problems of daily life, there is a good deal of stumbling, hesitation, groping and guessing on the subject's part. The directions which the subject reads from the typewritten copy are shown on page 331. At the bottom of that page is the diagram which reveals the problem. This diagram is not shown to the sub-

[3] Joseph Peterson, "Learning When Frequency and Recency Factors Are Negative," *Journal of Experimental Psychology*, 1922, 5, 270-300.

ject, and without it most subjects are lost during most of the time the learning is going on.

Method.—While the subject is reading, the experimenter arranges a screen which serves to keep the subject from getting any cue from the experimenter's facial expression as to whether he is right or wrong. It is the experimenter's responsibility to control his voice carefully in presenting the letters so that there can be no cue from differences in the emphasis with which either of the letters is spoken. The experimenter then says *N-V*. If the subject says *N*, he has thereby led himself into a figurative blind alley and according to the plan he has to go back to the beginning again; hence the experimenter says *N-V* again. Meanwhile he has recorded what the subject said. If in response to the second *N-V*, the subject chooses *V*, then the experimenter passes on to the next combination, *I-L*. If the subject chooses *I*, the next combination is read, but if he chooses *L*, then the experimenter says *N-V*. The chances that the subject will say either *N* or *V* are equal, so that out of a large number, we would expect half of the subjects to say *V*, but the chance of his getting *I* correctly by guessing is only one in four, and the probability that he will be able to go through all the combinations correctly by mere guessing is only one in 1,024.

Without any accurate record of results, one would jump to the conclusion that a person learned a task like this because, on the whole, he made the correct responses more frequently than he made errors. But an accurate record shows many puzzling changes in behavior that are entirely inexplicable in terms of either how many times a given choice has been made in the past or how recently it has been made.

That performance of a typical subject is shown on page 332. This table is to be read as follows: The first nine times *N-V* was presented the subject chose *N*. For the next four times he chose *V*, as indicated by the *x*, but each time that *I-L* was presented, *L*, the blind alley, was chosen. By the time the fiftieth error was made only twenty-five correct responses had been made and the subject had never been further than halfway through the maze. In all, one hundred and twenty errors were made.

Instructions to the Subject

A maze, you know, is a winding way to some goal, but it has many blind alleys which will lead you to error if you enter them. I have drawn a maze which I will show you when you have completed this experiment. Wherever there is a choice of two alleys, each pathway is designated by a letter. No two parts are lettered the same. I call out two letters at a time, and you are to choose one of them; then I call out two more; and so on, till you get to the goal. Whether the right letter comes first or second in the pair called out is determined wholly by a chance-order schedule, arranged by flipping a coin; hence you need not attend to which letter comes first. In fact, if you try to choose according to some predetermined plan or order, or try to make the letters you choose spell words, you will never learn the way to the goal. The problem is to see with how few errors you can get to the goal, and how soon you can learn to make no errors at all. You are through the experiment when you get to the goal the third successive time without any error. You will be told each time when the goal is reached, and also the number of errors made in reaching it. Remember, accent and order of calling out the letters have no significance. Don't attend to them. Keep in mind also that where we go in the maze depends on your own choices.

Note:—Please do not inform anyone else about the nature of this experiment. All subjects must be ignorant of it when they begin.

N	V*	I*	L	F	K*	E*	G	Q	B*	T*	O	A	C*	Y*	X	U	S*	H*	J
1-9																			
	x		10																
	x		11																
	x		12																
	x		13																
14-21																			
	x		22																
23-26																			
	x		27																
28-23																			
	x		34																
35-40																			
	x	x		41															
	x	x		42															
	x	x			x	x		43											
	x		44																
	x	x			x	x		45											
	x		46																
	x	x			x	x		47											
48-50																			
	x	x	–	51															
52-54																			
	x		55																
56-59																			
	x	x			x	x		60											
	x		61																
	x		62																
	x		63																
64																			
	x		65		x	x	66												
	x		67																
68-69																			
	x		70																
	x	x			x	x		71											
72-73																			
	x	x		74															
	x	x		75															
	x		76																
77-79																			
	x		80																
	x		81																
82																			
	x	x			x	x		83											
84-85																			
	x	x			x	x			x	x		86							
87-88																			
	x	x			x		89												
	x	x		90															
	x	x		91															
92																			
	x	x		94	x		93												
	x	x			x	x			x	x		95							
	x	x			x	x			x	x		96							
	x	x			x	x			x	x		97							
	x	x			x	x			x	x			x				x		98
	x	x			x	x			x	x			x		99				
	x	x		100															
	x	x		101															
	x	x			x	x			x	x			x		102				
	x	x			x	x			x	x			x		103				
	x	x			x	x			x	x			x		104				
	x	x			x	x			x	x			x		105				
	x	x			x	x			x	x			x		106				
107																			
108																			
	x	x		109															
	x	x		110															
	x	x			x	x			x	x			x		111				
	x	x		112															
	x	x			x	x			x	x			x		113				
114																			
115																			
	x	x		116															
	x	x		117															
	x	x			x	x			x	x			x		118				
	x	x			x	x			x	x			x		119				
	x	x			x	x			x	x			x	x			x	x	
	x	x			x	x			x	x			x		120				
	x	x			x	x			x	x			x	x			x	x	
62	60	41	19	15	27	25	3	6	18	18	0	4	14	2	11	0	3	2	1

The frequency and recency theories of learning fail to explain why, once having made nine responses of *N*, the subject finally, the tenth time, said *V*. Or after having chosen *L* seven times, he shifts to *I*. On the other hand, these factors can be used to explain why the subject reacted as he did in the choices 2 through 9 and for other limited parts of the experiment.

Thus we would conclude that the *frequency and the recency of an act do have some limited explanatory significance, but their precise relation to other factors, such as knowledge of results and consequences of the act, is not at all understood at present.* Since this whole field is highly controversial among professional psychologists, any positive statement regarding the efficacy of any one factor is entirely out of line with the objectives of this book. *We simply do not know in any precise way how the various factors that are known to have some effect on learning are interrelated.*

Schoolroom drill.—Somehow many repetitions are supposed to result in learning. Any more adequate methods of studying are apparently never taught in the public schools. Indeed, the teachers may not be aware that drill in itself is not productive of learning. Evidence of their belief in the efficacy of drill is observed when they assign a misspelled word to be written fifty or one hundred times. Multiplication tables, theorems, and methods of computation, as well as more specialized training in typewriting and shorthand and music, all make their painful bows to "practice makes perfect."

4. PRACTICE IN ERROR

Dunlap has pointed out [4] that there are three logical possibilities in connection with the relations between practice and learning, of which "practice makes perfect" is only one. As he states them, practice may facilitate learning (this is the most common notion, but we have been demonstrating its falsity); practice may have no effect on learning at all; practice may inhibit learning. The first

[4] Knight Dunlap, "A Revision of the Fundamental Law of Habit Formation," *Science,* 1928, 67, 360-62.

and most common of these statements he calls the alpha hypothesis, the second the beta, and the third the gamma. The most useful thing about an array of hypotheses of this kind is that they cause one to plan experiments to test them that would never even have been thought of in the absence of the hypothesis.

Dunlap's beta hypothesis has, for instance, resulted in several experiments in which the subjects practice their errors instead of practicing the correct ways of doing things.

If practice in itself has no effect on learning, its main function must be that of allowing other causal factors an opportunity to operate. Patently, one *does* have to practice, even if it should turn out that actually the *mere* repetition of an act does not account for what and how much is learned. One could never learn to operate a typewriter without actually manipulating a keyboard. But the point of the beta hypothesis is that, if practice allows favorable factors to function, it also allows an equal, or more than equal, opportunity for factors unfavorable to a certain performance to operate, whatever they might turn out to be.

In one experiment to test this hypothesis [5] forty night school students who studied shorthand acted as subjects. Dictation was given to them which contained an unusual number of words frequently misspelled. From their papers, which contained no erasures or corrections of any kind, a study of errors was made. If any error in spelling was found four times, and if the student could spell it correctly orally, the error was classed as a constant automatic error in typing. There were two students who made eight such errors apiece, and nine more who made four each. These words were then divided into two equal groups. Group one was to be practiced in error and group two practiced correctly. The student's attention was called to the fact that he was making automatic errors and he was instructed to write the words of group one incorrectly, i.e., as he had been making the error. These instructions were uniformly considered unusual, funny, mysterious. The practice in error was supervised to assure that the students would, as directed, type eight

[5] J. Q. Holsopple and V. A. Vanouse, "A Note on the Beta Hypothesis of Learning," *School and Society*, 1929, 29, 15-6.

full lines of each error. The words of the other group were assigned for the same amount of ordinary drill, i.e., typed correctly.

In an examination of the subsequently typed papers *not a single one of the eleven students made an error in the words which were practiced in error while all except one continued to make the errors which were supposed to have been drilled out of them* by practicing the correct responses.

5. BELONGING

Thorndike [6] is responsible for still another experiment which demonstrates on the one hand the inadequacy of mere repetition and on the other the positive adequacy of what he calls "the principle of belonging."

The list of sentences shown on page 336 was read to a group of students ten times. After the tenth reading, they were asked to answer the questions shown at the bottom of the page. It is clear that "Edward" follows "sadly" just as often as "Davis" follows "Edward," but because these presentations are sentences there is a closer meaningful connection between "Edward Davis" than there is between "sadly Edward." The average per cent correct from the end of one sentence to the beginning of the next was about 3.0; while from the first to the second word in the same sentence, it was 21.5. For the seventh question in the list, 81 per cent of the replies were correct.

If mere repetition were effective, all sequences that occur an equal number of times should be remembered equally well. They are not. But what Thorndike apparently fails to see is that "belongingness" itself needs to be explained. How do things come to belong together? A verb which in English "belongs" in the fore part of a sentence close to its subject, in German "belongs" at the end of the sentence separated from its subject by all manner of phrases and clauses. An adjective which "belongs" in a certain relation to the noun it modifies in French, "belongs" in a reverse location in

[6] Edward L. Thorndike, *Human Learning,* Chap. 2.

The Sentences Read and the Questions Asked

Alfred Dukes and his sister worked sadly.
Edward Davis and his brother argued rarely.
Francis Bragg and his cousin played hard.
Barney Croft and his father watched earnestly.
Lincoln Blake and his uncle listened gladly.
Jackson Craig and his son struggled often.
Charlotte Dean and her friend studied easily.
Mary Borah and her companion complained dully.
Norman Foster and his mother bought much.
Alice Hanson and her teacher came yesterday.

1. What word came next after *rarely?*
2. What word came next after *Lincoln?*
3. What word came next after *gladly?*
4. What word came next after *dully?*
5. What word came next after *Mary?*
6. What word came next after *earnestly?*
7. What word came next after *Norman Foster and his mother?*
8. What word came next after *and his son struggled often?*

English. And a question mark which "belongs" at the end of our sentences "belongs" at the beginning in Spanish. This belonging can only result from the formative factors of experience, whatever they might turn out to be, before the experiment in question is started. Belonging itself is derived, but once derived, it is an effective factor, as Thorndike's experiment shows.[7]

6. MOTIVATION AND LEARNING

The connection between the problems of motivation and learning can best be perceived by recalling the experimental situations in which motivation is studied in animals. We have shown how Warden and others (page 177) put an obstruction between a hungry rat and a dish of food. This arrangement permitted them to study the drive or "energy" with which an animal went about obtaining the food. The process of crossing a charged grill was very simple. In the maze experiments with animals there is also an obstruction interposed between the hungry animal and the food box. But this obstruction is of an entirely different nature from the electrically charged grill. It is a long, and in some instances a complicated, pathway which, to be mastered effectively, does not require so much brute force as it demands cleverness on the part of the animals.

So long as the maze remains constant and the degree of hunger or the amount and kind of reward is varied in different experiments, the maze technique can be used to measure the strength of different drive conditions (page 180). But the fundamental assumption in these experiments is that the cleverness—or, more technically, the maze-learning ability—of the different groups of animals

[7] Gestalt psychologists have denied that belonging must itself be learned. They have pointed out instances in which it appears that belonging is the "natural outcome" of situational relations quite independent of learning. We cannot enter here into an extended analysis of this controversial issue. There has been no experimental contribution to answer the question. See Wolfgang Köhler, *Gestalt Psychology,* Liveright Publishing Corp., New York, 1929, especially pages 352-59.

is the same. The assumption is probably warranted because large enough groups are used to iron out individual differences.

There is another possibility. If we are interested in the effect of alleys of different lengths or of turns in different directions or maze floors of different composition, these things can be varied and the motivating conditions kept constant. Then we are studying learning.[8]

Kuo's[9] apparatus allowed his animals to get to food by four alternative routes. One of them had an electric grill in the floor; as far as this one alley was concerned, the situation duplicated Warden's (cf. page 177), but the other three alleys presented possibilities of selection that Warden's setup did not offer. One of these three was arranged so that if the animal chose it he was confined for a short time. Another alley led to a long pathway with several turns in it before food was available; the last led directly to the food. In actual practice the position of the compartments was changed so that the easily learned position habits would not be confused with the effect of the different kinds of alleys.

We will not go into detail in examining the behavior of the thirteen rats Kuo studied, although their responses are interesting. It is sufficient for our purpose to observe that on the whole the electric shock compartment was eliminated first, the confinement compartment second, and then the long path. The short path compartment for most rats was the one eventually used exclusively. This result shows that *the consequences of an act are powerful determiners of whether or not it will be repeated*. A shock causes an actual withdrawal from the point where food is. As a consequence behavior for a time is variable and some other method of solution is tried. The confinement causes an interruption in the goal-directed activity and the consequent variability in performance is the same. Least interference with motivated activity comes about as a result

[8] There is still another possibility. When the maze is constant and when the motivating conditions are constant, some animals still learn more quickly than others. We have already discussed an experiment of this kind.

[9] Zing Yang Kuo, "The Nature of Unsuccessful Acts and Their Order of Elimination in Animal Learning," *Journal of Comparative Psychology,* 1922, 2, 1-27.

of the latter two paths. They survive the elimination process. We can infer from this that any condition which intercepts or deflects the activity of a goal-directed animal will finally be eliminated in favor of an alternative possibility in which the consummatory act can take place more promptly or more completely.

Human subjects have been shocked for taking the right pathway in ordinary finger mazes and some modifications of them. The promptness of their learning has been compared with a shock administered for going into the blind alleys. Under these conditions it sometimes happens that the correct path for which the subject is shocked—punished, if you will—is learned more promptly than the reverse condition, where he is punished for making the errors. The interpretation of these experiments is still being argued, some holding that they show that punishment cannot explain why errors are eliminated. But there is little agreement on this point; a final interpretation will have to wait for more experimental evidence.

7. GUIDANCE

If a typical subject who is trying to learn the mental maze is told, "Now here is a difficult problem. I am going to help you by telling you that the correct answer to the first combination that you will hear is *V*, not *N*," we might expect that more than half the total number of errors would be eliminated. Whether this reduction would actually result from instructions of this kind in this problem we have no way of knowing in the absence of an actual demonstration of its verity. But one frequently hears a teacher say, "Now you take my word that such-and-such is so. Then try to find out the answer to this, and this, and this on your own." The usual teaching techniques involve guidance and direction and limits as to the final outcome of a problem, particularly in the earlier stages of solution. After that wise teachers gradually withdraw their directional influence while foolish ones solve problems completely for their pupils and, as a consequence, develop a group of intellectually ineffectual dependents.

Carr and his students [10] have tried to find out whether a subject, either animal or human, can master a problem more quickly when his reactions to that problem are guided and directed than he can when he is compelled to solve the problem on his own initiative. The guidance that they used was mechanical in some instances, i.e., a maze, for example, had all of the blind alleys plugged so that no errors could be made in certain guided trials. In other cases the guidance was manual, in which case a person who knew the way through a maze actually led a person who didn't know by the hand. This technique may have been suggested by the etymology of *educate,* which comes indirectly from the Latin *educere,* "to lead out of." In still other cases the guidance consisted merely of information about errors, a function fulfilled by the professional teacher who marks errors on papers. In still other cases the guidance was given by verbal direction, a technique frequently used as a practical timesaving device in laboratory courses.

In all of the experiments which Carr reports, whether made with rats or human beings, the device used to measure the effectiveness of the learning was related to this timesaving feature of teaching. If a group of subjects required, on the average, thirty trials to learn a maze, and another group, after five guided trials, had to have twenty more to reach the same criterion of mastery, then it is clear that five guided trials are equal to ten unguided ones. Each guided trial is equal in learning effectiveness to two unguided ones. On the other hand, it might turn out that after five guided runs, an additional twenty-five trials would be required to meet the criterion. In that case since the total is thirty, there would be no advantage at all in the guided trials. Each guided run is equal to one unguided.

There is also the possibility that a group of subjects might be somewhat worse off after having had guidance. This would be true if they required more trials to learn than a comparison group which had not been guided.

Table A shows results of this kind for several different experiments with human subjects on mazes. The table is to be read as follows: When 2 guided trials are numbers 1 and 2, each guided

[10] Harvey Carr, "Teaching and Learning," *Journal of Genetic Psychology,* 1930, 37, 189-219. This is a summary of several experimental studies.

run is equivalent to 3.7 unguided. When trials 1 and 2 are undirected and 3 and 4 are guided, then each unguided trial is equal to —3.0 directed trials. The minus sign indicates that more trials were required by the guided group.

Note that guidance is never detrimental when instituted late in the practice, but neither is it very effective. On the other hand, *it may be positively detrimental, as shown by the minus sign, if insti-*

TABLE A

MECHANICAL GUIDANCE

Number of Guided Trials	Number of Undirected Runs That Are Equivalent to One Directed Run					
2	3.7 (1-2)	—3.0 (3-4)	0.6 (5-6)	1.6 (7-8)	4.3 (9-10)	3.0 (11-12)
4	1.8 (1-4)		0.15 (5-8)		1.7 (9-12)	
6	0.1 (1-6)			1.2 (7-12)		
8	—1.6 (1-8)				0.9 (9-16)	
12	—0.12 (1-12)					

TABLE B

MANUAL GUIDANCE

Number of Guided Trials	Number of Undirected Runs That Are Equivalent to One Guided Run			
2	3.8 (1-2)	5.9 (3-4)	3.2 (7-8)	0.4 (11-12)
4	0.9 (1-4)	2.0 (5-8)	1.0 (9-12)	
8	1.2 (1-8)			
12	0.9 (1-12)			
16	0.2 (1-16)			

tuted early in the practice. This statement is truer for the longer periods of guidance than it is for the shorter.

In another set of experiments the alleys in the mazes were not blocked, but a person who knew the maze pattern manually directed the subject. The results for this kind of guidance are shown in Table B.

Manual guidance was never detrimental, but in all those cases where the numbers in the table are less than one, guided trials are not as effective as the unguided. The larger the numbers, the more effective guidance is. These large numbers occur first, *where the amount of guidance is small,* and second, *where guidance comes early, but not at the very beginning of the learning process.*

Summary.—On the basis of far more data than we have given here, Carr concludes,

For the most part, the efficacy of the tuition [guidance] tended to decrease with the amount given and the later in the learning stage in which it was instituted. The most effective results are secured generally by giving a small amount of tuition [guidance] relatively early in the process. Detrimental results were generally secured when too much tuition [guidance] was given or when it was inserted at an inopportune time.

8. A PRACTICAL APPLICATION

If you read anything over twenty times you will not learn it by heart so easily as if you were to read it only ten, trying to repeat it between whiles, and when memory failed looking at the book.[11]

Gates's experiment was designed to answer the extremely practical question, "What are the relative values of learning by reading as compared to learning by recitation in the case of school children working under school conditions and with the ordinary schoolroom methods of attack?"

[11] Francis Bacon, *Novum Organum,* 1620, Trans. James Spedding, 1863, 229; cited by Gates, *op. cit.*

To satisfy the practical nature of his problem, Gates[12] secured his subjects from a grammar school in Oakland, California. All the grades from the first through the eighth, comprising somewhat more than three hundred individuals, took part in various parts of the study.

Some preliminary experiments indicated that material similar to the sample shown on page 344 could be used and at the same time was nearly enough like the kinds of things that children have to do in the classroom to form a reasonable task.

It was planned to provide for six different combinations of reading and recitation:

	1	*2*	*3*	*4*	*5*	*6*
Per cent of time reading	100	80	60	40	20	10
Per cent of time reciting	0	20	40	60	80	90

It is perfectly obvious that if a single group of subjects using a single text used method 1 and was compared with a different group of subjects using method 2, there would be no assurance that whatever differences were found would not be due to a difference in the groups. The problem of *equalizing* the groups and the materials, the time of day and the amount of previous practice was solved according to the following plan: At 9.00 A.M. of the first day, a group was given its first sitting under method 1, using text 1. A second group then studied the same text according to method 2; then group 3 worked according to method 3. The complete details of the plan are shown in the table on page 346. The personnel of each group—seven or eight individuals—remained constant for the duration of the experiment.

Method of studying.—A single squad was seated at the table in the experimental room, a copy of the material was passed out face downward before each pupil, and the following instructions were given:

On each of these cards is a biography (show a sample). Now the object of the test today is to see how many of these things you can learn in a certain short time.

[12] Arthur I. Gates, "Recitation as a Factor in Memorizing," *Archives of Psychology,* 1917, No. 40.

SAMPLE OF MATERIAL USED IN GRADES 5, 6, 7, AND 8

James Church, born in Michigan, February 15, 1869. Studied in Munich, and later studied forestry and agriculture. Director of Mt. Rose Weather Observatory in 1906. Studied evaporation of snow, water content, and frost.

John Clark, born in Indiana, June 4, 1867. Studied surgery and became a doctor in Philadelphia. Taught at Johns Hopkins. Has visited Italy and Russia. Has a brother in Vancouver.

Morton Clover, born in Ohio, April 25, 1875. Studied chemistry at Michigan. Worked in Manila for eight years. Wrote articles on the content of dogwood, of sugar, and acids. Now lives in Detroit.

Clarence Cory, born in Indiana, September 4, 1872. Studied in Purdue and Cornell universities. Now lives in Berkeley. Is Professor of Engineering and Dean of Mechanics. Since 1901 has been Consulting Engineer of San Francisco. Is a member of the British Institute.

George Curtis, born in Massachusetts, July 10, 1872. Studied geography at Harvard. Won gold medals at Paris in 1900. Member of Boston Scientific Society. Went on the Dixie Expedition in 1902.

The eighth grade used five biographies; the fifth and sixth used four. There were six texts of equal difficulty in all.

SAMPLE OF MATERIAL USED IN GRADES 3 AND 4

Harry is fourteen years old. His father is a farmer. Around the farm are red stones, blackberry bushes, red clay, green clover, and small trees. Harry is in the eighth grade and is tall and slender. He likes dancing and singing.

James was born in June, 1905. He is going to be a carpenter. He can make a chair, a stool, a box, a gate, and a window. His mother has white hair and wears a black dress. His father is fifty-five years old.

Harold was born in New York. He came to California when six years old. He is now fifteen years old and has a gun, a bicycle, a kite, a pair of skates, and a baseball suit. He is going to be a lawyer and live in Seattle.

Fred was born in March, 1898. He lives on 31st and Parker streets. He goes to business college. He is tall, has black hair and blue eyes, wears a gray suit and brown necktie. His home is made of brick and granite.

The fourth grade used four biographies; the third grade used three. In all there were six texts of equal difficulty.

We will proceed like this. I will give you two signals to start. At "Ready" you take the card at the corner like this and at "Go" you turn the card over and begin to study.

Now you are going to study for a while in one way and then later you are going to study in a very different way. To begin with you are to study by reading this material over and over from beginning to end [illustrate]. Remember you are to read only. You should never look away from the paper; never close your eyes to see if you can say the words; in fact never say a single word unless you are actually looking at it, actually reading it. Remember you are to read through from the first to the last every time.

After you have read the material through and through in this way for a while, I am going to give you a signal "Recite." When I say "Recite" you are to hold your paper in front of you so that when you are looking straight ahead, you look over the top of it and you can see it by glancing downward a little like this. Now you are to try to say to yourselves as much of the material as you can without looking at the card. When you cannot remember the next word look down at your card and then go on saying as many of them as possible without looking. Glance at the card again whenever you cannot remember. Go through the list from the first word to the last in this way and continue until the word "Time" is given. Remember you are not to look at the words unless you absolutely have to.

When the learning period is over I am going to ask you to write as much of this material as you can.

Method of scoring.—The sense material was scored by dividing the original texts into details, ideas, or facts that were mentioned, to serve as a guide. One credit was given for the correct reproduction of each of these "details" when they fell under the proper name. When a detail, such as a birthplace, was correctly reproduced but applied to the wrong person, one-half a unit was given. In some cases the credits of one-half or three-fourths were given to details or facts partly correct, depending upon the judgment of the grader.

Part of the sense material was scored by one individual and part by another, neither of whom was acquainted with the experiments in general. To test the reliability of the judgments, forty papers were scored independently by each grader. Variations of small magnitude were found, but these were due to variable errors

PLAN OF THE EXPERIMENT

	DAY 1	DAY 2	DAY 3	DAY 4	DAY 5	DAY 6	TOTAL
Method 1	Group 1	Group 2	Group 3	Group 4	Group 5	Group 6	All groups
	Trial 1	Trial 2	Trial 3	Trial 4	Trial 5	Trial 6	All trials
	Hour A	Hour F	Hour E	Hour D	Hour C	Hour B	All hours
	Text 1	Text 2	Text 3	Text 4	Text 5	Text 6	All texts
Method 2	Group 2	Group 3	Group 4	Group 5	Group 6	Group 1	All groups
	Trial 1	Trial 2	Trial 3	Trial 4	Trial 5	Trial 6	All trials
	Hour B	Hour A	Hour F	Hour E	Hour D	Hour C	All hours
	Text 1	Text 2	Text 3	Text 4	Text 5	Text 6	All texts
Method 3	Group 3	Group 4	Group 5	Group 6	Group 1	Group 2	All groups
	Trial 1	Trial 2	Trial 3	Trial 4	Trial 5	Trial 6	All trials
	Hour C	Hour B	Hour A	Hour F	Hour E	Hour D	All hours
	Text 1	Text 2	Text 3	Text 4	Text 5	Text 6	All texts
Method 4	Group 4	Group 5	Group 6	Group 1	Group 2	Group 3	All groups
	Trial 1	Trial 2	Trial 3	Trial 4	Trial 5	Trial 6	All trials
	Hour D	Hour C	Hour B	Hour A	Hour F	Hour E	All hours
	Text 1	Text 2	Text 3	Text 4	Text 5	Text 6	All texts
Method 5	Group 5	Group 6	Group 1	Group 2	Group 3	Group 4	All groups
	Trial 1	Trial 2	Trial 3	Trial 4	Trial 5	Trial 6	All trials
	Hour E	Hour D	Hour C	Hour B	Hour A	Hour F	All hours
	Text 1	Text 2	Text 3	Text 4	Text 5	Text 6	All texts
Method 6	Group 6	Group 1	Group 2	Group 3	Group 4	Group 5	All groups
	Trial 1	Trial 2	Trial 3	Trial 4	Trial 5	Trial 6	All trials
	Hour F	Hour E	Hour D	Hour C	Hour B	Hour A	All hours
	Text 1	Text 2	Text 3	Text 4	Text 5	Text 6	All texts

that compensated each other in the long run, producing, on an average, forty scores with very slight differences.

Results.—The results for the eighth grade and the third grade are shown here and are typical of the results from all the grades and from a few adults who also served as subjects.

	1	2	3	4	5	6
Grade 8	20.8	22.4	24.8	25.0	25.3	23.8
Relative score	87.8	94.6	105.0	105.5	106.8	100.0
Grade 3	8.7	10.3	11.2	14.2	13.1	12.1
Relative score	74.8	89.3	96.5	121.9	113.1	104.4

The relative score was computed by taking the average raw score of all methods and all grades as 100. Proportionally as the results from individual methods are above or below this average, they either exceed or fall short of 100.

We may conclude:

(1) The best results are obtained by introducing recitation after having devoted not more than 40 per cent of the time to reading.

(2) The *best* method for the various groups (condition 4) is from 17 to 47 per cent better than straight reading.

(3) Reading alone without recitation always gives the poorest performance.

(4) The lower grades benefit most from recitation.

Practical application.—Many students know no better method of studying than to read over and over again the material they are trying to study. According to the results of this experiment, this is the worst possible method to use. Frequent reviews, thinking the matter over by oneself, writing briefs of the main points, conversation with other students, and the like, are valuable because they throw into relief the portions that are hazy, inexact, and confused and because they fix more clearly in mind the material that is rehearsed.

Various opinions have been expressed with regard to methods of taking notes during lectures. Doubtless the method must be varied somewhat to suit the material that is presented, but the findings in the present study suggest a method which, although seldom employed, should bring good results. Instead of making onself a mechanism for transferring spoken words to paper with but little heed to their meaning, the student could devote his attention to a thorough understanding of the material presented, selecting the important points, organizing them into a systematic whole as the lecture progresses, and, for the most part, delaying until a later hour the writing of the notes. Later in the day or evening, the lecture could be rehearsed and an outline written down for future reference. While some disadvantages or, more likely, inconveniences of such a method may appear, certain advantages of an important nature are obvious. First of all, the student may develop better habits of attention during the lecture. He forces himself to pick out the essentials, to grasp the relations of ideas and to unify and to organize the material presented.

Summary of the chapter.—Modification of behavior is secured more promptly—other conditions remaining constant—when the learners are aware of their progress. As our second section showed, no learning results when the subject is kept completely in the dark. Sheer practice is not effective in bringing learning about. Neither the frequency with which a response has been made nor its recency will explain all the specific choices that subjects make in a mental maze. Our fourth experiment showed that if the errors rather than the correct responses are practiced, modification is more permanent in correcting certain kinds of errors in spelling. Practice is important in that it allows other factors that are causal to operate. One of these factors has been called belonging; another is knowledge of results; another is the consequence of an act.

Teaching involves an active attempt on the part of one person to modify the course of learning in another. One can generalize that guidance should come early in the learning process and that there should be only small amounts of it for the most positive facilitating effect. Making errors is not to be avoided for from errors some of the most instructive experiences come. The last experiment demonstrates that learning is an active process. One must participate; he cannot learn effectively when he passively reads material over and over.

In the problem of learning we are not interested alone in the acquisition of an act, but we also have some concern about how permanent the modification is. Our next chapter discusses some of the considerations that have to be taken into account when we say a person has or has not remembered what he has learned.

XVIII

REMEMBERING

ONE of the simplest questions that one can ask a person is, "How much of some poem, some course, some mathematical operation, or some remote childhood experience do you remember?" Nevertheless these simple questions have no simple answers. How much of a given experience is retained depends, among other things, upon the way in which retention is to be measured. If one requires a perfect reproduction immediately, with no aids of any kind and with no stumbling around, it is perfectly clear that a high standard is being set; the amount of forgetting a person does, measured in this way, would far exceed the amount he retains.

On the other hand, if a person is required to select only the items he has learned from those that he has not experienced before, the task becomes simpler and the amount that he could be said to have retained would be more.

1. RELATIVITY OF REMEMBERING

The exact relationship between five different methods of measuring retention has been studied by C. W. Luh,[1] who, at the time he made these experiments, was a graduate student at the University of Chicago.

Method.—In order to make experiments like this it is necessary to use large amounts of material of equal difficulty. If the memory for a task has been tested twenty minutes after it has first been learned, then that task cannot be used again when the experimenter

[1] C. W. Luh, "The Conditions of Retention," *Psychological Monographs,* 1922, 31, No. 142, 87.

wants to compare how much is remembered at one hour with the twenty-minute period. Another equally difficult task must be used, not the same one. If five different ways of measuring retention are to be compared, as in this experiment, then it would appear that five times as much material must be on hand as would be required for a single measurement. In this experiment there were five periods of delay after the original learning, twenty minutes, one hour, four hours, twenty-four hours and forty-eight hours. This would mean twenty-five tasks of equal difficulty. As will be explained later, Luh cleverly cut this number down to ten by combining the various retention measures. But even ten different and equally difficult tasks are not easy to provide.

The nearest approximation to this ideal is to be found in nonsense syllables. A series of twelve syllables was learned for each task. The syllables were presented one every two seconds by means of an automatic device. All series were learned to a criterion of one perfect reproduction at one sitting. Then the experiment proper started.

Twenty minutes after the learning, the subject was again seated in front of the exposure apparatus.

(1) He was required to anticipate each exposure of the twelve syllables. Since the rate of exposure was one every two seconds, he had two seconds in which to recall and spell each syllable. The number of times he was correct was recorded. Later the per cent of twelve was determined. The same procedure with a change in lists was repeated twenty-eight times with eight different subjects, the average per cent retained turning out to be about 68, as shown in Figure 65.

(2) The drum was started again and continued to run until the subjects could again anticipate correctly every syllable. Of course, fewer repetitions were required to relearn than to learn, so a comparison of the number of trials for relearning with the number for original learning always shows some retention. In this experiment nine different subjects gave on the average about 75 per cent retention after twenty minutes. For the other time intervals the results closely approximate the curve labeled "Relearning."

The possibilities from this list of syllables were then exhausted so that it had to be discarded. All the subjects then learned another list. This list gave three measures of retention:

(1) The subject was given a piece of paper with twelve lines on it and instructed to write the syllables that he had learned twenty minutes previously. On the average this gave 88 per cent

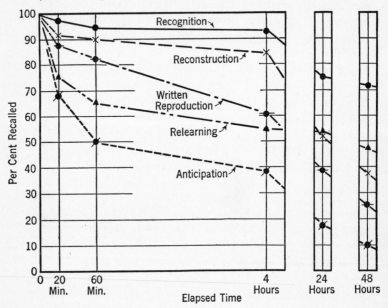

FIG. 65.—Percentage retained measured in five different ways.

retention. For the other intervals the results follow the curve labeled "Written Reproduction."

(2) Immediately following the subject's attempt at written reproduction, he was given a list of twenty-four syllables and required to check the twelve he had learned. There was a time limit of ninety seconds on this task. It revealed on the average a retention of about 98 per cent after the twenty-minute interval, and it consistently gave the highest retention over the whole range of delays, as is shown by its topmost position.

(3) Finally the subject was furnished with the twelve syllables he had learned and required to reconstruct the order of the original

presentation. This reconstruction method resulted in about 92 per cent accuracy at first. It was second place of all the methods for the first twenty-four hours, after which time it took third position.

If one asks what per cent of a list of nonsense syllables is retained four hours after learning, the answer depends on the method used to measure retention. It can be read from the graph. The same methods of measuring, however, give different results after forty-eight hours. The only generalization that can be made is that the anticipation method invariably shows the least retention; the recognition method, the most. The order of the other methods depends on how soon after the learning retention is tested. These results may not be true for other kinds of material or for other criteria of mastery. Obviously this is not a simple question.

2. PRACTICAL APPLICATION

Advertisers want to know whether newspaper and magazine advertising is more effective than radio. It is now becoming an old story to us that the answer to this kind of question, too, is not a simple one.

There are numerous nonpsychological considerations that would determine a choice of advertising medium in any special case. But there is also involved in the final consideration the psychological question: Is material which is presented orally retained better than the same material presented visually? Although this statement narrows the problem to workable proportions, it is still complicated by the consideration that whatever method of presentation proves to be better when retention is measured in one way may not prove to be better when retention is measured in another way.

Method.—Stanton [2] has investigated this problem, using fictitious advertising copy for the material. The same copy was presented on the printed page and delivered over a radio loud-speaker. There was no music or dialogue in the auditory presentation and

[2] Frank N. Stanton, "Memory for Advertising Copy Presented Visually vs. Orally," *Journal of Applied Psychology,* 1934, 18, 45-64.

no illustrations or display type in the visual copy. Every effort was made to eliminate all variables except the two avenues of presentation. To this end no attention-getting devices for either auditory or visual methods could be used.

Controls.—There were two groups of eight advertisements each. With one group of subjects, one set of advertisements (copy X) was presented visually and the other set (copy Y) presented by means of the loud-speaker. For another group of subjects this procedure was reversed. This procedure controls any inherent difficulty in retaining either copy. Another control consisted in making one ad in each set appeal especially to men and another especially attractive to women. The remaining six commodities were designed to appeal equally to the two sexes.

The fictitious trade names selected for the sixteen commodities in the two lists were two-syllable names chosen on the basis of a preliminary study with visual and auditory presentation. Confusing final consonants such as *s* and *f* were distributed equally in the two lists. No two names ended with the same syllable or syllables that sounded alike. The same precaution was maintained for the first syllable of each word. The two lists were balanced for similar products wherever necessary, *e.g.,* gasoline vs. oil, tea vs. coffee. The two lists of trade names and their products are printed below.

X SERIES	Y SERIES
Lorenz Powder	Barlow Cigarettes
Harvey Toothpaste	Parker Coffee
Bryan Gasoline	Crawford Bread
Warren Candy	Stewart Oil
Kenwood Soap	Robbins Shaving Cream
Douglas Cigars	Andrews Ginger Ale
Curtis Ink	Browning Hosiery
Randolph Tea	Wagner Mouthwash

A further attempt was made in the preliminary series to insure equal trade-name-commodity associations. A group of forty subjects, similar to those used in the experiment proper, participated. The experimenter read a list of fictitious trade names to the group, instructing its members to write the name of any product they could associate with the trade name. After collecting those responses, the experimenter repeated the fictitious trade names and with each one gave a product which he had arbitrarily selected to go with it. To all subjects this presentation was made orally. A portion of them received typed copies of the fictitious trade-name commodity lists which they read as the experimenter presented the list verbally. Immediate recall and aided recall tests were given. After an analysis of both sets of responses, those trade names for which there existed any consistent product associations other than the fictitious ones of the experiment were eliminated. Likewise cases where the fictitious trade-name-commodity associations ran extremely high or low with the experimental group were eliminated. The effort was to select material for which there was no naturally strong association between product and brand and also in which the formation of such associations was not extremely difficult.

Each piece of advertising copy was of approximately constant length—between 70 and 75 words—and included three mentions of the trade name and its product. The first mention occurred at the opening, another approximately in the middle, with the third at the close of the paragraph. In each mention the trade name always came first with the product immediately after. Care was exercised to keep all copy as nearly equal in complexity and sales appeal as possible. No dramatic statements or slogans were employed.

Subjects.—The subjects for this investigation were 160 students of both sexes enrolled in psychology courses at the Ohio State University during the summer quarter of 1933. They were divided into 4 groups to permit the necessary reversals of copy and method of presentation. The table shows how copy and method of presentation varied with the 4 groups. For instance, group A had copy X auditorially, followed by copy Y visually at the same sitting.

The ads were presented visually by the use of booklets which measured 6 inches in width and 9 inches in height and used an antique India stock for the text with a cover of dark blue paper. The instructions and fictitious advertising copy were set in 12 point, bold antique face, 18 picas, leaded two points. No emphasis was given to trade names or products by the use of caps, italics, or special type. Copy occurred only on every fourth page, making it necessary to use 40 pages in each booklet.

SCHEDULE OF COMPARISONS

GROUPS	A	B	C	D
Copy used and method of presentation	X aud.	Y aud.	X vis.	Y vis.
	Y vis.	X vis.	Y aud.	X aud.
Number of subjects	39	38	42	41

The copy prepared for the booklets was also used for the auditory presentation, made by a student announcer over a small portable public address system. The announcer read the copy to the groups. Several practice presentations were made by the announcer and the experimenter in order to eliminate possible stress or emphasis on any point. The trade names were not spelled out. The announcer and amplifying unit were outside the classrooms in which the presentations were made.

The following directions were given by the experimenter when the visual presentations came first (groups C and D):

Shortly, I shall pass out some booklets to you. Please place them so that the word "Front" on the upper half of the cover is facing you. When I give the signal you will please break the seal and turn at once to the first printed page. After you have finished reading it, please turn to the next page which will be blank and then look up to receive the starting signal. Ready . . . begin.

Further instructions for the visual part of the experiment were presented on the same paper with the same type as the advertising copy in order to facilitate adjustment of the subjects for the copy to come. The instructions read by the subjects were as follows:

On the following pages you will read a series of advertisements for familiar products. Will you please sit comfortably and read the copy carefully. Later you will be asked to answer some questions about the products and the trade names—the features of the products and the inducements to buy. Time enough will be allowed to read each advertisement through once. When you have finished reading the ad, please turn immediately to the next page in this booklet. The page will be blank. After you have done so await the signal from the experimenter before turning to the next advertisement. The time between readings will give you an opportunity to think over the ad just read. Throughout the experiment will you please remain quiet so as not to disturb your neighbor.

Before giving the signal to begin the experimenter gave an opportunity for questions, but none were asked in the entire experiment. Following this brief interval he gave the starting signal. At the end of each succeeding minute the signal to turn was given until all eight advertisements were read. The booklets were collected and after a pause came the following announcement through the loud-speaker which had been installed before the class convened.

In the following minutes you will hear a series of advertisements for familiar products. Will you please sit comfortably and listen carefully to the copy. Later you will be asked to answer some questions about the products and the inducements to buy. Between each advertisement there will be a pause during which you will have time to think over the ad just heard. Throughout the experiment will you please remain quiet so that you will not disturb your neighbor.

Recall and recognition tests were given at three different time intervals after the presentations, one day, seven days, and twenty-one days. Three subgroups of subjects were formed for this purpose by selecting every third name from the class rolls. On the test day the instructors read the names of the students who were to serve as subjects. They left their classes and met in a common room. Thus each group was tested only once.

The pure Recall Test forms were mimeographed and headed by the following directions to the subjects:

On the lower part of this sheet will you please list as quickly as possible all the products you can remember as having heard or read about in this experiment. List them in the order in which you recall them. Try to list both product and trade name, such as: Beechnut Chewing Gum, not just Chewing Gum. If you cannot do that, then please list either the product or trade name in the proper column. Please try to do your very best. Keep your eyes on your own sheet at all times. A sample is given below.

The Aided Recall Test forms were given as soon as all Recall blanks had been collected. Two forms of the Aided Recall Tests were designed to keep the commodity names on the blank in the same sequence as that in which they had been read in the booklet or heard through the loud-speaker or vice versa. This test form consisted of a series of sixteen blank lines with one commodity appearing to the right of each line. Only products actually used in the experiment were included in the list. The instructions on each form of the test were as follows:

On the lower part of this sheet you will find a list of products made up from the advertisements you heard and read about in the experiment. In front of each product on the list is a blank space. Write in the blank space the trade name for each product on the list that you can remember. Please keep your eyes on your own paper at all times. A sample is given below.

The Recognition Test blanks were made up likewise and consisted of sixteen blank lines, each of which was followed on the right by the product and four two-syllable fictitious trade names. One out of each four was correct and was to be recorded in the blank. The positions of the correct trade names were staggered down the page. Directions for this test follow:

On the lower part of this sheet you will find a list of products made up from the advertisements you heard and read in the experiment. In front of each product is a blank space in which you are to write the correct trade name of each product if you recognize the trade name in the group of four trade names appearing to the right of each product listed. Please keep your eyes on your own sheet at all times. A sample is given below.

For all three methods of measuring retention, the auditory recall is somewhat superior to the visual. The auditory method becomes increasingly superior to the visual in the recognition method, but not in the other two. Whether this advantage for the auditory presentation would continue if longer periods had been used we cannot say.

Throughout the experiment every precaution was taken to control all the variables by keeping them as constant as possible. Yet in searching the procedure and results for an answer to the reason for auditory superiority, one must not overlook the part played by the experimental situation. The auditory results are probably heightened somewhat as a result of the abnormal attention to the loud-speaker and the copy. But one must not overlook the visual advantages. Few printed advertisements receive the attention given to the visual copy in this study. The students were warned not to look inside the booklets, thus setting up a condition of expectancy. They were instructed to read every word of copy, which, of course, is not the case in normal visual advertising. Thus the effectiveness of both media was presumably increased. Here, as in the case of presenting the copy (visual void of illustrations, display faces, and so on; auditory without music or sound effects), the advantages and disadvantages are as nearly equal as possible with this setup. When we consider that the college student is a trained reader, such an experiment with other persons may even show a greater difference in favor of audition for certain economic levels.

3. REMINISCENCE

Retention curves do not always have the appearance of the ones we have just seen. Instead of a continuous decrement, some show an actual increase in the amount recalled as time progresses. In order to distinguish between the two types, those that show decrement have been called *curves of obliviscence,* and those that show increments have been called *curves of reminiscence.* Reminiscence can be observed only in partly learned materials. If material is perfectly learned, there can obviously be no more than 100 per cent recall.

Reminiscence was first studied in detail by Ballard,[3] an English

[3] P. B. Ballard, "Obliviscence and Reminiscence," *British Journal of Psychology,* Monograph Supplement, No. 1, 1913.

investigator, in 1913. Since he worked mostly with children and with poetry, he assumed that the effect was a result of these two factors. This conclusion is not justified, however, because other investigators have obtained reminiscent effects with other materials and with subjects of different ages. Ballard also thought that the degree of learning was effective. As pointed out above, reminiscence

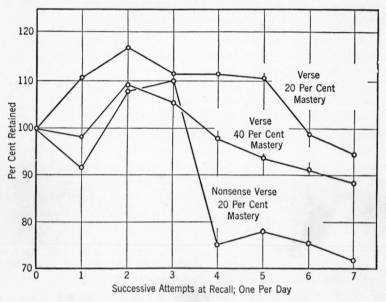

FIG. 66.—Retention curves showing reminiscence.

presupposes partly learned materials, but obliviscence has been observed with partly learned materials, too, so that although partial mastery is a necessary condition, it is not invariably effective in producing reminiscence.

The principal results of Ballard's experiment are shown in Figure 66. Verses from the "Wreck of the Hesperus" were practiced until about one-fifth could be recalled; this amount was taken as 100 and the percentage of later recalls was calculated on this basis. The same children attempted the recall seven different times so that the x-axis represents a complication between practice and time. Time alone could have been made the x-variable by using different groups of subjects for each point plotted on the graphs, but this control was not employed. We really cannot tell very much about the reminiscence effect from Ballard's work. His work is mentioned here only because it has been the source of several other experiments designed to explain the reminiscence that he was the first to discover. The educational implications of this work are clear. If we knew how to teach so that even better performance would be obtained a year after a course is finished than is obtained on a final examination given immediately after, the educational outlook would not be quite so somber as it appears when students promptly forget most of what they learn.

Williams [4] has performed an experiment designed to control some of the numerous variables encountered. He used 2,006 subjects in all, which were divided into four groups. Group 1 was composed of third and fourth graders; group 2 of sixth and seventh; group 3 of tenth and eleventh grades. A fourth group was made up of college students. These groups were further divided on the basis of the length of retention. Since no subject was used more than twice, after the student was tested for immediate retention he would be used but once again. If he was to be tested for retention on the seventh day, the seventh day comprised his second attempt at recall. A procedure of this kind requires large numbers of subjects.

The length of the material to be learned was varied with the age of the subjects so that all groups were able to reproduce only about 50 per cent of the material after five minutes spent in studying it. There were no definite time limits set for the reproduction. The younger subjects, in general, required more time.

There were two kinds of material: verse from "The Spider and the Fly," and fifty abstract monosyllabic words.

As in Ballard's experiment, the amount of immediate retention was taken as 100, and the percentages for later retention were compared to this figure as a base. As Figure 67 shows, there was definite evidence of reminiscence for the two younger age groups. That this is not alone an age-effect can be observed by comparing the solid curves with the dotted ones. Such a comparison shows the

[4] Osborne Williams, "A Study of the Phenomenon of Reminiscence," *Journal of Experimental Psychology*, 1926, 9, 368-87.

effect of a change in the material when age is held constant. The abstract words[5] without connective material are retained least, while for all age groups connected verse is retained better.

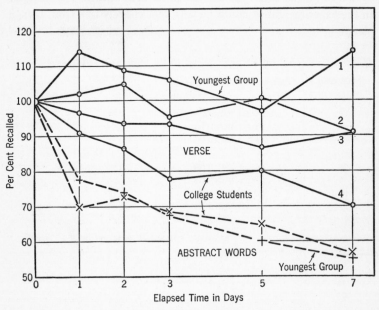

FIG. 67.—A group of retention curves showing both reminiscence and obliviscence.

4. BURTT'S EXPERIMENT

We have pointed out in previous experiments that even when there is no overt evidence that a person has ever learned a thing, it is possible to show that previous experience is still effective because he can relearn the same task in much less time. That even very early childhood experiences can be effective was shown by Burtt.[6]

[5] Only two of the curves for the abstract material are presented here, since the other two are very similar. Were they shown, the picture would merely be complicated without any real advantage in interpretation.

[6] H. E. Burtt, "An Experimental Study of Early Childhood Memory," *Journal of Genetic Psychology*, 1932, 40, 287-95.

Burtt read passages to his young son from Sophocles's *Oedipus Tyrannus* in the original Greek. At the time of the original reading the boy was between 15 months and 3 years of age, a mere infant, so that there was no assurance that he actually learned the material. In the experimental situation he was kept entirely free from toys or playthings.

SELECTION	AGE AT ORIGINAL LEARNING	REPETITIONS REQUIRED AT 8½	AVERAGE
1	15-18 months	382	
2	18-21 months	253	
3	21-24 months	385	340
4	24-27 months	379	
5	27-30 months	328	
6	30-33 months	226	
7	33-36 months	265	299
	Average for seven selections.....317		
A	8½ years	409	
B	8½ years	451	
C	8½ years	455	
	Average for three selections 435		

Beginning at fifteen months, three passages of twenty lines—240 syllables—were read daily for ninety days. At the age of eighteen months these three passages were dropped and three more were substituted. This procedure was continued until the child was three years old, whereupon the whole matter was dropped until he was eight and one-half years old.

In the twenty-one months between fifteen and thirty-six there were seven passages read. These seven and three others were learned at age eight and one-half years. The three new ones (A, B, C) were presumably of equal difficulty to the previously learned selections. The nature of the experiment was explained to the subject, but he was not told which selections had been learned previously and which had not been. For the first seventeen trials the experimenter merely read the selections in the same fashion that they had been read in the beginning. But with the eighteenth trial the subject anticipated wherever he could as the selection was read very slowly. As the experiment progressed he was supplying more and more words and phrases. This procedure, with minor changes, was continued until every word except the cue words at the beginning of each selection was anticipated. It required about eleven months for the first selection to be learned. It was then dropped from the schedule. In sixteen months all the selections had been learned.

The averages to be compared are, in the first place, 435 repetitions required for the new passages (A, B, C) and 317 for the ones heard previously—a saving of 27 per cent.

If we compare the repetitions required for material heard at less than two years of age and for new material, we find a 21 per cent saving. But during the latter half of the period, when 299 trials were required, we observe that the saving is 32 per cent. This finding is perfectly astounding. One would not be surprised perhaps at 5 per cent saving. But at eight and one-half years, to find that almost one-third fewer trials are required to learn material *only heard* in the years before three, indicates an influence exerted by the experiences of the early years that could hardly have been foreseen.

Burtt had not used all of his material in this experiment at eight and one-half years. When his young son was fourteen, he produced enough material to repeat the whole experiment. The procedure was the same as at eight and one-half. For the first eighteen trials, the material was simply read to the subject. Beginning with the nineteenth, every third trial made use of the prompting method in which the subject tried to anticipate as many words and syllables as he could while the passages were slowly read.

The results are shown in a new table (on page 365) which corresponds in significance to the table on page 363.

D, E, and F were new selections which correspond in significance to A, B, and C. The principal comparison is between the average of 162 trials for this new material and 149 for the material experienced between fifteen months and three years of age. This is a saving of thirteen trials or about 8 per cent. Since this saving is to be compared with the 30 per cent that was observed six years

Selection	Age at Original Learning	Repetitions Required at 14 Years	Average
1a	15-18 months	142	
2a	18-21 months	139	
3a	21-24 months	169	150
4a	24-27 months	151	
5a	27-30 months	145	
6a	30-33 months	169	
7a	33-36 months	127	148
D	14 years	169	
E	14 years	151	
F	14 years	166	162

previously, it is apparent that there has been a real loss in retention during the interval. It is likely that by the time the boy is of age, there will be no saving at all in favor of the infantile experiences.

5. MOTOR SKILLS REMEMBERED LONGER?

It is frequently observed that acts of skill, such as riding a bicycle, swimming, or ice-skating, are retained much better than verbal materials such as the Lord's Prayer, the Gettysburg Address, or a Shakespearean sonnet. There often seems at first glance, even from laboratory studies, to be some evidence that this common observation is true. Some remarkable retention has been shown in laboratory studies when people have been tested after several years of no practice in skills which they originally learned under rigid practice conditions. Typical experiments show that it is common to find a very rapid rise to an expert efficiency in certain kinds of juggling tasks even after three or four years of no practice. In a few trials the best performance during the original practice is exceeded. On the other hand, verbal material seems to be quickly forgotten.

One cannot be certain that the results of these numerous experiments are really commensurate because none of them were designed actually to compare the relative retention of skilled motor performances and verbal materials. It is probably true that most skillful acts are overlearned, while most verbal material is just barely learned. Differences in retention would then be due to this fact rather than to any implicit difference in the retention value of "motor" and "mental" acts.

McGeoch and Melton [7] planned an experiment which would show whether or not skilled acts are intrinsically more permanent. They compared maze learning and nonsense syllables and later added a rational learning problem.

Method.—The comparison of different learning tasks like these is not quite the simple task that it first appears. In the first place, even though the tasks are learned to one perfect trial for each one, there is no assurance that they have been learned equally well. The experimenters recognize this difficulty, but the only thing they can do about it is to require that all the learning meet the same criterion of perfection.

Comparisons were made for (a) the average number of trials required to meet the criterion; (b) the time required and (c) the number of errors made. After eight weeks a relearning of both tasks was required; and comparisons were made of (d) the savings scores.

[7] J. A. McGeoch and A. W. Melton, "The Comparative Retention Values of Maze Habits and of Nonsense Syllables," *Journal of Experimental Psychology,* 1929, 12, 392-414. The experiment actually described in these pages is not the original McGeoch and Melton experiment. We have chosen to describe an extension of the original reported by McGeoch under the title "The Comparative Retention Values of a Maze Habit, of Nonsense Syllables, and of Rational Learning," *Journal of Experimental Psychology,* 1932, 15, 662-80.

Subjects and materials.—A relatively easy stylus maze and an eight-syllable list of nonsense material composed the material. There was just one group of eighteen college students. Each subject learned both the maze and the nonsense syllables.

Half the group learned the maze on the first day and the syllables on the second. The other half of the group reversed this procedure. One week later and again at eight weeks they relearned both materials.

The results are shown in the table below.

MAZE SCORES

	ORIGINAL LEARNING (*Mean*)	RELEARNING (*Mean*)	SAVING (*Per Cent*)
Trials	17.2	30.5	−77.5
Time	572.1	437.4	23.5
Errors	130.8	90.7	30.7

NONSENSE SYLLABLES

Trials	24.2	15.4	36.5
Errors	119.0	53.7	58.9

It is clear that the nearer to 100 per cent the saving is, the more the retention. Zero per cent means that the same number of trials was required to relearn as to learn in the first place. If we keep this in mind and compare the trials for maze and nonsense material, it is clear that the retention of the maze is not so complete as the retention of nonsense syllables. The same is true of the errors. Time scores are not entered in the lower part of the table because the syllables were presented at a constant rate.

We would conclude, then, that the statement that motor skills (such as maze learning) are better retained than verbal materials is *not* true. *When we take all of the criteria into consideration, there is no clear-cut superiority for either kind of material.* We might *infer* that the seeming greater retention for some skillful acts is a product of the fact that they are more frequently overlearned.

6. THE TRANSFER OF TRAINING [8]

In an article in a nontechnical magazine which describes the kinds of things a boy should learn in order to become an effective adult in outlook and action, the notion is expressed that fencing is a valuable art. The speed and the dexterity necessary as part of the art of fencing are held to make the boy quick and accurate in his later accomplishments of an intellectual kind. The same idea motivates football coaches who are more interested in training for teamwork and co-operation than they are in winning games. Whatever we may think privately about the sincerity of most coaches, there must be some who are firmly convinced that teamwork learned now on the gridiron is later to be useful when the player sells bonds. The same idea is expressed when it is more romantically said that "the Battle of Waterloo was won on the playing fields of Eton." The technical term used by psychologists to cover phenomena of this kind is "transfer of training."

We have touched on this general topic in our first chapter, where we showed that selection is a better explanation of the superiority of Latin students over their fellows who are not taking Latin

[8] The whole notion of transfer of training poorly fits the framework of our modern understanding of psychological functioning. It is based on the notion that psychological functioning is like muscle functioning. It doesn't make any difference how an individual muscle cell is stimulated. It grows stronger with use whether that use comes in connection with rowing, hoeing, raking, sawing, or routine gymnastic exercise. The doctrine of formal discipline attempted to apply this same idea to reasoning, honesty, memory, attention, and the like. Experiments finally showed that this notion was false in the sense that transfer from one activity to another was always on the side of advantage for the delayed thing and always complete in the sense that nothing was wasted or lost. We now know that one thing learned can aid or hinder or have no effect on the learning of some subsequent performance. The aiding and the hindering can appear in different amounts. Whether it will be an advantage or a disadvantage to subsequent problems to learn one thing does not depend on the thing itself; it depends on the method used in instruction.

than any direct contribution to scholarship from the Latin experience itself.

In this section we reopen the problem with further observations on the influence one thing learned can have on another.

In an experiment performed some time prior to 1916 [9] it was concluded that the habit of producing neat arithmetic papers failed to develop a similar neatness in language and spelling papers. The extension of this generalization to other subjects or to other methods of teaching the same thing is not justified, however, in the face of experiments by Ruediger, [10] who showed that in his school system just exactly the reverse was true even when special effort was made to avoid *any* mention of neatness in other subjects except the one where the habit was to be acquired.

With these results before him, Woodrow [11] saw that these two diametrically opposed results could be explained if the *method* used in teaching were the effective factor in producing a transfer or its lack. He felt that there must be some difference between "unenlightened drill and intelligent teaching." If this is true, then rather than baldly stating that there is no transfer, we would conclude that the method used in teaching will determine whether there is transfer to specific situations where there has been no previous training.

This experiment deals with the possibility of teaching a general technique of memorizing. Its object is to show that training in certain kinds of memorizing may be given in two such widely different ways that in one case the individual will benefit little or not at all and in the other case enormously, when he turns to new kinds of memorizing. The experiment which was carried out on memorizing has, however, its analogy in any field of teaching where training is given in the hope that it will result in a better ability to undertake activities related to, though different from, the particular performances in which the individual is trained.

[9] Squire, reported in W. C. Bagley, *The Educative Process,* The Macmillan Company, New York, 1916, p. 208.
[10] W. C. Ruediger, "The Indirect Improvement of Mental Function through Ideals," *Educational Review,* 1908, 36, 364-71.
[11] Herbert Woodrow, "The Effect of Type of Training upon Transference," *Journal of Educational Psychology,* 1927, 18, 159-72.

Method.—The experiment program is shown in the table on page 372. Three groups of students were required: control, practice, and training groups. The control group contained 106 University of Minnesota sophomores; the practice group contained 34, and the training group 42, all members of classes in experimental psychology at Minnesota. All of the groups of subjects took a pretest and an end test. The control group was tested only at the beginning and the end of the experiment; it memorized no other material. After the pretest the practice group *merely memorized* different kinds of material in the four weeks and five days that the experiment was in progress; then they were tested finally. In addition to memorizing, the training group received *special instruction,* but the total time in instruction and memorizing was the same as the memorizing time of the practice group.

The nature of the tests of memory.—Up to this point we have been very vague about the nature of the pretests and the end tests. Theoretically the statement of the problem is very simple: We want to find out the relative merits of two kinds of training on a person's ability to memorize. In order to accomplish this end the conventional procedure is to give a test before and after the experience and compare these results with those obtained from another group that did not share the experiences in question. If we were interested in the effects of a special kind of diet on weight we could proceed in this straightforward manner, but unfortunately there is no single measure of "memory" as there is for weight in pounds. We cannot say that we have a pretest and an end test of a person's "memorizing ability" because there can be no such test. We must be more specific and say a test for memorizing names, dates, numbers, poetry, or whatever comprises the test, because we know from previous experiments that the relation between abilities in these different areas will not be high.[12]

There were six subtests in the group which composed the bat-

[12] The scores will all be positively correlated, but the magnitude of the correlations will not be high as a rule. In this experiment the average intercorrelation was $+0.38$, corrected for attenuation. The highest coefficient was between "prose" and "poetry" $+0.91 \pm 0.05$; the lowest between "memory span" and "Turkish-English vocabulary" $+0.06 \pm 0.08$.

tery of pre- and end-tests in this experiment. The end-test consisted of different material from the pretest, although the tasks required the same kind of performance on the part of the subjects. They are not necessarily of equal difficulty nor do they have to be for the comparisons that are required.

(1) *Rote memory of poetry:* The time required for learning verbatim was the measure used. The initial test was composed of twenty-eight syllables (four verses) from "Mistress Gilpin" and the end test, 128 syllables (five verses) from "Alice Brand." The second poem was harder to memorize than the first, so for all groups the times are longer on the end test.

(2) *Rote memory of prose:* Selections from Benjamin Franklin's *Autobiography* were used and the time required for perfect mastery was the score.

(3) *Memory for facts:* Twenty items of miscellaneous information, each from a dictionary of facts, composed the two tests. The subjects were allowed six minutes to study the facts and then after a thirty-second intermission, fifteen minutes to write all they could remember. The papers were scored by counting reproductions of the *substance* of each idea in the list. The maximum score was 99 in the pretest; 90 in the end test.

(4) *Turkish-English vocabulary:* Each test consisted of thirty Turkish words and their English equivalents. The subjects were allowed six minutes to study the vocabulary and then after a one-minute intermission the Turkish words were shown, one at a time, printed in large type on cards, while the subjects endeavored to write the corresponding English word. The number recognized was their score.

(5) *Memory for dates:* Lists of twenty obscure historical events were studied for six minutes. After one minute, as the names of the events were shown printed on large cards, the subjects tried to write the corresponding dates. The score was the total number of correct dates. Half credit was allowed when the last two figures of the date were correct even though the century was wrong. No credit was given when the century alone was right and the decade and specific year were wrong.

	CONTROL GROUP N-106 PRETEST	PRACTICE GROUP N-34 PRETEST	TRAINING GROUP N-42 PRETEST
Period I		20 min.: memorizing poetry	7 min.: listening to rules 13 min.: memorizing
Period II	These periods were dis- tri bu ted throughout four weeks.	25 min.: memorizing poetry	7 min.: listening to rules 18 min.: memorizing
Period III		28 min.: memorizing nonsense syllables	28 min.: listening to exposition and il- lustration of rules
Period IV		20 min.: memorizing nonsense syllables	5 min.: listening to review of previous period 15 min.: memorizing nonsense syllables
Period V		19 min.: memorizing nonsense syllables	9 min.: attending to blackboard talk on meaning of second- ary associations 10 min.: memorizing nonsense syllables
Period VI		25 min.: memorizing poetry	25 min.: memorizing poetry
Period VII		20 min.: memorizing poetry	20 min.: memorizing poetry
Period VIII		20 min.: memorizing nonsense syllables	20 min.: listening to review of methods and the situations in which to use them

FIVE-DAY INTERVAL

	END TEST	END TEST	END TEST
TOTAL	*None*	*177 min.*	*177 min.*

Total time memorizing poetry . . . . 90 minutes   76 minutes

Total time memorizing nonsense syllables . . . . 87 minutes   25 minutes

Listening to rules and illustrations . . . .   none   76 minutes

(6) *Memory span for consonants:* The consonants were presented orally, one each second, in lists varying from four to ten. At the conclusion of each reading the subjects wrote as many as they could. The point at which the chances were equal that the series would be right or wrong was determined.[13]

The activities of the practice group.—The practice group practiced the memorizing of poetry and nonsense syllables according to the schedule shown above. There was no discussion of principles, methods, or comparison of methods. They were not told *how* they were to memorize, except that they were told to memorize "by heart" and that when they finished one selection they would begin another. They were assured by the instructor that such practice would improve their memories. This was necessary in order to motivate them for the task.

The activities of the training group.—To the training group, on the other hand, the same practice was given, but in smaller amounts. The remainder of the time was devoted to instruction in certain rules for learning. The training, it was emphasized, offered an opportunity to practice those rules that had been learned. The practical application of these methods to material other than poetry and nonsense syllables was pointed out. The rules they were taught were:

(1) Learning is most effective if accomplished by wholes.

(2) A program of self-testing, or recitation, is effective.

(3) Rhythm and grouping of members and ideas should be used.

(4) Attention should be paid to the meaning by picturing or in some other way symbolizing the material.

(5) Alertness and concentration are very important.

(6) Confidence in ability to memorize is necessary.

(7) Secondary associations should be used.

That some of these methods may not be the best is beside the point. The experiment was not planned to determine relative merit of different methods of learning.

---

[13] The selection of 50 rather than 100 per cent is arbitrary, the reason for the selection being beyond the scope of this treatment.

Results.—Due to the fact that we must consider the effects of practice and training and mere practice on six different kinds of memory instead of on but one kind, the table of results seems formidable. But if one takes one item at a time and makes the proper comparison, the table finally seems to make sense. Let's try it. First, the control group furnishes a base. More time was required to

	Poetry	Prose	Facts	Dates	Vocabulary	Span
Pre-test						
Control	524	637	67.5	7.6	16.2	6.6
Practice	571	654	64.0	7.2	14.6	7.0
Training	539	731	64.0	6.5	13.6	6.4
End-test						
Control	696	454	64.2	9.8	16.1	7.0
Practice	737	487	61.0	9.9	15.1	6.6
Training	596	361	72.2	12.2	21.1	7.7
Gains						
Control	−172	183	−3.3	2.2	−0.1	0.4
Practice	−166	167	−3.0	2.7	0.5	−0.4
Training	− 57	370	8.2	5.7	7.5	1.3
Per Cent Gain						
Control	−32.8	28.7	−4.9	29.0	−0.6	6.7
Practice	−29.1	25.5	−4.7	37.5	3.4	−5.7
Training	−10.6	50.7	12.8	87.7	55.2	20.3

memorize the poetry selection of the end test than the pretest. Since no routine practice of any kind had been given the control group, we *must* conclude that the second selection was harder to memorize than the first. The number of facts remembered is slightly smaller for the end test. This could have meant a little more severity in grading or a little harder list of items. In any event the difference is small and may be attributed to accidental occurrences. The same conclusion can be arrived at in the case of the vocabulary test. In the other instances the differences are slight, except one. The prose test shows that the control group does much better at the end. This must mean, following the reverse of the argument above, that the second selection is definitely easier.

Confining our attention to the pretest results alone, it is perfectly evident that at the start the groups were not all the same in these six abilities. Our task would have been simpler had all three groups required exactly the same time to learn the poetry and the prose; had recalled the same number of facts, the same number of dates; had correctly associated the same number of Turkish-English equivalents and had had the same memory span for consonants. Aside from the time scores in poetry and prose, there does not seem to be a great difference, and fortunately the comparisons that we are interested in do not require that the groups be of equal ability. If we compare the control group with itself, the practice group with the practice group and the training group with itself, the gains and losses shown in the third part of the table emerge.

As we have seen, a longer time was required for the poetry passage on the end test. This shows up as a negative gain in the difference between the two times (524 and 696) shown as the first entry in this part of the table (—172).

Following this column down, one notes that the only great change is for the training group. Presumably had this group not had the training, it too would have required 172 seconds more time to memorize the second selection. As it is, although it does require more time for the second selection, it is only 57 seconds instead of 172. The group that practiced in a routine manner takes an intermediate position, but it is closer to the control group than it is to the training group.

Consistently following the table across, one sees that in every instance the gains are more or the losses are cut down. In two instances, losses are converted to gains. In every case the practice group remains closer to the control group than it does to the training group.

The conclusion is clear, *in all the aspects of memory investigated here, the special methods used with the training group result in better performance than does routine practice in larger amounts. Whether or not there is transfer to acts not specifically practiced depends upon the methods used in training. It may also depend on other factors which were not controlled in this experiment, but its dependence on method rather than content is evident from these data.*

Summary of the chapter.—The first experiment shows how five different answers can be obtained for the simple question of "How much of a given thing do you remember?" The second shows how these facts have to be taken into consideration in a practical case. Attempted recall does not always result in less and less being remembered as time goes on. Sometimes reminiscence is observed, but the factors responsible for it have not yet been wholly determined.[14] That an experience completely forgotten can have its effect on the promptness with which it can be relearned is shown in Burtt's two experiments with his young son. That "motor" acts are not retained any better than "mental" is shown in the fifth section. Finally, the influence that one thing learned can have on another is shown to be partly a matter of the method used in learning rather than the content.

[14] The controversy still continues. Lewis B. Ward, "Reminiscence and Rote Learning," *Psychological Monographs,* 1937, 49, pp. 64, presents evidence that reminiscence is to be observed in nonsense syllable learning with adults provided retention is measured within a few minutes after the original learning is accomplished. Other investigators have thought that reminiscence never could be observed with nonsense materials.

XIX

REASONING

FOR many centuries it was held that one of the distinguishing characteristics of man was his ability to reason. Reasoning was held to be entirely impossible in animals, whereas it was the most excellent accomplishment of man. Men who didn't act in a manner that others thought they should were frequently described as "bereft of reason," as though reason were something that could be put on and taken off like a coat. This was the position of the scholars and the churchmen, who grasped at any suggestion that man and animal formed two entirely different and unrelated systems of life. The common people, while for the most part accepting this dogma, held an ambiguous position. They observed their household pets and their farm animals doing certain things which gave the appearance of their having perceived certain relations. Their dogs and cats were, in many instances, endowed with an ability to reason and to understand that we now know is entirely beyond their capacities. This process of interpreting the behavior of animals in terms of one's own reactions is called "anthropomorphism." Scholars didn't like it, so they spent a great deal of time emphasizing the random and undirected character of animal behavior. Many books were written which "proved" that animals were incapable of reasoning. As is true so often in these extreme views, modern findings have shown both camps to be wrong, although there need no longer be ambiguity in a view which allows animals a limited ability to see relations and combine experiences in new ways.

The year 1910 marked the appearance of two small volumes which were to have a tremendous influence on all later studies of reasoning, or problem solving. In this year Ruger's study of puzzle solving published under the misleading title of "The Psychology of Efficiency"[1] and Dewey's *How We Think*[2] made their appearance. Dewey's revised edition should be read by every student who has any interest in the problems of thinking or reasoning.

1. RUGER'S STUDY

Ruger's volume was the report of an experimental study which he made of adult subjects who solved the kinds of puzzles that all of us have amused ourselves with at one time or another. A familiar example of the kind of task he used is to be found in the "twisted nail" puzzle. Two common nails are twisted together in such a way that they have to be turned just right with respect to each other before they can be got apart. If you will recall your own fumbling with the nails and how, after a great deal of twisting which got you nowhere, suddenly the nails seemed to fall apart without your being able to observe in what relation they were to each other when they came apart, you will have some notion of the problem which confronted Ruger's subjects. He found out that the highly touted reasoning ability of adult human beings is a gross misstatement of fact. His subjects made as many random undirected movements as any lower animal ever did. Many subjects arrived at solutions that took them entirely by surprise and that they could not repeat. Ruger concluded that *there was no sharp line of demarcation between the human being who could reason and the infra-human who could not.*[3] But aside from this generalization, important though it is, his experiments showed how problem solving, or reasoning, could be experimentally manipulated. This was an important methodological step, because the so-called "mental processes" had previously resisted the methods that had been used to study them.

[1] *Archives of Psychology,* 1910, No. 15.
[2] John Dewey, *How We Think,* 1910, D. C. Heath and Company, Boston, Rev. Ed., 1933.
[3] This generalization would not have been justified if based on Ruger's data alone. He worked only with human subjects but he had available in the work of others fairly complete descriptions of animal behavior. For an extensive treatment of the data and generalizations in the field of reasoning in animals see N. R. F. Maier and T. C. Schneirla, *Principles of Animal Psy-*

2. DEWEY'S CONTRIBUTION

Dewey's principal contributions were his analysis of the conditions under which reasoning occurs and his outline of a typical reasoning process. In the first decade of the twentieth century, before his book appeared, most psychologists had been interested in a rather futile argument about whether or not there could be any thinking without images of concrete objects and events. But Dewey's little book exerted a marked influence in turning the interest away from sterile controversies of this kind.[4] There is nothing experimental in his book, but it shows how the environment and the human organism together in interrelation must be considered if one is to set up experiments to answer questions about problem solving. It suggested that good reasoning was not wholly a matter of being born capable. It held that normal people can be trained to be more effective reasoners than they now are. Aside from its effect on psychology, it has had a tremendous influence on the course of education, particularly in the elementary school where there has been a complete revision of the curriculum because of the principles set forth in it.

Dewey showed that as long as the previously learned reactions were adequate for situations, no problem-solving activity occurred. But when none of these old patterns of response result in a consummatory activity, then the stage is set for a rather definite process which he outlines. It consists essentially of formulating an hypothesis and testing it out, generally, but not always, through the process of talking to oneself. If the hypothesis is substantiated by further observation, it is held to be true. He illustrates by pointing to an experience of his own in trying to find out for himself the

chology, McGraw-Hill Book Company, New York, 1935, especially pages 444-479.

[4] The controversy was not uninfluenced by others who held similar views, especially William James, James R. Angell and Harvey Carr. Cf. Fred S. Keller, *The Definition of Psychology*, 1937, D. Appleton-Century Company, New York, pp. 40-53, and Edna Heidbreder, *Seven Psychologies*, D. Appleton-Century Company, 1933.

function of a white pole that extends horizontally from the upper deck of a ferryboat. His first hypothesis was that "it might be a flag pole," but the further observation that there is no rope or any other kind of gear attached to the pole, added to its horizontal position, an unusual one for flag poles, leads him to discard this hypothesis. That it might be part of a radio apparatus is discarded because he recalled that ferryboats don't carry such equipment. That it is ornamental, a third hypothesis, is discarded because tugboats, usually not heavily ornamented, also have it. That it is useful in guiding the boat, a necessity in fact because the pilothouse is so far forward, is a fourth hypothesis which is finally satisfactory to him. Enquiry at the pilothouse verifies the latter hypothesis.

Substitutes for reasoning.—Now it is perfectly clear that a situation of this kind does not always result in the process just outlined. Professor Dewey could have appealed to the authority of the pilothouse in the first place and saved himself a great deal of trouble— a device not uncommonly practiced, by the way. An appeal to the untested authority of laymen results in numerous hypotheses which are accepted as true but which are really misconceptions (cf. Chapter II). But the value of problem-solving activity becomes apparent when we consider problems for which there is no authority until they are solved. The procedure in several scientific fields in solving problems of this kind is set forth in a small volume called *A Guide to Thinking.*[5]

Frustration and reasoning.—The problem-solving situation comes very close to being identical with the kind of stimulating conditions that we have described in terms of frustration (cf. Chapter XI). As a matter of fact, for many of us emotional reactions, grading from mild annoyance to serious displays of temper, are commonly employed in situations that demand analysis, hypothesizing, and testing. The reason is perfectly obvious. In the past we have met our problems in this manner. Solutions of an inadequate kind, generally avoidances and evasions, have removed the

[5] Olin Templin and Anna McCracken, *A Guide to Thinking,* Doubleday, Doran and Company, Garden City, 1927.

See also P. M. Symonds, *The Education and Psychology of Thinking,* McGraw-Hill Book Company, New York, 1936, especially pages 125-143.

necessity of the rigorous observing, defining, calculating and testing demanded in reasoned solutions. Because we have evaded responsibility in the past in this way, we continue to employ the method—it seems to result in a satisfactory arrangement.

Unclear reasoning.—What is termed "muddy" or "foggy" thinking is generally a matter of failing in the close observation required or in telescoping and reversing the various steps in the reasoning process. What is termed clear, logical thinking is a matter of fine discrimination in perceiving the factual elements, the suitability of the hypothesis, the adequacy of the tests and the arrangement of the various steps in a manner calculated to convince others.

One essential tool in laying the foundation for precise reasoning is the acquisition of accurate language habits, because most problem solving is done with language symbols rather than with real objects and events. Even where actual objects are to be manipulated later, the preliminary planning is done in terms of words and diagrams.

Language.—We have previously pointed out (page 102) the manner in which vocabulary is acquired by an infant. In releasing appropriate responses words become the equivalent of objects. If one says the word "candy" in the presence of a two-year-old, the child commences to make the identical responses that he would make were he actually about to receive candy. That is why it is sometimes found expedient to spell words in family conversation when youngsters are present. Later, spelled and written words become as effective as the auditory stimulus alone. This elaboration continues until foreign words and phrases or mathematical and technical symbols have significances in terms of the objects and operations they designate. As Watson [6] has said, "After words are once formed, the human ever has two worlds—a world of objects and a world of words which are substitutable for the world of objects." [7]

[6] John B. Watson, *The Ways of Behaviorism,* Harper & Brothers, New York, 1928, pp. 80 ff.
[7] A symbolic process once started can continue of its own momentum. Consider: a^1 represents the length of a line, a^2 represents a square of dimensions

Direction.—Aside from a lack of accurate language habits, another principal difference between good reasoners and poor ones is that the former group goes from one mode of attack to another one in its attempted solutions, while the latter persists sometimes for hours in a narrow attack that fruitlessly attempts to overcome the impossible. Many of these unsuccessful attacks are the result of habitual sets or attitudes.

Valuable suggestions for the solution of problems are frequently made by people who know very little about the problems at hand. Their very ignorance of conventional ways to do things in the problem under consideration is an aid to them in seeing new attacks that are completely overlooked by persons already intimate with the conventional methods. Previously learned patterns can never be appealed to for original solutions. That there are not more instances of originality by people without experience is probably due to the fact that information of a factual kind has to be available to the reasoners. Experience ordinarily provides these facts, but it also provides solutions which blind one to better ways of doing things.

Billings,[8] in subjecting the question as to whether the good reasoners in a given field are also the good ones in other fields, finds that they are, provided the necessary data for the solution of the problem are supplied.

Experiments [9] with normal and feeble-minded children have shown that the feeble-minded lacked the flexibility in mode of attack that characterized the normal. If rats are deprived of a part of their cerebral cortex, the same invariability and stereotypy is ob-

---

a; a^3 represents a cube of dimensions a; a^4, a^5, a^6, . . . , a^n, can all be written and manipulated according to the same rules that apply to the lesser superscripts; still they represent nothing tangible like a line, a square, or a cube. Where the referents are not clear, as in the case of some of the abstractions in the social sciences, words get us into trouble, as Stuart Chase points out in his *Tyranny of Words,* Harcourt, Brace and Company, New York, 1938. Every student of the social sciences should put this book on his must list.

[8] M. L. Billings, "Problem Solving in Different Fields of Endeavor," *American Journal of Psychology,* 1934, 46, 259-272.

[9] K. Gottschaldt, "Zur Methodik psychologischer Untersuchungen an Schwachsinnigen und Psychopathen." *Bericht über den V Kongress für Heilpädagogik,* 1931, cited by Maier.

served.[10] Both these experiments suggest that an inability to reason effectively may be actually due to the lack of gray matter—an inference so often made by our friendly critics, as well as by some who are not so friendly. But cerebral cortex is not the only factor in reasoning. There are numerous habits of thinking and attitudes that have nothing at all to do with gray matter but which still exercise a noticeable effect on reasoning and problem solving.

3. MAIER'S EXPERIMENT

Maier [11] has designed an experiment which was aimed at finding out how much rather general instruction in the breaking down of directional habits would be effective in reasoning problems. He used 384 students in elementary psychology at the University of Michigan as his subjects, dividing them into two groups. The experimental group received a twenty-minute lecture followed by a three-point program of "How to Reason." The program was merely a summary of the lecture. The control group went to work on the problems without any of the tuition that the experimental group had.

Individual work was required of all students. Their solutions to the problems were written out on paper. When a solution had been formed, it was presented to the instructor. He either accepted it, rejected it as impractical, or asked for a different solution. This work was all done as a part of a regular three-hour laboratory period.

The lecture on the nature of reasoning with the specific hints on how to reason follow:

(1) The solution of a problem, when it is the product of reasoning, consists of a pattern which is made up of parts of different past experiences.

(2) The pattern forms suddenly as does the hidden face in a puzzle picture.

[10] N. R. F. Maier, "The Effect of Cerebral Destruction on Reasoning and Learning in Rats." *Journal of Comparative Neurology,* 1932, 43, 45-75.
[11] N. R. F. Maier, "An Aspect of Human Reasoning," *British Journal of Psychology* (Gen. Sec.), 1933, 24, 144-55.

(3) Meanings of elements depend on the pattern of which they are a part. The sudden formation of a pattern therefore results in sudden changes of meaning.

(4) The solution-pattern overcomes a difficulty.

(5) The difficulty is what one sees it to be. It is not in the problem. (Illustrations were given which show how the same problem can be solved in different ways, each solution being the conquering of a different difficulty.)

(6) The particular difficulty one sees determines what one will do about it, i.e., what direction one will take (e.g., one doctor will seek a serum to immunize man to certain germs, another will seek a means for preventing the germ from traveling).

(7) All difficulties cannot be overcome. Hence one must find a difficulty which can be overcome.

(8) Most people see the same difficulty.

(9) The difficulties we see are often determined by our past contact with problems (e.g., other diseases have been conquered by the discovery of serums). Such difficulties are habitual difficulties and give rise to habitual directions.

(10) Habitual directions do not solve difficult problems. Problems are difficult when a successful direction is not obvious.

The hints on how to reason were as follows:

(1) Locate a difficulty and try to overcome it. If you fail, get it completely out of your mind and seek an entirely different difficulty.

(2) Do not be a creature of habit and stay in a rut. Keep your mind open for new meanings.

(3) The solution-pattern appears suddenly. You cannot force it. Keep your mind open for new combinations and do not waste time on unsuccessful attempts.

Three problems were used for both the experimental and control groups as follows:

(1) *The string problem.*—One string was fastened to the ceiling and was of such length that it reached the top of a heavy stationary table. Another string was fastened to the wall about six feet above the floor and was of such length that it reached to the floor. The problem was to tie the ends of the two strings together. This operation was difficult because when either string was held, the other was completely out of the subject's reach.

Simple solutions were demonstrated by the experimenter. These solutions are (1) hooking one string in with a pole; (2) increasing the length of one of the strings; and (3) tying one of the strings to a chair and placing the chair halfway between the cords in order to keep one string within reach while getting the other. These demonstration solutions were not to be used even in a modified form by the subjects.

The solution desired of the students was that of converting one of the strings into a pendulum.

(2) *The hatrack problem.*—Making use only of the material on the table, subjects were required to construct a hatrack sturdy enough to support a heavy coat. It was to be built in an empty room of ordinary size.

The only available materials which were useful were two poles (between six and seven feet in length) and a table clamp.

The problem could be solved by clamping the two poles together and wedging them between the floor and the ceiling. The clamp could be used as a hook. (Cotton waste was present in case a student wished to protect the ceiling.)

(3) *The candle problem.*—Lighted candles set on a table were to be put out from a fixed distance of eight feet. No one could extinguish the candles by blowing over that distance, but there was available a supply of glass and rubber tubing ranging from six to twelve inches in length. These pieces could be fastened together to form a long tube, but the tube was so flexible that it was useless until it was fastened by means of sturdy clamps to a long pole. The candle could then be blown out.

All problems were to be solved with the use of the materials on the table. In addition to the material which was applicable to the solutions, the table contained such things as washers, bolts, pliers and chalk. These were confusion materials. They represent objects which in life situations would be present along with the pertinent materials. They can be used as raw material out of which to formulate hypotheses regarding their use in the solution, but these hypotheses will necessarily be wrong.

Results.—In the second and third problems the experimental group showed a decided advantage over the control group. In the whole series of three problems the difference averages about 10 per cent. Regardless of whether this difference was 1 per cent, 10 per

	N	PROBLEM 1	PROBLEM 2	PROBLEM 3	AVERAGE
Experimental..	178	50.6	28.7	68.3	49.2
Control.......	206	49.0	22.3	47.8	39.7

cent, or 100 per cent, it means very little because the equality of the groups has to be assumed to start with. If the ability of the experimental group was only slightly above the control group *at the start,* then we could easily account for the apparent 10 per cent gain of the experimental group on this basis—the lecture and the hints would have meant nothing.

Extension of the experiment.—Maier planned another experiment with the idea of controlling this weak point in his evidence for the efficacy of suggestions on how to reason. This experiment involved the use of just one instead of two groups of students, so that there would be no question but that they were the same in initial ability. They solved two of three problems of a paper-and-pencil nature as follows:

(1) *The square problem.* Given three-quarters of a square; divide the area into four parts which are equal in shape and size.

(2) *The dot problem.* Given three rows of three dots each; pass through each of the dots with four straight lines without raising the pencil from the paper. Retracing a line is regarded as making a line.

(3) *The "T" problem.* Each student was given four blocks of wood. From these he was asked to construct a perfect "T."

One of the two first problems was selected for period I of ten minutes. Some students finished the problems. They were then given others to keep them busy, but those results don't concern us here. Period I was followed by period II, also of ten minutes' duration. It involved the control problem, one of the latter two above. Period III followed II and was a return to the first problem for those who hadn't solved it in the first period. Period IV was preceded by the lecture on reasoning already described. The problems were the same as for period II. The results follow:

	PERIOD	N	SUCCESSES	PER CENT SUCCESS
Control Problem	I	169	29	17.2
	III	140	26	18.6
Experimental Problem	II	169	30	17.8
	IV	139	52	37.4

The table shows that the control and experimental problems were of equal difficulty. The abilities of the groups were the same because they are composed of identical people. In a second ten-minute period (III) preceded by no lecture, 18.6 per cent of the 140 who failed to solve the problem in the first ten minutes, were successful. But when equally difficult problems were preceded by a lecture on "How to Reason," the per cent who were successful jumped to 37.4. We must therefore conclude that *this lecture just about doubled the successes that presumably would have occurred in the second ten-minute period without it.*

There were still some people who had not solved the problems. Maier concludes that *we cannot, by this method, equip a person to solve a problem, but we can aid him to clear the field so that a solution is not prevented from appearing by virtue of his persistence in previously learned modes of response.* This shows that *reasoning is in part a matter of overcoming or inhibiting habitual responses.*

4. KÖHLER'S EXPERIMENTS

Strikingly enough, the principal impetus for Maier's experiments and for the experiments of others [12] on reasoning and problem solving comes not from work on humans but from a series of experiments with nine chimpanzees conducted by Wolfgang Köhler.

The story of how Köhler came to make these experiments is an absorbing one. A professor of psychology of Berlin University, he was on a vacation tour in the late summer of 1914. His itinerary included a biological research station maintained by the University on the Island of Teneriffe, one of the Canary Islands. With the outbreak of hostilities, he was interned on the island for the duration of the War. The complete story of his experiments is told in a book called *The Mentality of Apes*.[13] A clearer, simpler, more interesting account of psychological experiments has never been written, before or since. A rapid reading of the entire book will repay any thoughtful student.

Köhler found that chimpanzees could, without any special training, use sticks to pull food lying just outside their cages but beyond their reach into the latitude of their grasp. Of course, the fact that they didn't have to be especially trained to use sticks as rakes does not mean that they hadn't *learned* previously to do so. But the significance of the observation is that animals lower than the great apes—the chimpanzees, the gorillas, the orangutans and gibbons [14]—are extremely inept in the use of even so simple a tool.

Longer poles were sometimes provided to see if they would be used to dislodge food placed beyond reach overhead. Here a most instructive observation was made. Instead of using a pole as a man

---

[12] Augusta Alpert, "The Solving of Problem Situations by Pre-School Children: An Analysis," R. H. Wheeler (editor), *Readings in Psychology,* Thomas Y. Crowell Company, New York, 1930, 114-44.

Edgar A. Doll and Cecelia G. Aldrich, "Problem Solving among Idiots," *Journal of Comparative Psychology,* 1931, 12, 137-69.

[13] Wolfgang Köhler, *The Mentality of Apes,* Harcourt, Brace and Company, New York, 1925.

[14] For descriptions of these forms see R. M. Yerkes and Ada Yerkes, *The Great Apes,* Yale University Press, New Haven, 1929.

would to knock down suspended fruit, the chimpanzees set the
poles up vertically under the food, and then, before they could fall
over, they quickly climbed the pole and secured the food in an
entirely nonhuman manner. Their natural agility prevented the
solution of the problem in the more indirect human way. The indirection easier for a human is not easier for the chimpanzee.

Nevertheless there was one humanlike response in the face of
a difficult problem. When food was suspended overhead and the
required solution was not immediately evident to the animal (as
when he was required to stack several heavy boxes one on top of
another so that the tower so constructed, if mounted, enabled him
to reach the incentive), the keeper was led to a position under the
food and by gestures and grunting the notion was conveyed to him
that his help was wanted. On several occasions the ape climbed to
his shoulders and used the keeper as a vaulting pole. A dependence
of this kind on a keeper of animals is perfectly analogous to the
appeal to authority mentioned as a deterrent in human reasoning.
It has been observed frequently in students who, asked to tie the
two strings together in Maier's experiment, literally withdrew from
the field all the while "registering" an appeal for help from the
instructor.

In other experiments with the chimpanzees a short stick within
reach could be used to obtain a long one out of reach. The long
stick would reach to the incentive, but the short one wouldn't. In
cases of this kind, which greatly increased the complexity of the
problem, the apes were sometimes observed to take a box which had
been previously successful for suspended food and, as if intending
to use it as a rake, push it in the direction of the food on the ground
beyond the bars. A box makes a very unsatisfactory rake at best;
to get it through the bars was impossible. But here, again, we have
a response perfectly analogous to responses that you have certainly
seen in other people even if you have not observed it in yourself.
I am reminded of a rather dense student who finally grasped the
notion of disparate images in connection with space perception. But
ever after in the face of difficult problems, however remote from
space perception, we were certain to hear something about disparate
images from this particular person. A response that had been suc-

cessful once was used again and again because the student lacked the ability to discriminate its suitableness in exactly the same way that the ape failed to perceive that the box which had been successfully used in another connection wouldn't go through the bars of his cage.

In all of these experiments, Köhler observed that a problem was difficult to the extent that it was impossible for the ape to survey the total situation. A stick placed in close proximity to the food was more likely to be used than one placed so that the chimpanzee could not see both the tool and the incentive at the same time. Items that are located together in space belong in Köhler's terminology to one constellation, whereas if they are more dispersed they may be grouped into different patterns. *Whatever is a part of one perceptual pattern is difficult to separate and to integrate with another.* This generalization is illustrated in another experiment that he made. Instead of the sticks used in some experiments, a small bush or sapling was planted in the cage, any branch of which would make a suitable wand or rake. But *it was a much more difficult problem to separate a branch from the plant and thereby make a stick than it was to use sticks already provided.* Things perceived in a certain setting, or belonging to a particular constellation, are so definitely a part of that setting that their utilization in some other setting is particularly difficult. This observation is as true of human problems as it is for the chimpanzee attempting to employ a stick which is not perceptually separate. Man's superiority over the chimpanzee in being able to make use of only the essential elements of a concrete situation depends in part on this ability to use words as symbols for the various parts of a specific situation. Words and symbols are more easily manipulated into new constellations than objects themselves are.

Köhler also investigated the possibilities of invention among the chimpanzees. If a chimpanzee is given two sticks, neither of which will reach the food alone but which can be jointed together so that they make a stick of sufficient length, will the chimpanzee ever succeed in manufacturing the long stick? Köhler found that only one of his animals was able to achieve the long stick. It happened this way:

. . . He pushes one of the sticks out as far as it will go, then takes the second, and with it pushes the first one cautiously towards the objective, pushing it carefully from the nearer end and thus slowly urging it towards the fruit. . . . (In this way he actually touches the fruit with the first stick several times.) . . . The proceeding is repeated; when the animal has probed the stick on the ground so far out that he cannot possibly get it back by himself, it is given back to him. But although in trying to steer it cautiously, he puts the stick in his hand exactly into the cut (the opening where they are to be joined) of the stick on the ground and although one might think that doing so would suggest the possibility of pushing one stick into the other, there is no indication whatever of such a practically valuable solution. Finally, the observer gives the animal some help by putting one finger into the opening of one stick under the animal's nose (without pointing to the other stick at all). This has no effect; Sultan, as before, pushes one stick towards the objective, and as this pseudo solution does not satisfy him any longer, he abandons his efforts altogether, and does not even pick up the sticks when they are both thrown through the bars to him. The experiment has lasted over an hour and is stopped for the present, as it seems hopeless, carried out like this. As we intended to take it up again after a while, Sultan is left in possession of his sticks; the keeper is left to watch him.

Keeper's report: "Sultan first of all squats indifferently on the box, which has been left standing a little back from the railings; then he gets up, picks up the two sticks, sits down again on the box and plays carelessly with them. While doing this, it happens that he finds himself holding one rod in either hand in such a way that they lie in a straight line; he pushes the thinner one a little way into the opening of the thicker, jumps up and is already on the run towards the railings, to which he has up to now half turned his back, and begins to draw a banana towards him with the double stick. I call the master; meanwhile, one of the animal's rods has fallen out of the other, as he has pushed one of them only a little way into the other; whereupon he connects them again."

All of this description shows that occasionally chimpanzees will be found who are able to fabricate very simple instruments. But since there has been no real follow-up in these studies, it is not clear how far it is possible for these animals to go. After the experiments are over the creatures revert again to a simple caged-animal existence in which care is provided by a keeper. The profound effects upon people of a protected life of an analogous kind have been observed to lead to a complete lack of accomplishment. It is probably equally true that an anticipation of every need has a deleterious effect on chimpanzees.

Aside from all this, another hindrance to more complex accomplishment on the part of chimpanzees is their complete lack of language mechanism. Although there is some use of symbolism,[15] Köhler and others have observed that there is very little value in allowing one chimpanzee who cannot accomplish a given act to observe another who can. This means that every animal has to learn all of his repertoire for himself. Cultural background is nonexistent for every generation starts *de novo*. If such a condition obtained among human beings we would still all be living in caves and hunting with clubs. Every human generation, for the most part, starts where the previous one has left off. Its accomplishments, through the symbolism of words, are built onto the accomplishments of people that it has never seen.

Further problems having to do with what are called the "higher mental processes" as well as those in which most of the data are in the animal rather than the human field are those relating to delayed response and to abstraction. The delayed response problem is simply this: If an animal, human, or infrahuman receives a stimulus now, he can apparently react to it a few seconds, a week, or a month from now, depending upon his position in the animal series. Hunter made the first experiment in this field in 1913. He found that if the experimenter expected a rat to select one of three doors that had just been lighted up in order to be rewarded there with food, the delay after the light had been turned off could be only about two seconds. He also worked with dogs and with one child and found correspondingly longer delays possible. Using a somewhat different method, Köhler found that chimpanzees could "delay" several hours. The mechanism of this response has never been identified. We know that it is not true that the stimulus is dammed up in the central nervous system somewhere and released at an appropriate

[15] J. B. Wolfe, "The Effectiveness of Token-Reward for Chimpanzees," *Comparative Psychology Monographs*, 1936, 12, 1-72.

time. Hunter thought that in rats bodily orientation was responsible for the response. If the rat remained "pointed" at the position where the stimulus had been he would choose correctly, but later work has shown that explicit bodily orientation does not have to be maintained. In people the response can be seen to be related to the language mechanism, but there is no generally accepted explanation. To go into the controversy extensively would take us too far afield. Interested students will find a summary of the literature to 1935 in Maier and Schneirla, *Principles of Animal Psychology*.[16]

The problem of abstraction involves essentially what Köhler was requiring of his apes when he furnished them with a small tree from which they could manufacture sticks that would reach food. They were to abstract "stick" from a collection of "sticks" called a tree. Abstraction is the essential mechanism in the problem of classification. When a series is arranged the individual items which have numerous properties are grouped according to some abstract quality. Rocks varying in size, shape, color, and so on, can be arranged in a "hardness" series quite independent of any other quality. The problem of classifying is one of the preliminary steps in any science. The growth of a young science depends on the adequacy, for their purpose, of the particular qualities which are to be abstracted. Thus in some early zoological classifications, bats were classed with birds because they fly. But it turned out that their flying was relatively unimportant in zoology and that the qualities of their reproductive mechanisms, together with other morphological considerations, throw them definitely into the classification "mammal."

Everywhere in science superficial resemblances are not important; the most useful classifications are made on the basis of hidden, unobtrusive qualities. We have seen how sleep and hypnosis were confused (Chapter XIV) on the basis of a most striking resemblance in the apparent behavior in the two states. Little progress was made in understanding hypnosis until it was shown that the resemblance was entirely superficial, like the resemblance of bats to birds and whales and porpoises to fish.

[16] McGraw-Hill Book Company, New York, 1936.

Because the perception of abstract qualities was so important in human activities it was deemed an indicator of higher thought processes [17] until recently, when it was shown that the lowly rat and other subhuman forms could abstract qualities like "triangularity" with sufficient accuracy to pass difficult test situations.[18] In the animal field there is a considerable literature growing up in "abstraction" or, as it is generally called, "equivalence of stimuli." [19]

Summary of the chapter.—To say that reasoning or thinking differentiates man from the lower animal forms is not true in the light of experimental evidence, which shows that the only difference in the behavior of the various animal forms is in the complexity of the problems that can be solved. Man has a tremendous advantage over forms that do not have language because reasoning and reflective thinking are most efficiently accomplished by means of symbols. Symbols once invented can be handled independently of the objects they originally designated so that in effect man possesses "two worlds." Aside from language, the use of tools by human beings as extensions and improvements of manipulatory organs like the hands is of the greatest significance.

Effective use of tools cannot be accomplished without the sensory, motor, and central nervous equipment possessed by man. The hope of future experimentation in the field of problem solving should be, according to one student [20] of the field, "directed at determining what the factors are which condition the success of one individual or genus, and the absence of which limits the achievements of another." Most of the work, he feels, has been of a pre-

[17] C. L. Hull, "Quantitative Aspects of the Evolution of Concepts: An Experimental Study," *Psychological Review Monographs,* 1920, 28, 85.
[18] P. E. Fields, "Form Discrimination in the White Rat," *Journal of Comparative Psychology,* 1928, 8, 143-58; "Studies in Concept Formation," *Comparative Psychology Monographs,* 1932, 9, 70.
[19] L. W. Gellerman, "Form Discrimination in Chimpanzees and Two-Year-Old Children," *Journal of Genetic Psychology,* 1933, 42, 3-50.
J. A. Gengerelli, "Studies in Abstraction in White Rats," *Journal of Genetic Psychology,* 1930, 38, 171-202.
H. Klüver, *Behavior Mechanisms in Monkeys,* University of Chicago Press, Chicago, 1933, pp. 387.
[20] Kenneth W. Spence, "Experimental Studies of Learning and the Higher Mental Processes in Infra-Human Primates," *Psychological Bulletin,* 1937, 34, 806-50.

liminary nature in an attempt to find out what animals can do in comparison to man and to one another. We do not now know how important previous habits are in comparison with structural equipment in determining the accomplishment of either man or animal. Among the many structural factors we do not know relatively which are more important. Aside from gross structural defects, as in some of the low-grade feeble-minded, we have no explanatory principles in this field.

One of the elements of habit equipment that is important in limiting reasoning has been demonstrated by Maier in what he calls "direction." He showed that if habitual ways of regarding problems could be overcome, solutions occurred in larger proportions. This observation is probably a special case of the difficulty Köhler noted in connection with his chimpanzees—an item perceived in one constellation is difficult to abstract from its concrete setting so that it becomes free for incorporation into new forms.

XX

LEARNING, THINKING, IMAGINING, DREAMING, AND THE BRAIN

EARLY theorizing about the part that the brain plays in determining behavior led to the mistaken notion that the brain somewhat resembles the wax cylinder of a dictaphone. Impressions made on it by experience were thought to be recorded in much the same way that the cutting head on this instrument makes grooves of varying depth in the soft wax surface. Memory was explained by actual physical impressions which remained engraved on the surface after the experience itself was long gone. In an extreme form this theory called for an exact location in the brain for each different thing a person could recall: a different brain cell stored each item of experience. Forgetting meant that with time the precisely engraved experiences lost their detailed contours, became fragmented and badly eroded. Things that one couldn't forget were incised so deeply through the intensity of the original experience, or through the constant recurrence of experiences of lesser intensity, that they resisted the smoothing effect of time.

Anatomical evidence.—Early anatomical evidence seemed to strengthen this theory. Locations were found on the exposed brains of animals that when directly stimulated resulted in fairly definite movements of individual muscle groups. From certain brain areas uniformly in different animals, movements of the digits, the hind legs, the forelegs, the head and lips could be elicited. All this was very impressive. It led to the notion that sense organs were connected with the muscles through the nervous system, like subscribers are interconnected by a telephone system. All the facts which violated this notion were unknown at the time this generalization was made.

As the nerve pathways from the eyes and the ears and the nose and the other sense organs were traced they seemed to lead uniformly to definite brain areas—from the eyes to the rear of the brain, and from the ears to the temporal region. From observations on the difference between man and animals and from clinical cases among men in which certain deficiencies were observed, other areas of the brain were supplied with theoretical properties when the anatomical evidence was not so direct. Thus there were centers isolated for reasoning in the frontal lobes because men, who could reason—compared with animals, who were not supposed to be able to reason—had a greater development of the frontal lobes. For the same reason, speech was located in the parietal lobes. There was even supposed to be a difference in the locations of written and spoken language.

All this development is quite independent of the story of phrenology (see Chapter II) which asserts that in the individual a difference can be discerned between the psychological properties and the *surface* contours of the skull. It is true, however, that Gall and Spurzheim, the founders of phrenology, made significant non-phrenological observations and thus contributed to our present understanding.

1. BEHAVIOR STUDIES WITH RATS

As we have pointed out, the sensory nerves from the retina of the eye, after a series of fairly complicated connections, finally end [1] in the outer layer of the brain on the extreme back surface. An area of this kind on the cortex is called a *projection area*. Anatomical evidence of this kind would lead one to believe that if these occipital lobes are invaded and destroyed in any way, the individual would become hopelessly blind.

Lashley has tested this hypothesis experimentally by having a

[1] They do not actually end here except for purposes of arbitrary classification. The occipital surface is a tremendous distributing and connecting center. Nerves can be traced from this area to motor end organs of wide distribution over the whole body.

group of white rats learn a problem which required a visual discrimination. A special apparatus presented two areas—one brightly lighted, the other dark. By always allowing the animals to eat after going through a passageway containing the light and by always giving them a slight shock if they entered the darkened passage, all of the animals soon learned to take the lighted alley without exception. The apparatus allowed the light to be presented first on one side and then on the other in some random order so that the experimenter could be certain that they were actually reacting to the brightness and not to the *position,* right or left, of the stimulus pattern. Since rats learn position habits very readily, a control of this kind is absolutely necessary.

After the problem had been learned, the skull of the animal was opened—under deep anesthesia, of course—and the exposed brain surface was destroyed by cautery. Ten days later, after they had recovered from the effects of the operation, the rats were tested for retention.

Animals so operated were no longer able to make brightness discriminations. The ten-day delay for the recovery from the operation did not cause the forgetting because normal animals who served as controls showed but slight decrease in their scores.

Another control experiment showed that *the same amount of brain substance destroyed in other regions produced no loss of the habit.* It would appear that the hypothesis has been substantiated. If an animal has to make brightness discriminations it would appear that he must have a complete visual projection area in the cerebral cortex.

But in an extension of this experiment it was shown [2] that animals devoid of cerebral cortex in the occipital region *could relearn brightness discriminations* which were lost as a result of the operation.

The only possible interpretation of these facts is that some other uninvaded part of the brain took over the function of the

[2] K. S. Lashley, "The Relation between Cerebral Mass, Learning, and Retention," *Journal of Comparative Neurology,* 1926, 41, 1-58.

areas that were destroyed.[3] Similar studies have been made on the auditory areas with the same conclusions and interpretations.[4]

If an auditory discrimination has been learned, it is destroyed along with the destruction in the temporal lobes; invasion of the other lobes causes no loss of the habit. But if the temporal area is destroyed first, and then the animal is trained in an auditory discrimination, he learns as readily as an intact animal. As a matter of fact, there is a very slight *advantage for the operated animals in* *both the brightness discrimination and the auditory problem.*

When the experimenter opens the skull and touches the surface of the brain with a cautery, he cannot be certain exactly how much of the brain tissue is going to be destroyed. Considerable skill is required in order to confine the injury to the cortex. If the subcortical structures are involved, the results for that animal have to be discarded. The experimenter knows in general whether the damage will be large or small, but a precise measurement must wait until after the behavior data are collected and the animal is finally sacrificed. After the animal's death, the entire brain is removed from the skull and preserved in the proper solutions. Even yet it is impossible to tell how much cortex was destroyed. The scar can be seen on the brain surface, but it has little relation to the amount of damage that is done immediately under the external surface. The subsurface damage can be observed only by making cross sections of the entire brain.

The results of studying these cross sections by means of a microscope are transferred to greatly enlarged charts that have been prepared beforehand. Figure 68 shows an injured area in the occipital lobes (visual area) taken from one of these reconstructions of a rat's brain; Figure 69 shows an injury confined to the auditory area. The areas shown in black are measured with an engineering instrument (planimeter) designed for measuring the areas of irregular figures. Then the per cent that this magnitude is of the total brain area is computed.

[3] K. S. Lashley, "Vicarious Function after Destruction of the Visual Areas," *American Journal of Physiology*, 1922, 59, 44-71.
[4] L. E. Wiley, "The Function of the Brain in Audition," *Journal of Comparative Neurology*, 1932, 54, 109-41, and "A Further Investigation of Auditory Cerebral Mechanisms," *Journal of Comparative Neurology*, 1937, 66, 327-31.

When these measurements and computations are made and related to the errors made in the retention tests, it turns out that within the occipital region where, as we have just seen, an extensive

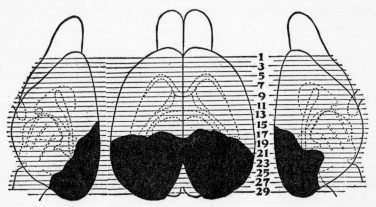

FIG. 68.—The reconstruction of an extensive injury to the occipital, or visual area. (After Lashley, courtesy of the University of Chicago Press.)

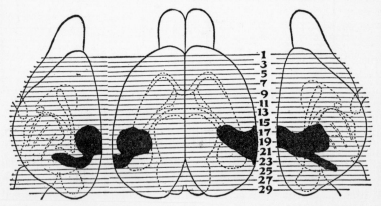

FIG. 69.—The reconstruction of an injury confined to the temporal, or auditory regions. (After Lashley, courtesy of the University of Chicago Press.)

lesion produces a complete loss of the brightness discrimination habit, lesser injuries produce smaller effects. The amount of interference with the habit is roughly proportional to the amount of damage that was done by the cautery. *A small lesion produces a few errors, but an extensive lesion produces a complete loss of the habit.* The same is true for the auditory habit.

Localization of the maze habit.—Learning a relatively more complex function like a maze does not depend upon any single sense department as a visual discrimination depends on the eyes and

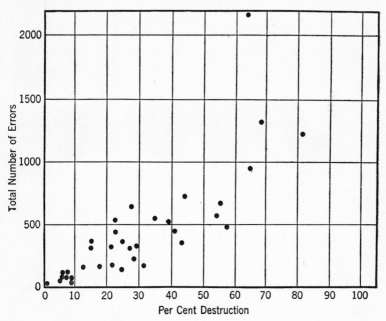

FIG. 70.—The relation between the per cent of destruction and the number of errors. (After Lashley.)

the visual projection areas in the brain. An animal deprived of the use of one sense department through an operation or through stimulus control [5] will depend upon other cues. Lashley has studied the effect of brain injury on the learning of simple mazes and has related the amount of destruction to the number of errors made in the process mastering the mazes.

[5] Making the entire field uniform so that no differences exist in excitatory field which can serve as cues at critical points. Presumably a complete control of this kind over all factors including internal ones in the animal would result in an insoluble problem.

Typical results showing this relation are exhibited in Figure 70. This diagram shows that *there is some relation between the number of errors made and the per cent of destruction*. The relationship is not very precise. The animal with the largest per cent of the cortex destroyed requires a little over 1,200 trials to learn a maze that requires almost 2,200 trials for one that has suffered about 15 per cent less destruction. Our interpretation would be that there are other factors, aside from that under observation, that determine how many errors a rat will make. One of them might be his ability before the operation was made. Another might be a lack of reliability in the maze, but in spite of these and other factors there still exists a definite trend to the data.

From a close study of the areas in which the destruction took place it was evident that, *unlike the visual and auditory habits, maze learning has no localization within the cortex*. It is the amount of destruction, not its locus, that is the determining factor in slowing up the learning.

2. CLINICAL OBSERVATIONS ON HUMAN BEINGS

There have been several cases of brain tumor in human subjects that have necessitated the removal of large portions of the brain. In three such cases reported by Dandy [6] one entire half of the brain was removed. Because subcortical structures were removed along with the cortex, the patients were hopelessly paralyzed on one side of their bodies, but there were no signs of deterioration or disorientation. As a matter of fact, there was marked improvement in the way the patients could carry on conversation. With the tumor they were showing signs of breakdown, but with the tumorous growth removed along with half the brain, they improved. Dandy was very much surprised by these results. He had expected the patients to show a considerable loss of ability to reason when one

[6] Walter E. Dandy, "Physiological Studies Following Extirpation of the Right Cerebral Hemisphere in Man," *Bulletin,* Johns Hopkins Hospital, 1933, 53, 31-51.

half of their frontal lobe complement was removed, but they did not do so.

Observations on monkeys.—More recently Carlyle Jacobsen [7] has studied the effect of removing the frontal lobes in monkeys. These observations are more convincing than those on human subjects because the whole thing can be planned beforehand, and the monkey can be trained before the operation and retrained afterward. We generally know little about human subjects beforehand, and more frequently than not observations on them afterward are made by surgeons who are more adept with a scalpel than in psychological discernment.

Jacobsen [8] found a distinct difference in the effects of frontal lobes removed in infant monkeys and in adults. Effects that were enduring with adults were only temporary with infants. This would make it appear that after specialization has taken place, to remove certain areas produces permanent effects, but before specialization has taken place some other part of the brain takes over the function of the destroyed area.

Jacobsen also found that the frontal lobes seemed to have a specific function in the delayed reaction tests that were given after the operation. Animals so operated were less capable in being able to solve a problem if there was any delay between the occurrence of a stimulus and the required response.

Summary of these studies.—The notion that particular parts of the brain are responsible for specific acts is in error. Some of the phylogenetically older parts of the brain do have specific functions, but the neopallium in rodents [9] and in infant primates is pretty

---

[7] Carlyle Jacobsen, "Functions of Frontal Association Areas in Primates," *Archives of Neurology and Psychology*, 1935, 33, 558-569, and *Comparative Psychology Monograph*, 1936, 13.

[8] Carlyle Jacobsen, F. V. Taylor, and G. M. Haslerud, "Restitution of Function after Cortical Injuries in Monkeys," *American Journal of Physiology*, 1936, 116, 85-6.

[9] This generalization is further substantiated in the work of N. R. F. Maier, who found that "reasoning" in the white rat was as nonspecific as Lashley had found maze learning to be. Cf. "The Effect of Cerebral Destruction on Reasoning and Learning in Rats," *Journal of Comparative Neurology*, 1932, 54, 45-75; "Cortical Destruction in the Posterior Part of the Brain and Its Effect on Reasoning in Rats," *Journal of Comparative Neurology*, 1932, 56, 179-214.

general in its function. Destruction of specific areas does not produce the effect one would expect if every experience had a specific location in the cortex. We infer that among primates specificity of function is more precise than it is among rodents, but even here clinical observations indicate that a considerable part of the cortex can be removed without seriously affecting behavior, particularly if the injury is made during infancy before specific patterns develop.

3. THINKING

What happens when a person thinks? Is it, as an older psychology taught, totally a matter of brain activity? Is it true that thinking is a function of the cerebral cortex in the same way that contraction is the function of a muscle? Or is it true that the motor segments are an integral part of the thinking process? Even when overt movement cannot be observed, however intently we scrutinize a thinking person, is it true that muscular movement is still present but at a low level of intensity? This latter notion, that thinking is a matter of implicit bodily movements—a kind of a shorthand, low energy-level way of dealing with things as a substitute for actually performing the movements of handling them—has been subjected to experimental test.

For many years the experimenters had to depend on mechanical devices fastened directly to various muscle-groups to magnify the tiny muscle changes (if any) that are present when we think. These devices were usually unsatisfactory because even if they showed no activity it was no proof that activity wasn't there. It was recognized that the instruments were very insensitive and that a considerable amount of activity might have been present in amplitudes too small to be recorded.

With the development of thermionic amplification—the same kind of amplifying that enables a radio set to pick up very feeble radio signals and make them audible—it became possible to amplify small potentials that come about as a result of nerve and muscle activity.[10] These potentials are very weak—sometimes in the relaxed

[10] Edmund Jacobson, "Electrophysiology of Mental Activities," *American Journal of Psychology,* 1932, 44, 677-94.

subject they are of the order of a millionth of a volt. After they are amplified they are made strong enough to affect a very sensitive string galvanometer, whose vibration under the control of potentials is then photographed on a moving film.

The increased sensitivity of this apparatus over the old mechanical and pneumatic devices had one drawback: the instrument sometimes turned out to be too sensitive. When most people lie with eyes closed in a darkened and partially soundproof room and are instructed to relax, unless they are actually sleeping the action-currents are still present to such an extent that the instructions "to *think* of something" produce no observable changes in the record. There is so much "spontaneous" activity that the increment produced by the special instructions is no more detectable in the total pattern than a thirteenth person's voice in a room where twelve are already loudly talking. But if a subject is trained to relax, the record becomes steadier and provides a stable base line against which comparisons can be made. Under these conditions the instructions to *think*—to solve a problem—result in easily observed differences in the record.

When the galvanometer is recording practically a straight line from the right biceps muscle, a signal is given to the subject to begin thinking or imagining a movement of the right arm. Within a fraction of a second the galvanometer string begins to swing and continues to do so until the signal to stop thinking is given. Control electrodes put on other parts of the body show that the action currents are confined to the regions that the subject is instructed to think about. *They do not involve the whole body.* Another control —"This time when the signal is given do not imagine a movement in the right arm, remain relaxed"—shows that the action currents are not due to the subject's hearing the signal.

In about half the cases where various subjects were required to: "Imagine writing your name"; "Imagine yourself rowing a boat"; "Imagine yourself boxing"; "Imagine scratching your chin"; and so on, it turned out that there was no great difference in the record when a comparison was attempted between the experimental period and the pre-experimental relaxed period. In some of these cases the subjects reported that they *visualized* themselves performing these acts rather than taking part in them. If the subjects were reported accurately, then potentials should be available for registration near the eyeballs. An analysis of records obtained from these points indicate that in imagining the Eiffel Tower, for instance, the eyeballs move slightly upward, somewhat as they actually would do if the tower were really seen.

In different subjects the *same muscles do not always contract during the imagination of a particular act or object*. But the results do indicate that *if these contractions are absent in one region, they will be found in another*. This principle explains why the instruction to "imagine using the right arm" is not *invariably* followed by action-potentials in the right arm; in some instances the subject merely visualizes the act, and if he does, movements are made in the region of the eye.

Aside from imagining an experience kinesthetically or visually a person may think about it in terms of words.[11] If he does, we might expect that electrodes in the muscles of the tongue or under-lip would pick up potentials associated with tiny muscular movements in these regions.

Instructions to the subject which were designed to bring out lip and tongue movements include: "Imagine counting"; "Imagine telling your friend the date"; "Recall certain poems or songs"; "Multiply numbers." Almost anyone would agree that tongue movements would be associated with these acts even though they refused to agree that "mental" processes did not accompany them. But the subjects were also instructed to "Think of 'eternity' "; "Think of electrical resistance"; "The meaning of 'incongruous'; of 'everlasting.' " Most people would hold that thinking of these abstractions is a purely "mental" process. During the experimental periods there are potentials for all these instructions which disappear in the relaxed subject. The vibrations occur in patterns which evidently correspond to those present in actual speech. The kinds of instruction given above are different from those like "Imagine moving your left arm," because here there are no arm-potentials. *Thinking in abstract terms is then a matter of incipient movement of the speech*

---

[11] There are, of course, other possibilities. These are merely the most frequent ways of imagining.

(Courtesy of Edmund Jacobson)

Fig. 71.—*Record 1.* The signal to begin imagining is shown at the top of the record by a white line. A similar line indicates the end of the imagining process. During the interval, lasting a little more than a second, the subject was to "imagine lifting a ten-pound weight with the right arm." The potentials are recorded during this interval as shown.

Record 2. The subject is to imagine lifting with the left arm. The right-arm record shows no electromyographic response.

Record 3. Two distinct volleys are separated by a relaxed period when the subject is instructed to "imagine hitting a nail twice with a hammer held in the right hand."

Record 4. The record shows typical responses in the imagining of rhythmical acts like rowing a boat.

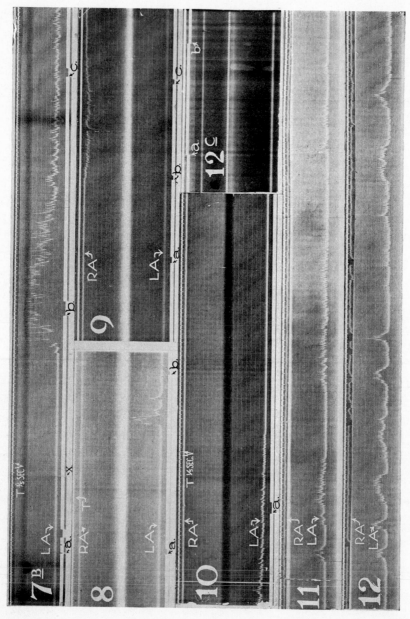

(Courtesy of L. W. Max)

Fig. 72.—Electromyographic Responses of the Deaf

Record 7B. Time in fifths of seconds is shown on the extreme top of the record. The electromyographic record from the left arm is marked *L A.* At signal *a* a card was illuminated in front of the subject who, although deaf, could speak. The card contained the following problem: "Is this true? If Paul is taller than Herbert and is also shorter than Robert, then Robert is taller than Herbert." At *b*, the subject said, "Yes, he is the tallest." During the solution there was no hand movement, but movement of the left hand accompanied speaking. The subject's report indicated that the absence of hand movements during the solution could be accounted for in the way the subject solved the problem. He said: "First read the card rapidly, then pictures of three boys; lined them up with tallest at right, then gave the answer . . ."

Records 8, 9, 10 do not concern us here.

Record 11. Electromyographic responses to the problem "Think the word 'Heavy' again and again till the light goes out." In the section shown there are three signings.

Record 12. Two overt signings of the word "Heavy" photographed with the sensitivity of the instruments greatly reduced.

Record 12c. A control experiment on a hearing subject instructed to "Think the word 'Heavy' again and again till the light goes out." The light was turned on at *a*, off at *b*. There was no response in either arm.

apparatus at so low a level that the ordinary subject overlooks it entirely. The reverse is also true: in imagining a left-arm movement no potentials are present in the speech regions.

4. DEAF-MUTES

In deaf-mutes the principal organs of speech are the fingers and hands rather than the tongue and lips. Deaf-mutes therefore become valuable subjects because it is much easier to attach electrodes to the hands, arms, or fingers than it is to put them on the tongue and lips. It was L. W. Max of New York University who first pointed out these advantages [12] and was the first to examine the action-potentials from these regions in deaf-mute subjects. The apparatus that he used was very similar to that used by Jacobson, although there were important technical differences that we cannot go into here.

Max found that he could get subjects to relax enough to provide a stable base line by allowing them time to get used to the experimental setup.[13] They were allowed to lie on a wide bed in a darkened quiet room. Under these conditions, although they were tense at first, most of the subjects learned to relax without any direct training in relaxation. In this respect his experiment is entirely different from that of Jacobson. One girl was unable to relax after a prolonged attempt before the experiment started. This preliminary general training was in the hands of an assistant. When Max himself took over the experiment in order to find out why the girl could not relax when the others could, a satisfactory record was secured in a short time. Higher responses returned when the same assistant again took charge. It turned out finally that the girl was in love with the assistant, and was therefore tense when he was around. Other subjects were tense because they thought that certain assistants were too brusque or unsympathetic. All records affected by factors like these had to be discarded.

[12] Louis W. Max, "An Experimental Study of the Motor Theory of Consciousness," *Journal of General Psychology*, 1935, 12, 159-75.
[13] Louis W. Max, "An Experimental Study of the Motor Theory of Consciousness," *Journal of Comparative Psychology*, 1937, 24, 301-44.

The subjects did not know that their finger movements were the principal interest of the experimenters. The electrodes were attached to the forearm over the flexores digitorum, the muscles which control finger movement. The potentials were thus picked up some distance away from the fingers themselves. There were eighteen deaf subjects and sixteen hearing subjects who were used as controls. Five of the eighteen deaf subjects were more intensively studied because they could relax better than the other thirteen. Some of the subjects volunteered because they were interested in the problem, others were in effect paid for serving for they were drawn from the relief rolls.

Two amplifiers and two string galvanometers were used. Generally the electrodes were placed on the two arms, two on each arm, so that simultaneous records could be obtained from these parts, but other segments, such as the eye and brow region and the legs, were also used as controls.

Analysis of hundreds of records from these subjects shows that *finger movements are present in deaf subjects when they are solving problems, imagining, and dreaming*. These movements are not present in hearing subjects. In hearing subjects this activity is present in the tongue and lips, could it be recorded satisfactorily. The finger movements of deaf subjects during a dream are sometimes complete enough so that someone who knows the manual language signs can infer what the dream is about in the same way that, with hearing subjects, ordinary speech sounds give enough significant information so that a listener can accurately reconstruct a dream of the sleep-talker.

The records shown in Figure 72 indicate the kinds of records that Max obtained from his subjects. We are particularly interested in records 11 and 12. Record 11 (Figure 72) shows an entirely implicit imagining response. The subject is totally unable to report any movement at all, but the instrument shows three distinct periods of activity corresponding to what the subject would call three entirely "mental" performances. The amplifiers and the galvanometers are more sensitive than the subject's own kinesthetic sense organs. Record 12 shows the electromyographic responses when the sensitivity of the instrument is greatly reduced and the same subject actually "signs" the same word that he merely "imagined" in record 11. The response in record 12 was entirely overt. It was evident to the subject and to everybody who watched him that there were two distinct responses; the word "heavy," chosen because in "signing" it calls for distinctive movements, was repeated once.

There are three comparisons that can be made from these two records. First, the two overt "signings" of the same word in record 12 do not result in exactly the same pattern of response; [14] second, there is no precise similarity between the implicit and the overt records; third, there are three *implicit* responses in the time that is required for two *overt* responses. These observations allow us to conclude that *implicit responses are considerably more rapid than equivalent overt responses*. The same conclusion is suggested when we observe that silent reading is faster than oral reading.

It should also be emphasized that nobody can read these electrical records. One cannot tell from the record *what* a person is thinking about; he can only infer that reasoning, imagining, or dreaming is taking place. That no one ever will be able to read a person's thoughts from these records is strongly suggested by theoretical considerations that we cannot go into here, but we must also remember that at one time it was "scientifically proved" that an airplane could never fly. Action-potential researches are about in the same stage of development that airplanes were in when this discouraging prediction was made.

5. "BRAIN WAVES" [15]

Electrical potentials of the brain, popularly known as "brain waves," were first discovered in animals in 1875, but not until the beginning of the 1930's were extensive experiments made nor did widespread interest in the phenomenon develop. In 1929,

[14] It has been said that no two responses of whatever kind are exactly identical.
[15] This section was written by Donald B. Lindsley.

Hans Berger,[16] a German investigator, first recorded electrical variations from the surface of the head of intact human subjects. In a series of well-controlled experiments he was able to show that *the electrical potentials are due to the activity of the brain itself* rather than to the activity of neighboring muscles, circulatory pulsations, eye movements, or other artifacts. He demonstrated that the electrical changes recorded from the surface of the scalp are practically identical, except for differences in magnitude, with those recorded directly from the exposed surface of the brain, a fact which has greatly facilitated the investigation of brain potentials in human subjects.

Several groups of investigators in this country and abroad have confirmed and extended many of Berger's original observations in normal and pathological cases. They have studied sleep, unconsciousness, anesthesia, hypnosis, epilepsy, mental deficiency, and other psychologic and neurologic disorders in human beings and have performed significant experiments on animals. Students interested in the details of this work will find Jasper's [17] recent review of it valuable.

In Berger's original experiments potential changes were led from two needle electrodes inserted through the scalp or from two large pad electrodes attached to the surface of the scalp, usually one over the forehead, the other over the back of the head. Many recent investigations have employed small metal plate electrodes which may be placed fairly close together on the surface of the scalp over localized regions and which are held comfortably and securely in place by collodion or bandages. An electrode paste or jelly usually serves as the conducting medium between an electrode and the surface of the skin. Because of the differences in the pattern of the electrical activity over different regions of the head it is important to know the position of the electrodes.

Two main types of waves were described by Berger, alpha and beta waves. The alpha waves are large, rhythmic oscillations which

[16] Hans Berger, "Über das Elektrenkephalogramm des Menschen," *Archiv für Psychiatrie und Neurologie,* 1929, 87, 227-70.
[17] H. H. Jasper, "Electrical Signs of Cortical Activity," *Psychological Bulletin,* 1937, 34, 411-81.

may be observed best when the subject is quiet and relaxed, with sensory stimulation at a minimum. In normal adult subjects alpha waves range in frequency from 8 to 13 per second with an average of about 10 per second. The potentials are of the order of 10 to 100 millionths of a volt. The beta waves are even smaller and faster and are often superimposed on the alpha waves. Their frequency ranges from about 20 to 50 per second. Although alpha and beta waves appear in records from most regions of the head, the alpha waves are more prominent over the occipital, parietal, and temporal regions, whereas the largest beta waves are usually found in the frontal region, particularly over the motor area.

Alpha waves are diminished in amplitude or abolished entirely by visual, auditory, tactual and pain stimuli, but the beta waves do not seem to be affected. "Mental" arithmetic or problem solving often diminishes or abolishes the alpha rhythm for the duration of the problem-solving process. The reason for this seemingly paradoxical effect—amounting to a reduction in the electrical activity of the brain with increased stimulation—is not clear for the physiological basis of the alpha and beta waves is not entirely understood.

According to the hypothesis proposed by Adrian and Matthews,[18] individual brain cells when "at rest"—that is, in the absence of external stimulation—are continuously and "spontaneously" charging and discharging. It has been shown in simpler organisms that when groups of nerve cells are "spontaneously" active they tend to discharge in unison. Thus the extremely minute potentials from single neurones, too small to be detected through the scalp and skull, are thought to produce alpha waves when the thousands of brain cells constituting a particular region discharge synchronously. An external stimulus disrupts the synchronous discharge of the cells and destroys the summation effect, thus reducing or abolishing the alpha waves.

Rhythmic alpha waves first appear in infants at about 3 months of age at a frequency of 3 to 4 per second. The frequency of alpha and other types of waves increases with age in children according to a definite growth function and reaches the fairly stationary adult

[18] E. D. Adrian and B. H. C. Matthews, "The Berger Rhythm: Potential Changes from the Occipital Lobes in Man," *Brain*, 1934, 57, 355-85.

level between 10 to 12 years of age. In normal adult subjects the frequency of the alpha waves varies little from day to day and even from year to year. Likewise the pattern of the waves, whether very rhythmic or very irregular, remains much the same. It has even been suggested that the pattern of the waves is correlated with certain characteristics of the personality but this finding has not as yet been substantiated.

Recent studies of brain potentials during various stages of sleep have indicated that changes in the frequency, amplitude, and pattern of the brain waves constitute an important index of the depth of sleep. Modifications of the brain potentials during unconsciousness and deep anesthesia are similar to those during sleep. Striking and characteristic changes occur in the brain potential records of epileptic patients slightly preceding and during convulsive seizures but a comparison of the records from normal and mentally deficient subjects has so far failed to reveal marked differences.

One thing is clear: "brain waves" are not even remotely related to the kind of electrical activity that is imagined to be responsible for one person's being able to read the mind of another. They are not capable of being transmitted over the distances required and no person has the receptive equipment required to pick them up.

Summary of the chapter.—The brain alone is not the organ of reasoning or learning or thinking or imagining or recalling or any other property of man. The greater elaboration of certain brain parts in comparison with other species makes it apparent that these parts are important to man, but to differentiate one person from another on the basis of microscopic differences in brain structure cannot now be done. It is even likely that it never can be done, and to expect to do it is to misunderstand the nature of psychological functioning.

The principal experiments on localization of brain function are reviewed. They show that the brain is much less specific in its function than might be expected. Characteristically, if one part is destroyed, another functions vicariously for it. The exceptions to this generalization are found in the subcortical nuclei which, if destroyed, result in permanent losses of function.

Experiments on the action currents present in imagery, thinking, problem-solving, and so on, show that the whole organism is involved in these processes—not just the brain. There is the further indication that to have a "mental experience" of these kinds means that objects and relations are dealt with in much the same way as if we were actually handling them, except that the implicit responses are a kind of muscular shorthand.

SUMMARY

PSYCHOLOGY is an attempt to understand why people behave as they do; but psychology is not the only subject-matter field concerned with understanding human beings. Novelists, philosophers, poets, biographers, among others, are engaged in the same activity. There is, however, a fundamental difference in the method of attack on the problem which characterizes psychology and sets it apart from all these literary activities. The method did not grow up overnight. Historically there have been many different systems of psychology and the future holds out promise for even more to come. Suffice it to say that first attempts were highly speculative and terribly abstract. They were literary and philosophical. Then, near the close of the last century, came the modern note. The notion developed that it would be wise to take over into psychology the scientific method that had proved to be so valuable in understanding the nature of the physical world. This procedure, it was thought, would enable psychologists to check up on *speculations* regarding the nature of man by actually studying men in the laboratory, just as the botanist studied plants and the geologist studied rocks. It was proposed to apply the same scientific instruments that other scientists used and to invent new ones that would enable the psychologist to penetrate beneath the obvious and superficial surface of psychological happenings. And herein lies a long story of psychological instrumentation which is interesting in its own right, but again can not be elaborated.

There is one fundamental difficulty hampering a complete application of scientific method to psychological events. It lies in the fact that it is easy enough to be objective and scientific with regard to mountains, rivers, canyons, trees or shrubs, or even other animals, but it is hard to be objective and analytical about other human beings, let alone oneself. We are reared to respond sentimentally and personally to members of our own families; this training carries over into other person-to-person relations and is cultivated by certain of our institutions, so that a very special training is required if one is to adopt a different attitude as an adult. If this book has helped anyone to cultivate an objective, detached, analytical attitude, one of its purposes has been fulfilled.

Some people object to the scientific point of view in dealing with other people because they think it cold, austere, harsh, hard, or severe. But it is not that, or at least it need not be. To be objective about other people means that one can better understand one's own mother, father, brothers, and sisters. When you understand why somebody else is the person that he is, you can evaluate and appreciate his performances and his failures with a sympathy and a warm understanding that you are not capable of as long as you believe him to be capricious, perverse, erratic, inexplicable. Unpleasant people are not unpleasant because they choose to be or because they were born under unfortunate planetary influences, but because the circumstances of their lives make them that way. The framework for understanding these things, offered in this book, consists in regarding human nature as the product of three factors—a person's structure, his immediate surroundings, and his past history. Since there is no method at present of actually quantifying these factors, there are various opinions concerning the weight they should have in explaining human behavior. Geneticists and biologists generally are prone to emphasize the inherited factors (structure); physiologists emphasize the momentary stimulus conditions, both external and internal; while psychologists, modern sociologists, and educators attribute greater efficacy to the biographical factors (Chapters I and II).

This whole volume was designed to show how the scientific method can be used to determine the relative importance of these factors in a general way. Although the formula for the scientific method—observing, classifying, hypothesizing, and testing the hypothesis—is very simple, the practical application of this formula to the problems of psychology is not. We have not thought about behavior in terms of the scientific interpretation long enough for the method to become second nature to us. Statements that ought really to be hypotheses are announced as dogmatic assertions. The scientific point of view is always the unassertive, undogmatic, tentative position which does not appeal to large numbers of people who want final answers.

Another difficulty has always been the fact that many speculations about human beings are framed in such a way as not to be susceptible to test. Every day we make observations on what we call another's "intelligence," his "will power," his "aptitudes," his "emotions." When we do this we imply or posit relationships between these abstractions and others equally remote from performance without considering the likelihood that we are talking meaningless twaddle (Chapter III).

1. STRUCTURE

The structure of a person's body is important in the determination of the behavior he exhibits. By "structure" we mean the microscopic anatomical details as well as the grosser features of physique that are open to the inspection of all. In saying this we are not implying that structure is the only or even the most important determinant of human destiny. Just how important it is depends upon what particular aspect of behavior is under consideration and what item of structure is held to be responsible (Chapter IV).

Unimportant structures.—We certainly know that the color of a person's hair or skin is related in no precise way to any of his psychological properties. The shape of his hands, the contour of his nose, and the size of his ears are all equally unimportant. Because these things are obvious, in many superficial analyses they were, and still are, held to be the causes of, or to be related to, capacities, talents, temperament, and general capability. We have shown that the important principle of control reveals that all such assertions are utter nonsense.

When we enter the field of the psychological differences between the various races of man, we get into a more controversial field—controversial largely because we have inadequate data with which to work. The evidence that is available indicates that here again those who attribute psychological differences to differences in the shape and size of eyes, head, lips, hair, color of skin, and bodily proportions are being blinded to other circumstances by these obvious and superficial differences between the various races. The point of view expressed and implied in this book stands for a skeptical attitude toward anybody who insists that a white man is superior because he is a Caucasian, or a Negro is inferior because he stems from African forebears (Chapter IV).

It has also been held that special talents are determined by structure—one frequently hears that "teachers are born, not made," or "he wasn't cut out to be a physician," "he is a born artist"—the implication being that there is some structural determinant for special aptitudes. No basis of fact supports these assertions. They are made by people who have failed to observe that motivational effects could account for talents of special kinds (Chapter III).

Important structures.—Undoubtedly some fraction of the feeble-minded are inadequate because they lack certain anatomical details in the nervous or glandular system. Just what is lacking we are unable to state with any certainty. Here again, a healthy and vigorous skepticism should greet those who proclaim that all feeble-mindedness is the result of structural deficiencies in the nervous system, or that the onset of senile dementia is determined by the slowing up of metabolic processes in the brain, or that involutional melancholia is caused by the cessation of menstruation alone. These are again only the outward, obvious differences. Controlled observations would undoubtedly uncover more important causal factors. One very important way in which structures are indirectly the causes of behavior lies in the manner in which other people react to our structural characteristics. If a girl is unusually tall, unusually thin, or greatly overweight, her treatment by her associates of both sexes differs from what it would be if she more nearly resembled the popular conception of a girl's physique. In the case of children, particularly, any distinguishing feature of structure or coloring is commented upon and evokes a variety of reactions in other people. The treatment thus accorded different children is varied enough to account for major differences in their actions that appear in later life.

There is also some evidence that glandular balance is important in the determination of behavior. One example of this lies in the field of sex, where the differences between masculinity and femininity have been laid at the door of the glands involved. There is evidence, however, that masculine and feminine behavior does not depend completely on glandular structures; effeminate men or masculine women are made more often by the treatment accorded them in childhood than by glandular imbalance. Even when this imbalance is serious enough to prevent the appearance of secondary sex characteristics, the very lack of these properties is noticed and commented upon by a person's associates. As a result it is difficult to know how much of the ensuing behavior is caused by the comparisons that are made with other people and how much is due to the malfunctioning glands themselves. Even a hyperactive thyroid gland, which normally produces an unusual amount of energy, may not be totally responsible for all the tension that is observed in people with overactive thyroids. Again, we respond differently to people who are tense, they make us tense, and we then add to their tension.

Inheritance.—Structures are primarily determined by patterns laid down in the very earliest stages of embryological growth. Of course, there has to be an available supply of the materials needed in growth or else stunting or malformation will result. But in the next generation size is restored to normal if adequate materials are available. To think of inheritance without at the same time thinking of an environment capable of supplying essential materials for growth is to become hopelessly muddled in abstractions. Nevertheless, by keeping the environment constant one can, by selective breeding alone, change in a marked degree whatever structural feature he sets out to change. Mice have been made as large as rats, and rats as large as cats. Presumably there are limits—cats have never been made as large as elephants. As far as human endeavor is concerned, the limitations set by biological restrictions are so wide that it is only rarely true that one's accomplishment is truly limited. These experiments with animals have implications for human problems, but one can expect inheritance to solve psychological problems only in so far as structures are important in the determination of psychological events—and, as we have been showing, structures are not so important as the traditional concepts have led us to expect. Inheritance means that one's *structure* is determined by the character of the germ cells of one's parents, and only that—it does not mean that *behavior* is biologically determined by one's ancestors (Chapters V, VI and VII).

Maturation.—The rate at which elaboration of bodily structure proceeds as one becomes older is important in determining superiority in childhood. These rates seem to be determined principally by heredity, and without any stimulation from the external environment or in spite of environmental deficiencies. This fact would be extremely important if there were any close relation between early superiority and later accomplishment. This relationship does not seem to be close enough to enable us to venture a prediction of mature capability based on childhood superiority (Chapters V, VI and VII).

Implications.—From the evidence presented in previous chapters as well as in this summary, it should be perfectly clear that man is first and last a biological creature, a fact so frequently overlooked in idealized descriptions. Biological factors establish definite limits on human accomplishment.

2. ENVIRONMENT

The conditions surrounding one at any time in the form of lights, sounds, odors, and so on, do determine behavior. They do not, however, dominate the picture so completely as they were supposed to do by earlier physiologists and psychologists, who believed that a person's actions were *principally* determined by stimuli coming from the outside.[1] Human behavior was thought of as being

---

[1] It is perfectly true that a single cell can not originate any kind of activity. The instigation for activity of the cells that compose our bodies must come from the outside of that cell, but the activity of one cell can stimulate another. Stimuli do not determine the nature of the reaction of a cell, but

generated by externally originated stimuli playing upon a fixed and passive human frame.

Today internal stimuli arising from tissue conditions are recognized as the principal source of a person's behavior. It is characteristic of this class of stimuli that they are insistent[2] *and result in heightened tensions in skeletal as well as visceral musculature. They are also the important source of glandular stimulation.*

External stimuli serve to guide and to modify processes already under way as a result of internal stimulation. This distinction between external and internal stimuli is an important one (Chapter VIII).

Some authors have found it convenient to differentiate between physical and social stimuli, principally to make the point that social stimuli result in responses completely out of proportion to their physical energy values. This is only a distinction between sensing and perceiving, and leads us to our final class of behavior causes.

3. BEHAVIORAL HISTORY

It should be perfectly obvious that a given stimulus can be sensed only in terms of a background of previous experiences in connection with that stimulus object as well as with others. Things are perceived only in settings. Whether a given element or some other one will stand out from a background depends on a person's past experience as well as on the nature of the energy distribution in the whole stimulating situation.

A human infant at first is a strictly biological organism. But from the first day onward his nurses and family use different techniques in handling him so that within even a few days individual babies commence to acquire different habits of sleeping, eating, and elimination. It has been observed that nurses in large hospitals treat infants left in their care in different ways—for instance, if an in-

merely serve to set the cell off, once it is stimulated. The character of the reaction is totally determined by the structure and physiological condition of the cell itself.

[2] Insistent because it is possible to move away from external stimuli, but internal stimuli we always have with us.

fant has some attractive characteristic they spend more time with him and give him an extra pat or two—even though they handle hundreds or even thousands of babies in a relatively short time. This extra attention soon causes the favored infant to *demand* more attention than his neglected brother receives or expects. Once at home, the newest member of a family is accorded the treatment dictated by the domestic, economic, and cultural background of the family group. In the higher socioeconomic levels the father takes a more active part in rearing a child. Lower levels are still dominated by an outmoded concept of "women's work." Mother, father, nurses, brothers, sisters, friends—his social environment—lead to the development of habits that result in characteristic ways of dressing, speaking, gesturing, and of thinking and acting generally (Chapters IX and X).

4. PERSONALITY

In common parlance all these habits are subsumed in the word "personality." The word has been used to cover such a wide variety of habits, attitudes, and opinions, in psychology as well as outside the discipline, that it has very little scientific value at the present time. If one is addressing a lay group, the word usually connotes an ability to "make friends and influence people" that is unfortunate for a sober consideration of the factors involved in "personality" make-up. To charlatans the word means some sort of mystic power which somehow directs one's actions and guarantees successful living. To the immature, personality means chic in dress and coiffure, and clever repartee. People who are not up to the minute in dress and action are even said to have *no* personality. All these ways of conceiving personality are extremely superficial. On the other hand, to the reflective thinker, *personality means individuality* in all these things, but more important than these, individuality *in the organization of complex habits of thinking and doing, particularly in the field of dealing with other people.* The crux of the matter seems to lie in the fact that we have to learn to deal with both the nonpersonal objects (and relations between them) and the people in our environment. Some of us learn to be expert in handling nonpersonal situations; let us say those paint brushes and spatulas that are involved in getting a painting upon canvas. In such a case we may be recognized as talented in art, but at the same time we may have failed so miserably in dealing with people that we have to work in an atelier as far removed from human contact as possible. In this case we would say that our personality development has been unusual, abnormal, esoteric, or eccentric—devoid even of rudimentary mastery of the techniques of person-to-person interrelations. Other and perhaps more common examples of the same principle are found in the "grinds" of the college campus, the technicians and experts of various kinds in business and industry who are endured only because of the value of their specialized skills. I do not mean to imply that all good students and all expert technicians are lacking an ability to deal with people or that adequate personality adjustment is characterized by a lack of talent in dealing with nonpersonal situations, but in our society there is always the danger that some such condition will develop because we make it possible for these people to make a living. We may even encourage them to be inept in interpersonal relations.

Psychology and Personality.—There is a distinct difference between scientific psychology and serious personality study. It lies in the fact that in the science of psychology we are interested in developing broad generalizations about the uniform behavior of countless people. We are interested principally in average performance, typical results, uniform conditions, prediction, measurement, and control. The psychologist's laboratory is not the place where one can find a genuine interest in the individual experimented upon, as a person. Usually we attach a great deal of apparatus to the subject, get him to react to certain specified stimulus conditions, and then get rid of him as quickly as we can so that we can analyze the pointer readings arranged in neat columns and the curves that he has left inscribed on paper as a record of his responses. All this is important, as this book in its several chapters has tried to show. There is, however, a legitimate field of human endeavor—personality study, if you will—which is interested in following through in an intimate manner the development of an integrated and organized system of habits, knowledge, attitudes, opinions, and prejudices that we know as John Jones. Personality study is thus based on general psychology, and without a knowledge of the basic principles of psychology one can accomplish little in understanding the development of any personality; but for many of its working hypotheses personality study leaves the field of general psychology to go into the special ones of child study, anthropology, social and abnormal psychology, and sociology. In order to be a competent student of personality adjustments one has to go far beyond the limitations of this book. Without this background it is hopeless to try to understand people except in the most superficial way.

It is true that many of the findings in general psychology have little or no bearing on personality study because there are equally important fields—physiology, biology, animal behavior—from which psychological researches gain their inspiration and direction. I have eliminated these from this volume in so far as my own bias will allow me to do. There are other fields of general psychology—learning, maturation, motivation, perception, emotion, and the conflict-frustration (Chapter XI) area where the implications for the psychology of individual adjustment are more obvious. At the risk of seeming somewhat repetitious, let us recall some of the principles developed in chapters devoted to these topics.

First, it appears that a human infant, in common with the young of all other higher animal forms, begins life under the control of internal stimulating conditions. Most of these conditions seem to result, at first, in a restless undirected activity involving considerable muscular tension. Various external stimulating situations serve to accomplish changes in the environment which bring an end to this activity (Chapter IX). Cessation of intense activity means muscular relaxation so that a balanced or quiescent state is reached. The relief of tension seems to be the prime prerequisite associated with learning so that whatever conditions surround the relief of these tensions are approached and appropriate activity is sought after (Chapters X and XVII). Whatever causes tension is avoided (Chapter XVII). When this stage is reached, we cease to say that the child is "driven," but rather speak of his behavior as "motivated." The variety of things and conditions that can serve as signals for approach reactions is positively enormous (Chapter X). If hunger pangs are relieved by foods of certain consistencies and flavors, then these kinds of stimuli cause approach reactions, but another child who gets different consistencies and flavors will refuse what the first prefers. Although we can observe these differences between the preferences of different families in our own culture, they are even more pronounced when we examine the preferences of different cultural groups. Since what is true for the approaching and accepting reactions is also true for avoiding and rejecting, we find wide differences between the kinds of things that people dislike. At a very early age behavior thus becomes goal-directed. The process of attaining these goals is the process of "living" as contrasted with "existing."

Language.—In human beings this process is complicated by the fact that words soon come to stand as substitutes for things, and as a consequence behavior can be motivated through the use of language alone. Because of the comparative ease with which words can be manipulated, all kinds of conflicts soon arise. One such conflict involves our saying one thing and doing another. Children are quick to observe this difference between word and act, and, if it occurs, that there are wide discrepancies between these two factors in our behavior as adults. Then children learn either to react in the same way and become people in whom no dependence can be placed, or else they come to distrust members of their own families and seek the security that is found in correspondence between word and deed in friends, teachers, and associates outside the family group.

Let us digress from the main developmental theme of this section for a moment to show how in still another way language is important in personal relations. Once a person has acquired a system of words, he keeps them with him always. Although by leaving the scene of the conflict to go home or to his room, he can escape from the minor irritations or serious conflicts involved in contact with either people or things, he can not escape from carrying along with him the language responses built up in these situations. These produce the same tensions in privacy that the actual situation does—a process commonly called "worrying." As a matter of fact, the tensions produced in this process may even be more pronounced than those involved in dealing with the situation directly because certain outcomes of proposed action having no correspondence with an actual outcome can be anticipated in words. This fact is commonly observed and finds expression in the formulation "anticipation is frequently worse than realization." Anticipations can be worked out in words inviting a favorable outcome rather than an unfavorable one, and where there is a discrepancy we speak of disappointment and disillusionment.

Both of these processes—worry (anticipating an unfavorable outcome) and disillusionment (anticipating a favorable outcome and later finding it to be different)—are distinctive experiences which involve the whole psychological individual and as such have an influence on personality development. Some people develop habits of either the one kind or the other and so find themselves always in some chronic state of dissatisfaction.

Planning an outcome in words, or in word substitutes, as in drawing plans for a machine or a building or in designing a costume, is of course an invaluable activity. We could not get along without it in our civilization. It is equally obvious that our civilization could not exist if it were not possible to plan and to design. But it will also be evident that human beings have been more successful in planning for machines, structures, and clothing than for the outcome of person-to-person interrelations. The reason for this is that our plans for dealing with the nonpersonal situations have specific and definite meanings in terms of the objects and events they represent, while there is no such correspondence between our plans for dealing with people and the actual behavior of the people in question. Part of the difficulty is that people are so complex. When we try to anticipate human behavior we are in effect drawing a plan for a complicated architectural structure by scratching with a stick in the sand without benefit of highly specialized drafting tools, T-square, and drawing board. But even if we had the best tools with which to work, we would find still another factor which would interfere with our ability to plan satisfactorily our dealings with people. In terms of our analogy, it is easy to see that even today we can have idealists and impractical people working out their dream-structures on drawing boards. That these designs are impractical is due to the fact that there is no correspondence between the design on paper and the properties of the materials that will finally have to be used. By the same token, in our dealings with people we will encounter dreamers who have such idealized conceptions of human behavior that no person ever existed or can exist to correspond with the dream. Teachers expect children to sit still, ministers expect people to be honest, professors expect students to thirst for knowledge, Sunday School teachers expect people to be moral—and all this universally and absolutely without regard to special conditions. A more realistic view of these matters would have it that morality and honesty are highly specific concepts; children can't be expected to sit still in view of their metabolic rates; a thirst for knowledge has to be especially cultivated.

Human behavior does not depend upon the language formulations of teachers, moralists, novelists, poets, philosophers, lawyers or politicians. It depends on the three factors—structure, environment, and the history of past reactions.

INDEX OF AUTHORS

INDEX OF SUBJECTS

INDIANAPOLIS